St. Louis

METROMORPHOSIS

St. Louis

METROMORPHOSIS

Past Trends and Future Directions

Edited by

Brady Baybeck & E. Terrence Jones

Published in the United States of America by Missouri Historical Society Press
P.O. Box 11940, St. Louis, Missouri 63112-0040

08   07   06   05   04   1   2   3   4   5

Library of Congress Cataloging-in-Publication Data

St. Louis metromorphosis : past trends and future directions / edited by Brady
Baybeck and E. Terrence Jones.
          p. cm.
Includes bibliographical references and index.
ISBN 1-883982-50-2 (pbk. : alk. paper)

1. Saint Louis Metropolitan Area (Mo.)—Social conditions. 2. Saint Louis
Metropolitan Area (Mo.)—Economic conditions. 3. African Americans—
Missouri—Saint Louis Metropolitan Area—Statistics. 4. Saint Louis
Metropolitan Area (Mo.)—Population—Statistics. 5. Saint Louis Metropolitan
Area (Mo.)—Race relations. I. Baybeck, Brady, 1971- II. Jones, E. Terrence
(Endsley Terrence), 1941-
          HN80.S2S7 2004
          306'.09778'66—dc22

                                                                    200401077

Distributed by University of Missouri Press

Design by Elaine A. Young, Hopscotch Communications Design Firm, St. Louis

Printed and bound in Canada by Friesens

∞ the paper used in this publication meets minimum requirements of the ANSI/NISO Z39.48-1992
(R 1997) (Permanence of Paper).

Cover photos by Mark Tranel

Table of Contents

Foreword

"Metromorphosis" is a delightful invention of a word, an imaginative and marvelously succinct way to tell the reader exactly what this book is about: the development and change of a metropolitan region. The past is where we discover who we are, how we got to be the way we are, and what choices contributed to the process. As we begin to understand the changes of our metropolitan region over the last five decades and analyze the results of the decisions made during those fifty years, we develop a basis for community discussion and a framework for proposing a mutual agenda for the betterment of our regional community. What has worked, and why do we think so? What has proved faulty or ineffective, and how can we fix it now? What in our regional past can we use for our future, and what should we discard? Professors Jones and Baybeck and their colleagues provide us here with some of the essential reference points for engaging in these conversations.

We in public history are conveners of public dialogue, facilitators in the construction of community narratives, and evaluators of multiple perspectives. Our colleagues in the academic world, as evidenced by the scholars represented in these fourteen chapters, are no less involved in the concerns of the community in which they study, research, write, and teach. We form a community of interest with all our neighbors in the St. Louis area. Knowledge of what we have done in the past fifty years is vital in the continued development of this community that depends on a place of commingled memory and leads to a common concern for mutual welfare. *St. Louis Metromorphosis* offers us a working knowledge of historic community issues and concerns within a factual framework on which to build an open and collaborative process.

Around and within the scholars' tables, figures, and statistics, the human story of our region emerges. While we acknowledge the ambiguity of the past, we also recognize specific burdens and legacies which should shape our contemporary community agenda. This is the story that we must tell, the one to which we add our own chapters and promulgate among ourselves and preserve for the generations after us. The past is not past. Every piece of it—genetic, cultural, ancestral, personal, or unremembered—is vested in us as it is in every generation. Every generation works on this all-encompassing legacy and then departs with new chapters finished and new possibilities exposed. All St. Louisans, even those yet unborn, will contribute their own stories and statistics, building on what we have left behind for them, for St. Louis is an unfinished project, a work in progress. In studying its past, we are preparing for its future, its "metromorphosis" into the region our children and grandchildren will inhabit. Let us leave them more beauty than burden in what we choose to do for our part in the story.

ROBERT R. ARCHIBALD, PH.D.
PRESIDENT, MISSOURI HISTORICAL SOCIETY

Preface

Years ending in "04" carry special importance for St. Louisans. A century ago, it was the World's Fair that had everyone meeting in St. Louis. Two centuries past, the Missouri side had just become part of a new nation and the Corps of Discovery was on its magnificent journey. In 2004, St. Louis is certainly older and hopefully wiser. It's an apt time to examine the past in order to illuminate the future.

In this volume, twelve scholars from four area universities (Saint Louis University, Southern Illinois University–Edwardsville, University of Missouri–St. Louis, Washington University) use decades of data to identify underlying trends, probe possible causes, and consider future consequences. Focusing primarily on the past half century, they examine demography, spatial expansion, economic transformation and restructuring, labor force developments, minority business location, transportation policies, residential segregation, neighborhood stability, family structure, homicide patterns, municipal competition, and educational practices.

By framing their investigations in decades rather than years, these analyses identify changes that are not readily apparent when the time horizon is shorter. Although the pace of change within the region often seems slow when experienced annually, St. Louis 2004 is distinctly different from St. Louis 1950 or St. Louis 1960. The residents are much more diverse and dispersed, the economy has shifted from a manufacturing to a service base, the two-parents-with-children household is no longer the norm, and a suburban municipality rather than the City of St. Louis is the prevailing residential location.

But there is continuity as well. Historic racial separation and its consequences remain the region's biggest challenge. Although whites are considerably more aware of racial divisions now than they were two generations ago, the legacy of a century and a half's slavery followed by legally mandated segregation remains all too real. As several contributors demonstrate, the consequences are still evident in residential patterns, economic opportunity, family structure, and educational equity.

The editors and authors are especially indebted to Dr. Alan Artibise, formerly Public Policy Research Center Director at the University of Missouri–St. Louis and now Dean of the College of Urban and Public Affairs at the University of New Orleans. He embraced this initiative and, as importantly, invested in it. Also crucial has been the enthusiastic support of Dr. Robert Archibald, the President of the Missouri Historical Society.

Behind the scenes, Ms. Becky Pastor, the Director of Communications for the UM–St. Louis Public Policy Research Center, did an extraordinary job editing copy and ensuring consistency. The Missouri Historical Society staff, most notably Lauren Mitchell, provided much encouragement and guidance. We appreciate their help.

The 1997 Peirce Report stressed that the St. Louis region is blessed with many strong colleges and universities that could and should do more to contribute to the metropolitan area's vitality. This volume represents the first time that social scientists from the region's four research universities have collaborated on a book-length analysis of the St. Louis area. As scholars and citizens, it is our contribution to a better tomorrow for the place where we both work and live.

St. Louis
METROMORPHOSIS

.

Chapter 1

The St. Louis Region, 1950–2000: How We Have Changed

David Laslo
University of Missouri–St. Louis

Over the past fifty years, the population of the St. Louis region has undergone an enormous transformation in its composition and distribution. These changes have been driven in large part by a restructuring of the local economy from one based on the manufacturing of durable goods, principally automobile assembly and steel, to one based on services, a restructuring that has mirrored changes in the national economy (Primm 1981). It has also been transformed by changing social norms and an increasing tolerance for new and different living arrangements (Frey, Abresch, and Yeasting 2001, 36–37). All of these changes present a dramatically different picture of the St. Louis region from the one in 1950.

With the release of each decennial census since 1950, the process of analyzing the results has traditionally become a source of concern and a cause for introspection among residents and civic leaders. Comparing the numbers and identifying the key trends have generally focused first on the rise or fall of the region's population and its rank among the nation's metropolitan areas. These analyses have also generally focused on how the region's population has steadily moved from the City of St. Louis and its adjacent suburbs to the counties to the east, west, and south. But these statistics tell only part of the story. A closer examination of census data between 1950 and 2000 brings to light a number of other trends that are familiar but less sensational than the broader growth and migration trends. Underlying these trends are many that show how different the region is in the first decade of the twenty-first century than it was in 1950.

This chapter first compares and contrasts the most significant changes in the region in 1950 and in 2000. Focusing largely on the trend in population growth and the growth in the land area that is defined as the

St. Louis region, it traces the population trends over the fifty-year period. The chapter then examines selected demographic and social characteristics. These include the growth and suburbanization of the nonwhite population, the aging of the population, the change in the rate of household and family formations, the trends in living arrangements, the distribution of family income, and the changes in housing types and its distribution. The analysis finds that the St. Louis region has become a place not too unlike the nation, but one that is also at the forefront of many trends.

Fifty Years of Population Change

When the 1950 census was taken, the St. Louis region consisted of five counties and had a population of 1,681,281, ranking it ninth in the nation. One hundred years earlier, in 1850, it had ranked eighth in the nation, but had risen to fourth by the turn of the century (U.S. Bureau of the Census 2002). By 2000, the region had grown to twelve counties with a population of 2,603,607. This represented an increase of seven counties and 922,326 persons, a population increase of 54.9 percent. But its ranking had fallen to eighteenth in the nation. A comparison with the increase in the population of the nation shows that the St. Louis growth rates have been much slower after 1960; the city experienced an actual population loss between 1970 and 1980 as the region struggled through the economic pain of a national manufacturing restructuring (Bluestone and Harrison 1982, Teaford 1990). Table 1 compares the change in population between 1950 and 2000 in St. Louis and the nation as well as its rank in the nation.

Losing an average of 10,172 persons annually for fifty years, the City of St. Louis has served as a population feeder for St. Louis County and other outlying counties for the entire fifty-year study period. In the 1960s, 1970s, and early 1980s, the foremost receptor of out-migrants from the City of St. Louis was St. Louis County. But more recently, out-migration from the city and St. Louis County has fueled population increases in St. Charles, Jefferson, and Franklin Counties in Missouri and Madison and Monroe Counties in Illinois. St. Charles County grew at one of the fastest rates in the nation between 1990 and 2000 (U.S. Bureau of the Census 1992 and 2002).

With the addition of the seven counties over the fifty-year period, the land area of the region has grown by 3,950 square miles or by 152.1 percent (see Figure 1). This has lowered the overall density of the region's population by 250 persons per square mile or by -38.6 percent. However, the contrast in densities between the counties that made up the region in 1950 and those that have been added since then is dramatic. Density in the original five 1950 counties has actually increased during the fifty-year period, rising from 647.3 persons per square mile in 1950 to 832.9 in 2000. This contrasts with the density in the seven new counties, which has risen to only 111.4 persons per square mile in 2000 from 100 persons per square mile in 1950. Again, the principal driver of these changes has been the steady out-migration from the City of St. Louis.

Table 1. Population of Saint Louis Region and United States: 1950–2000

Year	Saint Louis Population	Percent Change	Rank	United States Population	Percent Change
1950	1,681,281	--	9	151,325,000	--
1960	2,060,103	22.5	9	179,323,000	18.5
1970	2,363,017	14.7	10	203,302,000	13.4
1980	2,355,460	-0.3	12	226,542,000	11.4
1990	2,444,099	3.8	17	248,709,000	9.8
2000	2,603,607	6.5	18	281,421,000	13.2
1950–2000	922,326	54.9		130,096,000	86.0

Source: U.S. Census, 1950–2000.

Figure 1. Map of the St. Louis Metropolitan Region

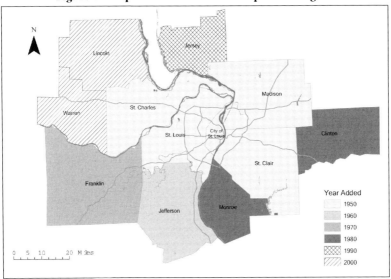

Source: U.S. Census, 1950 and 2000.

The population density of the City of St. Louis has declined from 10,643.4 persons per square mile in 1950 to 4,325.3 in 2000, a decline of nearly 60 percent. St. Clair County experienced population gains through the 1970s, but since then has steadily lost population, lowering its density from 432.1 persons per square mile in 1970 to 379.9 in 2000. Conversely, St. Louis County and St. Charles County have increased their population density from 773.2 and 50.2 persons per square mile respectively in 1950 to 1,161.6 and 478 in 2000. Table 2 provides a history of the region through its population change between 1950 and 2000 and the years the counties were added to the definition of the region (U.S. Bureau of the Census 1950–2000). Table 3 shows the change in population, land area, and density in the 1950–2000 period.

Table 2. History of St. Louis Regional Population: 1950–2000

County	1950	1960	1970	1980	1990	2000
St. Charles	29,834	52,970	92,954	144,107	212,907	283,883
St. Louis	406,349	703,532	951,353	973,896	993,529	1,016,315
City of St. Louis	856,796	750,026	622,236	452,085	396,685	348,189
Madison	182,307	224,689	250,934	247,691	249,238	258,941
St. Clair	205,995	262,509	285,176	267,531	262,852	256,082
Total 1950 Counties	1,681,281	1,993,726	2,202,653	2,085,310	2,115,211	2,163,410
Jefferson		66,377	105,248	146,183	171,380	198,099
Franklin			55,116	71,233	80,603	93,807
Clinton				32,617	33,944	35,535
Monroe				20,117	22,422	27,619
Jersey					20,539	21,668
Warren						24,525
Lincoln						38,944
Total Post-1950		66,377	160,364	270,150	328,888	440,197
Total Region	1,681,281	2,060,103	2,363,017	2,355,460	2,444,099	2,603,607

Source: U.S. Census Bureau, 2000; PPRC UM–St. Louis.

Overall, the region's population increase of 54.9 percent over the fifty-year period represents a modest average annual growth rate of 1.1 percent. This contrasts with the 86 percent increase in the nation's population or an annual average growth rate of 1.7 percent. Although the region experienced modest population gains in 1990 and 2000 following the loss between 1970 and 1980, it has not been enough to keep the region's ranking from declining to eighteenth in 2000, a drop of nine positions from 1950 (see Table 1). The 6.5 percent increase in the region's population between 1990 and 2000 is far below the average growth rate of the top-fifty region of 17.9 percent (MIDAS 2003; U.S. Bureau of the

Census 2000). In fact, as Table 2 indicates, the original five-county region in 1950 actually peaked in population in 1970 at 2,202,653. Since then, this part of the region has declined by 39,243 persons and stood at 2,163,410 in 2000. The population growth of the region can be largely attributed to the counties that have been added since 1950, as those seven counties now contribute 440,197 persons to the region's total. The process of population decentralization has increased the land area of the region at a much faster rate than the growth rate in population. In 2000, the seven counties added to the region since 1950 make up 60.3 percent of the land area, but are the home to only 16.9 percent of the population (see Table 3). Figure 2 compares the average annual growth rates of the counties in the region with those of the region and the nation.

Table 3. Change in Regional Land Area and Population Density: 1950–2000

	1950	1960	1970	1980	1990	2000
MSA in square miles	2490.1	3146.9	4069.0	4931.6	5300.8	6319.6
Population per square mile total	675.2	633.6	541.3	422.8	399.0	342.3
Population per square mile in 1950 counties	675.2	800.7	884.6	837.4	849.4	868.8
Population per square mile in post-1950		101.1	101.6	110.6	117.0	113.7
Pct. growth in MSA population		22.5	14.7	-0.3	3.8	6.5
Pct. growth in MSA land area		26.4	29.3	21.2	7.5	19.2
Proportion of original MSA: population		96.8	93.2	88.5	86.5	83.1
Proportion of original MSA: land area		79.1	61.2	50.5	47.0	39.4

Source: U.S. Census Bureau, 2000; PPRC UM–St. Louis.

While these larger population and land area trends are significant for the story they tell about the St. Louis region's place in the nation, an inward look reveals other insights into how the region has changed during the past fifty years. These include the growth of nonwhite populations, the age distribution of the population, household and family formation rates, household types and size, income distribution, and housing unit growth and change.

The Suburbanization of the Nonwhite Population

The number and proportion of persons in the St. Louis region that are nonwhite has grown steadily over the 1950 to 2000 period. (Because the 1950 census did not distinguish among races that were not white, the term nonwhite is used for comparative purposes and includes all nonwhite

Figure 2. Average Annual Growth Rate, 1950–2000

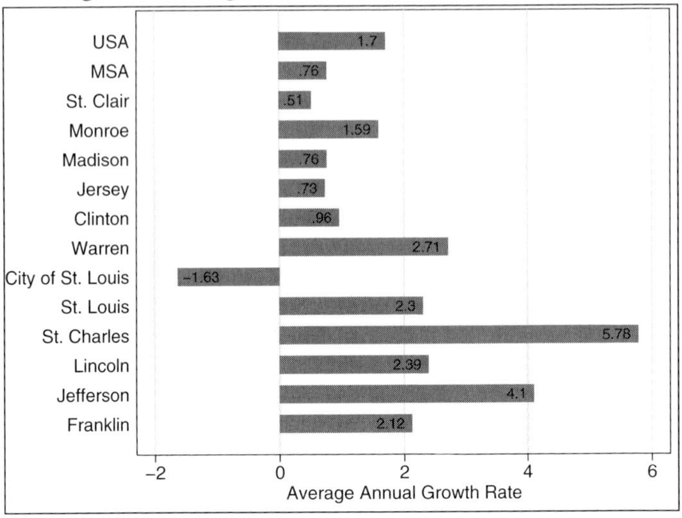

Location	Average Annual Growth Rate
USA	1.7
MSA	.76
St. Clair	.51
Monroe	1.59
Madison	.76
Jersey	.73
Clinton	.96
Warren	2.71
City of St. Louis	-1.63
St. Louis	2.3
St. Charles	5.78
Lincoln	2.39
Jefferson	4.1
Franklin	2.12

Source: U.S. Census, 1950 and 2000.

races). In fact, the nonwhite population has grown at a much faster rate than the white population. The data presented in Tables 4 and 5 show the distribution and percentage of nonwhite population in the St. Louis MSA (metropolitan statistical area) during the fifty-year period. In every county of the MSA, the minority population has grown, albeit at significantly different rates. In 1950 the nonwhite population was concentrated in St. Louis and St. Clair County; it has continued to grow proportionately in those counties while dispersing across the region in greater numbers. In 1950, 70.6 percent of the region's nonwhites resided in the City of St. Louis, while 20.3 percent resided in St. Clair County. In some of the outlying counties, the nonwhite population remains small in number and as a proportion of the total population, but it has increased significantly by percentage since 1950.

One of the most significant trends to emerge from the 2000 census is the proportion of nonwhites that reside in the City of St. Louis (56.2 percent) and the number of nonwhites now residing in St. Louis County (235,485). The City of St. Louis has long had the largest concentration of the nonwhite population in the region, and it is now a majority nonwhite population. This is a marked change from 1950, when nonwhite populations (mostly blacks) made up 18 percent of the population. The out-migration from the city has included both whites and nonwhites, but whites have left at a much faster rate. Similarly, St. Clair County and St. Louis County have experienced significant increases in the proportion

Metromorphosis

of nonwhite population. St. Clair County increased its proportion of nonwhite population from 16.8 percent in 1950 to 32.1 percent in 2000, and St. Louis County's nonwhite population increased from 4.2 percent of the population in 1950 to 23.2 percent in 2000.

Also noteworthy is that the largest concentration of nonwhite population in the region now resides in St. Louis County, having surpassed the City of St. Louis by 235,485 to 195,523 in 2000. The 235,485 nonwhites in St. Louis County in 2000 now represent 41.6 percent of the nonwhites in the region. The City of St. Louis's share is 34.5 percent, while St. Clair County's share has held steady at 19.5 percent. Overall, the nonwhite population in the region has grown nearly 160 percent or by 349,903 persons over the past fifty years, rising from 12 percent of the total population in 1950 to 21.7 percent in 2000. In comparison, the white population has increased by 572,423 persons or 39.1 percent during the same period, indicating that 37.9 percent of the increase in population in the St. Louis region over the fifty-year period can be attributed to growth in the nonwhite population. There have been large-scale movements in the minority population within the region. Moreover, given the nonwhites' higher annual average growth rate, the region will experience a continued rise in the share of the total population that is nonwhite.

Table 4. St. Louis Regional Nonwhite Population: 1950–2000

County	1950	1960	1970	1980	1990	2000	1950–2000 Difference
Franklin	469	552	717	1,033	1,200	2,371	1,902
Jefferson	836	855	1,041	1,742	2,403	4,997	4,161
Lincoln	580	552	553	644	812	1,509	929
St. Charles	776	916	1,408	3,093	7,483	15,127	14,351
St. Louis	17,067	19,880	49,351	121,792	157,297	235,485	218,418
City of St. Louis	154,223	216,022	257,244	209,509	194,600	195,523	41,300
Warren	268	357	433	540	631	1,008	740
Total Missouri	174,218	239,134	310,747	338,353	364,426	456,020	281,802
Clinton	23	119	238	476	1,256	2,065	2,042
Jersey	61	49	99	147	193	405	344
Madison	9,662	12,059	13,703	16,459	19,021	25,296	15,634
Monroe	13	17	19	94	160	340	327
St. Clair	34,607	48,146	64,408	76,617	74,986	82,112	47,505
Total Illinois	44,366	60,390	78,467	93,793	95,616	110,218	65,852
St. Louis Region	218,585	299,524	389,214	432,146	460,042	566,238	347,653

Source: U.S. Bureau of the Census, 2000; PPRC, UM–St. Louis, 2002.

Table 5. St. Louis Regional Percent Nonwhite Population: 1950–2000

County	1950	1960	1970	1980	1990	2000	1950–2000 Increase
Franklin	1.3	1.2	1.3	1.5	1.5	2.5	406.0
Jefferson	2.2	1.3	1.0	1.2	1.4	2.5	497.6
Lincoln	4.3	3.7	3.1	2.9	2.8	3.9	160.4
St. Charles	2.6	1.7	1.5	2.1	3.5	5.3	1850.1
St. Louis	4.2	2.8	5.2	12.5	15.8	23.2	1279.8
City of St. Louis	18.0	28.8	41.3	46.3	49.1	56.2	26.8
Warren	3.5	4.1	4.5	3.6	3.2	4.1	275.7
Total Missouri	12.6	14.6	16.8	18.5	19.1	22.8	161.8
Clinton	0.1	0.5	0.8	1.5	3.7	5.8	9039.6
Jersey	0.4	0.3	0.5	0.7	0.9	1.9	563.3
Madison	5.3	5.4	5.5	6.6	7.6	9.8	161.8
Monroe	0.1	0.1	0.1	0.5	0.7	1.2	2459.9
St. Clair	16.8	18.3	22.6	28.6	28.5	32.1	137.3
Total Illinois	10.1	11.1	13.0	15.9	16.2	18.4	148.4
St. Louis Region	12.0	13.7	15.8	17.9	18.5	21.7	159.0

Source: U.S. Bureau of the Census; PPRC, UM–St. Louis.

The Aging of the Regional Population

In 1950, the nation and the St. Louis region were in the midst of an unprecedented population surge in births (Frey, Abresch, and Yeasting 2001, 9). Persons born between 1946 and 1965 became known as baby boomers, as young servicemen returning from World War II and people born too late to serve in the military, married and bore children in previously unmatched numbers, leaving their mark on the nation's history for its wartime service and its progeny (Frey, Abresch, and Yeasting 2001, 7). The sheer size of this generation of St. Louisans has pushed upward the median age of the population as its first members reached age fifty in 1996. With increasing life expectancy for both males and females due to advances in medical and health care, the region's population will continue to be dominated by this generation. Figures 3 and 4 show the age and sex breakdown for the region's population in 1950 and 2000.

In 1950, the large "bulge" in persons age four and under reflects the first members of the baby boom generation as it began its ascent toward becoming the largest in St. Louis's and the nation's history. By 2000, the size and full effect of the baby boomers can be seen in Figure 3, which shows the age and sex breakdown of the regional population in 2000. The age cohorts between 35–40 and 50–54 display the size of the baby boom generation as it has advanced in age over the fifty-year study period. In

2000, this generation accounted for 30.1 percent of the total population. During the fifty-year period, the median age of the population in St. Louis advanced from 32.5 in 1950 to 36.5 in 2000, and the proportion of persons over the age of sixty-five increased to 12.9 percent, up from 8.5 percent in 1950.

Figure 3. St. Louis Region Age Distribution. Total Population, 1950

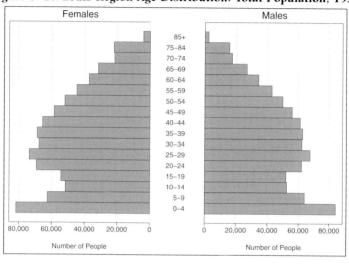

Figure 4. St. Louis Region Age Distribution. Total Population, 2000

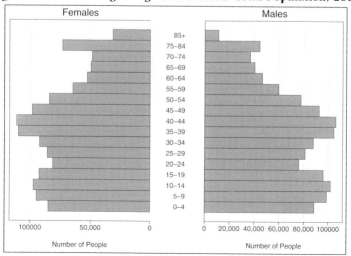

Also evident in Figure 4 is women's longer life expectancy, which is evident in the larger number of females in the upper age cohorts. Today, women are expected to live 5.8 more years than men (Frey, Abresch, and Yeasting 2001, 162). Another significant feature is the next demographic "bulge" found in the 5–9 to 15–19 age cohorts composed of the baby boomers' children. Popularized as Generation Y, this segment represents approximately one out of five (22 percent) St. Louisans in 2000 and will begin to move into leadership roles and prominent occupational positions within two decades. In the short run, the smaller generation of persons between 20 and 34, termed Generation X, will move through the early stages of career and family building in the decade ahead. In 2000, nearly one out of every five was a member of this generation.

The age distribution of the population by race presents a different picture. In 1950, the image created by the population pyramid of age distribution for the St. Louis region for whites and nonwhites looked remarkably similar but with nonwhites being a smaller group overall (12 percent of the total population). Figures 5 and 6 show the distribution of white and nonwhite populations by age in 1950. Each distribution shows the base of its pyramid as the largest cohort in the 0–4 age category. However, by 2000, the age distribution of each race had changed dramatically. Figures 7 and 8 show the age distribution of whites and nonwhites in 2000. Lower fertility rates among whites and higher mortality rates among nonwhites have, in large part, created significantly different age distributions (U.S. Bureau of the Census 1992, 9). Largely reflecting the total population pyramid, the age distribution of whites shows the demographic "bulges" created by the baby boomers. The relatively small base of the pyramid suggests that the trend of slow growth in the white population may continue and that recent growth may be attributed to lower mortality rates vis-à-vis fewer wars and longer life expectancy. Conversely, the pyramid of the nonwhite population in 2000 (Figure 8) suggests that the trend in higher rates of growth may continue. The largest age cohorts are found in the youngest age categories, giving them a large foundation for continued growth. This is an indication that the nonwhite population is younger overall than the white population, and it also may suggest that the nonwhite in-migration that does occur in St. Louis is by larger-than-average households or families.

The Changing Composition of Households and Families

Throughout the 1950–2000 period, the number of households and families in the St. Louis region continued to increase, but did so for variety of social and economic conditions that caused the rates to vary significantly during each decade. Most significant of these trends was the decline in "traditional" family households, most often described or thought of as a married couple living with their own children. As a result, the rise in the rate of the formation and the proportion of non-family households has been the most notable change over the fifty-year period both in St. Louis and the nation. The number of households continued to increase each decade, but were composed of a wider range of living arrangements and were, on average, smaller in size. Table 6 compares the formation rates for all households, family households, and married-couple households for each of the censuses between 1950 and 2000 (U.S. Bureau of the Census 1950–2000). Table 7 shows the average household size, the proportion of family and married-couple households as a proportion of all households, and the proportion of married persons fifteen years and older during the same period.

Figure 5. St. Louis Region Age Distribution. White Population, 1950

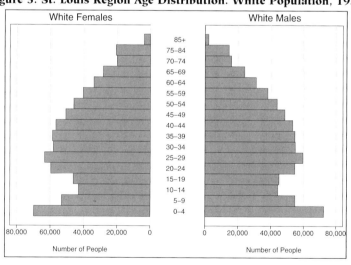

Figure 6. St. Louis Region Age Distribution. Nonwhite Population, 1950

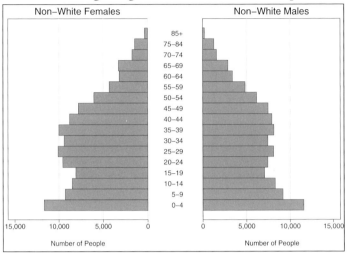

Figure 7. St. Louis Region Age Distribution. White Population, 2000

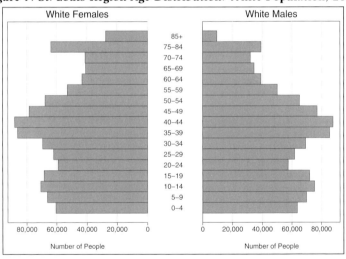

Metromorphosis

Figure 8. St. Louis Region Age Distribution. Nonwhite Population, 2000

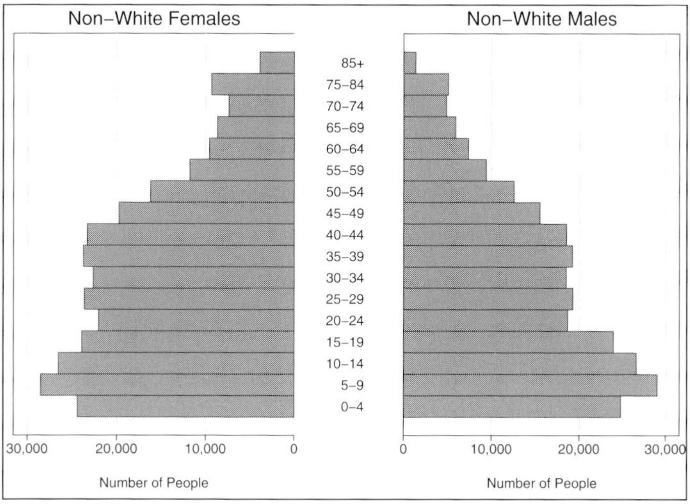

Table 6. Household Type Rates of Change: 1950-2000

	1950–60	1960–70	1970–80	1980–90	1990–2000	1950–2000
Population Change						
St. Louis	22.5	14.7	-0.3	3.8	6.5	54.9
USA	18.5	13.4	11.4	9.8	13.2	86.0
Household Change						
St. Louis	26.2	17.8	13.8	10.2	16.5	117.4
USA	21.2	20.2	27.4	15.6	12.2	140.4
Family Change						
St. Louis	18.5	12.2	4.3	4.1	5.6	52.4
USA	15.6	14.6	13.5	13.1	9.0	85.4
Married Couple Change						
St. Louis	16.5	9.3	-2.4	1.6	-0.4	25.7
USA	15.2	13.9	7.7	8.6	5.7	62.3
Non-Family Change, MSA						
St. Louis	99.7	49.8	54.5	27.8	41.8	737.7
USA	67.4	51.3	87.1	22	19.9	593.0

Source: U.S. Census, 1950–2000.

As indicated in Table 7, the average household in 1950 in St. Louis consisted of 3.25 persons, slightly smaller than the national average of 3.37 (U.S. Bureau of the Census 1950, 2000). By 2000, the St. Louis average household size had fallen to 2.37, again smaller than the national average of 2.62 (U.S. Bureau of the Census 1950–2000). The reason most often cited as contributing to the decline in the average household size has been a decrease in the fertility rates among all racial groups, but most prominently among whites (U.S. Bureau of the Census, Households 1992, 9). Other factors contributing to these changes included changing social norms in the 1960s and 1970s that led to increasing divorce rates that, in turn, contributed to the increase in the rate of household formations (Frey, Abresch, and Yeasting 2001, 120–21). As women entered the labor force in greater numbers by the 1970s, the postponement of marriage and childbearing also contributed to the increase in household formations (Frey, Abresch, and Yeasting 2001, 104–05). Other reasons often cited for the increase in household formations have been grandparents raising children; an increase in one-person households, both young and old; social tolerance for same-sex households; and cohabitation as an alternative to marriage (Frey, Abresch, and Yeasting 2001, 122–26).

Table 6 shows that the rate of household formations was greatest in St. Louis and the nation between 1950 and 1970 before reaching a low point between 1980 and 1990. Indicative of higher divorce rates and the postponement of marriage and childbearing were the rate of family and married-couple household formation, which were consistently below the rate of all household formations. Also from Table 7, it can be seen that the proportion of family and married-couple households declined significantly from 90.5 percent and 81.6 percent of all households in 1950 to 63.5 percent and 47.2 percent in 2000 (U.S. Bureau of the Census 1950–2000).

This trend is also reflected in the proportion of one- and two-person households shown in Table 8, which compares household size between St. Louis and the nation. In 1950, one-person households composed only 9 percent of all households, while the largest proportion (42 percent) had three to four persons. By 2000, the proportion of one-person households had tripled to 27.4 percent, while three- to four-person households declined to less than a third of all households (31 percent). In 2000, St. Louis ranked ninth in the nation in one-person households (U.S. Bureau of the Census 2000, 3). Households with five or more persons declined by half during the fifty-year period, representing 18 percent in 1950 and declining to 9.6 percent in 2000. In respect to these trends, St. Louis was nearly identical to the nation (U.S. Bureau of the Census 1950–2000).

Table 7. Average Household Size and Percent of Household Types: 1950–2000

	1950	1960	1970	1980	1990	2000
Average Household Size						
St. Louis	3.25	3.23	3.15	2.77	2.60	2.37
USA	3.37	3.33	3.14	2.76	2.63	2.62
Families as Percent of Households						
St. Louis	90.5	85	80.9	74.1	70	63.5
USA	89.2	85	81.2	72.3	70.8	68.8
Married Couples as Percent of Families						
St. Louis	90.4	88.8	86.4	81	78.6	74.4
USA	87.7	87.9	86.9	82.5	79.2	76.8
Married Couples as Percent of Households						
St. Louis	81.6	75.3	69.8	59.9	55.2	47.2
USA	78.2	74.3	70.5	59.6	56	52.8
Percent Non-Family Households						
St. Louis	9.5	15	19.1	25.9	30	36.5
USA	10.8	15	18.8	27.7	29.2	31.2
Percent Married Persons						
St. Louis	51.5	47.9	46.0	45.5	44.6	46.5
USA	49.2	47.0	46.9	46.3	45.3	42.7

Source: U.S. Census, 1950–2000.

Overall, people in the St. Louis region are living in a wider variety of arrangements and in households that are almost one person less, on average, than they were in 1950. While family and married-couple households are still the most common households, non-family households of all varietys have increased t over one out of three (36.5 percent) households in 2000, up from under one out of ten (9.5 percent) in 1950.

The Pattern of Income Distribution

In 1950, the median family income of the St. Louis region was $3,383, 8.7 percent below the national median of $3,705 (U.S. Bureau of the Census 1950). A worker in the durable goods industry, such as automobile assembly, made $3,483 a year (Derks 2000, 78). However, over the next decade, the region's economy was able to supply local families with a median income that exceeded the nation by 10.9 percent, comparing a median of $6,275 for the St. Louis region to $5,660 for the nation. And since then, the region's median family income has consistently exceeded that of the nation, although the difference had fallen to 8.1 percent in 2000. Table 9 shows a comparison of the region and the nation's median family income over the 1950 to 2000 period.

Table 8. Household Size: 1950–2000

MSA	1950	1960	1970	1980	1990	2000
1 person household	9.0	13.5	17.5	23.1	25.9	27.4
2 person household	30.9	29.5	29.1	30.3	31.0	32.0
3–4 person household	42.0	35.6	32.4	33.0	32.7	31.0
5+ person household	18.0	21.4	21.0	13.7	10.4	9.6
USA						
1 person household	9.3	13.1	17.1	22.7	24.6	25.5
2 person household	28.1	27.8	28.9	31.4	32.3	33.1
3–4 person household	41.2	36.5	33.0	33.2	32.8	31.0
5+ person household	21.4	22.6	20.9	12.8	10.3	10.4

Source: U.S. Census, 1950–2000.

A closer look at a comparison of the distribution of family income in the St. Louis region and the nation reveals that the region is increasingly mirroring the nation in the way income is distributed among its families. Table 10 compares the distribution of income in 1950 and 2000. In 1950, proportionately, St. Louis had fewer families in the lower income categories and significantly more in the upper income categories. For example, St. Louis had about half (52.9 percent) the proportion of the families in the lowest income category as that of the nation. Likewise, St. Louis had about a third more (32.1 percent) proportionately in the highest income category. By 2000, the difference in the proportions in the lowest and highest categories had narrowed significantly. In the lowest category in 2000, St. Louis had proportionately fewer families, but the difference was only 17.7 percent. At the other end of the income spectrum, the region had proportionately more families in the highest income category, but the difference was only 4 percent. Furthermore, comparing the proportions between the St. Louis region and the nation in 2000 shows that the distributions are very similar with only small differences, indicating that over the 1950–2000 period, St. Louis has experienced a relative decline in its positive difference from the nation.

Another view of how the St. Louis region's distribution of family income has changed over the fifty-year period can be seen by comparing the median family income of the five original counties with the median for the region and the nation. Table 11 shows how the five original counties have compared to the regional and national medians of family income. From this analysis, the impacts of the economic restructuring of the regional economy that began in the late 1960s and the subsequent population decentralization that occurred can be seen. The two counties most heavily engaged in heavy manufacturing operations, the City of St. Louis and St. Clair County, experienced steady declines in their median family incomes relative to the region and the nation over the entire fifty-year period. Other counties, such as St. Charles and St. Louis in Missouri and Madison in Illinois, have experienced trends that are very different.

Table 9. St. Louis and United States Median Family Income: 1950–2000

Year	St. Louis Median Family Income	USA Median Family Income	Percent Difference
1950	3,383	3,705	-8.7
1960	6,275	5,660	10.9
1970	10,584	9,586	10.4
1980	21,984	19,917	10.4
1990	38,146	35,225	8.3
2000	54,113	50,046	8.1

Source: U.S. Census, 1950–2000.

As Table 11 shows, St. Louis County has remained above the region's and nation's medians over the entire fifty-year period. However, the most recent census data indicates that median family income declined between 1990 and 2000. This may be an indication that the continued process of population decentralization is now affecting St. Louis County. Having the opposite experience is St. Charles County which, since 1970, has posted median family incomes increasingly above the region and national medians. Madison County has had a mixed experience relative to the region and the nation. Since 1960, the median family income of Madison County has been higher or practically the same as the medians of the nation. However, when compared to the region's median family income, the county has been below it since 1970.

In general, the distribution of family income in the St. Louis region over the fifty-year period reflects the population shifts that have occurred within the area. The region has fared well, posting medians consistently above the nation's. But at the same time, population decentralization is reflected in the declining medians of three of the five counties that made up the region in 1950. In 2000, only St. Louis County and St. Charles County of those original five, have median family incomes above the region's and the nation's. Madison County's median was practically identical to the nation's. Together these are indications that families with higher incomes have continued to move to less central locations.

Table 10. Family Income Distribution: 1950 and 2000

1950	St. Louis Percent	USA Percent	St. Louis Difference	Percent St. Louis Difference
< $999	10.6	22.4	-11.8	-52.9
$1,000-$1,999	10.2	16.2	-6.0	-37.3
$2,000-$,2999	19.4	18.2	1.2	6.5
$3,000-$3,999	22.8	16.8	6.0	35.9
$4,000-$4,999	14.2	10.1	4.1	40.8
$5,000-$6,999	14.1	9.8	4.3	44.2
$7,000+	8.7	6.6	2.1	32.1

2000	St. Louis Percent	USA Percent	St. Louis Difference	Percent St. Louis Difference
<$15,000	8.3	10.1	-1.8	-17.7
$15000-$24,999	8.9	10.7	-1.8	-17.1
$25,000-$34,999	11.2	12.0	-0.8	-6.8
$35,000-$44,999	11.4	11.7	-0.3	-2.7
$45,000-$59,999	16.1	15.5	0.6	4.2
$60,000-$99,999	28.2	24.7	3.5	14.1
$100,000+	15.9	15.3	0.6	4.0

Source: U.S. Census, 1950 and 2000.

Housing and Home Ownership

The St. Louis region's population decentralization between 1950 and 2000 has often been described as a "push" and "pull" process. The "push" of population out of central locations is conditions that would influence an individual or household to move—factors such as crime, congestion, or a lack of job opportunities. The "pull" influences would include new housing choices, public school options, and increased job opportunities. For the St. Louis region, all these factors have had an influence on the internal movement of population, but the creation of new housing choices has been the most evident and is generally accepted as the first stage of the decentralization process. The expansion of the region's housing stock has roughly paralleled the rise in population and households. This growth has occurred in all the counties of the region and has had the general effect of raising the proportion of households that are home owners. Table 12 shows the growth of single-family housing units in the twelve counties that now make up the region and their proportion of single-family units.

Table 12 shows the relationship between housing and population. Over the fifty-year period the region has consistently created housing units at rates above the rate of population growth and household formations. The only exception has been the rate between 1990 and 2000, which was double the rate of housing unit increase during the same period. This may suggest that the housing stock in 2000 was of sufficient size and type to provide housing for the new households created between 1990 and 2000.

Table 11. Percent Difference from Median of Region and United States

	Difference from St. Louis Median Family Income				
	Madison	St. Clair	St. Charles	St. Louis	St. Louis City
1950	3.2	-6.7	-11.9	18.2	-5.3
1960	1.2	-6.9	-5.7	20.0	-14.7
1970	-3.2	-9.8	2.6	19.0	-22.7
1980	-2.6	-12.5	9.9	14.9	-30.6
1990	-6.4	-16.3	17.0	18.5	-36.4
2000	-6.3	-12.4	19.0	14.0	-39.8
	Difference from United States Median Family Income				
	Madison	St. Clair	St. Charles	St. Louis	St. Louis City
1950	-5.8	-14.8	-19.5	7.9	-13.5
1960	12.2	3.2	4.5	33.0	-5.4
1970	6.9	-0.4	13.2	31.4	-14.6
1980	7.5	-3.4	21.3	26.9	-23.4
1990	1.3	-9.3	26.7	28.4	-31.1
2000	1.3	-5.3	28.7	23.2	-34.9

Source: U.S. Census, 1950–2000.

Table 12. St. Louis Regional Population and Housing Unit Change: 1950–2000

	Population Change	Percent Change	Households Change	Percent Change	Housing Units Change	Percent Change
1950–1960	378,822	22.5	129,762	26.2	154,036	30.4
1960–1970	302,914	14.7	111,475	17.8	124,223	18.8
1970–1980	-7,557	-0.3	101,881	13.8	113,860	14.5
1980–1990	88,639	3.8	85,642	10.2	106,679	11.9
1990–2000	159,508	6.5	152,381	16.5	86,904	8.6
Total	922,326	54.9	581,141	117.4	585,702	155.1

Source: U.S. Census, 1950 and 2000.

Overall, the region increased its housing stock one and half times (155.1 percent) while its population and households increased 54.9 percent and 117.4 percent respectively during the same period. This was a rate that was higher than the increase in units at the national level of 135.9 percent (U.S. Bureau of the Census 1950 and 2000). This can be attributed to "push" factors, such as obsolete and older housing stock, but also to "pull" factors relating to the creation of housing types that were consistent with contemporary housing type demand. This demand for housing has been predominantly for single-family detached housing.

The desire to live in a single-family detached home is evident in a comparison of the number and proportion of single-family housing units between 1950 and 2000 (see Table 13). The proportion of single-family units in the region's housing stock has increased from 60.2 percent in 1950 to 71.3 percent in 2000, an increase of 473,629 or 115.5 percent. This is considerably higher than the nearly unchanged national proportions of 65.9 percent in 1950 and 65.8 percent in 2000. Nearly half of that increase occurred in St. Louis County, where 227,955 single-family units were added over the fifty-year period. Also noteworthy is the eleven-fold increase in single-family housing units in St. Charles County. Overall, eight out of ten (80.9 percent) units created between 1950 and 2000 were for single families, well above the 65.7 percent of single-family units created in the nation.

The desire for home ownership can be seen in data for owner-occupied units in the expanded twelve counties. In 1950, just over half (57.4 percent) of the units in the twelve-county area were owner occupied, a proportion similar to the nation's 54.8 percent (see Table 14). By 2000, the proportion of owner-occupied units had increased to 71.3 percent, higher than the national rate of 66.2 percent. Likewise, the number of units created between 1950 and 2000 that were owner occupied in St. Louis exceeded the nation, 84.7 percent to 73.5 percent.

These data also highlight the pattern of population decentralization. The rate increase in owner-occupied units in the counties added since 1950 was approximately two times the rate in the original five counties: 132.9 percent in the five 1950 counties and 341.9 percent in post-1950 counties. Almost half of the increase in owner-occupied units is found in St. Louis County. At opposite ends of the spectrum of change were St. Charles County, where owner-occupied units increased almost fifteen times (1,469.9 percent), and the City of St. Louis, which experienced a 23.6 percent decline in owner-occupied units. The St. Louis region has a greater proportion of single-family units and owner-occupied units than the nation.

Summary and Conclusions

The St. Louis region has changed dramatically since 1950. It has increased its land area by one and a half times (152.1 percent) while increasing its population by only about half (54.9 percent) over the fifty-year period. This has lowered the population density overall, but the region's population remains centered in the counties that made up the region in 1950, where the density of population increased by 24.2 percent from

647.3 in 1950 to 832.9 person per square mile in 2000. The counties added to the region since 1950 have an overall density of only 111.4 persons per square mile. These developments provide numerous challenges that include supporting a transportation infrastructure that has expanded faster than the population and tax base and an increase in the number and levels of governance. These factors will be compounded by changes in the population's composition (age and race) and demands for services.

Table 13. St. Louis Regional Single-Family Unit Change: 1950 and 2000

County	1950	2000	Change 1950–2000	Percent 1950–2000
IL, Madison County	41,180	85,497	44,317	107.6
IL, St. Clair County	42,698	76,810	34,112	79.9
MO, St. Charles County	6,768	84,528	77,760	1148.9
MO, St. Louis County	96,592	324,547	227,955	236.0
MO, St. Louis city	75,011	76,978	1,967	2.6
Total 1950 Region	262,249	648,360	386,111	147.2
IL, Clinton County	5,836	10,582	4,746	81.3
IL, Jersey County	4,393	7,238	2,845	64.8
IL, Monroe County	3,515	8,994	5,479	155.9
MO, Franklin County	10,491	28,478	17,987	171.5
MO, Jefferson County	11,885	56,219	44,334	373.0
MO, Lincoln County	4,657	10,783	6,126	131.5
MO, Warren County	2,278	8,279	6,001	263.4
Total Post 1950	43,055	130,573	87,518	203.3
Total 1950–2000	305,304	778,933	473,629	155.1
Total units	507,213	1,092,915	585,702	115.5
Percent single-family	60.2	71.3		
Percent of new units			80.9	
USA percent single-family	65.9	65.8		
Percent of new units			65.7	

Source: U.S. Census, 1950 and 2000.

Two other significant developments are the growth of the nonwhite population and its gradual process of decentralization across the twelve-county region in 2000. The region's nonwhite population has grown from 12 percent in 1950 to 21.7 percent in 2000, increasing by 160 percent over the fifty-year period, while the white population increase was 39.1 percent. These changes over the fifty-year period would signal a shift in the pattern of regional politics and changes in the mix of local service demands.

Table 14. St. Louis Regional Owner Occupancy Change: 1950 and 2000

County	1950	2000	Change 1950–2000	Percent 1950–2000
IL, Madison County	35,923	75,243	39,320	109.5
IL, St. Clair County	36,591	64,860	28,269	77.3
MO, St. Charles County	5,310	83,363	78,053	1469.9
MO, St. Louis County	86,425	299,670	213,245	246.7
MO, St. Louis city	89,811	68,639	-21,172	-23.6
Total 1950 Region	254,060	591,775	337,715	132.9
IL, Clinton County	4,098	10,231	6,133	149.7
IL, Jersey County	2,896	6,292	3,396	117.3
IL, Monroe County	2,471	8,237	5,766	233.3
MO, Franklin County	7,245	27,275	20,030	276.5
MO, Jefferson County	8,012	59,624	51,612	644.2
MO, Lincoln County	3,170	11,178	8,008	252.6
MO, Warren County	1,632	7,630	5,998	367.5
Total Post-1950	29,524	130,467	100,943	341.9

The aging of the regional population is also a significant change as it too will represent a shift in service demands. As the baby boomer generation continues to age over the next several decades, it will bring new service demands in health care and transportation. Likewise, the differences in the age distribution of whites and nonwhites will point to growing differences by race in local service demand and representative politics. The larger proportion of younger nonwhites relative to whites also points to an increase in the proportion of nonwhites in the population over the next several decades.

The composition of households changed dramatically over the 1950 to 2000 period and in this regard, the St. Louis region mirrors the changes in the nation. The growth of non-family and married-couple households has been motivated over the fifty-year period by changing social norms and economic conditions. The social and economic trends that began in the 1960s and 1970s, and that have affected the rate of household formations of all types since then, have left their mark on the St. Louis region, as a smaller and a more varied range of household types will also have impacts on service demands such as education, health care, and social services.

The distribution of income in the St. Louis region as measured by median family income indicates that the region's families have fared well relative to the nation. However, the distribution of family income varies significantly within the region as three (Madison, St. Clair, and the City of St. Louis) of the original five counties in 1950 have median family incomes that fell below the medians of the region and the nation by 1970. The city had a median in 2000 that was only about two-thirds (65.1 percent) of the nation's and approximately 60 percent of the region's median. Conversely, the wealth of the region remains concentrated in St. Louis County as its median has consistently been above the regional and national marks. Also influencing the distribution of family income within the region is the rapid rise in the median family income of St. Charles County since 1950. The wide disparity in the distribution of family income across the region is believed by many observers of urban and regional development to have a negative impact on the region's ability to grow and provide its citizens with adequate basic services. If true, the region will face an uphill battle as it competes in the coming decades for new jobs and a general prosperity.

As the population of the St. Louis region has continued to decentralize over the fifty-year period, it has added to its housing stock at rates similar to the rate of household formations. The addition of 585,702 new housing units since 1950 "pulled" St. Louisans initially to St. Louis County, where the bulk of new housing has been created over the fifty-year period. However, the creation of new housing choices in outlying counties such as St. Charles, Jefferson, Franklin, Lincoln, Warren, and Monroe has reinforced the trend of population decentralization. These data provide a picture of St. Louis as a region dominated by single-family housing and its creation as the prime mover of population within the region. Its continued creation will continue the process of decentralization.

References

Bluestone, Barry, and Bennett Harrison. *The Deindustrialization of America.* New York: Basic Books, 1982.

Derks, Scott. *The Value of a Dollar: Prices and Incomes in the United States 1860–1999.* Lakeview, Conn.: Grey House Publishing, 2000.

Frey, William H., Bill Abresch, and Jonathan Yeasting. *America by the Numbers: A Field Guide to the U.S. Population.* New York: The New Press, 2001.

MIDAS (Metropolitan Information and Data Analysis Services), Public Policy Research Center, University of Missouri–St. Louis. "Analysis of Metropolitan Statistical Area Data, from U.S. Bureau of the Census, American Fact Finder." St. Louis: Author, 2000.

Primm, James Neal. *Lion of the Valley.* Boulder, Colo.: Pruett Publishing Company, 1981.

Teaford, Jon C. *The Rough Road to Renaissance: Urban Revitalization in America, 1940–1985.* Baltimore: John Hopkins Press, 1990.

U.S. Bureau of the Census. *Current Population Reports: Households, Families and Children: A 30-Year Perspective.* Washington, D.C.: U.S. Government Printing Office, 1992.

___. *U.S. Census Brief: Households and Families in 2000.* Washington, D.C.: U.S. Government Printing Office, 2002.

Chapter 2
The Dynamics of Density in the St. Louis Region

Brady Baybeck
University of Missouri–St. Louis

The conventional wisdom about St. Louis is that the region is rapidly decentralizing. Numerous articles in the local newspaper have lamented the loss of farmland to suburban housing and the loss of population in the urban core, and these anecdotes seem to be validated by empirical studies. For example, a recent study ranked the St. Louis metropolitan area the seventeenth least dense region out of the top fifty in the nation (Lang 2003, 107); other data, using different measures, confirm this finding (U.S. Bureau of the Census 2000, Table GCT-H1). The central city has lost population while suburbs now extend at least forty miles from the traditional historic downtown on the Mississippi River. Areas in the region that were once distinctly rural are now decidedly urban; conversely, because of abandonment, areas within the central city now rival rural areas for quaintness and country-like quiet.

In many ways, the St. Louis metropolitan area seems to represent the future of the United States for residential density—overall, physical densities of the built environment seem quite low, and the vast majority of citizens live a suburban existence. In the United States, 80 percent of the nation live in a metropolitan area, while only 38 percent live in a central city. In St. Louis, this percentage is even lower, with only 13 percent of the region's population living within the boundaries of the central city (U.S. Bureau of the Census 2000). At first glance, St. Louis appears to be a leading citizen of the suburban nation (Duany, Plater-Zyberk, and Speck 2000).

Yet anecdotes and comparative studies gloss over the dynamics of density occurring within a metropolitan area. This chapter examines how density in St. Louis living patterns—physically, spatially, and aspatially—has changed over the past forty years. While it is true that the average residential density is declining in the United States in general and in St. Louis in particular, and that the average citizen no longer lives in a dense urban environment, density is in reality a dynamic, heterogeneous process. Some parts of the region are emptying out, achieving densities that are essentially rural, while others are changing in character from rural to suburban or perhaps even to urban. There are also spatial patterns to these phenomena. Using data on St. Louis collected from the 1970 through 2000 censuses, I examine the following questions: What does density mean and how does one define it? What are the patterns of density in the St. Louis metropolitan area, and how have these patterns changed in the past forty years? Finally, what are the implications of this changing density for the region?

The argument of this chapter is found in the answers to these questions and revolves around the idea that density is a complicated concept. The conventional wisdom, which argues that St. Louis is the victim of a rapidly decentralizing region, is at best half correct. In order to understand the dynamics of density one needs to examine changes on a variety of indicators at various levels. Using this idea, I find that, in St. Louis, what constitutes "urban" is rapidly ratcheting downward—an urban neighborhood is not as urban as it used to be, while increases in rural density do not cover the losses in the urban areas. The new reality of population and housing density in St. Louis is a suburban one: most people in a region, regardless of what their neighborhood actually looks like, are living in densities that could be called suburban. Although this chapter confirms the conventional wisdom, it does suggest that we take a more nuanced approach to conceptualizing living and development patterns in St. Louis.

What Is Density?

Residential density measures the degree or closeness to which people live in proximity to one another in the built environment. In the global development context, measures like people per some geographic unit are used to measure the degree to which places, cities, or nations are overcrowded (United Nations 1996). Although the nations themselves may not rank high in terms of density, the cities in Africa and Asia have extremely high population densities. In this context, high density is considered detrimental, as it tends to bring with it the problems associated with poverty—disease, violence, and other afflictions associated with substandard, overcrowded housing and too-close communities.

In the United States, density is a somewhat different concept. Very few areas of the United States reach the high population densities of Asia, Europe, or developing nations. Even the residential densities of Manhattan, in New York City, are not as high as those in the cities of the developing world, and residential density does not necessarily translate into overcrowding and poverty. In fact, what makes the United States different from the rest of the world (except, perhaps, for Canada and Australia) is its decentralized character. With its reliance upon the automobile for personal transportation, the preponderance of owner-occupied, detached, single-family housing, and the spatial separation of work from home and play, density is relatively low (Jackson 1985, 6).

In geographic as well as in other terms, the United States has always been decentralized, but this trend has clearly accelerated since World War II. Older portions of metropolitan areas have become less dense, with fewer families occupying more space. New developments tend to turn greenfields into housing, increasing density, but these developments are not dense in the traditional urban sense of the word. For example, an apartment building in a central city may have been converted into 12 units from the original 25, with the renovated apartments being larger and the space being utilized differently. Based upon this factor alone, ceteris paribus, the density would drop by half. Conversely, a rural plot of land containing 1 square mile of area (640 acres) may go from one farmhouse to a planned unit development of 100 homes. This would increase the density by 99 percent in terms of housing units per square mile but still not make the neighborhood urban. The density in places like this could conceivably increase by thousands of times. Thus, over the entire region, decentralization has occurred, but some areas have increased in density while others have decreased.

The factors leading to these shifts are the result of broad as well as place-specific trends. In terms of broad trends, the typical family is smaller, so, by definition, there are fewer people taking up space in each housing unit. Furthermore, as the wealth of the nation has increased, the definition of "adequate," in terms of housing, has shifted. Americans in the housing marketplace now expect more amenities such as larger homes, more rooms, and more parking for their automobiles. Today the average home takes up more geographic space than average homes of the past; for example, the average house size has increased from 1,660 square feet in 1973 to 2,320 in 2002. (U.S. Bureau of the Census 2003). These factors apply to rural, urban, and suburban parts of metropolitan areas.

There are place-specific factors that are changing density as well. In some inner cities, abandonment and urban renewal have fundamentally changed the character of certain neighborhoods. Stadiums, parks, and other commercial or industrial developments have removed what were once dense neighborhoods from the housing marketplace. In many cities, multi-unit dwellings have been renovated to contain fewer units. In the suburbs, new homes tend to be larger, and neighborhoods are designed to be dependent upon the automobile. Car-dependent development takes up more space across the board—residential, commercial, and industrial portions of the metropolitan area require more space because of the need for efficient circulation of the transportation network and because of the need for parking at each location.

These factors combined suggest that the United States is more decentralized, and perhaps less dense, than it used to be. This notion, however, is only partially correct. Density has decreased in some portions of the metropolitan area, but it has increased in others. The decrease comes as the historically developed urban areas (the "core") contain fewer people; the increase comes as new developments are built in the suburbs and exurbs. In other words, metropolitan areas are less dense overall but the concept is more complicated than a single number could possibly convey.

Why does density matter? Although the jury is still out as to whether declining density is good or bad, it is clear that changes in density have an enormous impact upon the local environment and the people who live within it (for an example, see Dreier, Mollenkopf, and Swanstrom 2001, chapter 2). Socially, the density of a place structures formal and informal interaction; if one lives in a subdivision with single-family homes on five-acre lots, the opportunities for interacting with neighbors as well as the need to do so are very different from someone who lives in a condominium in a fifteen-story high rise (Putnam 2000, chapter 12). In political terms, political conflict and patterns of representation are structured by density and the numbers of people who live within certain geographically determined communities. Who represents whom, and how closely, are framed by geographic boundaries (Rusk 1995, 7). Finally, and probably most important, is the effect of density on local policy. Service preferences and the public needs of a community—for example, the transportation network—are driven by the degree to which people live in proximity to one another. In the subdivision with five-acre lots, policy needs are different from those in the fifteen-story high rise. Clearly, density is an important component of metropolitan life; in the next section, I discuss why much care needs to be taken when trying to capture the dynamics of shifting density in the St. Louis metropolitan region.

Measuring Density

The indicator most often used to measure density is persons per square mile. This is relatively easy to calculate; all that is necessary is a count of persons and the spatial area of some aggregate unit such as a metropolitan area, county, or neighborhood. The count data are freely available from the U.S. Bureau of the Census and can be merged with various geographic data such as the county or tract. Although the simple measure—the number of people divided by the number of square miles at some spatial unit—is useful as a rough indicator of people's proximity to one another, it is subject to two major caveats.

First, the density measure of people per square mile does not take into account factors such as commercial or industrial development, open space, or land that cannot be developed. The physical space of a metropolitan area may contain large amounts of space where no one actually lives, which would mean that people per square mile does not capture the closeness in which the population actually lives. As the size of the physical area increases—to, say, the metropolitan area—this becomes more of a problem.

Second, a single measure of people per square mile, for any area, may hide much of the diversity and heterogeneity of development within a unit. Generally speaking, within every metropolitan statistical area (MSA), development runs the gamut from rural to suburban to urban—some areas are still being farmed, while others are high-density, high-rise city neighborhoods. Throwing these areas into one measure means that a single measure of density would be an inaccurate representation of the reality in which people live because of the canceling-out effect. For example, an MSA with a density of 2,000 people per square mile could actually contain neighborhoods where thousands of residents live at densities of 10,000 people per square mile or more, and it could also contain large physical spaces where less than 5 people per square mile live. Similarly, a neighborhood may contain both apartment buildings and single-family homes, and the density of the neighborhood would reflect the central tendency of the two and may not be a particularly accurate representation of reality. In other words, a measure of density is contingent upon the spatial unit chosen for analysis (Longley et al. 2001, 299).

The problems of measurement raised by these issues can be ameliorated in two ways: multiple measures of residential density and multiple units of analysis. Using multiple measures—population density, housing density, and people per housing unit in this analysis—gives a more complete picture of the dynamics underlying how people live. For example, housing density (the number of housing units per square mile) captures the physical aspects of residential development. Multiple units of analysis enable seeing how changing the boundaries of measurement alters the results. This is important to capture accurately the process of density within a region. There is also a tradeoff between ease of interpretation and accuracy—the fewer the units (for example there is only one metropolitan area but it contains many neighborhoods), the easier the interpretation— yet at the same time, much within-unit variation is masked. Using a smaller unit, while better at capturing variation within a place, is more difficult to interpret. I err on the side of comprehensiveness and include multiple units of measurement.

Quantifying Changing Density

I examine three measures of density, for three units of analysis, at four points in time. This seemingly complicated analysis is required to fully understand the dynamics of density in the St. Louis metropolitan region. The three measures are people per square mile, housing units per square mile, and people per housing unit. Each captures one if not more aspects of density. People per square mile is a blunt measure of the proximity of people within one spatial unit. The second indicator, housing units per square mile, better measures physical density in terms of urban development. The final measure, people per housing unit, calculates the aspatial side of density; it examines within housing density and does not necessarily depend upon the scale of the geography being examined.

The three units of analysis evaluated are the metropolitan area, the county, and the tract. Metropolitan area is included as it is a common unit at which regions are evaluated, and this level of analysis provides an easy-to-understand single measure for each indicator. Counties are included as units because they reflect the political geography of the St. Louis MSA; they are also the first step in recognizing the heterogeneity of density within a metropolitan area. St. Louis County and Jefferson County are very different places, for example, and comparing the changes on the three indicators is useful. The final unit, the tract, is used as a proxy for neighborhoods. Census tracts are drawn and tabulated by the Census Bureau and are meant to be relatively equal in terms of population. They are also drawn to be as homogeneous as possible on a variety of size, race, and income indicators. The physical size of the tracts varies substantially, but the general idea is that one can get an accurate picture of a neighborhood by examining its census tract.

Finally, I examine these indicators and their units through time, from 1970 to 2000, using the results of each decennial census (U.S. Bureau of the Census 1970, 1980, 1990a, 2000; GeoLytics, Inc. 2002). Although the gap in years between the censuses is quite large, they are the best, most reliable spatial-temporal data available. Estimates on some of these indicators are available in the years between the censuses, but usually only at the unit of the MSA or county, and usually not for any time before 1990. Using the four decades available from the Census Bureau and from GeoLytics provides the most accurate portrayal of the temporal dynamics of density in the St. Louis metropolitan region.

These three concepts combine to provide a subtle picture of the dynamics of density in St. Louis. Density cannot be reduced to one simple number, and to capture the spatial and temporal dynamics one must incorporate spatial heterogeneity and measures across time.

The St. Louis Region: Not Just Sprawl

The St. Louis metropolitan area, like many other regions in the Rust Belt of the United States, is experiencing two distinct and opposite internal forces. On the one hand, the inner core's population is steadily declining and, along with it, the density. The outer core, however, has become increasingly more dense as residential, commercial, and industrial development spreads throughout what were once rural areas (Brookings Institution 2002, 17–43). These changes, whether occurring as a "natural" result of increasing wealth in a capitalistic society, or due to government policies that promote sprawl, are substantial. The changes are also obvious enough that an observant short-term resident notices differences when traveling about the region.

Figure 1 is a map of the eight-county region examined in this analysis. Within the corporate boundaries of the City of St. Louis—relatively small at 62 square miles—one notices immediately the consequences of disinvestments and suburbanization. There are many areas within the city where the land is vacant, the buildings that used to exist having been demolished at some point, and the neighborhood feels decidedly rural. However, examining the city a bit deeper for subtler clues reveals how fundamentally the concept of density has changed within the city. Touring around the neighborhoods, one notices that in the back alleys, there are buildings that were obviously service apartments at one time, holding domestic servants, relatives, or non-relative tenants. Even the interiors of the many older homes that exist (according to the 2000 census, the median year built for homes in the city is prior to 1940), one sees evidence that the basement or third floor was at one time used as living quarters for the people noted previously. There are also many "four flats"—where four or more families lived within the same building—but many of them have been converted into single-family or two-family homes.

The City of St. Louis was at one time very densely populated, full of large families, immigrants, and others who lived in close proximity to one another. St. Louis is an old city, founded in 1764 (Primm 1981, 9), and its density was at one time extremely high; in 1950, for example, its residential density was nearly 14,000 people per square mile. However, in the past fifty years this density has decreased substantially, both qualitatively and quantitatively, as the population has dropped from 850,000 in 1950 to 348,000 in 2000 (U.S. Bureau of the Census 1990b). The boundaries of the city have not changed, so density by definition has decreased. But what type of density now exists in the city?

On the outskirts of the metropolitan area, one notices a distinctly different set of circumstances. Fields and flood plains once filled with agricultural crops have become, seemingly overnight, residential subdivisions. Forests that were once hunting grounds have become planned-unit developments, with the houses often surrounding a golf course. Density in these areas has clearly increased substantially; where zero (or near zero) people lived one hundred, fifty, or even ten years ago, entire communities containing numerous families now exist.

Nowhere is this trend more evident than in St. Charles County, the bulk of which lies beginning approximately 20 miles to the western boundaries of the City of St. Louis. Although European settlements in the county are nearly as old as those in St. Louis City—the major city, St. Charles, was founded in 1768, according to Primm (1981, 66)—the population remained relatively small until the westward surge of recent decades. St. Charles County's population increased from approximately 30,000 in 1950, to 213,000 in 1990, to nearly 300,000 in the 2000 census, an increase of 900 percent from 1950 and 41 percent in the most recent intercensal period (U.S. Bureau of the Census 2000). Cities to the west of the City of St. Charles have experienced even higher rates of growth, and the developments that preceded the people are primarily subdivisions consisting of single-family homes. The rural character of the county has changed, and with it the density, but to what has it changed?

The two questions presented above have a common theme—to what extent has density changed in the St. Louis region? The descriptions also suggest that density is more complicated than the derogatory term *urban sprawl* implies.

Metropolitan Density: A Slow March Upward. The metropolitan area is the bluntest unit of analysis to use when measuring density. As noted previously, many parts of the region remain rural and bear little resemblance to the neighborhoods of the urban or suburban core. Yet an explanation of the measures through time suggests some intriguing trends.

The data are presented in Table 1. In terms of people per square mile, density tracks perfectly with the population dynamics of the region. This is not surprising, as in this case the denominator (land area) remains constant throughout the analysis. Overall, population density has increased 4 percent, moving from 530 in 1970 to 553 people per square mile in the 2000 census. Interestingly, on this indicator, population density of the region actually decreased from 1980 to 1990, when the region lost population due to deindustrialization and losses in the defense industry. The current measure of 553 people per square mile is not a particularly accurate indicator of the average St. Louisan's living arrangement, however, as at the neighborhood level 553 people per square mile would be a very sparsely settled neighborhood, less than 1 person per acre.

Figure 1. Map of the Eight-County St. Louis Metropolitan Region

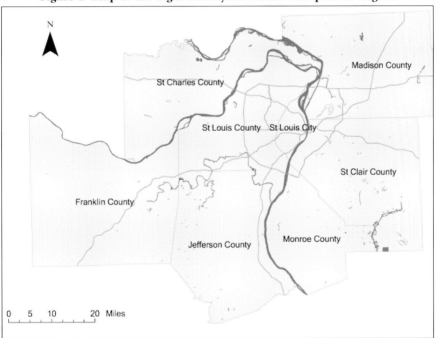

The more illuminating indicators for the metropolitan area are the housing units per square mile and the measure of people per housing unit. Housing density has increased at a greater rate than population density (32 percent versus 4 percent), which suggests that although there are more people, they live in even more houses. In one sense, housing density is a more accurate reflection of the true density at which people live—it measures the physical development of a place, and the increase experienced in the St. Louis metropolitan area means that more land in the region has been developed for housing. Even in the decade that the region lost population, from 1970 to 1980, housing density increased from 197 to 220 housing units per square mile, an increase of 12 percent. The trend toward higher density is seemingly independent of the population trends.

The increasing density across housing units does not translate into higher concentrations within those units, however, as shown by the last measure, people per housing unit. This has decreased through time, from 3.2 in 1970 to 2.6 in 2000, a decline of 19 percent. That on average fewer people are occupying each home is not surprising since couples are having fewer children, individuals are waiting longer to marry, and people are living longer lives after the children leave the home. Even though the density of the region as a whole is increasing, most citizens would not truly experience the rise—there are fewer people living within each of the homes.

County Density: Increasing but Decreasing. Counties are a useful subgroup with which to view density because they represent meaningful political boundaries within a metropolitan area. A citizen living in Jefferson County, for example, lives in a different political and perhaps social realm than a citizen living in the mainline suburban county of St. Louis County. Also, decisions about density—planning, zoning, and transportation—are usually made at the county level. Viewing the shifting densities at the within-region unit of the county, then, is useful.

The results of the county analysis are presented in Tables 2 through 4. Since the metropolitan area has been broken up into counties due to political decisions made more than a century ago, the metropolitan area itself can be treated as a distribution of observations. In alphabetical terms the eight counties range from Franklin to St. Louis Counties. The values calculated for the metropolitan area as a whole are different from the quantities generated for the counties, which are a distribution. The county mean represents the central tendency of the county observations throughout the metropolitan area, while a percentage change measure of the mean represents the average change of the distribution. This gives rise to seemingly strange outcomes—the mean may be decreasing through time, but the percent change measure may increase, or vice versa.

The basic density measure (people per square mile), presented in Table 2 and Figure 2, demonstrates that some counties have experienced substantial increases in density, while a relative few have decreased considerably. St. Charles County, for example, has experienced an enormous increase in density (205 percent), from 166 people per square mile in 1970 to 507 in 2000. In fact, six of the eight counties have increased, a direct function of their population increases. These increases are centered in the suburban and exurban counties, with the largest increase occurring in counties far away from the urban core of the City of St. Louis.

Table 1. Metropolitan Density Data, 1970–2000

	Year				Percent Change
	1970	1980	1990	2000	1970–2000
People per square mile	530	518	533	553	4%
Housing units per square mile	176	197	220	233	32%
People per housing unit	3.2	2.8	2.6	2.6	-19%

Figure 2. Bar Chart, Residential Density at the County Level, 1970–2000

The percentages at the county level, however, mask the decentralization in the St. Louis region. The two counties that decreased in density—St. Louis City in Missouri and St. Clair County in Illinois—also happened to be, at one time, the most populated counties in their respective states. Particularly in St. Louis City, the depopulation has been severe. In 1970, the density of the city proper was 10,048 people per square mile, equivalent to today's Philadelphia. By 2000, the city had fallen to a density of 5,623, comparable to St. Paul, Minnesota (U.S. Bureau of the Census 2000, STF1). This density is still higher than all other counties in the region by a substantial margin. But because of the severity of the loss, and because of the magnitude of the difference between St. Louis City and every other county, the mean density of the metropolitan area is decreasing. The average county, however, is increasing—the mean increase is a positive 46 percent—because six of the eight counties experienced an increase in population density.

The housing density measure, housing units per square mile (Table 3 and Figure 3), is more instructive regarding the trends in physical development occurring in the St. Louis metropolitan area. As before, the average housing density is decreasing due to the losses in St. Louis City as structures are demolished due to abandonment or redevelopment. The city has lost 30 percent of its housing units over the past thirty years, from around 232,000 in 1970 to 176,000 in 2000. Yet, as before, the average county increased in density, and this increase is substantial. More important, in every case the increase in housing density is greater than the increase in population density.

Table 2. Residential Density, in People per Square Mile, Counties of the St. Louis Metropolitan Area, 1970–2000

	Year				Percent Change
	1970	1980	1990	2000	1970–2000
MSA mean	1,640	1,323	1,236	1,169	46%
Franklin County	60	77	87	102	70%
Jefferson County	160	223	261	302	88%
Madison County	346	341	344	357	3%
Monroe County	48	52	58	71	47%
St Clair County	422	403	396	386	-9%
St Charles County	166	257	380	507	205%
St. Louis County	1,873	1,917	1,956	2,001	7%
St. Louis City	10,048	7,316	6,406	5,623	-44%

Table 3. Housing Density, Counties of the St. Louis Metropolitan Area, 1970–2000

Housing Units per Square Mile	Year				Percent Change
	1970	1980	1990	2000	1970–2000
MSA mean	601	557	556	566	81%
Franklin County	21	29	35	41	98%
Jefferson County	51	76	96	115	127%
Madison County	113	129	139	150	33%
Monroe County	16	19	23	28	75%
St Clair County	135	147	156	157	16%
St Charles County	50	88	141	188	278%
St. Louis County	574	706	791	834	45%
St. Louis City	3,851	3,261	3,148	2,848	-26%

Finally, the relatively aspatial measure of people per housing unit (Table 4) demonstrates how fundamentally density is decreasing in all counties of the St. Louis region and suggests that there is a distinct convergence to a central tendency across all counties. Traditionally suburban counties such as St. Louis County, where families with children are the predominant category, have declined substantially on this measure. Even St. Charles County, currently the place to be for young families, has experienced a decline of 22 percent, from 3.6 in 1970 to 2.8 in 2000. As the average household family size has decreased, so has the density as measured by people per housing unit.

Figure 3. Bar Chart, Housing Density at the County Level, 1970–2000

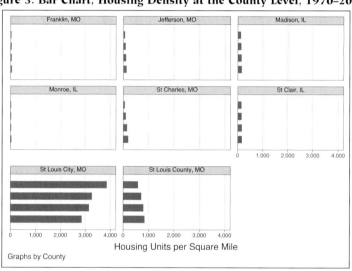

Table 4. Density in People per Housing Unit, Counties of the St. Louis Metropolitan Area, 1970–2000

People per Housing Unit	Year				Percent Change 1970–2000
	1970	1980	1990	2000	
MSA mean	3.3	2.9	2.7	2.6	-20%
Franklin County	3.2	3	2.8	2.7	-17%
Jefferson County	3.5	3.1	2.9	2.8	-22%
Madison County	3.2	2.8	2.6	2.5	-21%
Monroe County	3.3	2.9	2.7	2.7	-18%
St Clair County	3.3	2.9	2.8	2.6	-20%
St Charles County	3.6	3.1	2.9	2.8	-22%
St. Louis County	3.4	2.8	2.6	2.5	-25%
St. Louis City	2.9	2.5	2.4	2.4	-18%

Figure 4. Histogram of Changing Residential Densities, Neighborhoods of the St. Louis Metropolitan Area, 1970–2000. Number of Neighborhoods = 505

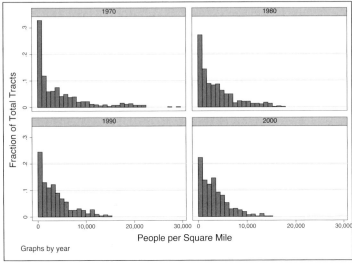

Source: CensusCD.

An interesting exception to this trend is the City of St. Louis. Since 1970, the City had the lowest value on the number of people per housing unit. This is not particularly surprising, given that urban centers and inner cities have high numbers of the elderly, of young professionals, and of other solitary households. The city's decline has slowed relative to the other counties, and has seemingly evened out at 2.4. Unlike the other measures of density (people and housing units per square mile), St. Louis City has appeared to stabilize on this one.

Taken together, the density measures at the county level suggest some interesting trends for density in the region. First, there are clear winners and losers. In both physical and human terms, the inner counties are decreasing in density while the suburban and exurban counties are increasing. The urban way of life is far less crowded than it used to be; the suburban way of life is more congested but nowhere near the urban densities. In addition, densities at all measures seem to be converging to some value, an average that actually represents the central tendency. The typical life experience for St. Louisans is approaching a decentralized suburban existence, even in what would be called, relatively speaking, urban environments.

Neighborhood (Tract) Density: It's the Distribution! The concept of density is scale dependent: the measure value depends upon the boundaries drawn for the units. The larger the unit, the easier the number is to interpret because there is less data complexity. Yet the measures at the large units generally do not accurately portray how the average citizen lives. To accomplish this, a smaller unit of analysis is necessary, which adds to the complexity of interpretation but is more substantively compelling and accurate.

The lowest unit for which density data can be obtained reliably through time is the census tract. This measure is analogous to the neighborhood with generally defined social boundaries. Tracts are drawn to be a relatively constant size (3,000 to 5,000 people) and are used by many scholars as a proxy for the neighborhood. The boundaries, once drawn, are generally maintained—or split, but rarely dissolved—so that stable spatial boundaries can be observed through time (U.S. Bureau of the Census 1994, ch. 10).

There are 505 neighborhoods (tracts) in the eight-county region. For each neighborhood, the density measures represent the proximity with which residents live near one another; for example, residents in a neighborhood with a large value on the persons per square mile measure are assumed to live in higher-density, urban neighborhoods. Measures at this unit of analysis, then, are the closest to capturing how the physical setting operates in an individual resident's life.

Measuring neighborhood density at this unit complicates the analysis. Rather than reduce it to a single number, one must examine distributions, measures of central tendency and dispersion, and spatial patterns across the neighborhoods. In order to account for the differential size in the neighborhoods, one must also weight the data for population size, which gives a better perspective on the typical neighborhood in the region. Finally, outliers must be accounted for, so measures such as medians (along with averages or means) must be calculated as well. In this section, I sort through these messy data issues to get to the core point: the central tendency of neighborhood density is decreasing overall—and quite rapidly—but this decrease is not the result of a common tendency throughout the data.

The change in density through time, for the people per square mile measure, is presented in Table 5. The results for the weighted neighborhood means are similar to those for the counties; on average, the number of persons per square mile has decreased across neighborhoods (from 6,351 people per square mile to 3,223), yet most individual neighborhoods have increased in density. What is most interesting is the change in the standard deviation for the distribution, which has decreased from 6,167 in 1970 to 2,853 in 2000. Figure 4 presents this phenomenon visually in the form of a histogram. Rather than seeing a zero-sum pattern of abandonment in one area and overcrowding in another, there is a convergence to a declining mean. Some neighborhoods are losing density while others are gaining, but the neighborhoods with losses do not go to zero, nor do the gaining neighborhoods obtain densities considered urban. Another visual presentation, Figure 5's scatterplot, demonstrates this graphically. The neighborhoods to the left of the line have gained in density, while those to the right have lost. The losses of the high density neighborhoods are clearly not made up by the gains. Finally, the median density measures support this finding. Even though the mean and standard deviation measures have varied widely through time, the median has remained remarkably constant, with a slight increase from 2,588 in 1970 to 2,748 in 2000.

Table 5. Residential Density, Neighborhoods of the St. Louis Metropolitan Area, 1970–2000. Number of Neighborhoods = 505

People per Square Mile;	Year				Mean Percent Change
n = 505	1970	1980	1990	2000	1970–2000
Mean density per square mile (weighted)	6,351	4,277	3,645	3,223	5%
Standard deviation (weighted)	6,167	3,953	3,260	2,853	102%
Median density per square mile (unweighted)	2,588	2,575	2,824	2,748	-11%
Source: CensusCD.					

Some geographic context helps. Figure 6a is a map of the percent change in residential density for the neighborhoods. Figure 6b presents the gainers and losers on this measure, as well as the low, high, and typical (average) density neighborhoods. There is an obvious, albeit imperfect, spatial pattern. The neighborhoods that have lost density over the thirty-year period tend to be within the outer beltway of I-270, with the largest losses occurring near the central business district of the City of St. Louis, near the Mississippi River. There are some neighborhoods with increasing density within I-270, particularly the areas surrounding Clayton, an emerging urban area that is becoming the de facto central business district of the region, and Washington University. The only neighborhoods in the City where density has increased are one near St. Louis University, in the central corridor, and one on the far north side. The neighborhood near St. Louis University has become more dense because of the construction of new student dormitories; the neighborhood in the north side has increased due to a new housing development built there, although the density actually decreased from 1990 to 2000. The City does appear to have some short-term dynamics, in that 17 neighborhoods, out of 113, increased in density between 1990 and 2000.

Figure 5. Scatterplot of Residential Density in 2000 on Residential Density of 1970, Neighborhoods of the St. Louis Metropolitan Area. Number of Neighborhoods = 505

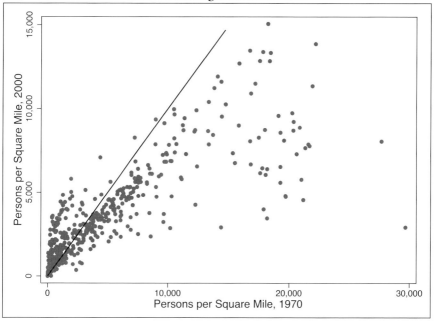

Source: CensusCD.

The distinctions of magnitude of density loss and gain are best described by comparing them. Noted in Figure 6b are three neighborhoods, chosen based upon their values on the residential density measure in 1970: a very low density neighborhood in St. Charles County; the highest density neighborhood, located in the City of St. Louis; and the neighborhood closest to the 1970 average, located in the central corridor of St. Louis County. The experience of these neighborhoods is somewhat typical of their peers.

The low-density neighborhood has experienced tremendous growth, increasing by 249 percent, from 10.6 people per square mile in 1970 to 37.1 in 2000. Yet, in comparison to 1970's most dense neighborhood, the density still has a long way to go before it is considered urban. Although 1970's densest neighborhood, in the City, lost 90 percent of its residential density, the buildings and development are still far more urban in character than most—its 2000 density of 2,917, while substantially below the 2000 average, is well above that of the rapidly densifying counties. The most interesting neighborhood is the one closest to the average in 1970. This neighborhood has a rather high density in 2000, even though its residential density has declined from 1970 to 2000 by 17 percent. In fact, residential density increased from 1990 to 2000, demonstrating that populations do increase in already somewhat dense areas. If one were to do the arithmetic, the increase in density in this neighborhood, in people, is greater than that of the rapidly increasing neighborhoods of St. Charles County.

The housing density measure, housing units per square mile, illustrates the complex dynamics of changes in the physical environment through time, and the results are presented in Table 6 and Figure 7. One would expect, with suburbanization, that housing density would increase substantially in the suburbs while remaining stable or decreasing in urban areas. This is not necessarily the case. In some parts of St. Louis City, the decline in housing has been precipitous. The City neighborhood with the

**Figure 6a. Map of Neighborhood Change in Residential Density, 1970–2000.
Number of Neighborhoods = 505**

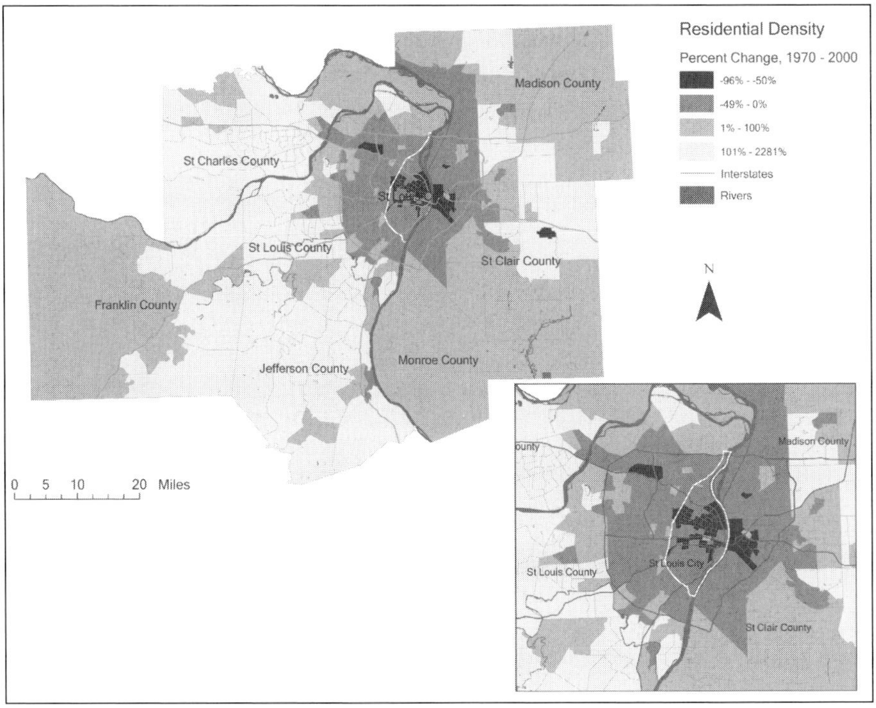

Source: CensusCD.

largest decline in residential density lost 87 percent of its housing units. Where there were once 4,709 units of housing, there are now 613, a substantial drop in both percentage and actual terms.

Unlike the residential density measure, however, new housing units take up the slack. A neighborhood in St. Louis County, in the suburb of Chesterfield and near the Missouri River, experienced a 900 percent increase in housing density, and the number of housing units increased from 498 to 4,944, an almost equal gain to the loss in the previously

Table 6. Housing Density, Neighborhoods of the St. Louis Metropolitan Area, 1970–2000. Number of Neighborhoods = 505

Housing Units per	Year				Percent Change
Square Mile; n = 505	1970	1980	1990	2000	1970–2000
Mean density per square mile (weighted)	2,241	1,722	1,601	1,554	39%
Standard deviation (weighted)	2,360	1,761	1,626	1,485	128%
Median density per square mile (unweighted)	815	972	1,122	1,160	24%
Source: CensusCD.					

Figure 6b. Map of the Low, High, and Typical Neighborhoods, 1970 Residential Density. Number of Neighborhoods = 505. Source: CensusCD.

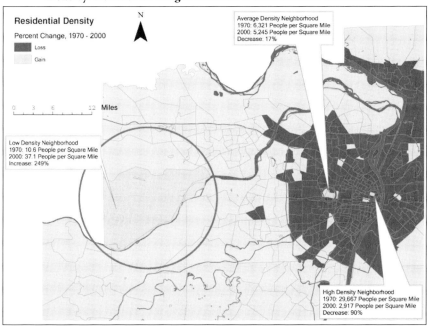

Residential Density

Percent Change, 1970 - 2000
- Loss
- Gain

Average Density Neighborhood
1970: 6,321 People per Square Mile
2000: 5,245 People per Square Mile
Decrease: 17%

0   3   6   12   Miles

Low Density Neighborhood
1970: 10.6 People per Square Mile
2000: 37.1 People per Square Mile
Increase: 249%

High Density Neighborhood
1970: 29,667 People per Square Mile
2000: 2,917 People per Square Mile
Decrease: 90%

described City neighborhood. Although not all neighborhoods in the suburban areas increased as much—the average percentage gain is 200 percent—the changes in housing unit density are substantial.

Overall, though, housing density is stickier than population density. Housing, once built, tends to remain (unlike people), and the distribution changes reflect this. The average neighborhood housing density has decreased, but not at the same pace as population density. The standard deviation has also decreased, but the convergence to the mean is not as pronounced, as the histogram in Figure 8 indicates. Finally, the scatterplots, when compared with the population density scatterplots, demonstrate the phenomenon. If density is decreasing, neighborhoods lose population density much faster than they do housing density.

Comparing the low, average, and high neighborhoods in 1970 to where they are in 2000 and to the others yields results similar to the population density measure (see Figures 9a and 9b). The low and high neighborhoods in 1970 housing density are the same as the lows and highs for the population density. The changes in the housing density in the urban areas are similar to those of the suburban and exurban areas—housing density increased at a greater rate, or decreased at a slower rate, than population density.

The average neighborhood of 1970 is different from the residential density case, and is a reflection of the different densities in which St. Louisans lived in 1970. Located in Florissant, in north St. Louis County, the neighborhood with the approximately average housing density had a value of 2,239 housing units per square mile—far below the average 1970 residential density of 6,351 people per square mile. This neighborhood remained remarkably stable on this measure, decreasing only 6 percent over the thirty-year period and actually increasing from 1990 to 2000. This neighborhood also remained above the 2000 average for all neighborhoods, which is a function of housing being a physical and virtually immovable commodity. People can move; houses really cannot.

The final measure, people per housing unit, reinforces the trends previously identified, and the results are presented in Table 7 and Figure 10. The number of people per unit has dropped substantially from 1970 to 2000, although this decline is flattening as the mean approaches 2.5 people per housing unit. Like the previous two measures, the standard deviation is decreasing; neighborhoods with a high degree of crowding are becoming less frequent, and like the other measures there appears to be a convergence to a mean. This is the first neighborhood measure where the changes in the median agree with the changes in the mean. As family or household size decreases—a trend that is international in scope, not just limited to the St. Louis region—the region, by this measure, is becoming less dense.

Figure 7. Histogram of Changing Housing Densities, Neighborhoods of the St. Louis Metropolitan Area, 1970–2000. Number of Neighborhoods = 505

Source: CensusCD.

Figure 8. Scatterplot of Housing Density in 2000 on Housing Density in 1970, Neighborhoods of the St. Louis Metroplitan Area. Number of Neighborhoods = 505

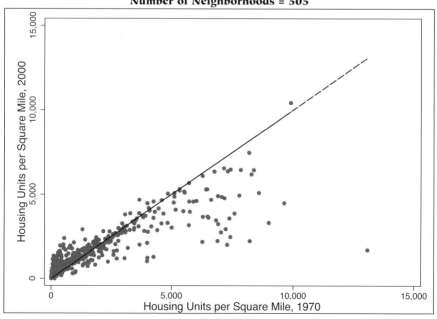

Source: CensusCD.

Yet this trend toward decreasing aspatial density is far from uniform, and the neighborhoods increasing in the people per housing unit measure (see Figure 11) are currently undergoing a marked shift in demographics—both socioeconomic and racial. They are directly affected by abandonment in other neighborhoods; the City's poor population, which has remained relatively constant, apparently is moving into neighborhoods adjacent to the distressed neighborhoods. Neighborhoods increasing in both physical and aspatial density are typically near Washington University and St. Louis University. Although these neighborhoods are increasing in densitybecause of an influx of college-age residents, one would be hard pressed to take this as anything but localized around the campuses. In this case, increasing density is not an indicator of true poverty, but neither is it an antidote to declining density. Taken together, these measures suggest that the decentralization of the St. Louis region is not as clear-cut as the conventional wisdom seems to indicate. One needs to take a measured view of the shifting densities in order to understand what is really happening to the physical environment in the metropolitan area. Clearly, some places are emptying out, at rates that make the challenges those neighborhoods face quite stark. Yet, the increase in density, coupled with decentralization, is not so uniform as most tend to think.

Figure 9a. Map of Neighborhood Change Housing Density, 1970–2000. Number of Neighborhoods = 505

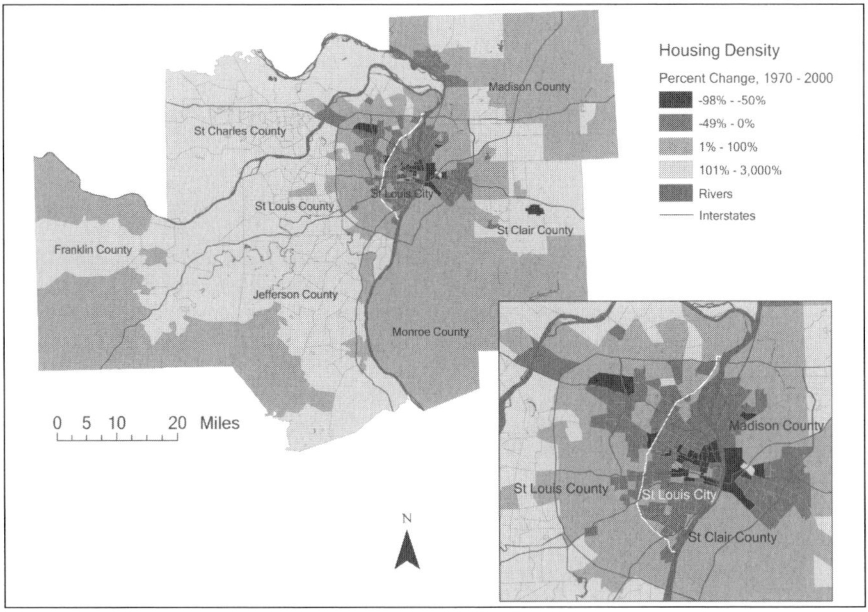

Source: CensusCD.

Figure 9b. Map of the Low, High, and Typical Housing Density, 1970, St, Louis Metropolitan Area. Number of Neighborhoods = 505

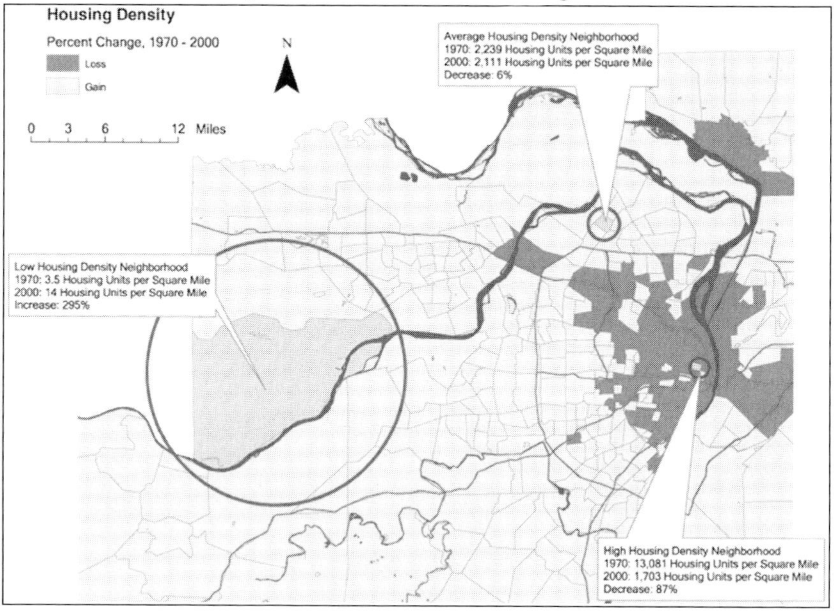

Source: CensusCD.

Table 7. People per Housing Unit Density, Neighborhoods of the St. Louis Metropolitan Area, 1970–2000. Number of Neighborhoods = 505

People per Housing Unit;	Year				Percent Change
n = 505	1970	1980	1990	2000	1970–2000
Mean housing units per square mile (weighted)	3.3	2.9	2.7	2.6	-21%
Standard deviation (weighted)	0.46	0.41	0.39	0.36	11.7%
Median housing units per square mile (unweighted)	3.4	2.9	2.7	2.6	-23%
Source: CensusCD.					

Rethinking Density

The conventional wisdom, particularly in the local media, is that the St. Louis region is becoming a "donut"—hollow in the center and well-developed on the outside (Getz & O'Connor 2001; Judd & Swanstrom 1998, 425). While St. Louis is decentralizing overall, the process is not necessarily straightforward. Urban areas, particularly neighborhoods, are complicated units subject to a vast number of social, economic, and political forces. When regional actors discuss "sprawl," they need to consider four factors.

First, examining density at the level of the metropolitan area hides, and perhaps misrepresents, important intra-regional dynamics. Even though metropolitan-level density is an easy concept to interpret, fully under-standing the dynamics of density requires examining distributions within a region. Going down to the county or neighborhood level gives a far better sense of how measures of density are changing through time. It would be more productive to view density as the complicated process that it is—as a distribution of neighborhoods, perhaps even blocks, which vary widely throughout any region.

Second, in all cases, for all neighborhoods and counties, housing density is increasing at a faster rate than population density (in the cases where density is declining, housing density is decreasing at a slower rate). This housing indicator represents the true shift in density within the St. Louis region; houses per square mile have increased even if population has not (which is borne out by the people per housing unit measure). Overall, people just occupy more physical space than their predecessors.

Figure 10. Histogram of People per Housing Unit Density, Neighborhoods of the St. Louis Metropolitan Area, 1970–2000. Number of Neighborhoods = 505

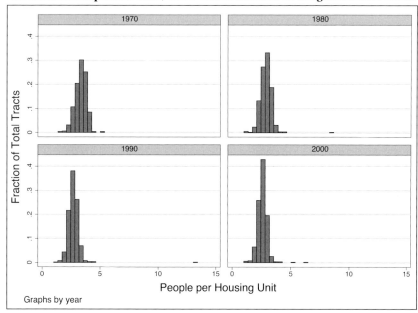

Source: CensusCD.

This is a trend not unique to St. Louis, which runs quite consistently, although not perfectly so, through all counties and neighborhoods. Households have decreased in size across all units of analysis here, and people are living less closely than they used to. With the exception of the poorest and college neighborhoods, on average people are not living inhomes or apartments with a large contingent of other occupants. This change, probably a function of the increasing material prosperity of

Figure 11. Map of Increasing v. Decreasing People per Housing Unit, Neighborhoods of the St. Louis Metropolitan Area, 1970–2000. Number of Neighborhoods = 505

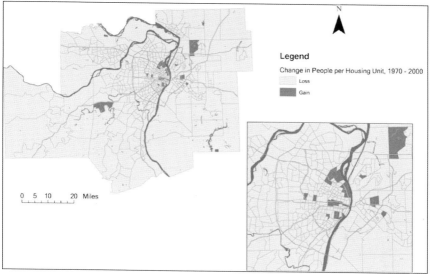

Source: CensusCD.

society, means that aspatial density is decreasing. As population increases, the need for housing consistent with current preferences increases as well. Within our homes, we just lead less dense lives, which has a large effect upon the measures of density we utilize and how we interpret them.

Third, the shifts in density at the county level indicate how much the notion of "urban" has changed for the St. Louis region. The mean county density has decreased over time even though the vast majority of counties (six out of eight) have actually increased on the two density measures. This is because St. Louis City has dropped by nearly 50 percent in terms of density. What constitutes urban densities—the places where people live in close proximity to each other—has changed dramatically. People are not living as near to each other as they used to, although the housing densities have not dropped as precipitously.

Finally, the underlying dynamic is that of a convergence to a mean, where the urban-rural split within the region is not as distinct as it used to be. Somewhat surprisingly, urban neighborhoods and rural neighborhoods seem to be moving toward a common value, which not coincidentally is that of a typical inner ring suburban neighborhood. And these inner ring suburban neighborhoods seem to be holding steady at this mean value. As the region seems to disperse outward, neighborhoods—whether they consist of city blocks or tract-home subdivisions—are becoming more similar. As our society becomes wealthier, the densities are becoming more alike, and our shared experience of proximity is converging to a reasonably consistent number across neighborhoods. The differences in the future will likely be even more marginal—the residents of the St. Louis region are not as far apart or as close together physically as they think.

References

Brookings Institution Center on Urban and Metropolitan Policy. *Growth in the Heartland: Challenges and Opportunities for Missouri*. Washington, D.C.: Brookings Institution, 2002.

Dreier, Peter, John Mollenkopf, and Todd Swanstrom. *Place Matters: Metropolitics for the Twenty-First Century*. Lawrence: University Press of Kansas, 2001.

Duany, Andres, Elizabeth Plater-Zyberk, and Jeff Speck. *Suburban Nation: The Rise of Sprawl and the Decline of the American Dream*. New York: North Point Press, 2000.

GeoLytics, Inc., in conjunction with the Urban Institute. *CensusCD Neighborhood Change Database (NCDB) 1970–2000 U.S. Census Tract Data*. East Brunswick, N.J.: GeoLytics, Inc., 2002. More information available at http://www.censuscd.com.

Getz, Jim, and Phillip O'Connor, with contributions by Jennifer LaFluer and Dawn Fallik. "Monroe County Grew by 23 Percent." *St. Louis Post-Dispatch*, accessed from http://www.stltoday.com, 2001.

Jackson, Kenneth T. *Crabgrass Frontier: The Suburbanization of the United States*. New York: Oxford University Press, 1985.

Judd, Dennis R., and Todd Swanstrom. *City Politics: Private Power and Public Policy*. New York: Longman, 1998.

Lang, Robert E. *Edgeless Cities*. Washington, D.C.: Brookings Institution Press, 2003.

Longley, Paul A., Michael F. Goodchild, David J. Maguire, and David W. Rhind. *Geographic Information Systems and Science*. New York: John Wiley and Sons, Ltd., 2001.

Primm, James Neal. *Lion of the Valley: St. Louis, Missouri*. Boulder, Colo.: Pruett Publishing Company, 1981.

Putnam, Robert D. *Bowling Alone: The Collapse and Revival of American Community*. New York: Simon & Schuster, 2000.

Rusk, David. *Cities Without Suburbs*. 2d ed. Washington, D.C.: The Woodrow Wilson Center Press, 1995.

United Nations. *"An Assessment of Urban Environmental Problems and Policies in Selected ECA Member States."* Paper presented for the ninth session of the Conference of African Planners, Statisticians, and Population and Information Specialists, Addis Ababa, Ethopia, March 11–16, 1996. Available at http://www.un.org/popin/confcon/uneca9603/psdpi96.html.

United States Bureau of the Census. *Census of the United States*. 1970, 1980, 1990a, 2000. Accessed through http://www.census.gov.

___. *Geographic Areas Reference Manual*. Washington, D.C.: U.S. Bureau of the Census, 1994.

___. "Median and Average Square Footage of Floor Area in New One-Family Houses Completed by Location." 2003. Accessed through http://www.census.gov/const/C25Ann/sftotalmedavgsqft.pdf.

___. "Population and Housing Unit Counts: United States." 1990b. Accessed through http://www.census.gov/prod/cen1990/cph2/cph-2-1-1.pdf.

___. *Statistical Abstract of the United States*. 2000. Accessed through http://www.census.gov/prod/www/statistical-abstract-us.html.

Chapter 3
The Transforming Economy

Mark Tranel
University of Missouri–St. Louis

In academic terms, the metropolitan St. Louis[1] economy is a B student. POLICOM Corporation, a national economics research firm, annually measures and ranks the "economic strength" of U.S. metropolitan areas for the purpose of studying the characteristics of strong and weak economies (POLICOM 2003). It measures economic strength as a combination of both the rate of growth and the consistency of the growth over a twenty-five-year period. St. Louis has averaged a B, although it has improved from a B- to an A- over the last eight years.

2002	2001	2000	1999	1998	1997	1996	1995
A-	B+	B+	B	B	B-	B-	B-

An overall B grade masks, however, the diversity in the metropolitan St. Louis economy. Some sectors would have earned an A rating while others are barely holding onto a C.

Based on economic activity (the value of sales, receipts, or shipments), metropolitan St. Louis is a manufacturing and wholesale trade economy. Those two sectors account for over $100 billion in activity ($57 billion wholesale and $51.5 billion manufacturing), compared to $26.5 billion for the service sector. Manufacturing and wholesale trade are responsible for $9.5 billion in annual payroll, just 2 percent less than the $9.9 billion for services. If, however, one asks what most people in the metropolitan St. Louis economy do, the response is that the service sector dominates. There are about 450,000 people working in the service sector (the majority being 150,000 in health care and 100,000 in accommodations

---

[1] For this chapter, metropolitan St. Louis is defined as the eight-county region served by the federally designated metropolitan planning organization: in Missouri, St. Louis, St. Charles, Franklin, and Jefferson Counties and the City of St. Louis; in Illinois, St. Clair, Madison, and Monroe Counties.

and foodservices), compared to about 237,000 in manufacturing (171,000) and wholesale (66,000).

St. Louis is not alone in being a predominantly manufacturing and wholesale economy. As Table 1 shows, Cleveland's manufacturing sector has both a larger sales volume and more employees. Milwaukee and Minneapolis have more manufacturing employees than St. Louis, but not as large an industry by sales volume. Denver and Minneapolis have more employees in the wholesale sector, but Minneapolis's sales volume is considerably larger than that of both Denver and St. Louis. For all of these metropolitan areas, the manufacturing/wholesale sectors are larger by sales volume than services, although the service sector has more employees.

Table 1. St. Louis Compared to Other Central U.S. Metropolitan Areas in Manufacturing, Wholesale, and Services Sectors

City	Manufacturing		Wholesale		Services	
	Sales	Employees	Sales	Employees	Sales	Employees
St. Louis	51,488,137	170,766	57,134,255	66,406	26,412,376	448,812
Cincinnati	35,239,117	139,924	D	D	14,099,430	338,533
Cleveland	53,188,994	255,158	45,381,353	80,340	27,894,776	489,130
Denver	26,465,891	115,133	54,606,933	69,748	32,099,826	447,352
Indianapolis	26,773,226	106,283	28,933,918	42,968	15,680,470	276,200
Kansas City	31,014,921	95,231	46,070,822	53,535	19,085,981	307,338
Milwaukee	36,323,066	184,012	30,083,310	47,661	16,849,919	300,368
Minneapolis	44,599,702	234,192	81,848,998	98,760	34,152,490	562,140

Source: U.S. Census Bureau, 1997 Economic Census.
Note: Sales data in $1,000.
Note: D = withheld to avoid disclosure.

Specifically comparing the manufacturing and service sectors, manufacturing is the dominant economic activity by sales volume in all eight counties (see Table 2). In Franklin, Jefferson, and Madison Counties the largest portion of payroll also comes from manufacturing. Manufacturing is particularly important in Franklin County. Payroll for the manufacturing sector is almost three times the payroll for the service industry and, by the measure of sales volume, manufacturing is six times the activity level of services. In Madison County the manufacturing payroll is a little less than twice the services payroll, but, by sales volume, manufacturing is seven times the activity level of services.

The largest subregional economy in metropolitan St. Louis is St. Louis County: in manufacturing, it has 38 percent of all establishments and 46 percent of all employees; in wholesale it has 55 percent of all establishments and 58 percent of all employees; in retail it has 43 percent of all establishments and 51 percent of employers; in services it has 44 percent of all establishments and 40 percent of all employees; in professional and technical services it has 56 percent of all establishments and 59 percent of all employees.

To document how the economic sectors in metropolitan St. Louis have changed over time, the following sections use U.S. Bureau of the Census's County Business Patterns data to compare the structure of economic activity for three years: 1987, 1992, and 1997. In March 1987, the metropolitan St. Louis area employed approximately 993,000 individuals working for 57,000 companies. In March 1997, those numbers increased to 1,164,000 workers and 64,000 companies. This is a gain of 17.2 percent employed and 11.3 percent in companies over the ten-year period.

Table 2. County-Level Comparison of Manufacturing and Services in Metropolitan St. Louis

County	Manufacturing		Services	
	Sales/Shipments	Payroll	Sales/Shipments	Payroll
City of St. Louis	8,605,466	1,243,627	4,385,105	1,704,172
St. Louis County	25,347,905	3,359,780	10,974,121	4,097,664
St. Charles County	4,432,880	431,886	1,317,612	475,432
Jefferson County	1,199,342	168,185	424,097	145,355
Franklin County	1,836,298	284,438	308,737	99,480
St. Clair County	1,763,491	249,320	1,344,480	480,376
Madison County	7,676,517	743,827	1,120,654	393,430
Monroe County	NA	NA	57,956[1]	24,254[1]

Source: U.S. Census Bureau, 1997 Economic Census.
Note: Data in $1,000.
[1]For Monroe County, manufacturing data was not available and the services data did not include educational services, accommodation, and food services.

The Importance of Manufacturing

The manufacturing sector has shown the highest relative decrease in percentage of regional employees over the ten-year period. However, it is still in absolute terms the third largest in percentage of individuals employed, 17.15 percent of all workers. The total number of manufacturing firms actually increased from 3,154 to 3,341, although as a percentage of total business establishments it decreased from 5.51 percent in 1987 to 5.24 percent in 1997.

From 1987 to 1997 the number of individuals employed in manufacturing dropped from 203,692 to 199,668. Although this is only a 2 percent drop, it is a decrease in percentage of total employed in the region from 20.5 percent to 17.1 percent. Many of these people were employed by the Boeing Company (McDonnell Douglas Corporation until 1997), which had 40,000 employees at the start of the decade. As of February 2001, it employed only 16,400.

Boeing and automobile manufacturers (Chrysler, Ford, and General Motors) and many of their suppliers are all included in the industrial classification "transportation equipment." In 1987 and 1992 County Business Patterns did not disclose how many employees they had at their various locations, so an overall trend cannot be established. However, numbers are available for 1997. That year 45,121 workers were employed by transportation equipment firms, which accounts for 23 percent of all those employed in the manufacturing industry, with 37,027 of these workers employed in St. Louis County, where Boeing and two automobile plants are located.

The manufacturing industries that increased in number of establishments from 1987 to 1997 are apparel and other textile products; lumber and wood products; furniture and fixtures; printing and publishing; petroleum and coal products; rubber and miscellaneous plastics products (an increase of 36 percent in the number of firms); transportation equipment; and miscellaneous manufacturing industries.

One of the reasons for continued strength in the metropolitan St. Louis manufacturing base is foreign direct investment. In a Department of Commerce study, St. Louis ranked seventeenth nationally for foreign-owned establishments (Bureau of Economic Analysis, Survey of Current Business 1999). The foreign direct investment was disproportionately new construction on previously undeveloped suburban land. Metropolitan St. Louis ranked twelfth in such establishments but twentieth in foreign-owned acquired establishments. The metropolitan area was in the top five for Canadian- and German-owned and in the top ten for French-owned greenfield establishments. For existing businesses acquired by foreign ownership St. Louis was ranked in the top ten for Canadian ownership and in the top twenty for French ownership.

The Milken Institute, a California-based economic research corporation, conducted a study of the structure of high-tech economic activity (DeVol and Wong 1999). The study examined the impact of high technology on the growth of metropolitan areas. The report ranked metropolitan St. Louis thirty-fourth of the top fifty high-tech metropolitan areas on a composite index equivalent to the percent of national high-tech real output multiplied by the high-tech real output location quotient. While this ranking classifies St. Louis as a "Tech-Pole" (metropolitan areas that attract high-tech), using a measure of high-tech real output growth for the period 1990–98, St. Louis did not make the top fifty metropolitan areas.

The Milken study definition of high-tech ("industries that spend an above-average amount of revenue on research and development and that employ an above industry-average number of technology-using occupations") includes nine manufacturing and five service industries.

There are 195 high-tech manufacturing firms in metropolitan St. Louis using Milken's definition. Nearly half (45 percent) of the high-tech firm manufactures are either surgical, medical, and dental instruments/supplies or drugs. There also are concentrations in electronic components and accessories and laboratory apparatus and analytical, optical, measuring, and controlling instruments. Not including Boeing workers, about 80 percent of metropolitan St. Louis high-tech manufacturing workers are employed in these four industries. There are 19,500 workers at the other 194 high-tech firms and 16,400 at Boeing.

The Research and Planning Division of the Missouri Department of Economic Development prepared a report on manufacturing diversity in Missouri counties, comparing 1990 to 1999 (MoDED 2003). Manufacturing diversity measures the distribution of various industries in a particular area—measured by the proportionate distribution of the labor force. The City of St. Louis has a fully diversified index. While St. Louis County was fully dependent and St. Charles County significantly dependent on aerospace at the start of the last decade, they both moved to significantly diversified in the last ten years. Franklin and Jefferson Counties were consistently significantly diversified.

The type of manufacturing activity varies across counties. As shown in Table 3, the leading subsector in the City of St. Louis is chemical; in St. Louis and St. Charles Counties it is transportation equipment; in Jefferson, St. Clair, and Madison Counties it is primary metals; and in Franklin County it is fabricated metal products.

Table 3. County-Level Comparison of Manufacturing Subsector Activity

Geographic Area	Subsector	Percent of Manufacturing
City of St. Louis	Chemical	34 %
St. Louis County	Transportation equipment	70 %
St. Charles County	Transportation equipment	D
Jefferson County	Primary metal	20%
Franklin County	Fabricated metal product	16%
St. Clair County	Primary metal	27%
Madison County	Primary metal	30%
Monroe County	NA	NA

Source: U.S. Census Bureau, 1997 Economic Census.
Note: For Monroe County, manufacturing data was not available.

Growth in Services

For the metropolitan St. Louis area, the industrial sector with the largest percentage of employees as well as the greatest number of establishments over the ten-year period is the service industry. The percentage working in the service industry grew from 29.67 percent in 1987 to 34.09 percent in 1992 to 37.08 percent in 1997. The number of service establishments as a percentage of total establishments in the metropolitan area increased from 34.65 percent in 1987 to 36.21 percent in 1992 and to 38.09 percent in 1997. There were three notable changes within the services industry classification: health services, business services, and engineering/management services.

Health Services

The health services industry in metropolitan St. Louis had the largest percentage of employees and establishments over the ten-year period. In 1987 there were 90,891 employees and 4,230 establishments, in 1992 there were 115,869 and 4,575, and in 1997 there were 130,869 and 4,843 respectively. As of March 1997, the health services field employed 11.22 percent of all workers in metropolitan St. Louis and included 7.59 percent of all establishments. This represents an increase of 43.8 percent in the number of employees and a 14.5 percent in the number of establishments since 1987. The total number of establishments did not increase at the same rate as the number of employees because of mergers of health service organizations over the last several years. In fact, according to the February 2–8, 2001, *St. Louis Business Journal* listing of the fifty largest employers, BJC Health leads metropolitan St. Louis with 19,033 employees.

The counties with the largest percentage of employees in the health field in 1997 were St. Clair (10,881 of 73,753 employees) at 14.8 percent, Madison (10,782 of 81,652) at 13.2 percent, and Jefferson (4,234 of 34,841) at 12.2 percent. St. Louis County had the largest absolute number of employees and establishments, 57,501 and 2,599 respectively. Within the health services industry in every county, the largest percentages of employees were working in hospitals, followed by nursing and personal care facilities, then offices and clinics of medical doctors.

Business Services

The next largest area of service growth and total percentage of employment in metropolitan St. Louis is business services. Employment in business services increased over 50 percent from 1987 to 1997. In 1987, there were 58,158 employees at 3,554 establishments. In 1992 there were 63,035 employees at 3,345 establishments, and in 1997 88,604 employees at 4,203 establishments. This is an increase of 52.3 percent in employees over the ten-year period, with a gain of 18.2 percent total businesses, although there was a 6 percent decline from 1987 to 1992. In 1987, 5.85 percent of metropolitan workers were employed in this industry. By March 1997 that percentage increased to 6.59 percent.

Because of data withheld due to disclosure in several of the counties, total metropolitan percentages were not computed at a detailed classification level for business services. However, examining St. Louis City and County shows that in business services the largest percentages of employment in 1997 were services to buildings, personnel supply services, and computer and data processing services. They all grew as percentages of total employment and establishments from 1987 to 1997 as well as within their fields.

The computer and data processing field in 1987 for St. Louis City and County combined consisted of 8,738 employees working in 342 establishments. By 1997 there was a growth to 15,209 employees working in 897 establishments. This is an increase of 74 percent in the number of employees, but 162 percent in the number of establishments.

There is a high and growing demand for telecommunications and information technology related jobs, but the supply is not growing at the same rate. The labor shortage has contributed to the increase in personnel supply services. Not only does this classification include employment agencies, but also temporary services. Personnel supply services in 1987 for St. Louis City and County combined consisted of 10,270 employees working in 229 establishments. By 1997 there was a growth to 22,776 employees working in 388 establishments. This is an increase of 122 percent in the number of employees and 69 percent in the number of establishments. This is also an increase from 19.7 percent of total percentage of business service employees employed in this classification to 30.2 percent of total percentage of business service employees from 1987 to 1997. This growth is likely due to the increase in the number of temporary workers that many companies use because they cannot find qualified workers on their own.

The third area within business services that has a large percentage of employees and establishments is services to buildings. For the City of St. Louis this is the largest subclassification for employees and third in establishments. The concentration of large office buildings downtown accounts for the demand for this service category since they include those affiliated with building maintenance. For the City of St. Louis, the number of employees in 1987 was 3,917, which was 25 percent of all business service employees. By 1997 the number of employees in this area increased to 6,787 (an increase of 73 percent), which was 32 percent of all business service employees.

Engineering and Management Services

Engineering and management services is the final service component that showed significant change. In 1987, there were 1,208 companies employing 13,551 individuals. In 1992 there were 2,243 such businesses employing 25,145 workers, and in 1997 there were 2,719 with 27,612 employees. This is an increase of 104 percent in employers and 125 percent in the number of firms. Over 60 percent of these businesses were located in St. Louis County in 1997. In 1997 in St. Louis County, approximately 25 percent of this service sector consisted of engineering and architectural services; 29 percent accounting, auditing, and bookkeeping; 7 percent research and testing services; and 39 percent management and public relations firms.

There are 2,320 high-tech service firms in metropolitan St. Louis. Over three quarters (77 percent) of these firms are either computer programming; data processing and other computer-related services; or engineering, architectural, and surveying services. There are 45,000 high-tech service industry employees in metropolitan St. Louis. Telephone communications services represent a disproportionately large percentage of the workers. Eleven percent of the high-tech service firms are telephone communications services, but they employ over one-third (33 percent) of all high-tech service workers.

Wholesale

In the wholesale sector, as shown in Table 4, the greater portion of activity in nondurable goods (other than groceries) is transshipment of farm and petroleum products. The largest segment of employment in the wholesale sector is durable goods, especially those handled by merchant wholesalers.

Wholesale trade accounts for 8.43 percent of all establishments in metropolitan St. Louis and 6.58 percent of all employees. This industrial category has declined in percentage of total jobs and firms over the ten-year period, although the total number of businesses and employees has increased (from 67,645 and 4,963 to 76,598 and 5,380 respectively).

Table 4. The Wholesale Sector in Metropolitan St. Louis

Type	Establishments	Sales	Employees
Merchant Wholesalers			
Durable goods	2,457	12,211,767	31,276
Nondurable goods	1,188	15,838,660	17,832
Manufacturers' Sales			
Durable goods	250	10,590,569	6,070
Nondurable goods	150	11,882,164	7,348
Agents/Brokers			
Durable goods	548	3,272,209	2,474
Nondurable goods	212	3,338,886	1,406

Source: U.S. Census Bureau, 1997 Economic Census.
Note: Sales data in $1,000.

The City of St. Louis has the largest share of wholesale trade firms as a percentage of total businesses, 10.5 percent, followed by St. Louis County at 9.7 percent. For both the City and County the largest group within this classification is professional and commercial equipment. This category includes photographic equipment, office equipment, computer equipment, and medical equipment. Over the ten years the number of establishments increased from 164 to 461 (a 181 percent increase) and the number of employees increased from 2,477 to 8,117 (a 227 percent increase) for St. Louis City and County combined. Professional and commercial equipment establishments as a percentage of total wholesale establishments increased from 4.2 percent to 11.5 percent during this time frame.

Retail Trade

Second to service industries in the percentage of employees as well as number of establishments is retail trade. In 1997, 19.39 percent of employees in metropolitan St. Louis worked in retail occupations and 21.67 percent of establishments were retail. This level has stayed fairly consistent over the ten-year period as far as number of employees, but has decreased in total percentage of establishments from 23.73 percent in 1987. The only retail establishment subcategory that showed an increase is eating and drinking places, a function of lifestyle changes and the economy. People have less time to cook and more money to spend since many families have two incomes. As a result they are eating out more because they can afford to and because it saves time. As in several other industries, the overall decline in the number of retail establishments coupled with the consistent number of employees most likely is the result of the trend in the 1990s of merging organizations.

F.I.R.E

A total of 6.98 percent of metropolitan St. Louis employees work in the area of finance, insurance, and real estate (F.I.R.E.). This sector includes 10.19 percent of business establishments. In this particular industry the total number of establishments has shown a sharp increase from 1992 to 1997 after experiencing a decline from 1987 to 1992. In 1987 there were 74,198 employees in 5,013 establishments. This decreased in 1992 to 60,118 employees (18.9 percent decrease) and 4,861 establishments (3 percent decrease). However, by 1997 these numbers increased to 81,237 employees and 6,498 establishments, an increase of 35 percent and 33.6 percent respectively since 1992. The three professional groups that caused this pattern were insurance agents, brokers and service, and real estate.

The trend in the insurance agent numbers can be attributed to the change in the way the insurance industry has operated nationally over the last ten to fifteen years. After years of consolidation among independent insurance agencies, the number of independent agents has leveled. The number was at a high of 53,000 nationally in 1987. It declined to 46,500 in 1992. This would explain the decrease shown in the St. Louis area from 1987 to 1992. The industry now consists of insurance agents who no longer represent one company, but independently compare several insurance companies and find their clients the best overall coverage package.

Real estate is the largest industry in the finance, insurance, and real estate classification. It also showed a recovery from a decline in estab-lishments from 1987 to 1992 to an increase from 1992 to 1997. This trend is probably the result of the several years it took for the real estate bust of the late 1980s to level. By the middle of the 1990s, with the economy picking up, several sectors in the real estate industry began rebounding, including retail real estate and new construction.

The real estate industry in metropolitan St. Louis, especially commercial real estate, is growing and changing. The core of St. Louis commercial real estate firms has changed dramatically over the last several years as they shifted their emphasis from simply brokering real estate deals and managing multi-tenant office buildings to carrying out complex real estate responsibilities for corporations that have started to reduce and in some cases eliminate their in-house departments. These include such services as establishing branch offices for large companies and handling legal environmental issues, interior design, and many other aspects of corporate services that used to be performed internally.

Geographic expansion has stimulated commercial and residential development throughout the multi-county metropolitan area. Over the past half century, the economic geography of metropolitan St. Louis has evolved into a polycentric structure. Interest by both investors and developers in greenfield and floodplain development expanded office, retail, and warehouse projects into the outer reaches of the metropolitan St. Louis real estate market. Languorous growth in population, however, has kept commercial real estate markets in equilibrium during the economic boom of the 1990s. Residential construction was the only exception. Comparing population change to building permits indicates a new single-family unit was built for every baby born during the last decade.

Historic tax credits and brownfield incentives encouraged office and hotel development downtown. Downtown office space recently has increased through renovation projects, whereas there has been new construction in Clayton. The downtown space has proven attractive to smaller, new technology businesses needing to attract a younger employee base. New office development in St. Charles County was constructed for decentralized technology functions of larger corporations such as MCI WorldCom Inc. and MasterCard International Inc. Build-to-suit projects have increased office space in the various submarkets. There is investor activity, but nationally, metropolitan St. Louis is not seen as a strong market.

A notable development in industrial space is expansion into Illinois through projects including Gateway Commerce Center in Edwardsville and the Lewis and Clark Enviro-Tech Business Park in Wood River. In retail, three big-box power centers have been completed in recent years with new major chains entering the market or chains already in the market expanding.

Consolidations and evolving business practices in the health care sector have produced a unique real estate challenge. St. Louis leads the nation in hospital closings and lags behind in putting vacant hospital buildings to new uses.

Construction

The construction industry stayed relatively constant between 1987 and 1997. In 1987, construction businesses accounted for 9.43 percent of businesses, and by 1997 the percentage was 9.88. This translates into an increase from 5,403 establishments to 5,977 establishments (a 10.6 percent rise). Although the number of employees increased from 60,386 to 63,449 (a 5 percent increase), the growth in construction employment was outpaced by the rise in total employment in the metropolitan St. Louis area, which is why the total percentage number from 1987 to 1997 showed a decrease from 6.08 percent to 5.45 percent. The construction industry has remained vibrant due to the strong housing markets in the outlying counties of metropolitan St. Louis, major highway projects, Metrolink, and the Lambert Field expansion.

All these construction activities will be continuing into the immediate future. The major concern with the construction industry is the age of the workers. The average construction worker in the St. Louis area is fifty-two years old, and many in this industry take early retirement. It is also not as prevalent as it has been in the past for fathers to pass construction jobs down to their sons. As a result the construction industry faces a shortage of 8,000 to 10,000 workers in the next seven or eight years. This trend is already having an effect, as the number of construction employees cannot keep pace with the number of establishments over the ten-year period studied.

Transportation and Public Utilities

Transportation and public utilities had extremely uneven performance. On the whole there was a decrease in the sector's percentage of total employment but an increase in percentage of establishments over the ten-year period, from 7.28 percent to 6.71 percent and from 4.02 percent to 4.22 percent respectively. The absolute number of employees did increase from 72,296 to 78,152 (8.1 percent) and the number of establishments from 2,303 to 2,694 (17 percent).

Most of the activity in this sector is transportation related. The largest component is trucking and warehousing, which expanded employment by 20 percent and the number of firms by 3.5 percent. Over the same time, the number of employees in local and interurban transit dropped by 23 percent (1,700 jobs), and the number of firms declined by 10 percent. All counties in the metropolitan area benefited from the growth in trucking and warehousing, but the geographic changes in local and interurban transit were very different, particularly in St. Louis City and County. The City lost half its work force in this category (over 2,500 jobs), but St. Louis County added over 600 jobs. The other counties in the region saw employment increases in local and interurban transit ranging from 20 to 150 employees.

Transportation by air experienced modest expansion (3 percent) in the number of jobs but an 8 percent growth in the number of firms.

Transportation services employed 7 percent fewer people but there were 17 more firms, an increase of about 4 percent. Communication is the other sizable, and growing, activity in this sector. The number of communication jobs increased by 14 percent. The number of firms stayed about the same (a 2 percent increase). The electric, gas, water, and sanitary utilities, while critical local infrastructure, account for only about 8,000 jobs and 120 firms in the region.

Nonemployers

While their impact is not typically examined, the nonemployer firms in the metropolitan St. Louis economy provide jobs for approximately the same number of people as the area's seven largest corporations. There are about 90,000 nonemployer firms. Nonemployers typically are self-employed individuals or partnerships operating businesses that they have not chosen to incorporate. Self-employed owners of incorporated businesses typically pay themselves wages or salary, so that the business is an employer.

Nonemployer firms can be a significant portion of the total employment in a particular economic subsector. As shown in Table 5 there are five subsectors where nonemployer firms add substantially to the total employment in metropolitan St. Louis. For example, there are about 60,000 employees working for professional, scientific, and technical services firms, and another 21,000 in nonemployer firms. There are about half as many people working in nonemployer firms in the "other services" subsector as there are in employer firms.

Economic Development Strategies

While the various sectors of the metropolitan economy have evolved considerably over the last decade, St. Louis has lagged in economic growth. On measures such as personal income growth and job growth, it performs worse than the Midwest region and the nation. The millennial year 2000 proved to be a stimulus for several studies that recommended action for both the public and private sectors to expand the metropolitan St. Louis economy. These studies examined the existing business structure, either generally or in specific sectors or subsectors, and recommended an approach to capitalize on existing clusters of activity to grow more businesses.

**Table 5. Ten Largest Subsectors of Non-Employer Firms
in Metropolitan St. Louis**

Economic Subsector	Employees	Non-employers
Professional, scientific, and technical services	59,511	20,966
Other services	33,822	15,441
Real estate and rental and leasing	17,872	13,324
Arts, entertainment, and recreation	25,132	5,798
Educational services	3,124	2,029
Source: U.S. Census Bureau, 1997 Economic Census.		

In the 1990s there was a rush by economic development professionals in St. Louis and across the nation to apply cluster theory as an alternative to smokestack chasing. Rather than competing with other metropolitan areas, and indeed other nations, over the relocation of large existing companies, cluster theory proposed a means to locally grow an existing base of related businesses. Largely stimulated by the concepts of Harvard Business School professor Michael E. Porter, cluster theory was subject to the usual debates among academics over definition and measurement (Bergman and Feser 1999). But it spread rapidly in the economic development community after publication of his very readable 1990 description of the respective roles of the public sector and the private sector in stimulating growth in regional industries (Porter 1990). Porter's work particularly emphasized the role of innovation in stimulating growth, thus tending to focus on technology clusters.

Porter capitalized on the response to his economic development theory in 1994 by establishing Initiative for a Competitive Inner City (ICIC). ICIC provided research and program services to local governments. With funding from the Danforth Foundation and other corporate sponsors, ICIC assisted in the development of the St. Louis Inner City Competitive Assessment and Strategy Project. The Project documented the plight of the inner city of St. Louis as well as the region. For the period 1995–2001, as might be expected, the inner city lost 3 percent of its jobs; metropolitan area job growth was only 1.1 percent, compared to 2.7 percent in Kansas City, 2.9 percent in Minneapolis, and 3.9 percent in Memphis.

With great fanfare and energy the Project announced in 2001 the formation of the St. Louis Inner City Competitive Alliance (ICCA). ICCA pursued an agenda to enhance work force readiness and the City government's business outreach capacity. It also targeted four clusters for development: metal manufacturing, transportation and logistics, construction services, and commercial services. Despite an initial flurry of activity, over the next several years ICCA did not have a significant impact on wealth creation and employment expansion for three reasons. First of all, it was in the city but not of the City. ICCA had a broad alliance of business, civic, and nonprofit leaders, but the City of St. Louis government never embraced it. The City's political and economic development leadership was not engaged in the Assessment and Strategy Project or in the Alliance. The City pursued its own existing business outreach agenda, never integrating with the Alliance. Second, the moment passed. The Project's September 2000 report (St. Louis ICCA and Strategy Project 2000) stated, "We live in a historic moment. Favorable economic conditions provide a unique opportunity to improve the future of the inner city and its residents." The triumvirate of technology stock collapse, economic recession, and September 11, 2001, quickly changed the favorable economic conditions. And finally, the inner city cluster initiative was overwhelmed by another cluster initiative: the BioBelt.

With funding from Civic Progress and the Danforth Foundation, the St. Louis Regional Chamber and Growth Association (RCGA) commissioned the Battelle Memorial Institute to prepare a strategy for the plant and life sciences industry cluster. The goal of the initiative Battelle proposed was "to position St. Louis as the international center for plant sciences and a major international center in life sciences" (Battelle Memorial Institute 2000). The Battelle report identified five strategies: establish an international reputation, build an entrepreneurial culture, tap intellectual capital resources, improve the business climate, and strengthen the work force. The marketing appellation given to this strategy was "the BioBelt: the Center of Plant and Life Sciences." Whereas the ICCA was strategically focused on the inner city, the BioBelt wrapped around the entire metropolitan area.

The plant and life sciences venture promised great rewards for metropolitan St. Louis but required a substantial investment necessary to implement the strategy. The Battelle action plan included twenty activities across the five strategies identified above, at a five-year cost of approximately $275 million. The implementation of the action plan achieved critical viability when the Danforth Foundation announced in 2003 a commitment of $124 million to plant and life sciences activities in metropolitan St. Louis.

While the BioBelt has achieved success in its marketing and fundraising objectives, it faced serious challenges in becoming the signature industry for metropolitan St. Louis. As Battelle stated in its report, the plant and life sciences industry cluster employed in 1997 only 23,000 workers in a labor market of over 1.1 million. While this industry cluster has considerable growth potential and marketing appeal, it will require a high rate of growth over a sustained period to have a significant impact on economic conditions in the metropolitan area. The capacity for sustained high growth was dealt a considerable setback in fall 2003. Battelle warned in its report, "The region will have considerable difficulty building a plant and life sciences base if St. Louis does not remain a major airline hub." St. Louis lost its hub status when American Airlines reduced the number of daily flights at Lambert Airport by almost half and shifted much of the remaining service to smaller, regional planes.

There are alternative cluster analysis theories that do not put emphasis on technological innovation. The Missouri Department of Economic Development prepared "Target Missouri II: Creating a Foundation for the 21st Century Economy," a business development strategy for the state that included a second targeted industry report for metropolitan St. Louis. Their study was based on scoring industries on six characteristics developed by Tim Padmore and Harvey Gibson (Padmore and Gibson 1998). Rather than identifying the industries with the highest potential for innovation, the Padmore and Gibson approach determines clusters that drive the local economy. The highest rated industrial clusters in the Target Missouri II St. Louis analysis are motor vehicles and equipment, aerospace, hydraulic cement, primary nonferrous smelting and refining, railroad, and communications (see Table 6). Most of this list does not have the panache to lend itself to a marketing campaign such as the BioBelt. These are, however, the industries that have the most effect on the metropolitan St. Louis economy and should not be overlooked in economic development growth strategies.

Table 6. Projected Growth Sectors

Industry
Motor vehicles and equipment
Aerospace
Hydraulic cement
Primary nonferrous smelting and refining
Railroad
Communications
Water and sanitation
Wholesale trade
Refrigeration and service industry machinery
Medical equipment, instruments, and supplies
Drugs
Soap, cleaners, and toilet goods
Miscellaneous plastics products

Source: Missouri Department of Economic Development.

To continue the analogy used at the beginning of this chapter, not only has the metropolitan St. Louis economy improved its academic grade, but it also has chosen a major, plant and life sciences. Is this the best major for St. Louis? Edward Hill defines a good city as one that has "the ability to adapt to external change so that people can prosper in the new economic and social environment" (Hill 1997). As has been shown here, the metropolitan St. Louis economy changed considerably in the last two decades, but the resulting prosperity was not equitably distributed. The millennial economic development studies were designed to proactively adapt to external change by selecting industry clusters to achieve global renown and economic reward. Data from twenty-first-century economic censuses will measure if this strategy distributes rewards as widely as earlier twentieth-century adaptations.

References

Battelle Memorial Institute. *Plant and Life Sciences Strategies for St. Louis: The Technology Gateway for the 21st Century.* St. Louis: Author, 2000.

Bergman, Edward M., and Edward J. Feser. "Industrial and Regional Clusters: Concepts and Comparative Applications." In *The Web Book of Regional Science*, edited by Scott Loveridge. Morgantown: Regional Research Institute, West Virginia University, 1999.

Bureau of Economic Analysis. *U.S. Department of Commerce, Survey of Current Business.* Washington, D.C.: Author, 2002.

DeVol, Ross, and Perry Wong. *America's High-Tech Economy: Growth, Development and Risks for Metropolitan Areas* [online]. Santa Monica, Calif.: Milken Institute, 1999. Available at http://www.milkeninstitute. org /publications/publications.taf?function= de tail&ID=15&cat= Res Rep.

Hill, Edward W. "Policy Lessons from Cleveland's Economic Restructuring and the Accompanying Case Study." Report for Maxine Goodman Levin College of Urban Affairs (February 1997): 1.

Missouri Department of Economic Development. "Target Missouri II: The St. Louis Metro Region Industry Study." Jefferson City, Mo.: Department of Economic Development, 2003. Available at http://www.ded.mo.gov/business/researchandplanning/industry/targetii/tm2_slrreg_execsum.sh.

Padmore, Tim, and Harvey Gibson. "Modeling Systems of Innovation II: A Framework for Industrial Cluster Analysis in Regions." *Research Policy* 26 (1998).

POLICOM. *Economic Strength Rankings* [online]. 2003. Available at http://www.policom.com/rankalph.htm.

Porter, Michael E. *The Competitive Advantage of Nations.* New York: Free Press, 1990.

St. Louis Inner City Competitive Assessment and Strategy Project. *St. Louis Inner City Competitive Assessment and Strategy Project: Creating Jobs, Income and Wealth in the Inner City.* [St. Louis, Mo.?]: The Project, 2000.

Chapter 4

The Past, Present, and Future of the St. Louis Labor Force

David Laslo
University of Missouri–St. Louis

In the decades ahead, one of the foremost challenges to maintaining economic growth in the St. Louis region will be providing a work force that has the skills and workplace competencies to meet the needs of local industry and commerce. Unlike in previous decades, when women and minorities joined the labor force in new and higher levels that generally met the labor demand of local industry, the labor demand of the future will require more than higher numbers of labor force participants. Workers possessing skills in numerous technologies and who are flexible and adaptive to rapid change are the prototype of the future (Judy and D'Amico 1997). Compounding this challenge will be a declining number of labor-force-age persons in the decades ahead. If the region's economy and population continue growing at their current historical rates, the gap between labor demand and the number of labor-force-age persons will be significant. Accordingly, the region must begin to plan now for significant changes in work force preparation.

This chapter illustrates how the St. Louis labor force changed between 1950 and 2000. The most salient features of these changes have been the growing participation rates of women and minorities, the age of the labor force, and the continued decentralization of jobs within the region. The first part of this chapter will examine the decentralization trends in labor force and the shifting distribution of workers in the region's counties. This includes the changing distribution of labor force characteristics such as educational attainment, occupation, age, labor force participation, and unemployment rates. The second part will examine the same labor market characteristics by gender and race and will include comparisons with the national economy over the 1950–2000 study period. The third part will provide a projection of the economy and potential labor force to the year

2040. These projections will provide a hypothetical look at potential gaps between labor force needs and the available number of workers. A final section will summarize and draw some brief conclusions regarding these changes and the potential challenges they present for the future of the St. Louis region.

Changing Characteristics and Distribution of the Labor Force

The changing distribution of the labor force across the St. Louis region between 1950 and 2000 mirrors the movement of population during the same period. The relationship between the movement of jobs and people has been well documented, and the long-standing trend of population decentralization from the center of the region is the salient demographic feature of the period. At the same time, the structure of the economy has transformed itself from a preponderance of durable goods production to one dominated by commercial activities that provide or perform services (Bluestone and Harrison 1982). This has had the effect of altering the occupation structure of the labor force as well as the distribution of workers as industries have sought locations outside the region's center.

Tables 1 and 2 show how the region has grown between 1950 and 2000 and how the amount of employment has followed that growth. As the area has expanded from five counties in 1950 to twelve in 2000, the number of employed persons has grown by 83.1 percent. During the same period, the nation's level of employment has grown by 128.1 percent, reflecting the slower-than-average growth of the region relative to other regions. As the tables show, the process of decentralization has fueled multiple increases in employed persons in many of the outlying counties, in particular those closest to the center: St. Charles (1185.3 percent) and Jefferson (623.6 percent), Warren (305.0 percent), Lincoln (256.1 percent), and Franklin (226.7 percent).

Similarly, Table 2 shows that in 1950 nearly three out of four jobs were found in the City of St. Louis (50.1 percent), St. Louis County (21.4 percent), and St. Clair (9.9 percent). By 2000, that proportion had fallen to a little over six out of ten jobs (60.5 percent), but the decrease was largely due to the City of St. Louis's decline: 61.5 percent over the fifty-year period. Because of its size and location, St. Louis County has the largest number of jobs (499,887) and proportion (40.3 percent) of regional employed persons, although these numbers are down from 1990's 507,771 employed persons and 1980's 45.1 percent share. Although it has the third highest number of jobs at 141,273, the City of St. Louis's proportion has fallen from just over half in 1950 (50.1 percent) to 11.4 percent in 2000.

It was surpassed in the 1990s by St. Charles County (12.1 percent), and followed closely by Madison (9.9 percent), St. Clair (8.8 percent), and Jefferson (8.0 percent).

Table 1. MSA Employment by County: 1950–2000

County	1950	1960	1970	1980	1990	2000	1950–2000
Madison	69,665	80,757	93,229	101,999	113,109	122,344	75.6
St. Clair	72,573	85,859	96,020	96,210	105,606	109,362	50.7
St. Charles	11,629	18,359	34,811	66,875	112,457	149,473	1185.3
St. Louis	156,526	263,200	384,409	469,768	507,771	499,887	219.4
St. Louis City	366,524	294,000	231,765	173,066	161,629	141,273	-61.5
Jefferson	13,683	21,462	37,563	61,307	82,394	99,005	623.6
Franklin	13,994	16,735	20,240	29,256	37,582	45,725	226.7
Clinton	8,317	8,043	9,568	13,073	15,050	17,107	105.7
Monroe	5,239	5,827	6,869	8,495	10,867	14,477	176.3
Jersey	5,344	5,614	6,448	8,226	9,139	10,312	93.0
Lincoln	5,187	5,010	6,257	8,427	13,077	18,471	256.1
Warren	2,979	2,998	3,445	5,816	8,964	12,065	305.0
Total 12 Counties	731,660	807,864	930,624	1,042,518	1,177,645	1,239,501	69.4
MSA	676,917	763,637	898,037	1,020,049	1,155,604	1,239,501	83.1
USA (000s)	59,072	68,144	80,898	104,450	123,473	134,769	128.1

▨ = counties included in census definition of the St. Louis region.

Source: MIDAS, PPRC, UM–Saint Louis, U.S. Census Bureau, 1950–2000.

Tables 3 and 4 depict the pattern of employment growth in the region in the context of the region's changing size between 1950 and 2000. The region was defined by only five counties in 1950, and the work-age population (person sixteen years and older) increased by 670,663 persons, or 51.4 percent, and totaled seven counties by 2000. The five counties that composed the region in 1950 still are home to 83.3 percent of all working-age persons. Likewise, the civilian labor force is still centered in these five counties, with 82.7 percent, although as shown in Tables 1 and 2, the shifts within those counties have been considerable. However, with a higher rate of labor force participation since 1950, particularly among women, the civilian labor force increased 85.9 percent to 1,310,974 from 705,132.

Table 2. Percent of MSA Employment by County: 1950–2000

County	1950	1960	1970	1980	1990	2000
Madison	9.5	10.0	10.0	9.8	9.6	9.9
St. Clair	9.9	10.6	10.3	9.2	9.0	8.8
St. Charles	1.6	2.3	3.7	6.4	9.5	12.1
St. Louis	21.4	32.6	41.3	45.1	43.1	40.3
St. Louis City	50.1	36.4	24.9	16.6	13.7	11.4
Jefferson	1.9	2.7	4.0	5.9	7.0	8.0
Franklin	1.9	2.1	2.2	2.8	3.2	3.7
Clinton	1.1	1.0	1.0	1.3	1.3	1.4
Monroe	0.7	0.7	0.7	0.8	0.9	1.2
Jersey	0.7	0.7	0.7	0.8	0.8	0.8
Lincoln	0.7	0.6	0.7	0.8	1.1	1.5
Warren	0.4	0.4	0.4	0.6	0.8	1.0
Total 12 Counties	100.0	100.0	100.0	100.0	100.0	100.0
MSA Percent of Total	92.5	94.5	96.5	97.8	98.1	100.0

▨ = counties included in census definition of the St. Louis region.

Source: MIDAS, PPRC, UM–Saint Louis, U.S. Census Bureau, 1950–2000.

These developments are reflected in Tables 5 and 6, which show the rates of unemployment and labor force participation for the St. Louis region in the fifty-year study period. Table 5 shows that unemployment rates for the region peaked in 1980 at 7.6 percent, a period when global and national restructuring were having a negative effect on local employment as many manufacturing operations closed or left the region. Reflecting the trends of population and job decentralization, the City of St. Louis and St. Clair County consistently have had the highest rates of unemployment. In spite of relatively prosperous times in the 1990s, the City of St. Louis and St. Clair County continued to rank above the region's rate of unemployment and above all other counties.

These counties also have the lowest rates of labor force participation, at 60.4 percent (City of St. Louis) and 63.7 percent (St. Clair County) and are well below the current rate of 66.7 percent for the region. Overall, the regional rate has increased from 54.9 percent in 1950 to the aforementioned rate of 66.7 percent in 2000, due largely to the surge in work force participation by women since about 1970 (U.S. Census 1950–2000). In 1950, the rate of labor force participation for the five counties that composed the region was largely the same, ranging from 56.2 percent in the City of St. Louis to 53.0 percent in St. Louis County. However, with the movement of population and jobs in these counties and to the seven counties added since then, the range has widened significantly, ranging from 74.6 percent in St. Charles County to 60.4 percent in the City of St. Louis.

Table 3. Total Work-Age Population by MSA and County: 1950–2000

County	Total Work-Age Population					
	1950	1960	1970	1980	1990	2000
Madison	137,195	156,516	171,612	187,035	192,440	199,865
St. Clair	157,843	178,324	189,290	194,371	196,515	191,351
St. Charles	22,385	34,435	57,903	101,561	154,768	208,483
Saint Louis	302,544	478,555	645,287	744,550	775,060	781,692
City of Saint Louis	685,042	555,346	446,445	349,946	306,308	263,523
Total 1950 Region	1,305,009	1,403,176	1,510,537	1,577,463	1,625,091	1,644,914
Percent 1950 Region	100.0%	97.0%	93.6%	89.1%	87.0%	83.3%
Jefferson		43,445	67,186	103,681	125,583	147,900
Franklin			36,705	51,459	59,985	70,392
Clinton				23,689	25,794	27,663
Monroe				15,135	16,963	21,167
Jersey					14,587	16,817
Lincoln						28,297
Warren						18,522
Total Post-1950 Region		43,445	103,891	193,964	242,912	330,758
Percent Post-1950 Region		3.0%	6.4%	10.9%	13.0%	16.7%
MSA Total	1,305,009	1,446,621	1,614,428	1,771,427	1,868,003	1,975,672

Source: MIDAS, PPRC, UM–Saint Louis, U.S. Census Bureau, 1950–2000.

Table 4. Civilian Labor Force by MSA and County: 1950–2000

County	Civilian Labor Force					
	1950	1960	1970	1980	1990	2000
Madison	73,358	85,045	98,846	111,719	121,596	129,123
St. Clair	76,207	91,750	102,218	107,260	117,126	117,266
St. Charles	12,055	19,205	36,710	71,999	116,870	155,339
Saint Louis	159,807	269,613	398,024	496,356	531,474	523,613
City of Saint Louis	383,705	310,890	247,586	194,784	181,306	159,127
Total 1950 Region	705,132	776,503	883,384	982,118	1,068,372	1,084,468
Percent 1950 Region	100.0%	97.2%	93.5%	88.9%	86.6%	82.7%
Jefferson		22,481	39,688	67,688	88,060	103,682
Franklin			21,408	32,071	39,984	47,370
Clinton				14,145	15,987	17,687
Monroe				9,169	11,331	14,849
Jersey					9,640	10,957
Lincoln						19,359
Warren						12,602
Total Post-1950 Region		22,481	61,096	123,073	165,002	226,506
Percent Post-1950 Region		2.8%	6.5%	11.1%	13.4%	17.3%
MSA Total	705,132	798,984	944,480	1,105,191	1,233,374	1,310,974

Source: MIDAS, PPRC, UM–Saint Louis, U.S. Census Bureau, 1950–2000.

Tables 7, 8, and 9 present the breakdown of the region's labor force by age for the period 1960 to 2000. There are several key trends that will have ramifications for the future growth of the St. Louis economy. The first is the decline in the proportion of younger workers between the ages of sixteen and twenty-four. As shown in Table 7, since reaching a peak of 22.7 percent in 1980 the proportion of workers between the ages of sixteen and twenty-four has declined to 15.9 percent in 2000. This is significant since the large proportion of workers between the ages of twenty-five and sixty-four will begin to decline by 2020 as the leading edge of the baby-boom generation will reach its mid-70s and the number of workers behind them is much fewer (Frey 2001, 9).

Table 8 shows the number of workers between the ages of twenty-five and sixty-four in the labor force has risen since 1980 as the full effect of

Table 5. Unemployment Rate by MSA and County: 1950–2000

County	\multicolumn{6}{c}{Unemployment Rate}
	1950	1960	1970	1980	1990	2000
Madison	5.0%	5.0%	5.6%	8.7%	6.9%	5.2%
St. Clair	4.3%	6.2%	5.7%	9.7%	9.3%	6.5%
St. Charles	3.5%	4.4%	5.2%	7.1%	3.8%	3.8%
Saint Louis	2.0%	2.4%	3.4%	5.3%	4.4%	4.5%
City of Saint Louis	4.5%	5.4%	6.4%	11.1%	10.8%	11.2%
Jefferson		4.5%	5.3%	9.4%	6.4%	4.5%
Franklin			5.5%	8.8%	6.0%	3.5%
Clinton				7.4%	5.8%	3.2%
Monroe				7.3%	4.1%	2.5%
Jersey					7.0%	5.9%
Lincoln						4.6%
Warren						4.3%
MSA Total	3.9%	4.4%	4.9%	7.6%	6.3%	5.4%

Source: MIDAS, PPRC, UM–Saint Louis, U.S. Census Bureau, 1950–2000.

the baby boom and the next generation, Generation X, entered the labor force (Frey 2001, 10–11). These numbers will decline as a proportion of the total as the lower number of persons in the sixteen to twenty-four age group move into this category.

Numerous factors affect the labor force participation rate of persons over sixty-five years of age. As Table 9 shows, the rate of participation had declined steadily between 1960 and 1990. However, the rate increased to 3.4 percent in 2000, a twenty year high, surpassing the rate of 3.1 percent in 1980. Among many influences on the decision to stay in the labor force beyond the age of sixty-five, the most prominent are rising health-care costs, fears of social security solvency, and longer life expectancy. It is likely that remaining in the work force will be more financially necessary than retirement and living off social security and savings, and participation rates may exceed historical highs in the decades ahead. In general, the range of participation rates across all counties in 2000 is less than those of the earlier decades, as the rate of participation in counties that were more recently rural was much higher in the 1960s and 1970s and kept persons working much longer.

Table 6. Labor Force Participation Rate by MSA and County: 1950–2000

County	Labor Force Participation Rate					
	1950	1960	1970	1980	1990	2000
Madison	53.8%	54.8%	58.0%	60.0%	63.5%	64.8%
St. Clair	53.9%	53.5%	57.0%	58.4%	62.7%	63.7%
St. Charles	54.1%	55.8%	63.5%	71.0%	75.8%	74.6%
Saint Louis	53.0%	56.4%	61.9%	66.9%	68.8%	67.1%
City of Saint Louis	56.2%	56.1%	55.6%	55.8%	59.3%	60.4%
Jefferson		51.8%	59.2%	65.4%	70.3%	70.2%
Franklin			58.4%	62.4%	66.7%	67.3%
Clinton				60.8%	62.8%	64.5%
Monroe				60.6%	67.0%	70.2%
Jersey					66.1%	65.2%
Lincoln						68.5%
Warren						68.0%
MSA Total	54.9%	55.6%	59.0%	62.9%	66.5%	66.7%

Source: MIDAS, PPRC, UM–Saint Louis, U.S. Census Bureau, 1950–2000.

A key characteristic of any labor force is its education attainment, and Tables 10, 11, and 12 show the proportion of persons aged twenty-five or older with some college or more for each county, for both sexes combined and for each gender. Education attainment was chosen as a measure that was a fair indication of an educated work force and one that is increasingly necessary in today's economy. As expected, educational attainment has risen over the 1950–2000 period, from 11.1 percent in 1950 to 54.7 percent in 2000. St. Louis County consistently had the greatest proportion of college-educated workers, but all counties have significantly higher levels over the years. In general, the more central and urbanized counties such as St. Clair, the City of St. Louis, St. Louis, and St. Charles have higher educational attainment levels than more recently rural counties such as Lincoln, Warren, Jefferson, and Franklin in Missouri and Clinton, Jersey, and Monroe in Illinois. The difference between levels of education attainment in St. Louis County and St. Charles County has continued to narrow since 1980.

Table 7. Percent of Labor Force Age 16–24: 1960–2000

County	1960	1970	1980	1990	2000
Madison	15.4	18.2	23.6	17.8	17.3
St. Clair	14.3	18.8	22.4	16.8	15.6
St. Charles	18.9	20.0	22.9	16.0	15.6
Saint Louis	13.1	18.8	21.9	15.1	14.8
City of Saint Louis	16.3	20.2	23.9	17.2	18.3
Jefferson	14.6	18.4	22.8	17.2	16.3
Franklin	21.3	19.5	24.3	18.2	15.8
Clinton	18.3	17.5	25.9	18.2	16.7
Monroe	15.6	16.4	22.9	14.5	14.7
Jersey	19.3	19.6	25.2	19.8	18.8
Lincoln	14.5	15.7	21.3	15.1	17.2
Warren	15.4	19.2	22.7	16.9	15.1
MSA Total	14.9	19.1	22.7	16.2	15.9

Source: MIDAS, PPRC, UM–Saint Louis, U.S. Census Bureau, 1960–2000.

The analysis of the data by gender in Tables 11 and 12 shows the great strides in education attainment made by both sexes, women in particular. From a regional perspective, the level of education attainment is nearly identical for men and women, 56.7 percent for men and 53.0 percent for women. However, the dramatic rise in education attainment between 1970 and 2000 for women can be seen in Table 12, where the advances made by women since 1970 saw their education attainment rise from 15.1 percent to 53.0 percent. As expected from the analysis provided by Table 10, St. Louis County and St. Charles County have the largest proportion of college-educated persons. Again, for men and women, the more recently rural counties in Missouri and Illinois have the lowest levels. For both men and women, the period between 1980 and 1990 saw the greatest increase in education attainment, with the level increasing 72.4 percent for women and 54.0 percent for men.

Table 8. Percent of Labor Force Age 25–64: 1960–2000

County	1960	1970	1980	1990	2000
Madison	80.0	77.6	73.5	79.4	79.5
St. Clair	78.0	72.0	69.1	75.6	77.2
St. Charles	76.8	77.2	75.0	82.1	81.7
Saint Louis	82.6	77.2	74.8	81.4	81.0
City of Saint Louis	78.1	73.8	71.4	79.2	78.2
Jefferson	82.1	78.9	75.4	81.1	81.6
Franklin	72.4	75.8	72.3	79.5	80.9
Clinton	76.4	75.0	68.6	77.4	78.1
Monroe	77.0	78.4	73.9	82.1	82.2
Jersey	72.7	75.4	71.8	77.6	78.0
Lincoln	77.7	76.8	74.5	82.0	80.4
Warren	74.8	74.5	72.1	79.8	80.6
MSA Total	79.9	75.8	73.4	80.2	80.2

Source: MIDAS, PPRC, UM–Saint Louis, U.S. Census Bureau, 1960–2000.

Occupations reflect the higher level of educational attainment. They are also indicative of the economic restructuring that the regional economy has undergone during the same period, whereby manual and unskilled labor occupations are continually being replaced with the application of technology and occupations requiring more education and technical and specialized training. Tables 13, 14, and 15 show the proportion of persons in managerial, professional, sales, and technical occupations for the region and for both men and women by county between 1960 and 2000. On a regional level this transformation in occupations has been dramatic: more than three out of four (78.2 percent) workers in 2000 held a management, professional, sales, or technical position, rising from 42.4 percent in 1960. At the county level, the highest proportion of workers in these occupations is found in the more highly urbanized ones such as St. Louis (89.8 percent), St. Charles (77.4 percent), and the City of St. Louis (72.5 percent). Conversely, the counties with the lowest proportions in these occupations are those that have been more recently rural, such as Warren (57.0 percent), Lincoln (54.1 percent), and Franklin (57.3 percent). Based on the new classification of occupations introduced in 2000, no county in the

Metromorphosis

region had a proportion of workers in these occupations less than the 54.1 percent in Lincoln County. Between 1960 and 1990, the number of workers in these occupations increased by 110.3 percent.

Table 9. Percent of Labor Force Age 65+: 1960–2000

County	1960	1970	1980	1990	2000
Madison	3.8	3.5	2.4	2.3	2.9
St. Clair	3.9	3.9	3.0	2.6	3.3
St. Charles	4.1	2.6	1.9	1.5	2.5
Saint Louis	4.1	3.7	3.1	3.2	4.0
City of Saint Louis	5.5	5.8	4.5	3.4	3.4
Jefferson	3.2	2.5	1.7	1.5	2.0
Franklin	4.4	4.6	3.3	2.3	3.3
Clinton	4.6	5.5	3.7	3.1	4.4
Monroe	7.0	4.8	3.1	3.1	3.1
Jersey	6.5	4.9	2.9	2.5	3.2
Lincoln	7.8	7.3	4.1	2.6	2.3
Warren	9.8	6.2	5.1	3.2	4.3
MSA Total	4.6	4.2	3.1	2.8	3.4

Source: MIDAS, PPRC, UM–Saint Louis, U.S. Census Bureau, 1960–2000.

Examining these trends by gender shows that this shift in occupations has been particularly dramatic for women, increasing by 179.0 percent between 1960 and 1990. This is indicative of the significant increase in the labor force participation rate of women during the same period. For men, the increase of 58.1 percent has been less dramatic since men still hold the majority of occupations that require some form of physical strength over technical expertise and professional training. As shown in Tables 14 and 15, the proportion of men in these occupations has been lower than women in all counties in the 1960–90 period. This is due to the inclusion of clerical and administrative occupations in this occupation category. In 1960, 55.5 percent of women held one of these occupations, compared to only 35.9 percent of men. By 1990, just under half (49.2 percent) of all male workers held this position while nearly three out of four women held one of these occupations.

Table 10. Education Attainment by MSA and County: 1950–2000

County	Percent Some College or More					
	1950	1960	1970	1980	1990	2000
Madison	8.5	9.9	14.0	23.7	39.8	50.3
St. Clair	7.7	9.6	13.8	25.3	42.0	51.8
St. Charles	8.8	10.7	16.6	29.5	50.6	59.5
Saint Louis	18.6	21.8	28.1	39.7	55.9	64.0
City of Saint Louis	9.1	9.8	11.6	20.9	35.8	43.8
Jefferson	6.1	7.9	10.7	19.0	33.5	43.0
Franklin	5.5	6.8	9.2	15.8	31.5	42.1
Clinton	5.7	5.8	10.7	17.0	33.0	42.4
Monroe	5.2	7.5	9.6	17.2	37.2	54.6
Jersey	7.3	7.9	11.7	19.0	33.3	43.2
Lincoln	5.9	8.1	9.8	13.2	26.3	33.5
Warren	7.3	9.3	10.7	16.5	29.1	39.2
MSA Total	11.1	13.8	18.8	29.8	46.2	54.7

Source: MIDAS, PPRC, UM–Saint Louis, U.S. Census Bureau, 1950–2000.

At the county level, this trend in occupation shift has been remarkably consistent for both men and women, with the notable exception being St. Charles County. Based on its rapid population increase since approximately 1980, its proportion of workers in these occupations has risen the fastest, with the number of men increasing over seven times (771.1 percent) and women increasing nearly 13 times (1290.0 percent). St. Louis County continues to have the largest proportion of workers in these occupations for both men (60.7 percent) and women (80.6 percent), an indication of its full development in the post-industrial period that began shortly after World War II.

The Changing Face of the St. Louis Labor Force: Age, Race, and Gender

As the previous section has demonstrated, the labor force in the region in 2000 is very different from the one that was working in 1950. The twin forces of economic restructuring and the entry of an ever-increasing number of women and minorities has changed the face of the labor force. It is no longer dominated by men working in a wide range of occupations. Today, the labor force features occupations that require higher levels of education and specialized training and, more important for women, do not require high levels of physical strength. The application of information, communications, and other scientific technology to production processes and service delivery systems has allowed a wider range of persons to enter the labor force and to earn adequate incomes.

Table 11. Male Education Attainment by MSA and County: 1950–2000

County	Percent Some College or More					
	1950	1960	1970	1980	1990	2000
Madison	9.3	11.5	17.3	29.4	44.2	52.3
St. Clair	8.8	11.7	17.1	30.4	45.5	53.7
St. Charles	8.5	11.3	19.4	35.5	55.1	62.2
Saint Louis	22.5	27.1	34.7	47.4	61.6	67.3
City of Saint Louis	10.7	11.6	13.6	24.9	39.5	45.4
Jefferson	6.3	8.9	12.0	22.5	35.6	42.6
Franklin	5.4	7.2	10.0	18.1	32.9	41.6
Clinton	5.2	5.9	11.6	21.0	34.2	41.2
Monroe	6.1	8.1	10.8	21.8	38.7	54.5
Jersey	5.4	7.3	12.5	21.7	32.6	40.5
Lincoln	5.1	7.7	9.9	13.9	25.5	32.6
Warren	7.8	9.3	12.0	18.3	30.8	38.5
MSA Total	13.1	16.8	23.1	35.8	50.6	56.7

Source: MIDAS, PPRC, UM–Saint Louis, U.S. Census Bureau, 1950–2000.

The transformation of an economy dominated by goods-producing activities to one that emphasizes services has also allowed persons to work longer. Together, these changes have helped the region's economy maintain a modest level of growth between 1950 and 2000.

The data in Tables 16 and 17 compare change in the labor force participation rate, unemployment rate, the total work-age population, and the civilian labor force (CLF) of the St. Louis region and the United

States between 1950 and 2000. As noted in the previous section, participation rates have risen from about half of work-age persons to approximately six out of ten. However, the participation rates for men, both whites and nonwhites, have actually declined over the fifty-year period, declining from 81.3 percent and 72.7 percent respectively in 1950 to 76.7 percent and 61.3 percent in 2000. In contrast, the participation rates of women of all races have nearly doubled. The rate for white and nonwhite women increased from 31.1 percent and 35.2 percent respectively in 1950 to 60.5 percent and 60.1 percent in 2000. This increase in participation has been the most prominent contributor to the growth in the labor force between 1950 and 2000 (see Table 16). Also during the 1950 to 2000 period, labor force participants in the region have had a slightly harder time finding or holding a job, as the unemployment rates between 1950 and 2000 have been higher than the nation (see Table 17). This difference in unemployment rates can be attributed in large part to the dismal employment picture that often accompanies the economic restructuring that occurred during the 1970s and 1980s.

Table 12. Female Education Attainment by MSA and County: 1950–2000

| County | Percent Some College or More | | | | | |
	1950	1960	1970	1980	1990	2000
Madison	7.6	8.4	11.1	18.7	36.0	48.4
St. Clair	6.7	7.8	10.9	20.9	39.0	50.1
St. Charles	9.0	10.1	13.8	23.8	46.3	57.0
Saint Louis	15.1	16.9	22.2	33.0	51.0	61.2
City of Saint Louis	7.6	8.2	10.0	18.0	33.0	42.4
Jefferson	5.9	6.9	9.4	15.5	31.6	43.4
Franklin	5.7	6.5	8.5	13.7	30.2	42.5
Clinton	6.2	5.7	9.9	13.2	31.8	43.6
Monroe	4.3	6.9	8.5	13.0	35.8	54.7
Jersey	8.9	8.5	10.9	16.5	33.9	45.7
Lincoln	6.7	8.6	9.7	12.5	27.1	34.4
Warren	6.7	9.3	9.4	14.8	27.4	40.0
MSA Total	9.3	11.0	15.1	24.6	42.4	53.0

Source: MIDAS, PPRC, UM–Saint Louis, U.S. Census Bureau, 1950–2000.

Metromorphosis

Table 13. Percent Managerial, Professional, Sales, & Technical by County: 1960–2000

County	1960	1970	1980	1990	1960–90 Pct. Change	2000*
Madison	34.9	45.2	48.9	56.2	125.3	72.8
St. Clair	37.4	46.7	50.7	56.6	86.0	73.2
St. Charles	34.6	46.4	54.1	61.9	996.7	77.4
Saint Louis	55.7	63.0	65.0	70.1	142.5	89.8
City of Saint Louis	37.6	45.3	48.9	55.9	-18.3	72.5
Jefferson	28.9	37.5	41.8	47.7	534.2	62.3
Franklin	26.1	33.0	36.4	42.8	268.2	57.3
Clinton	27.5	36.6	38.2	45.0	205.4	63.8
Monroe	30.7	37.0	45.7	52.5	218.9	75.5
Jersey	31.1	35.1	37.7	47.0	146.2	66.0
Lincoln	25.5	30.7	33.4	40.3	311.7	54.1
Warren	25.4	37.3	38.0	41.0	382.7	57.0
MSA Total	42.4	51.8	55.5	61.2	110.3	78.2

Source: MIDAS, PPRC, UM–Saint Louis, U.S. Census Bureau, 1960–1990.
*Not strictly comparable due to changes in occupation classification system.

The age distribution of the region's labor force has mirrored that of the nation between 1950 and 2000. Table 18 shows a comparison of the age distribution of the labor force of the region and nation, while Tables 19 and 20 compare the age distribution for men and women. In comparison to the nation, the region's age distribution is almost identical, with the largest differences occurring in the 1970s and 1980s when workers between twenty-five and sixty-four were about 2 percentage points lower. By 2000, the age distribution of the region is nearly identical to the nation (see Table 18). Comparing the region and nation by gender reveals greater variations as men between the ages of sixteen and twenty-four in the region have been consistently below the nation, reflecting the higher median age of the region and a lower participation in the armed forces (see Table 19). Differences among the number of men sixty-five years or older were mixed between 1950 and 2000 as the loss of manufacturing jobs and in other industries may have alternately caused men in this age group to retire or stay in the labor market longer based on industry trends. By 2000, the age distribution of the region and nation are nearly identical.

Table 14. Percent Managerial, Professional, Sales, & Technical by County:
Males, 1960–2000

| County | Males | | | | 1960–90 |
	1960	1970	1980	1990	Pct. Change
Madison	26.5	33.0	34.7	41.7	71.1
St. Clair	29.8	33.2	35.8	41.3	26.7
St. Charles	26.6	36.3	43.4	50.3	771.1
Saint Louis	50.5	54.5	56.1	60.7	74.4
City of Saint Louis	30.2	31.8	36.1	43.4	-36.3
Jefferson	22.1	26.2	28.2	32.1	314.5
Franklin	22.6	23.9	27.4	29.3	135.7
Clinton	20.6	26.4	26.8	31.2	111.2
Monroe	23.6	24.5	32.4	35.0	111.8
Jersey	22.7	25.1	25.6	32.9	83.5
Lincoln	19.3	20.0	23.0	24.9	157.9
Warren	18.9	27.3	26.5	28.9	239.0
MSA Total	35.9	41.2	44.3	49.2	58.1

Source: MIDAS, PPRC, UM–Saint Louis, U.S. Census Bureau, 1960–1990.

The comparison of the age distribution of women in the region and nation between 1950 and 2000 shows a distinctly different pattern. As shown in Table 20, the proportion of women between sixteen and twenty-four was significantly higher than those of men from 1950 through 1990. This is an indication that in the earlier decades (1950–60), women were less likely than men to attend college and were more likely to work in some capacity before entering prime childbearing age. For women over sixty-five, differences from men were similarly greater between 1950 and 1960, but by 1970, had practically become the same. Comparing genders in both the region and the nation showed little variation for women but showed a larger number of men between twenty-five and sixty-four in the region from 1950 to 1970 and a smaller proportion in the sixteen to twenty-four category. By 2000, the differences have largely disappeared because of the larger proportion of men working between 1950 and 1970 when goods-producing and manual labor jobs dominated male occupations and the region's economy.

Table 15. Percent Managerial, Professional, Sales, & Technical by County: Females, 1960–2000

County	1960	1970	1980	1990	1960–90 Pct. Change
		Females			
Madison	54.9	67.7	69.1	73.5	186.9
St. Clair	24.6	42.1	55.2	69.3	157.8
St. Charles	56.3	66.5	69.3	76.2	1290.0
Saint Louis	68.2	77.8	76.7	80.6	262.2
City of Saint Louis	49.2	61.7	62.1	68.1	-1.0
Jefferson	49.3	62.0	63.0	67.3	830.2
Franklin	33.6	49.9	49.5	59.6	459.5
Clinton	45.5	55.8	55.0	61.2	317.1
Monroe	49.8	65.6	65.2	74.8	355.5
Jersey	53.0	56.7	56.5	65.2	216.7
Lincoln	42.7	53.4	49.5	59.8	502.8
Warren	45.2	58.1	56.1	56.2	565.4
MSA Total	55.5	69.1	70.0	74.6	179.0

Source: MIDAS, PPRC, UM–Saint Louis, U.S. Census Bureau, 1960–1990.

Table 16. USA and MSA Comparison, 1950–2000: Labor Force Participation

	1950	1960	1970	1980	1990	2000
USA labor force participation rate	53.5%	55.3%	55.5%	62.0%	65.3%	63.9%
MSA labor force participation rate	54.9%	55.3%	58.6%	62.9%	65.9%	66.5%
MSA male	80.2%	79.3%	78.6%	76.4%	75.5%	73.4%
MSA white male	81.3%	80.7%	80.3%	78.7%	77.2%	76.7%
MSA nonwhite male	72.7%	70.2%	68.0%	67.1%	66.7%	61.3%
MSA female	31.6%	34.7%	42.1%	50.3%	57.8%	60.4%
MSA white female	31.1%	34.0%	41.1%	50.1%	57.6%	60.5%
MSA nonwhite female	35.2%	39.0%	47.8%	53.9%	59.2%	60.1%

Source: MIDAS, PPRC, UM–Saint Louis, U.S. Census Bureau, 1950–2000.

Table 17. USA and MSA Comparison, 1950–2000: Change in Work-Age Population, Civilian Labor Force, and Unemployment Rate

| | Percent Change | | | | | |
	1950–60	1960–70	1970–80	1980–90	1990–2000	1950–2000
Total work-age population, USA	12.4%	18.3%	14.6%	12.0%	10.8%	89.2%
Total work-age population, MSA	9.6%	11.0%	11.6%	12.5%	7.2%	63.7%
Civilian labor force, USA	15.4%	18.7%	29.1%	18.2%	9.1%	128.1%
Civilian labor force, MSA	11.5%	17.3%	19.9%	17.9%	8.5%	100.4%

| | Percent Change | | | | | |
	1950	1960	1970	1980	1990	2000
Unemployment rate, USA	4.7%	5.0%	4.3%	6.4%	6.2%	5.7%
Unemployment rate, MSA	3.9%	4.4%	4.9%	7.7%	6.3%	5.6%

Source: MIDAS, PPRC, UM–Saint Louis, U.S. Census Bureau, 1950–2000.

Table 18. Age Distribution of Labor Force for USA and MSA: 1950–2000

MSA	1950	1960	1970	1980	1990	2000
Total in armed forces	1.5	0.7	0.9	0.8	0.8	0.5
Total CLF 16–24	17.4	14.9	19.1	22.7	16.2	15.9
Total CLF 25–64	76.4	79.9	75.8	73.4	80.2	80.2
Total CLF 65+	4.7	4.6	4.2	3.1	2.8	3.4
	100.0	100.0	100.0	100.0	100.0	100.0

USA						
Total in armed forces	1.7	2.4	2.4	1.5	1.4	0.8
Total CLF 16–24	17.6	16.0	20.4	22.7	16.6	15.7
Total CLF 25–64	75.9	77.1	73.3	72.8	79.0	80.1
Total CLF 65+	4.8	4.4	3.9	3.0	3.0	3.3
	100.0	100.0	100.0	100.0	100.0	100.0

Source: MIDAS, PPRC, UM–Saint Louis, U.S. Census Bureau, 1950–2000.

Metromorphosis

Table 19. Age Distribution of Labor Force for Males, USA and MSA: 1950–2000

USA—Males	1950	1960	1970	1980	1990	2000
Total in armed forces	2.3	3.5	3.7	2.4	2.2	1.3
Total CLF 16–24	15.4	14.8	18.5	21.2	15.8	15.2
Total CLF 25–64	76.9	77.2	74.0	73.3	78.8	79.9
Total CLF 65+	5.4	4.6	3.9	3.1	3.2	3.6
	100.0	100.0	100.0	100.0	100.0	100.0
MSA—Males						
Total in armed forces	2.1	1.0	1.4	1.3	1.2	0.7
Total CLF 16–24	14.7	13.0	15.9	20.9	15.3	15.2
Total CLF 25–64	77.9	81.4	78.6	74.7	80.7	80.6
Total CLF 65+	5.3	4.7	4.2	3.1	2.8	3.4
	100.0	100.0	100.0	100.0	100.0	100.0

Source: MIDAS, PPRC, UM–Saint Louis, U.S. Census Bureau, 1950–2000.

As has been documented previously, women have made tremendous strides in their level of educational attainment. The data presented in Tables 21–26 compare the education attainment for men and women by race between 1950 and 2000. Comparing the data presented in Tables 21 and 22 for all men and women in the region and the nation, it shows the familiar pattern of higher-education attainment for men in the earlier decades, but a convergence of the levels between men and women by 1990 and 2000. However, in comparison with the nation, the region has consistently had lower levels of education attainment, and a higher proportion of persons in the region has less than a high school education. In part a reflection of the economy in earlier decades that did not require higher levels of education, the education attainment for men and women was lower than the nation until about 1980 for men and 1990 for women, when the proportions were nearly identical. By 2000, the region's men and women over the age of twenty-five years had proportions of some college education that were greater than the national average.

Comparing the education attainment for white men and women in the region and the nation reveals a striking contrast. Tables 23 and 24 show distinctly different comparisons with the nation, as white women have consistently had significantly lower proportions of persons with some college or more, with the differences between the region and the nation increasing over the fifty-year period between 1950 and 2000. In contrast, white men in the region have consistently had proportions of some college

Table 20. Age Distribution of Labor Force for Females, USA and MSA: 1950–2000

USA—Females	1950	1960	1970	1980	1990	2000
Total in armed forces	0.2	0.1	0.1	0.3	0.3	0.3
Total CLF 16–24	23.4	18.8	23.8	24.7	17.6	16.3
Total CLF 25–64	73.4	77.0	72.2	72.2	79.3	80.3
Total CLF 65+	3.1	4.1	3.8	2.8	2.8	3.1
	100.0	100.0	100.0	100.0	100.0	100.0
MSA—Females						
Total in armed forces	0.1	0.1	0.1	0.2	0.3	0.2
Total CLF 16–24	23.7	18.8	24.3	25.1	17.3	16.6
Total CLF 25–64	72.8	76.8	71.4	71.6	79.7	79.9
Total CLF 65+	3.3	4.3	4.3	3.1	2.7	3.3
	100.0	100.0	100.0	100.0	100.0	100.0

Source: MIDAS, PPRC, UM–Saint Louis, U.S. Census Bureau, 1950–2000.

or more, which was similar to the nation, but after 1980 have had a greater proportion than the nation. At the opposite end of the spectrum, greater proportions of white men and women do not reach high school, as the nation's proportion of some high school or high school has been consistently higher than the region.

The strides made in education attainment by nonwhite men and women between 1950 and 2000 have been substantial. The proportion of nonwhite women attaining some college or more has risen from 5.6 percent in 1950 to 48.1 percent in 2000. Similarly, that level of attainment for nonwhite men has risen from 5 percent in 1950 to 43.8 percent in 2000. Tables 25 and 26 compare the proportion of nonwhites by gender for the region and nation between 1950 and 2000. For nonwhite women in the region, their greatest strides have been made since 1980, when their proportion of some college or more was less than half of nonwhite men (See Tables 25 and 26). By 2000, their proportion was greater than both nonwhite men in the region and nonwhite women in the nation. For nonwhite men in the region, the story is less dramatic. By 1980, nonwhite men in the region had a reached a nearly identical proportion of college education attainment, 35.8 percent for the region to 37.7 percent for the nation. However, since 1980, nonwhite men in the region have increased their proportion by 8 percentage points in 2000 to 43.8 percent while the

Metromorphosis

nation's increase was 17.7 percentage points to 55.4 percent. Like white women in the region, nonwhite women are rapidly narrowing the pronounced education gap that existed in 1950. Unlike white men who have achieved a greater proportion of some college or more education attainment over the 1950 to 2000 period, nonwhite men in the region have fallen behind the national trend for nonwhite males.

Table 21. MSA Education Attainment for Females: 1950–2000

Attainment	1950	1960	1970	1980	1990	2000
Elementary or less	289,990	286,177	234,826	166,112	95,627	55,367
High school or less	185,470	266,657	350,894	400,440	391,787	369,137
Some college	28,785	39,814	55,198	97,387	212,843	270,629
Four years + college	21,985	28,854	48,852	87,828	145,602	208,393
Not reported	22,275	0	0	0	0	0
Total	**548,505**	**621,502**	**689,770**	**751,767**	**845,859**	**903,526**
Percent of Total	**1950**	**1960**	**1970**	**1980**	**1990**	**2000**
Elementary or less	52.9	46.0	34.0	22.1	11.3	6.1
High school or less	33.8	42.9	50.9	53.3	46.3	40.9
Some college	5.2	6.4	8.0	13.0	25.2	30.0
Four years + college	4.0	4.6	7.1	11.7	17.2	23.1
Not reported	4.1	0.0	0.0	0.0	0.0	0.0

Source: MIDAS, PPRC, UM–Saint Louis, U.S. Census Bureau, 1950–2000.

The distribution of occupations in the region between 1950 and 2000 reflects the general shift in occupations due to the restructuring of the economy. The dominance of managerial, professional, technical, sales, and administrative occupations in the new "information" economy is pronounced, accounting for almost two-thirds (62.2 percent) of all occupations in 2000. Occupations such as precision production, crafts, repair occupations, operators, fabricators, and laborers now account for only 22.5 percent of all occupations in 2000, down from 43.6 percent in 1950 (see Table 27).

The data presented in Tables 28 and 29 show the distribution of occupations in the region between 1950 and 2000 for men and women. For men in the region, occupations such as precision production, crafts, repair occupations, operation, fabrication, and labor, which are associated more with an industrial economy, still accounted for 36.8

percent of all male occupations in 2000, a decline from over half (52.2 percent) of male occupations in 1950. For women in the region, the new information economy has provided more employment opportunities, as physical strength is less important to the majority occupations in 2000. As a result, over nine out of ten (92.7 percent) occupations held by women in 2000 were in managerial, professional, technical, sales, administrative, and services, up from 66.4 percent in 1950. Likewise, only 24.2 percent of women held occupations in precision production, crafts, repair occupations, or operators, fabricators, and laborers positions in 1950, but declined further to 7.2 percent in 2000 (see Table 29).

Table 22. MSA Education Attainment for Males: 1950–2000

Attainment	1950	1960	1970	1980	1990	2000
Elementary or less	258,715	255,355	195,985	124,521	68,767	41,473
High school or less	145,660	202,995	259,485	283,244	291,111	300,611
Some college	29,305	41,114	56,654	98,186	187,592	226,931
Four years + college	35,025	51,425	80,148	129,558	180,715	220,456
Not reported	23,410	0	0	0	0	0
Total	492,115	550,889	592,272	635,509	728,185	789,471
Percent of Total	**1950**	**1960**	**1970**	**1980**	**1990**	**2000**
Elementary or less	52.6	46.4	33.1	19.6	9.4	5.3
High school or less	29.6	36.8	43.8	44.6	40.0	38.1
Some college	6.0	7.5	9.6	15.4	25.8	28.7
Four years + college	7.1	9.3	13.5	20.4	24.8	27.9
Not reported	4.8	0.0	0.0	0.0	0.0	0.0

Source: MIDAS, PPRC, UM–Saint Louis, U.S. Census Bureau, 1950–2000.

Table 23. MSA Education Attainment for White Females: 1950–2000

Attainment	1950	1960	1970	1980	1990	2000
Elementary or less	247,560	234,956	194,631	133,768	77,204	42,400
High school or less	168,175	221,188	303,210	322,470	319,923	289,012
Some college	26,660	34,440	48,705	78,425	173,020	213,353
Four years + college	20,395	25,961	44,825	70,727	125,376	178,064
Not reported	19,105	0	0	0	0	0
Total	481,895	516,545	591,371	605,390	695,523	722,829
Percent of Total	**1950**	**1960**	**1970**	**1980**	**1990**	**2000**
Elementary or less	51.4	45.5	32.9	22.1	11.1	5.9
High school or less	34.9	42.8	51.3	53.3	46.0	40.0
Some college	5.5	6.7	8.2	13.0	24.9	29.5
Four years + college	4.2	5.0	7.6	11.7	18.0	24.6
Not reported	4.0	0.0	0.0	0.0	0.0	0.0

Source: MIDAS, PPRC, UM–Saint Louis, U.S. Census Bureau, 1950–2000.

Table 24. MSA Education Attainment for White Males: 1950–2000

Attainment	1950	1960	1970	1980	1990	2000
Elementary or less	218,855	206,860	160,953	108,570	53,969	30,397
High school or less	133,360	170,968	225,431	246,962	237,660	234,562
Some college	27,640	37,246	51,753	85,609	160,121	188,522
Four years + college	33,695	49,114	77,184	112,962	163,636	197,312
Not reported	19,370	0	0	0	0	0
Total	432,920	464,188	515,321	554,103	615,386	650,793
Percent of Total	**1950**	**1960**	**1970**	**1980**	**1990**	**2000**
Elementary or less	50.6	44.6	31.2	19.6	8.8	4.7
High school or less	30.8	36.8	43.7	44.6	38.6	36.0
Some college	6.4	8.0	10.0	15.5	26.0	29.0
Four years + college	7.8	10.6	15.0	20.4	26.6	30.3
Not reported	4.5	0.0	0.0	0.0	0.0	0.0

Source: MIDAS, PPRC, UM–Saint Louis, U.S. Census Bureau, 1950–2000.

Table 25. MSA Education Attainment for Nonwhite Females: 1950–2000

Attainment	1950	1960	1970	1980	1990	2000
Elementary or less	42,430	51,221	40,195	32,344	18,423	12,256
High school or less	17,295	45,469	47,684	77,970	71,864	77,120
Some college	2,125	5,374	6,493	18,962	39,823	54,473
Four years + college	1,590	2,893	4,027	17,101	20,226	28,473
Not reported	3,170	0	0	0	0	0
Total	66,610	104,957	98,399	267,886	150,336	172,322
Percent of Total	**1950**	**1960**	**1970**	**1980**	**1990**	**2000**
Elementary or less	63.7	48.8	40.8	12.1	12.3	7.1
High school or less	26.0	43.3	48.5	29.1	47.8	44.8
Some college	3.2	5.1	6.6	7.1	26.5	31.6
Four years + college	2.4	2.8	4.1	6.4	13.5	16.5
Not reported	4.8	0.0	0.0	0.0	0.0	0.0

Source: MIDAS, PPRC, UM–Saint Louis, U.S. Census Bureau, 1950–2000.

Table 26. MSA Education Attainment for Nonwhite Males: 1950–2000

Attainment	1950	1960	1970	1980	1990	2000
Elementary or less	39,860	48,495	35,032	15,951	14,798	10,597
High school or less	12,300	32,027	34,054	36,282	53,451	63,213
Some college	1,665	3,868	4,901	12,577	27,471	36,014
Four years + college	1,330	2,311	2,964	16,596	17,079	21,363
Not reported	4,040	0	0	0	0	0
Total	59,195	86,701	76,951	81,406	112,799	131,187
Percent of Total	**1950**	**1960**	**1970**	**1980**	**1990**	**2000**
Elementary or less	67.3	55.9	45.5	19.6	13.1	8.1
High school or less	20.8	36.9	44.3	44.6	47.4	48.2
Some college	2.8	4.5	6.4	15.4	24.4	27.5
Four years + college	2.2	2.7	3.9	20.4	15.1	16.3
Not reported	6.8	0.0	0.0	0.0	0.0	0.0

Source: MIDAS, PPRC, UM–Saint Louis, U.S. Census Bureau, 1950–2000.

Metromorphosis

Table 27. MSA Occupations: 1950–2000

Classification	1950	1960	1970	1980	1990	2000*
Managerial, professional, technical, sales, and administrative	42.1	42.4	51.8	55.5	61.2	62.2
Clerical	16.9	16.8	20.1	19.0	17.8	na
Services, except private households	8.5	8.6	9.9	13.1	13.0	14.8
Services, private household occupations	2.2	2.0	1.3	0.5	0.3	0.0
Farming, forestry, and fishing	1.8	1.9	1.2	1.3	1.1	0.5
Precision production, craft, and repair occupations	14.8	14.3	14.1	12.0	10.6	8.8
Operators, fabricators, and laborers	28.8	24.1	21.7	17.6	13.8	13.7
Other	1.8	6.8	0.0	0.0	0.0	0.0

Source: MIDAS, PPRC, UM–Saint Louis, U.S. Census Bureau, 1950–2000.
*Not strictly comparable because of change in occupation classifications in 2000.

Table 28. MSA Male Occupations: 1950–2000

Classification	1950	1960	1970	1980	1990	2000*
Managerial, professional, technical, sales, and administrative	36.7	35.9	41.2	44.3	49.2	50.3
Clerical	10.0	8.8	8.7	7.6	7.2	NA
Services, except private households	7.0	6.1	8.0	9.8	10.6	12.1
Services, private household occupations	0.2	0.1	0.1	0.1	0.0	0.0
Farming, forestry, and fishing	2.4	2.6	1.7	1.9	1.8	0.8
Precision production, craft, and repair occupations	20.5	20.8	21.7	19.9	18.2	16.3
Operators, fabricators, and laborers	31.7	28.2	27.3	24.0	20.2	20.5
Other	1.5	6.3	0.0	0.0	0.0	0.0

Source: MIDAS, PPRC, UM–Saint Louis, U.S. Census Bureau, 1950–2000.
*Not strictly comparable because of change in occupation classifications in 2000.

Table 29. MSA Female Occupations: 1950–2000

Classification	1950	1960	1970	1980	1990	2000*
Managerial, professional, technical, sales, and administrative	54.3	55.5	69.1	70.0	74.6	75.0
Clerical	32.5	32.9	38.5	33.7	29.7	na
Services, except private households	12.1	13.5	12.8	17.3	15.7	17.7
Services, private household occupations	6.7	5.8	3.2	1.1	0.7	0.0
Farming, forestry, and fishing	0.4	0.4	0.3	0.5	0.4	0.2
Precision production, craft, and repair occupations	1.9	1.3	1.8	1.8	2.0	0.7
Operators, fabricators, and laborers	22.3	15.7	12.7	9.3	6.6	6.5
Other	2.3	7.8	0.0	0.0	0.0	0.0

Source: MIDAS, PPRC, UM–Saint Louis, U.S. Census Bureau, 1950–2000.
*Not strictly comparable because of change in occupation classifications in 2000.

The Future of the St. Louis Labor Force

The face and distribution of the labor force in the region in 2000 is very different from 1950. During the fifty years, these changes have helped sustain a modest rate of economic growth in spite of the painful restructuring in the 1970s and 1980s. The large-scale entry of women and minorities has been most responsible for the growth in the region's labor force. Perhaps as important has been the large size of the baby boom generation, the persons born between 1946 and 1965 (Frey 2001). This generation's size has provided a demographic-based boost to the region's labor force as its youngest members entered in the early 1960s and were completely in the labor force by the early 1980s.

However, the generations behind the baby boomers are smaller and will not be able to fully replace this generation as it leaves the labor force in the coming decades. Maintaining growth in the labor force over the coming decades will present the region with new challenges if it is to continue to grow its economy at even a modest rate.

Based on the historical growth performance of the economy and the trend in the age structure of the region between 1950 and 2000, projections for the years 2020 and 2040 are presented in Table 30. These projections provide a hypothetical scenario in which a significant gap develops between the number of persons sixteen years or older (the work-age population) and the employment currently necessary to maintain the fifty-year historical growth rate in the regional economy. In this scenario, it is assumed that everything relating to economic and demographic trends remains unchanged from its current and historical basis in 2000. Under this scenario a gap of approximately 265,000 workers will develop unless necessary and vital steps are taken. Without a sufficient labor pool local business will not be able to expand, and mobile capital will not be attracted to the region. However, attracting larger numbers of workers will provide only a partial solution to the challenge of maintaining local economic growth.

The advent of the post-industrial, information economy has challenged and will continue to challenge industry, educators, and regional leaders with creating a local labor force prepared for the new economy. The rapid rate of change due to the increased introduction of new and better technologies has shaped a new workplace and redefined how work is done. This new concept will require workers to be more adaptive and flexible to the inevitable rapid pace of change in markets and workplaces. In order to prepare existing and future workers for their new settings, existing processes and systems that deliver training and education will need to be adapted and retooled. Regions that are able to make these adaptations will be able to capture a greater share of future economic growth.

Table 30. Populaton, Labor Force, and Employment Projections

	2000	2020 Projection	2040 Projection	2000–2040 Pct. Change
Population*	2,603,607	2,732,965	2,842,432	9.2
Population 16+*	1,999,296	2,141,097	2,247,526	12.4
Percent	76.8%	78.3%	79.1%	--
Labor force* **	1,329,532	1,466,651	1,584,506	19.2
Not in labor force	669,764	674,446	663,020	--
Employment***	1,334,095	1,596,693	1,910,980	43.2
Employment deficit	-4,563	-130,042	-326,474	--
Percent of employment	-0.3%	-8.1%	-17.1%	--
Population/employment Ratio	2.0	1.7	1.5	--

Source: MIDAS, PPRC, UM–Saint Louis, U.S. Census Bureau, 1950–2000.
*Population, population 16+, and labor force from 2000 census.
**Estimates for 2020 and 2040 based upon a predicted rise in participation from 66.5% in 2000 to 68.5% in 2020 and 70.5% in 2040.
***Employment estimates based upon the average annual growth rate between 1950 and 2000.

One way of closing the hypothetical gap of the future is to make new and existing workers more productive. Increasing the productivity of the labor force has been a key feature to the success of the national economy and has been a major reason for the continued success of the nation'smanufacturing sector while it has experienced a long and steady decline in employment. This has been accomplished through the application of technologies and the preparation of workers in utilizing those technologies. But as the pace of change increases, training and educating existing and future workers will require institutions such as universities to adapt their response time to labor demand. Creating new programs and partnerships with specific industries will require these institutions to streamline and adapt their decision-making systems so that worker and industry needs are met in mutually consistent time frames. Many forward-thinking educators have noted that the future success or even the survival of these institutions will depend on their ability to adapt to the new pace of labor demand and the change in the way workers/students will demand that their education and training be delivered (Judy and D'Amico 1997).

Summary and Conclusions

Many changes have taken place in the composition and distribution of the region's labor force between 1950 and 2000. As part of the fifty-year pattern of population decentralization that has added seven counties to the definition of the region, the labor force has become less concentrated in the center and has grown in large percentages in counties that were primarily rural and agricultural. Counties such as St. Charles and Jefferson in Missouri have grown by multiples of twelve and six, respectively. Though the City of St. Louis was once the site of half the employment in the region, the share of employment there has fallen to only about one out of ten. The growth in the land area of the region has not been matched by the growth in employment, as only 17.3 percent of the civilian labor force resides in the seven counties added since 1950. And compared to the growth in employment in the nation, the region's growth has been modest. Growing 83.1 percent over the fifty-year period between 1950 and 2000—from 676,917 to 1,239,501—it represents only about two-thirds of the 128.1 percent growth in employment experienced by the nation.

Spurring the decentralization of population and jobs during this period has been a major restructuring of the economy in which the dominant commercial activities are now found in service industries that have supplanted the manufacture of durable goods. Because of this restructuring, the pattern of occupations has shifted and the number of workers in 2000 in managerial, professional, technical, sales, and administration or service occupations is at an all-time high. Over nine out of ten women in the region work in one of these occupations in 2000, up from three out of four in 1950, while the proportion of men working in these occupations has risen from a little over four out of ten to approximately six out of ten in 2000.

Also since 1950 the face of the region's labor force has changed from one dominated by men to one that is nearly equal parts men and women. This change has been the salient feature of the changes in the labor force as women are now participating at record levels and rates. Similarly, the participation rates of minorities has risen as higher levels of education attainment and the breaking down of some social barriers have provided increased employment opportunities. These increases in the labor force participation rates of women and men have been the major contributor to growth in both the size of the civilian labor force and the level of employment. The participation rates for men have actually declined slightly over the same period as social security, Medicare, retirement benefits, and savings from dual-earner households have allowed men to retire. Without these increases in participation by women and minorities it is unlikely that the region's and the nation's economy would have been able to grow at the rate it did over the period between 1950 and 2000.

Further changes in the labor force relating to its age distribution indicate that there lie challenges ahead to maintaining current levels of economic growth. Since 1980, the proportion of persons in the twenty-five- to sixty-four-year-old category has risen, while the proportion of persons in the sixteen- to twenty-four-year-old category has declined and the proportion of persons over sixty-five years old has risen. This is an indication that as the oldest members of the work force retire or leave for a variety of reasons, there will be fewer workers to replace them. This will create many opportunities for workers with high levels of skills and technical training and will create many more types of working arrangements such as telecommuting and the opportunity for older workers to work longer. And in order to maintain business expansion and economic growth in the region it will be necessary to find ways to make workers of the future more productive.

Based on historical growth rates, projections of future employment and the work-age population show that the region will fall short in providing the necessary number of workers. This will mean that if the region is to grow at its current rate in the decades ahead, industry in partnership with training and education institutions, such as public universities, will need to design programs and service delivery systems that will be in step with the rapid pace of change in labor demand and worker/student demand. Long-standing methods of delivery of education and knowledge will be under increased scrutiny as the pressures of fewer workers and the need for higher productivity from existing workers increase over the decades ahead.

References

Bluestone, Barry, and Bennett Harrison. *The Deindustrialization of America.* New York: Basic Books, 1982.

Duderstadt, James J. "Higher Education in the 21st Century: Navigating the Public Research University through the Stormy Seas of a Changing World." Lecture, University of Missouri–Columbia, March 6, 2003.

Frey, William H., Bill Abresch, and Jonathan Yeasting. *America by the Numbers: A Field Guide to the U.S. Population.* New York: The New Press, 2001.

Judy, Richard, and Carol D'Amico. *Work Force 2020: Work and Workers in the 21st Century.* Indianapolis, Ind.: Hudson Institute, 1997.

Russell, Cheryl. *Demographics of the U.S.: Trends and Projections.* 2d ed. Ithaca, N.Y.: New Strategist Publications, 2003.

U.S. Bureau of the Census. *Households, Families and Children: A 30-Year Perspective.* Washington, DC: U.S. Government Printing Office, 1992.

U.S. Department of Labor. *Report on the American Work Force.* 4th release. Indianapolis, Ind.: Your Domain Printing, 2001.

Chapter 5

Racial Inequality and Developmental Disparities in the St. Louis Region

Scott Cummings
Saint Louis University

As a metropolitan region, St. Louis is deeply concerned about its public image. This partially reflects its preoccupation with its grand heritage as the gateway to the west, its former position as a Midwest industrial giant, and its once secure reputation as a major player in America's business and commercial heartland. Primm (1981) explains that in the late 1900s, St. Louis rivaled Chicago as the industrial "lion" of the Midwest: "Still a leading agricultural entrepot and commercial hub, it was second only to Chicago as a railroad center, and it was a humming industrial metropolis." In 1900, St. Louis was the fourth largest city in America, behind New York, Chicago, and Philadelphia. In the aftermath of the City's grandest event, the 1904 World's Fair, "visions of glamorous growth danced before the eyes of St. Louis boosters" (Primm 1981, 419).

From its pinnacle at the turn of the century, St. Louis has undergone a series of profound developmental changes in its regional economy, in the racial and demographic composition of its residents, and in its relative ranking as a major American city. Today, it is struggling to secure a postindustrial future, and its civic leaders are aggressively seeking a new and more positive urban identity. Over the past four decades, St. Louis, along with Detroit, Philadelphia, and New Orleans, emerged as a poster city symbolizing the worst aspects of the nation's urban crisis. The infamous photograph capturing the implosion of the Pruitt-Igoe public housing project in 1972 branded St. Louis as the prototype of what was wrong with American cities (von Hoffman 2003). St. Louis became known as a place where racial polarization and economic decline conspired to produce extreme forms of social inequality, poverty, and downtown deterioration. Given its proud tradition and wistful recollection as the place "that for seven months in 1904…[became…the most cosmopolitan city on earth," it is not surprising that many St. Louis boosters are unhappy about its current public image (Primm 1981, 422).

Civic organizations, chambers of commerce and economic development entities, planning bodies, and public officials strive to counter the negative perceptions of the metropolitan area in a wide variety of brochures, pamphlets, reports, and advertising material. Over the past decade, the region's metropolitan planning organization, the East-West Gateway Coordinating Council, has published a robust assessment of how St. Louis compares with thirty-five other regimes on a number of important performance measures. The publication, *Where We Stand* (East-West Gateway Coordinating Council 2002), reflects the region's ongoing concern about its relative low rank among metropolitan rivals. Another civic association, FOCUS St. Louis, teamed with the Missouri Historical Society to publish *St. Louis Currents* (FOCUS St. Louis 1997), a cooperative effort that began in 1986. In the most recent edition, Losos (1997) contends that three policy dilemmas confront the St. Louis region: (1) racial polarization, (2) urban sprawl, and (3) the growing need for regional cooperation. Few local policy observers would disagree with her analysis.

This chapter examines contemporary evidence about the extent to which popular notions of racial and economic inequality and developmental and regional disparities in St. Louis are consistent with the most recent facts on the subject. Is St. Louis's image as a racially polarized region accurate? What are the underlying causes of racial polarization? What can be done to reduce racial inequality in the region? The purpose is to identify important social and economic trends that have significantly influenced urban development in St. Louis, and explain how these trends have created racial disparities in the quality of life among its residents. Three specific issue areas and trends are covered: deindustrialization and regional development disparities, racial and economic inequality, and racial disparities in the quality of life available to the region's citizens. The chapter concludes with a discussion of what contemporary policy analysts call civic capacity, and explores what is required of the region's political and business leadership to address these three important public policy issues.

St. Louis as the Urban Crisis Prototype: Reputation and Record

There is much evidence supporting the regime's current reputation as one of the prototypes of America's urban crisis, and justifying the intense civic concern about how to reverse this widely held perception. Between 1970 and 2000, the St. Louis region grew by fewer than 150,000 people. Between 1950 and 2000 more than 500,000 people abandoned the City of St. Louis, leaving many of its neighborhoods in a serious state of deterioration and decay. During this same period, business and industry were significantly restructured and the City's dominant position in the region's economy was radically undermined. In 1951, over 85 percent of the region's jobs were located in the City of St. Louis. By 1997, less than 30 percent were. Between 1970 and 1990, St. Louis City lost approximately 82,061 manufacturing jobs. During this same period, the counties surrounding the City gained more than 44,000 manufacturing jobs. As the center city declined, the suburbs surrounding it grew and prospered. While the City's stature became increasingly consistent with its negative public image, its suburbs developed into places where the good life was highly visible.

Despite the high quality of life apparent in the suburbs, the current political fragmentation in the St. Louis metropolitan area reflects long-standing disparities of wealth and power across the region. Jones (2000) reports no less than 92 separate political jurisdictions in the St. Louis metropolitan area. In St. Louis County alone, local government service delivery is divided among more than 150 political jurisdictions. According to Jones (2000), these separate governments insulate the wealthy from the myriad urban problems left behind in St. Louis City. Stein (2002) suggests that upper- and middle-income whites create political and legal barriers between themselves and the African American poor living in the City through maintenance of strict building codes and restrictive land use policies within their separate suburban jurisdictions.

Over the past four decades, the restructuring of the regional economy has produced extreme forms of racial inequality and reinforced the multiplication of separate political jurisdictions isolating the City from its suburbs. Governmental fragmentation contributes to an absence of consensus among business and civic leaders over a common regional public policy agenda. To understand how changes in the local economy have influenced development disparities and undermined political consensus, it is important to examine more closely how the organization of business and commercial activity in the regional economy has changed over the past fifty years. Such an analysis of change is essential to a better understanding of why racial inequality has such a strong influence on the region's negative public image.

Regional Developmental Disparities

There are several ways to depict the developmental disparities that characterize St. Louis's regional economy and explain how they have influenced race relations in the inner city. The Metropolitan Statistical Area (MSA) has shown relatively little growth since 1970. While the region grew by less than 150,000 people over the past three decades, dramatic population shifts took place within the MSA. The City of St. Louis dropped from 856,796 residents in 1950 to 348,189 in 2000. During the same period, the suburban regions surrounding the city displayed remarkable growth. Between 1950 and 2000, a relatively constant number of families and individuals spread across geographic space in a manner that produced extreme forms of suburban sprawl in the St. Louis region.

During this time, business and industry were significantly restructured, and the city's dominant position in the region's economy was radically undermined. As discussed in Chapter 4 of this volume, the dynamics of employment and geography have changed substantially in the St. Louis region. In 1951, over 85 percent of the region's jobs were located in the City of St. Louis. Over the ensuing four decades, the dominance of the City over the region's economy steadily declined, relatively and absolutely. In 1951, approximately 419,813 employees were working in the City of St. Louis. By 1997, this figure was 276,542.

During this same period, St. Louis County emerged as the dominant location of economic activity. In 1951, less than 10 percent of the region's work force was located in St. Louis County. By 1997, nearly 60 percent of region's work force was located there. In 1997, approximately 580,200 individuals were employed in St. Louis County, a figure substantially greater than that reported by the City at its peak economic capacity in 1951.

Figure 1 analyzes the geographic distribution of firms. In 1951, more than 80 percent of all firms were located in the City. By 1997, less than 20 percent of the region's firms were located there. Similar to the labor force data, the relative economic position of St. Louis County gradually surpassed that held by the City during the 1970s. By 1997, the County was home to nearly 60 percent of the region's firms. The analysis of firms shows that the County housed more firms in 1997 (30,314) than did the City in 1951 (23,427).

Figure 1 also shows the gradual emergence of St. Charles, Jefferson, and Franklin Counties as critical players in the regional economy. The trend lines suggest that St. Louis County is beginning to lose economic ground to its surrounding counties in a manner similar to its earlier eclipse of St. Louis City. Nonetheless, the City and County remain the primary centers of regional economic activity.

Figure 2 displays the gradual erosion of St. Louis City's domination of the region's payroll. In 1951, the City accounted for over 85 percent of the region's first-quarter payroll. By 1997, only 30 percent of the region's first-quarter payroll was being earned in the City. On the other hand, about 60 percent of the region's payroll was being earned in St. Louis County by 1997. A small trend line between 1990 and 1997 suggests that the relative position of the County is declining at the expense of income being earned in St. Charles County.

Figure 1. The Proportion of Total Firms by Political Jurisdiction

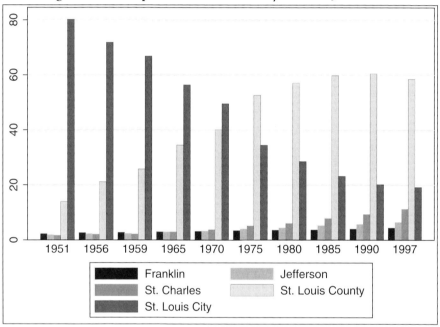

It is clear from the figures that regional disparities have increased significantly between 1950 and 1997. Not only has the relative position of the city eroded but recent evidence also suggests that St. Louis County may be entering a period of similar decline as business and industry continue their migration to the western and northern suburbs. Regional disparities in economic development within the St. Louis metropolitan area have been influenced by national and global patterns of disinvestment and deindustrialization. According to Bluestone and Harrison (1984, 6), deindustrialization refers to:

widespread, systematic disinvestment in the nation's basic productive capacity. Controversial as it may be, the essential problem with the U.S. economy can be traced to the way capital—in the forms of financial resources and of real plants and equipment—has been diverted from productive investment in our basic national industries into unproductive speculation, mergers and acquisitions, and foreign investment. Left behind are shattered factories, displaced workers, and a newly emerging group of ghost towns.

Figure 2. The Proportion of First Quarter Payroll by Political Jurisdiction

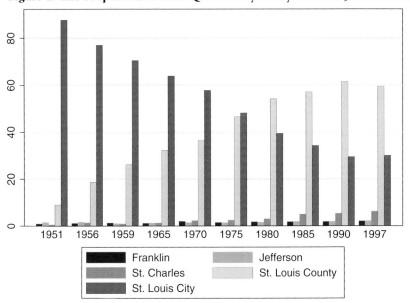

While the "ghost town" metaphor may be extreme, parts of north St. Louis have experienced extreme population loss over the past three decades. Based upon the analysis of county business data, the 1970s and 1980s were the periods in which the city experienced its greatest economic decline. This is when St. Louis County eclipsed the city as the center of regional economic activity. Between 1965 and 1980, St. Louis City lost approximately 71,117 jobs and 7,377 firms. Table 1 shows a partial timeline of watershed events in St. Louis's recent experience with deindustrialization and disinvestment. The table identifies the firms that closed or cut back their operations, the geographic location of the firm, and the approximate number of jobs that were eliminated. Between 1970 and 1990, St. Louis City lost approximately 82,061 manufacturing jobs. During this same time, the counties surrounding the City gained more than 44,000 manufacturing jobs. The bulk of these jobs (35,229) appeared in St. Louis County.

Metromorphosis

Table 1. A Timeline of Plant Closings and Shutdowns in the St. Louis Metropolitan Region

Company	Location	Year	Jobs Shed	Jobs?	Closure (X)
Boeing	St. Louis County	1999	2,000	Yes	
Sunmark Candy Co	St. Louis County	1999	125	No	X
Switzer Candy Company	St. Louis City	1998	220	Yes	X
Trans World Airlines	St. Louis City	1997	160	No	
Nations Bank	St. Louis City	1997	300	No	
Ritepoint	St. Louis County	1996	100	Yes	X
Magna Bank	St. Louis City	1996	200	No	
McDonnell Douglas	St. Louis County	1996	230	Yes	
McDonnell Douglas	St. Charles County	1995	800	Yes	
Pet Inc.	St. Louis City	1995	400	No	X
Brown Shoe Company (JVL Plant)	St. Louis City	1995	90	Yes	X
Crown Cork & Seal	St. Louis City	1994	180	Yes	X
Cupples Products	St. Louis County	1994	150	Yes	
Esco Electronics	St. Louis County	1994	100	No	
Lee/Rowan	St. Louis County	1994	300	Yes	X
Brown Shoe Company	St. Louis County	1994	410	No	
Chevron Company	St. Louis County	1994	160	Yes	X
Moog Automotive	St. Louis County	1994	260	Yes	X
Southwestern Bell	St. Louis County	1993	190	No	
General Electric (Engine Plant)	St. Louis City	1993	60	Yes	X
Southwestern Bell Corp	STL City & County	1992	900	No	
McDonnell Douglas	St. Louis County	1992	700	Yes	
Brown Shoe Company	Franklin County	1992	450	Yes	X
Union Camp Corporation	St. Louis City	1992	96	Yes	X
Sheraton Hotel	St. Louis City	1991	300	No	
Bristol Meyers Co	St. Louis County	1991	325	Yes	X
Chrysler Corp	St. Louis County	1991	2,100	Yes	
Monsanto Co.	St. Louis City	1991	168	Yes	
General Dynamics	St. Louis County	1991	170	No	X
Esco Electronics	St. Louis County	1991	373	Yes(180)	
Penaljo Shoe Company	Jefferson County	1990	300	Yes	X
PPG Industries	Jefferson County	1990	273	Yes	X
Care Unit Hospital	St. Louis City	1990	142	No	
St. Louis Sun	St. Louis City	1990	194	No	X
Crane Defense Systems	St. Louis County	1990	200	Yes	X
Bridal Originals	St. Louis City	1990	200	Yes	X
Southwestern Bell	St. Louis City	1990	325	No	
McDonnell Douglas	St. Louis County	1990	4,700	Yes	
Monsanto Co.	St. Louis County	1990	300	No	
Westinghouse Electric	St. Louis County	1990	337	Yes	X
TOTAL 1990–2000			**18,988**		**20**
Chrysler Corp	St. Louis County	1989	1,900	Yes	
Chase Hotel	St. Louis City	1989	300	No	
Westinghouse Electric	St. Louis City	1989	300	Yes	X
Dillard's Warehouse	St. Louis City	1989	300	Yes	X
Missouri Rolling Mill Corp	St. Louis City	1989	170	Yes	X
Colonial Baking Co.	St. Louis City	1988	400	Yes	X
Cuppples Products	St. Louis City	1988	400	Yes	X
Emerson Electric	St. Louis County	1988	250	Yes	

Table 1 (Cont'd). A Timeline of Plant Closings and Shutdowns in the St. Louis Metropolitan Region

Emerson Electric	St. Louis County	1988	250	Yes	
American Freight System	St. Louis City	1988	300	No	
Chrysler Corp	St. Louis County	1987	600	Yes	
General Motors (Trucks)	St. Louis City	1987	1,600	Yes	X
General Electric (Lightbulb Plant)	St. Louis County	1986	465	Yes	X
City Hospital	St. Louis City	1986	300	No	X
Monsanto Co.	St. Louis City	1986	350	Yes	
Kroger Food Stores	STL City & County	1986	2,000	No	X
McLean Trucking	St. Louis City	1986	150	Yes	X
Emerson Electric	St. Louis County	1986	100	Yes	
Mallinckrodt	St. Louis City	1986	200	Yes	
TWA	St. Louis City	1986	1,500	No	
General Motors (Wentzville)	St. Charles County	1986	1,000	Yes	
Monsanto Co.	St. Louis County	1986	200	No	
MCI Communications	St. Louis City	1986	130	No	
Seven-Up	St. Louis County	1986	105	No	X
Union Pacific Railroad	St. Louis City	1986	300	No	
Nooter Corporation	St. Louis City	1985	300	Yes	
Charter Hospital	St. Louis City	1985	154	No	
Moog Automotive	St. Louis County	1985	264	Yes	
Spielberg Manufacturing Co.	Jefferson County	1985	360	Yes	X
City Hospital & Charter Hospital	St. Louis City	1985	1200	No	
Monsanto Co.	St. Louis City	1985	250	Yes	
Carboline Co.	St. Louis County	1985	75	Yes	
AT&T	St. Louis City	1985	139	No	
Peabody Holding Co.	St. Louis City	1985	100	No	X
St. Louis County Hospital	St. Louis County	1985	173	No	
Monsanto Co.	St. Louis County	1985	710	No	
St. Louis Ship	St. Louis City	1985	306	Yes	X
Carter Carburetor	STL City & County	1984	3,000	Yes	X
Trans World Airlines	St. Louis City	1984	400	No	
St. Louis Ship	St. Louis City	1984	128	Yes	
St. Louis Ship	St. Louis City	1983	667	Yes	
Missouri Pacific Railroad	St. Louis City	1983	141	No	
Wagner Electric Co	St. Louis County	1983	1,300	Yes	X
Sheraton Reservations Corp.	St. Louis City	1983	200	No	
Atlas Tool & Manufacturing	St. Louis City	1983		Yes	X
McCabe Powers Body Co.	St. Louis County	1983		Yes	X
Combustion Engineering	St. Louis City	1983	500	Yes	X
General Motors (Trucks)	St. Louis City	1982	1,300	Yes	
Amcar (Division of ACF)	St. Louis City	1982	1,200	Yes	X
Yellow Freight System	St. Louis City	1981	270	Yes	
Wagner Electric	St. Louis County	1981	220	Yes	
Carter Carburetor	STL City & County	1981	907	Yes	
Reynolds Metals Co.	St. Louis City	1981	325	Yes	X
Missouri Portland Cement Co.	St. Louis County	1981	155	Yes	X
Alpha Portland Cement Co.	St. Louis City	1981	130	Yes	X
Missouri Pacific Railroad	Franklin County	1981	121	Yes	
Scullin Steel	St. Louis City	1981	680	Yes	X
Sealtest Dairy	St. Louis City	1981		Yes	X

General Motors (Corvette)	St. Louis City	1981	2,000	Yes	X
General Motors (Caprice, Impala)	St. Louis City	1980	5,000	Yes	X
Chrysler Corp	St. Louis County	1980	5,200	Yes	X
Amcar (Division of ACF)	St. Louis City	1980	800	Yes	
Other Plant Closings, 1981-84					
Amsco/Division of Abex Corp	St. Louis County	n/a	n/a	Yes	X
Hager Hinge Co	St. Louis City	n/a	n/a	Yes	X
Lexington United Corporation	St. Louis City	n/a	n/a	Yes	X
Perfection Manufacturing	St. Louis City	n/a	n/a	Yes	X
TOTAL 1980–89			**41,995**		**32**
NL Industries	St. Louis County	1979		Yes	X
Chrysler Corp	St. Louis County	1979	1,700	Yes	
Obear Nester	East St. Louis, IL	1979	650	Yes	X
Carter Carburetor	STL City & County	1979	700	Yes	
General Motors	St. Louis City	1979	3,200	Yes	
Falstaff Brewery	St. Louis City	1977		Yes	X
Chrysler Corp	St. Louis County	1975	4,900	Yes	
International Shoe Co	Franklin County	1975	60	Yes	X
Rockmore Co	St. Louis City	1975	200	Yes	X
LJ O'Neill Shoe Company	St. Louis City	1975	200	Yes	X
Mo Pac	Jefferson County	1975	267	Yes	X
Chrysler Corp	St. Charles County	1975	7700	Yes	
McDonnell Douglas	St. Louis County	1967-72	12,300	Yes	
TOTAL 1967–79			**31,877**		**7**

The figures, the tables, and the analyses in other chapters of this volume clearly show that the city has been consistently losing jobs, businesses, and payroll to the suburbs. Another way to explain the transformation of St. Louis's regional economy is to conduct a shift-share analysis (Bendavid-Val 1991; Hoover and Giarranti 1984). Shift-share analysis is used to determine how much of a region's growth is due to national and industry-specific trends as opposed to local trends, local initiatives, and locally competitive advantages. If a region generates more jobs than what national economic and industry-specific (or industry-mix) growth rates would indicate, then that region could be said to have a competitive advantage within certain industrial sectors relative to the rest of the nation. The technique can also be used to examine business performance within specific geographic components of a region's economy.

Table 3 shows growth rates in the national economy as a whole and within specific sectors between 1981 and 1994. This represents a critical period in St. Louis's recent experience with deindustrialization and disinvestments (see Table 1). Table 2 also shows local growth rates within three specific jurisdictions: St. Louis City, St. Louis County, and St. Charles County. In St. Louis City, contractions in the local economy as a whole and within specific sectors were severe. While the national economy grew by 29.2 percent, local job creation in the City was essentially stagnant (-1.3 percent). Growth in St. Louis County mirrored the national average (28.5 percent), and in St. Charles County job growth rates well exceeded it (111.9 percent).

Within specific sectors, performance differences across the region were also extreme. For St. Louis County, rates of economic growth and job creation closely followed national norms. Within some sectors, St. Louis County job growth rates exceeded the nation as a whole, including manufacturing, transportation and public utilities, and finance, insurance, and real estate. Even more impressive were the rates of growth within St. Charles County's economic sectors. Rates of job growth there far exceeded national averages in nearly all sectors. Growth rates in construction, manufacturing, transportation and public utilities, wholesale and retail trade, finance, insurance, real estate, and services were especially dramatic. St. Louis City, on the other hand, fell behind county and national norms in nearly all sectors. The contraction within manufacturing (-41.1 percent), wholesale trade (-11.6 percent) and retail trade (6.7 percent), finance, insurance, and real estate (4.6 percent), and services (41.7 percent) were especially noteworthy.

The shift-share procedure estimates the number of jobs that would have been created within local jurisdictions, assuming that all sectors of the economy grew at the national rate of 29.2 percent. The results appear in Table 3. In the table, N represents the number of jobs that would have been created in each sector between 1981 and 1994 based upon national growth rates (the actual number of jobs that existed in 1981 is used as the base to calculate N). R represents the number of jobs that were actually created within each sector between 1981 and 1994. The last column in the table (R-N=M+S) represents the net relative changes in job creation that the shift-share procedure must explain. In St. Louis City, for example, nearly all sectors produce negative numbers. This is a rough estimate of the number of jobs that could have been created had the local economy kept pace with national growth rates. The only sector that kept pace with overall national norms in St. Louis City was the service sector, where approximately 9,595 additional jobs were created. While jobs in the service sector were created at rates comparable to national norms (assuming an aggregate growth rate), the wages and benefits accompanying them were far below those lost in the industrial and manufacturing sectors. More important, the analysis indicates that, overall, 88,320 jobs were not created in the city due to economic restructuring.

Table 2. Job Growth Rates in St. Louis City, St. Louis County, and St. Charles County, 1981–94

| | Employment | | Change, 1981–94 | |
Nation	1981	1994	Absolute	Percent
Agricultural services, etc.	302,694	586,069	283,375	93.62%
Mining	1,107,726	607,721	-500,005	-45.14%
Contract construction	4,286,069	4,709,379	423,310	9.88%
Manufacturing	20,428,330	18,098,123	-2,330,207	-11.41%
TPU	4,613,030	5,713,515	1,100,485	23.86%
Wholesale trade	5,260,928	6,365,973	1,105,045	21.00%
Retail trade	15,039,998	20,320,266	5,280,268	35.11%
F.I.R.E.	5,409,780	7,002,431	1,592,651	29.44%
Services	17,814,081	33,253,032	15,438,951	86.67%
Other	587,766	76,791	-510,975	-86.94%
TOTAL	74,852,383	96,735,294	21,882,911	29.23%
St. Louis City				
Agricultural services, etc.	184	342	158	85.87%
Mining	500	138	-362	-72.40%
Contract construction	11,213	9,768	-1,445	-12.89%
Manufacturing	78,776	46,427	-32,349	-41.06%
TPU	24,850	24,238	-612	-2.46%
Wholesale trade	25,187	22,262	-2,925	-11.61%
Retail trade	32,967	35,194	2,227	6.76%
F.I.R.E.	21,738	22,737	999	4.60%
Services	76,464	108,409	31,945	41.78%
Other	1,256	137	-1,119	-89.09%
TOTAL	273,135	269,652	-3,483	-1.28%
St. Louis County				
Contract construction	27,040	27,890	850	3.14%
Manufacturing	102,116	99,213	-2,903	-2.84%
TPU	23,986	32,893	8,907	37.13%
Wholesale trade	33,568	36,450	2,882	8.59%
Retail trade	86,396	104,536	18,140	21.00%
F.I.R.E.	27,373	41,324	13,951	50.97%
Services	106,947	183,242	76,295	71.34%
Other	2,299	212	-2,087	-90.78%
TOTAL	411,980	529,458	117,478	28.52%
St. Charles County				
Agricultural services, etc.	101	638	537	531.68%
Mining	72	54	-18	-25.00%
Contract construction	2,500	5,470	2,970	118.80%
Manufacturing	6,581	10,543	3,962	60.20%
TPU	2,105	3,289	1,184	56.25%
Wholesale trade	973	2,571	1,598	164.23%
Retail trade	8,556	19,277	10,721	125.30%
F.I.R.E.	1,378	2,226	848	61.54%
Services	8,041	21,482	13,441	167.16%
Other	336	19	-317	-94.35%
TOTAL	30,643	64,931	34,288	111.90%

Table 3.Sectoral Analysis of Job Creation in St. Louis City, St. Louis County, and St. Charles County, 1981–94

Nation	*N	R	*R-N=M+S
Agricultural services, etc.		283,375	
Mining		-500,005	
Contract construction		423,310	
Manufacturing		-2,330,207	
TPU		1,100,485	
Wholesale trade		1,105,045	
Retail trade		5,280,268	
F.I.R.E.		1,592,651	
Services		15,438,951	
Other		-510,975	
TOTAL		21,882,911	
St. Louis City			
Agricultural services, etc.	54	158	104
Mining	146	-362	-508
Contract construction	3,278	-1,445	-4,723
Manufacturing	23,026	-32,349	-55,375
TPU	7,264	-612	-7,876
Wholesale trade	7,362	-2,925	-10,287
Retail trade	9,636	2,227	-7,409
F.I.R.E.	6,354	999	-5,355
Services	22,350	31,945	9,595
Other	367	-1,119	-1,486
TOTAL	79,837	-3,483	-83,320
St. Louis County			
Agricultural services, etc.	502	1,336	834
Mining	157	107	-50
Contract construction	7,904	850	-7,054
Manufacturing	29,849	-2,903	-32,752
TPU	7,011	8,907	1,896
Wholesale trade	9,812	2,882	-6,930
Retail trade	25,254	18,140	-7,114
F.I.R.E.	8,001	13,951	5,950
Services	31,261	76,295	45,034
Other	672	-2,087	-2,759
TOTAL	120,422	117,478	-2,944

Table 3 (Cont'd). Sectoral Analysis of Job Creation in St. Louis City, St. Louis County, and St. Charles County, 1981–94

St. Charles County			
Agricultural services, etc.	30	537	507
Mining	21	-18	-39
Contract construction	731	2,970	2,239
Manufacturing	1,924	3,962	2,038
TPU	615	1,184	569
Wholesale trade	284	1,598	1,314
Retail trade	2,501	10,721	8,220
F.I.R.E.	403	848	445
Services	2,350	13,441	11,091
Other	98	-317	-415
TOTAL	**8,957**	**34,288**	**25,331**

Even in St. Louis County, the shift-share procedure suggests that job creation fell behind national norms in several important sectors including contract construction (-7,054), manufacturing (-32,752), wholesale trade (-6,930), and retail trade (-7,114). As suggested by Table 4, however, overall job creation in St. Louis County largely kept pace with national norms. In the county about 2,944 jobs were not created due to failure to keep pace. In St. Charles County, however, nearly every sector shows job creation rates that exceed national norms. In several sectors, rates of job creation showed significant net gains including contract construction (2,239), manufacturing (2,038), retail trade (8,220), and wholesale trade (11,091). Overall, about 25,331 additional jobs were created in St. Charles over what national estimates would predict.

The bottom part of Table 3 shows estimates of the effects of industry-specific trends and growth rates after subtracting the overall national growth rate of 29.2 percent from sector-specific job creation rates. In this procedure, the percentage of national growth rates for each industry (as displayed in Table 2) less the national growth rate of 29.2 percent gives the percentage shown in the fourth column of Table 3. These percentages are then multiplied by the level of employment separately within each industry for the three jurisdictions for 1981 to produce an industry mix factor, M. This latter designation shows the number of jobs that should have been created had industry-specific growth rates (less the national average) been duplicated in each jurisdiction. This procedure is a more accurate way to measure job creation performance because it assumes variation between sectors. The analysis shows that in St. Louis City, about 27,327 fewer jobs were created than might be expected if national and sector-specific growth rates had been matched. The most sluggish sector was manufacturing in all three jurisdictions; the most robust sectors were services and retail trade in all three.

Last, Table 4 decomposes the effects of national and industry-specific effects on job growth in St. Louis City, St. Louis County, and St. Charles County. S is the local share effect or the portion of job creation due to any locally competitive advantage that may exist in a region which would cause job growth in that geographic area to be higher than what might be expected given national and industry-specific growth trends. The reverse is also possible. If S is negative, then the jurisdiction could have a comparative or competitive disadvantage, given national or industry-specific trends. Based upon the logic of shift-share analysis, the data show consistent competitive disadvantages in nearly all sectors of the city's economy. Consistent with the plateaus of economic activity revealed in Figures 1 and 2, the data also suggest that St. Louis County is beginning to encounter the emergence of disadvantages in selected sectors including manufacturing and wholesale and retail trade. St. Charles County, on the other hand, is showing competitive advantages in nearly all sectors of its local economy. These economic tendencies have obvious ramifications for general population trends. Of particular significance, however, is their importance for racial inequality in the region.

Racial Inequality and Developmental Disparities: Beyond Simple Discrimination

The disparities in growth rates across the St. Louis region have very significant ramifications for racial and economic inequality in the inner city. Perhaps most important, one does not have to assume widespread patterns of prejudice and discrimination in order to explain the emergence of racial inequity as a serious problem for the city and its residents. Nor does one have to assume that high levels of inter-group antagonism and conflict are behind the city's negative reputation as a place where racial disparities are the norm. Independent of its causes, racial inequality in the metropolitan area is clearly one of the region's most serious social problems. The St. Louis region is characterized by sharp differences in racial inequality and extremely high levels of concentrated poverty in the City, especially in its northern communities and neighborhoods. Additionally, higher levels of concentrated poverty among African Americans are now beginning to appear in selected inner ring suburbs of St. Louis County.

Consistent with the analysis of structural inequalities found in Chicago's urban economy reported by Wilson (1987), poverty and racial

Table 4. Locally Competitive Advantages in Regional Job Creation, 1981–94

Nation	R	*N	M	S
Agricultural services, etc.	283,375			
Mining	-500,005			
Contract construction	423,310			
Manufacturing	-2,330,207			
TPU	1,100,485			
Wholesale trade	1,105,045			
Retail trade	5,280,268			
F.I.R.E.	1,592,651			
Services	15,438,951			
Other	-510,975			
TOTAL	21,882,911			
St. Louis City				
Agricultural services, etc.	158	54	118	-14
Mining	-362	146	-372	-136
Contract construction	-1,445	3,278	-2,171	-2,552
Manufacturing	-32,349	23,026	-32,022	-23,353
TPU	-612	7,264	-1,337	-6,539
Wholesale trade	-2,925	7,362	-2,075	-8,212
Retail trade	2,227	9,636	1,935	-9,344
F.I.R.E.	999	6,354	43	-5,398
Services	31,945	22,350	43,913	-34,318
Other	-1,119	367	1,459	-2,945
TOTAL	-3,483	79,837	9,491	-92,811
St. Louis County				
Agricultural services, etc.	1,336	502	860	-26
Mining	107	157	-80	30
Contract construction	850	7,904	-165	-6,889
Manufacturing	-2,903	29,849	1,180	-33,932
TPU	8,907	7,011	-479	2,375
Wholesale trade	2,882	9,812	-237	-6,693
Retail trade	18,140	25,254	1,065	-8,179
F.I.R.E.	13,951	8,001	28	5,922
Services	76,295	31,261	43,816	1,218
Other	-2,087	672	2,425	-5,184

disparity in St. Louis are among the most severe in the nation. The size of the urban underclass in St. Louis City represents one of the most pressing challenges to those reducing racial disparities in the region's labor markets, and addressing the growing mismatch between those who need work and the places where jobs are being created. According to

Checkoway (1992), St. Louis is one of the poorest and most distressed cities in the nation. Similar patterns of racial inequality are found in East St. Louis (Shaw 2000).

The St. Louis Public School system reports that over 80 percent of its students fall below the official poverty level, and that public school teachers can expect an approximate 40 percent turnover of students enrolled in their classes each year. Over 70 percent of students were eligible for free or reduced lunches in 1998. Approximately 40 percent of students enrolled in the St. Louis Public Schools in 1997 did not complete high school and contribute to an average dropout rate of 16.2 percent, one of the highest in the nation. Currently, the city public schools are deep in financial crisis, and the board was recently compelled to close sixteen schools in order to remedy a major budget deficit.

Tables 5 and 6 show a variety of data describing the magnitude of racial inequality in the St. Louis region. The tables also show the size of the region's underclass, and its growing concentration in St. Louis City and in the inner ring suburbs of St. Louis County. Like many metropolitan regions, St. Louis has experienced extreme racial polarization between the City and suburbs. Between 1950 and 2000, the city became increasingly black and poor while the suburbs remained predominately white and affluent. The relationship between the restructuring of St. Louis's regional economy and these demographic shifts is evident.

On the Missouri side of the St. Louis MSA, there were approximately 381,442 African American residents reported in the 2000 census. Among those individuals, more than 97 percent resided in just two political jurisdictions, St. Louis City (46.7 percent) and St. Louis County (50.7 percent). Within the five largest jurisdictions (St. Louis County, St. Charles County, Jefferson County, Franklin County, and St. Louis City), African Americans accounted for only 19.7 percent of the total population. And while 46.7 percent of African Americans live in St. Louis City, nearly 69 percent of the region's whites reside in the surrounding suburbs.

Not only has the African American population become increasingly concentrated in the city and the older suburbs of St. Louis County, income disparities between black and white residents have increased over time. In 1990, a black family's median income was about 53.5 percent of that among white families (Manning 1998). In 1970, however, the median income of black families was about 60 percent of that found among white families. A recent study reported that the poverty rate in the city increased from 19.9 percent of the total population in 1970 to about 24 percent living in poverty in 1990 (Manning 1998). Most significant, according to the study, the disparity rate between African American and white poverty found in St. Louis was among the five highest found in the cities studied.

Table 5 presents additional information showing the racial disparities in the St. Louis metropolitan region and their relationship to the geographic polarization that has emerged over the past four decades. Those African Americans living in St. Louis City reported the lowest average personal income among the five geographic areas displayed ($7,154). In the four-county area, white residents consistently claimed more than 90 percent of total aggregate personal income. FOCUS St. Louis (2002) reports that while African Americans are disproportionately clustered in service, clerical, and operative positions, whites tend to occupy managerial, professional, and technical occupations. These patterns largely reflect the racially and geographically segmented labor markets that characterize the St. Louis regional economy.

Table 6 shows levels of educational attainment among whites and African Americans living in St. Louis City and St. Louis County, the two jurisdictions in which most of the region's population reside. The data show that in 1990 African Americans lagged considerably behind whites in educational attainment levels in both jurisdictions. While African Americans residing in the county revealed higher graduation rates from colleges than those reported by black residents of the city, both were considerably behind the proportion of whites graduating from institutions of higher education. Census data also show that rates of formal education among the African American population have not changed much over time. In 1970, about 20.8 percent of the city's African American population reported they had graduated from high school. In 1990 this figure had increased to only 27.3 percent. In the county, about 25 percent of African Americans reported they had graduated from high school in 1970. By 1990, this figure increased to only 26.6 percent. The lowest levels of educational attainment were found among African American males living in St. Louis City, thereby amplifying the difficulties involved in moving this population into the work force.

The population in greatest need of job training and work force development assistance is African Americans in the city and county. In terms of sheer numbers, however, numerous white residents also report low levels of formal education. About 46,287 African Americans and 47,687 white residents of the city reported less than a high school education in 1990. In the county, 19,230 African Americans and 96,163 whites reported less than a high school education. Overall, therefore, about 68.7 percent of the total population with less than a high school education in St. Louis City and St. Louis County is white and 31.3 percent is African American.

Table 5. Aggregate Personal Income by Race for Persons 15 Years and Older, 1990

	Pct. of Aggregate Personal Income	Total Persons, All Ages	Average Personal Income
Franklin County			
White	98.93%	79,455	11,648
Black	0.65%	754	8,108
American Indian, Eskimo, or Aleut		134	
Asian or Pacific Islander		172	
Other race		88	
Total Other Race (Not White or Black)	0.41%	394	9,824
TOTAL		80,603	
Jefferson County			
White	98.75%	168,968	12,246
Black	0.54%	1,168	9,656
American Indian, Eskimo, or Aleut		566	
Asian or Pacific Islander		508	
Other race		170	
Total Other Race (Not White or Black)	0.71%	1,244	11,943
TOTAL		171,380	
St. Charles County			
White	97.32%	205,761	15,474
Black	1.81%	4,667	12,661
American Indian, Eskimo, or Aleut		420	
Asian or Pacific Islander		1,456	
Other race		603	
Total Other Race (Not White or Black)	0.87%	2,479	11,527
TOTAL		212,907	
St. Louis County			
White	89.99%	836,603	19,905
Black	8.37%	139,044	11,145
American Indian, Eskimo, or Aleut		1,732	
Asian or Pacific Islander		13,899	
Other race		2,251	
Total Other Race (Not White or Black)	1.63%	17,882	16,889
TOTAL		993,529	
St. Louis City			
White	67.27%	202,276	14,246
Black	31.40%	187,995	7,154
American Indian, Eskimo, or Aleut		1,331	
Asian or Pacific Islander		3,566	
Other race		1,517	
Total Other Race (Not White or Black)	1.33%	6,414	8,879
TOTAL		396,685	

Table 6. Educational Attainment Level among Whites and African Americans: St. Louis County and St. Louis City, 1991

Educational Attainment Level	St. Louis City White	St. Louis City African American	St. Louis County White	St. Louis County African American
Less than high school	32.6 %	43.6 %	16.8 %	24.6 %
High school or GED	26.8 %	27.3 %	26.6 %	26.8 %
Some college	20.3 %	21.1 %	26.1 %	31.5 %
Bachelor's degree or higher	20.3 %	8.0 %	30.5 %	17.1 %

Source: U.S. Census Bureau, 1990.

The relationship between these disparities and the restructuring of St. Louis's regional economy clearly establishes the importance of what Wilson (1996) refers to as the "disappearance of work." Wilson (1996, 34) notes:

> Joblessness and declining wages are also related to the recent growth in ghetto poverty. The most dramatic increases in ghetto poverty occurred between 1970 and 1980, and they were mostly confined to the large industrial metropolises of the Northeast and Midwest, regions that experienced massive industrial restructuring and loss of blue-collar jobs during that decade. But the rise of ghetto poverty was not the only problem. Industrial restructuring had devastating effects on the social organization of many inner-city neighborhoods in these regions.

Many of the neighborhoods now populated by African Americans were those occupied by working and middle-class white families during the postwar period of industrial and manufacturing prosperity in St. Louis City. Many of the jobs held by these individuals during this period of prosperity offered good pay and benefits, often secured through union organizing and collective bargaining arrangements. Middle- and working-class white residents left these neighborhoods, largely in response to the economic restructuring of the region and the layoffs that followed in its wake (see Table 2). While white flight and racial antagonism probably contributed to the sweeping demographic changes that occurred in St. Louis during the 1970s and 1980s, disinvestment and deindustrialization undermined the economic vitality of the city's neighborhoods and severely compromised its ability to sustain the delivery of urban services, especially public education. More significantly, the white working and middle classes of St. Louis were directly affected by economic restructuring because this population disproportionately occupied the higher-paying union jobs found in the city's declining manufacturing and industrial sectors. The by-products of these sweeping changes in the regional economy are extreme disparities between the urban neighborhoods of St. Louis City and those communities located in the surrounding suburbs. The racial consequences of these disparities on the quality of life found in the region's communities and neighborhoods are vitally important to understand.

Quality of Life in City and Suburban Neighborhoods

Urban policy analysts have identified numerous risk factors at the neighborhood level that strongly influence life choices and options among families and children (Hawkins and Catalano 1992). The immediate geographic area in which a person lives strongly influences a wide variety of positive life options, choices, and opportunities. A person's community or neighborhood also shapes the probability of exposure to a variety of risks, perils, and hazards. Some neighborhoods are safe; others are dangerous. Some neighborhoods offer employment and business opportunities; others are characterized by high levels of unemployment and illegal enterprise.

Jargowsky (1997, 5) explains, "neighborhoods can influence the choices children make, the breaks they get, the way they are treated by family, peers, and employers, In the extreme, if living in destitute neighborhoods leads children to adopt self-destructive values and behaviors, the result is a vicious cycle of poverty."

These same observations were advanced in the Kerner Commission (1968, 263) report more than thirty years ago when the authors observed that certain urban environments make children "better candidates for crime and civil disorder than for jobs providing an entry into American society."

In the St. Louis region, the spatial separation of races (see Chapter 8) closely parallels the separation of income groups. Not only are upper-income whites separating themselves from their middle- and lower-income counterparts but also the African American middle class is separating itself from its lower-income counterparts left behind in the city. According to Jargowsky (1997, 18), "when the poor are residentially isolated from the non-poor, they are spatially and socially cut off from mainstream resources, opportunities, and role models." Jargowsky (1997) reports that St. Louis consistently shows one of the highest rates of concentrated poverty in the nation.

Jargowsky's findings are consistent with numerous other racial disparity measures reported in the most recent edition of *Where We Stand* (East-West Gateway Coordinating Council 2002). Based upon five economic variables measuring central city/suburban disparities, St. Louis was ranked tenth among the more than thirty regions examined. The report showed that upper-income African Americans in St. Louis received close to six times the amount of sub-prime-rate home refinance loans than did upper-income whites. These sub-prime figures were higher than any other region examined. On the basis of twelve socioeconomic measures, St. Louis was ranked eleventh on a disparity index calculating the overall ratio of African American to white inequality. The region also ranked high in racial disparities in infant mortality (#6), racial disparities in unemployment (#9), and racial disparities in overall housing opportunities. On this latter measure, St. Louis reported the highest disparity rate among the thirty-two regions studied.

Jaret, Reid, and Adelman (2003) reported very high rates of concentrated poverty and racial disparities in the St. Louis region. According to 2000 census data, St. Louis's black per capita income was 55.7 percent of white income (Adelman, Jaret, and Reid 2003). Among 150 metropolitan regions studied, St. Louis was ranked 109th; these figures mean that 108 other U.S. metro areas revealed lower racial disparities in per capita income than St. Louis. The authors indicate that racial disparities in the region have not changed significantly since 1990. Based on 1990 census data, St Louis's rank was 107th. Over the past decade, racial disparities in income have remained relatively stable.

Based upon measures of educational disparities, St. Louis ranked 97th among the 150 metro areas studied. Educational disparities were based upon the differences in the proportion of white and black residents who did not complete high school. The data were drawn from the 2000 census. They also show that racial disparities in unemployment were relatively high in St. Louis. St. Louis was ranked 123rd among the 150 regions studied. The real-life consequences of these regional disparities are manifested at the neighborhood level where African Americans carry out their daily lives.

The city's neighborhoods are highly segregated, as Chapter 8 of this volume demonstrates. Figure 3 shows those with the highest proportions of African American residents. Twenty-four neighborhoods in the city are hyper-segregated, with more than 90 percent of their residents being of African American descent. In another eleven neighborhoods, between 70 percent and 89 percent of residents are African Americans. Overall, about 45 percent of the city's neighborhoods are more than 70 percent African American in racial composition. In terms of actual numbers, approximately 54.4 percent of the city's total African American population resides in neighborhoods that are essentially one-race communities (90–100 percent African American); another 14.8 percent reside in communities that range between 70 and 89 percent African American. Overall, therefore, about 63.2 percent of the city's African American population resides in highly segregated neighborhoods.

Figure 3. Racial Isolation in St. Louis Neighborhoods. Neighborhood Average = .5638; Standard Deviation = .3637; Range = 1% to 99%

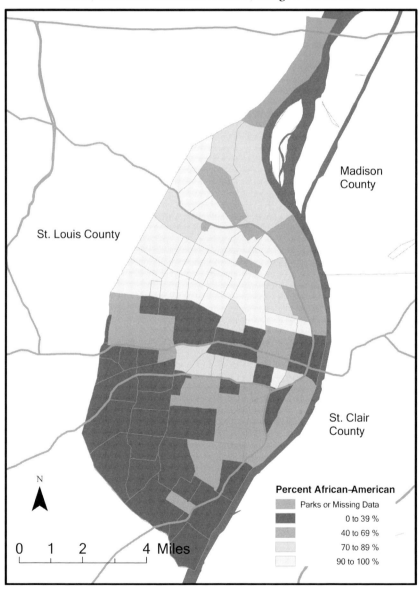

Figure 4 shows the range of average per capita household incomes across the city's neighborhoods. In 1997, the average per capita income in all St. Louis neighborhoods was $14,157. Per capita incomes ranged from a low of $6,496 to a high of $40,053. Based upon the analysis of standard deviation units, high-risk neighborhoods can be considered those in which

Figure 4. Average Per Capita Income in St. Louis Neighborhoods, 1997.
Neighborhood Average = $14,157;
Standard Deviation = $6,496; Range = $5,472 to $40,053

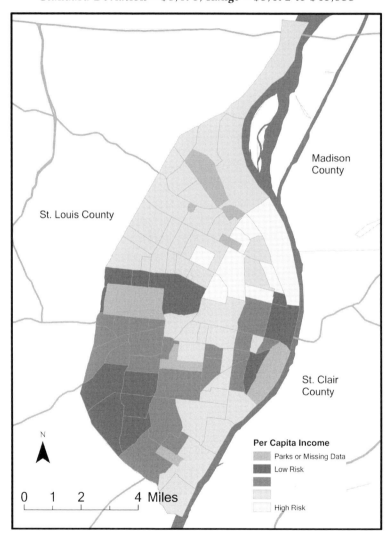

the average per capita income is below $7,660 per year. Those neighborhoods containing residents with an average per capita income more than $7,660 but less than $14,157 can be defined as moderate to high-risk areas. As can be seen from Figure 4, the poorest households in St. Louis are concentrated in the northern neighborhoods and selected communities in the southern part of the city.

Another way to measure concentrated poverty is to examine the range of average household incomes across the city's neighborhoods (Figure 5). The average household income in 1997 was $33,165. Average incomes ranged from a low of $14,219 in one neighborhood (Carr Square) to a high of $72,683 in another neighborhood (Wydown-Skinker). Based upon an analysis of standard deviation units, high-risk neighborhoods were identified as areas with average household incomes below $22,425. Moderately high risk neighborhoods were identified as areas below the citywide average ($33,165) but higher than $22,425. Consistent with the data appearing in Figure 4, St. Louis's poorest families are also clustered in its northern neighborhoods (e.g., The Ville, JeffVanderLou, College Hill, and Covenant/Blu/Grand), and in selected neighborhoods in the southern part of the city.

Figure 6 displays rates of unemployment across the city's neighborhoods. In 1997, the percentage of total unemployment (based upon the total civilian labor force) for all St. Louis neighborhoods was 12.5 percent. The range of unemployment across all neighborhoods was between 2 percent and 26 percent. High-risk neighborhoods were defined as those reporting an unemployment rate higher than 19 percent. The moderately high-risk neighborhoods were those reporting unemployment rates between 12.5 percent and 18 percent. Consistent with the income data reported in Figures 4 and 5, the city's northern neighborhoods tend to be disproportionately composed of residents who are unemployed and poor. This observation also applies to selected neighborhoods in the southern part of the city.

Another way to describe the magnitude of racial disparity in St. Louis City is to measure the degree of association among the various deprivation indices appearing in Figures 3 through 6. Table 7 shows the degree of association among the deprivation indices examined. The four risk indices are highly interrelated. Of greatest significance is the high degree of association between the racial composition of the neighborhood, poverty, and unemployment. The city's African American population disproportionately resides in neighborhoods with very high levels of unemployment and very low levels of per capita and household incomes.

**Figure 5. Average Household Income in St. Louis Neighborhoods, 1997.
Neighborhood Average = $33,165; Standard Deviation = $10,739;
Range = $14,219 to $72,683**

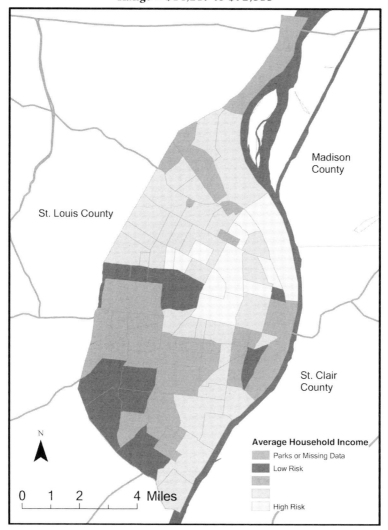

Figure 6. Percentage Unemployed (Total Civilian Labor Force) in St. Louis Neighborhoods, 1997. Neighborhood Average = 12.5%; Standard Deviation = 6.5%; Range = 2 to 26%

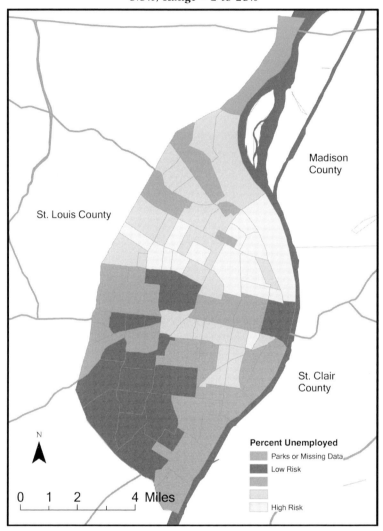

Table 7. Degree of Association among Deprivation Indices

	X_1	X_2	X_3	X_4
X_1: Racial isolation	1.0	.841	-.585	-.662
X_2: Percentage unemployed		1.0	-.607	-.674
X_3: Average household income			1.0	.929
X_4: Average per capita income				1.0
Note: All Pearson correlation coefficients are significant beyond the .01 level.				

Metromorphosis

Table 8 summarizes the composite scores of risk factors measuring economic deprivation. A deprivation score of 16 means the neighborhood ranked at the highest levels of risk (scale score of 4) on all outcome measures. These neighborhoods are the most racially isolated and the poorest and have the highest levels of unemployment. A deprivation score of 4 means the neighborhood ranked at the lowest levels of risk (scale score of 1) on all outcome measures. The neighborhoods in Table 8 are divided into four categories of risk, from highest to lowest. Based upon the prevention theories advanced by policy researchers such as Hawkins and Catalano (1992), exposure to these risk factors will increase the probability that high-risk behaviors will also be found in these neighborhoods.

Table 8. Identification of Neighborhood Risk Based upon Deprivation Indices

Risk	Risk Score	Neighborhoods
High Risk	16	Carr Square, College Hill, Fairground, JeffVanderLou, the Ville
	15	Fountain Park, Lewis Place
	14	Academy, Covenant/Blu/Grand, Hamilton Heights, Kingsway East, near north Riverfront
Moderately High Risk	13	Hyde Park, Kings Way West, Mark Twain, O'Fallon, Old North St. Louis, Peabody-Darst-Webbe, Penrose, St. Louis Place, the Great Ville
	12	Baden, Forest Park South, Gate District, McRee Town, North Riverfront, Tiffany, Walnut Park West
	11	Benton Park West, Fox Park, LaSalle Park, Mark Twain-I-70, North Point
Medium Risk	10	Columbus Square, Dutchtown, Gravois Park, Marine Villa, Midtown
	9	Benton Park, Carondelet, Downtown West, McKinley Heights, Mount Pleasant, Patch, Riverview, Shaw
	8	Lafayette Square, Tower Grove East
	7	Compton Heights, Ellendale, Franz Park, Hi-Pointe, Kings Oak, the Hill
Low Risk	6	Bevo Mill, Cheltenham, Clayton-Tamm, Clifton Heights, Holly Hills, Skinker-DeBaliviere, Southwest Garden, Tower Grove South
	5	Boulevard Heights, DeBaliviere Place, Downtown, Princeton Heights, Soulard, Wydown-Skinker
	4	Central West End, Lindenwood Park, North Hampton, South Hampton, St. Louis Hills

In addition to economic deprivation, prevention theorists also identify various forms of community disorganization and instability as important risk factors within neighborhood settings. Two important sources of neighborhood instability are residential mobility and high rates of population change. As discussed earlier, St. Louis has undergone radical changes in its population over the past fifty years. Even between 1990 and 2000, high rates of population change characterized many city neighborhoods. During this period, each of the neighborhoods lost an average of approximately 622 residents. Overall, 67 of the city's neighborhoods (85 percent) lost population. The lowest rate of loss was 15 residents (Tiffany); the highest rate of loss was 3,509 residents (Jeff-VanderLou). Only 11 city neighborhoods gained residents between 1990 and 2000.

Figure 7 shows the comparison across neighborhoods based upon rate of population decline. The unstable neighborhoods were those that lost more than 20 percent of their residents between 1990 and 2000. The moderately unstable neighborhoods were defined as those that lost between 10 percent and 20 percent of their residents between 1990 and 2000. Stable neighborhoods were those that gained population between 1990 and 2000. High rates of population decline tend to be found in the city's northern neighborhoods. High rates are also found in some neighborhoods located in the southern part.

Another measure of community instability related to rapid demographic change is the number of vacant and abandoned properties. According to census information, the average vacancy rate for all St. Louis neighborhoods was 18.6 percent in 2000. Vacancy rates ranged from a high of 52 percent in some neighborhoods to a low of 3 percent. Figure 8 shows the comparison of vacancy rates across all neighborhoods in the city. Based upon analysis of standard deviation units, highly unstable neighborhoods were defined as those with a 28 percent or higher rate of abandoned and vacant properties. Moderately unstable neighborhoods were defined as those with vacancy rates higher than the city average (18.6 percent) but lower than 28 percent. Stable neighborhoods were defined as those with 8 percent or lower rates of vacant and abandoned properties. High rates of vacant and abandoned properties tend to cluster in the city's northern neighborhoods. High rates of abandonment, however, are also beginning to appear in some of the southern neighborhoods.

High rates of property vacancy and abandonment are also linked to low levels of home ownership. High home ownership levels are important indices of community stability and commitment to a sense of place. Residents who invest in home ownership are typically more committed to building community institutions and display a greater sense of what many contemporary policy analysts call "social capital" (Putnam 2001).

In 2000, about 55.5 percent of all households in the city were renter occupied. Rates of rental occupancy ranged from a low of 14 percent in one neighborhood to over 90 percent in downtown and in Midtown.

Figure 7. Percentage of Population Decline in St. Louis Neighborhoods. Average Population Loss = 622 Residents; Range = 15 to 3,509

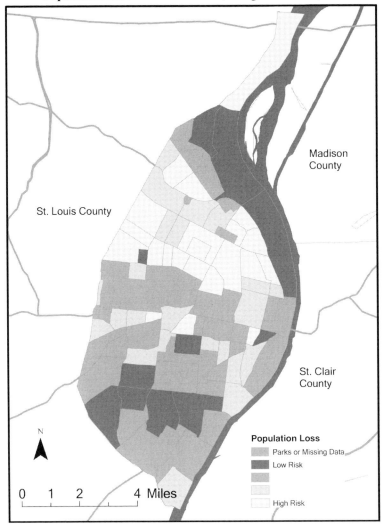

Figure 9 shows the comparison of rental occupancy rates across all of the city's neighborhoods. Higher-risk neighborhoods were defined as those with more than a 75 percent rental occupancy rate. Moderately high-risk neighborhoods were defined as those with rental occupancy rates higher than the citywide average (55.5 percent) but lower than 75 percent. Low-risk neighborhoods were those with rental occupancy rates below 35 percent. Reflecting their high rates of poverty, the city's northern neighborhoods revealed the highest proportion of renter-occupied units. Selected neighborhoods in the southern part of the city also contained a high proportion of households occupied by renters.

Another measure of community stability is the average sales price of housing in a neighborhood. A depressed housing market in a neighborhood signifies a low level of desirability and is a precursor of urban decline. Data

Figure 8. Proportion of Housing Vacancies in St. Louis Neighborhoods, 1997.
Neighborhood Average = 18.6%; Standard Deviation = 10.17%; Range = 3 to 52%

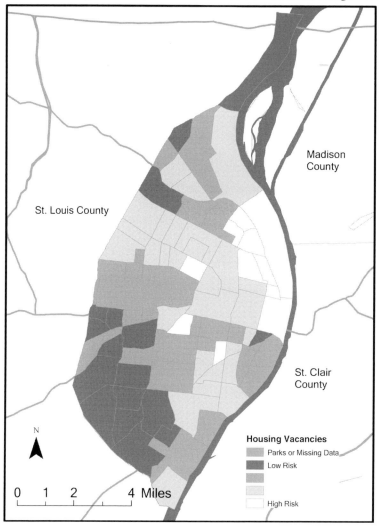

describing the five-year average sales price (1993–97) for all single-family housing in the city is a good measure of neighborhood residential desirability. The average sales price over the period for all single-family houses in the city was $54,979. Average sales prices at the neighborhood level ranged from a low of $8,000 to a high of $189,062. Figure 10 shows the comparison of the five-year average sales prices across all St. Louis

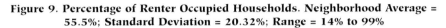

Figure 9. **Percentage of Renter Occupied Households. Neighborhood Average = 55.5%; Standard Deviation = 20.32%; Range = 14% to 99%**

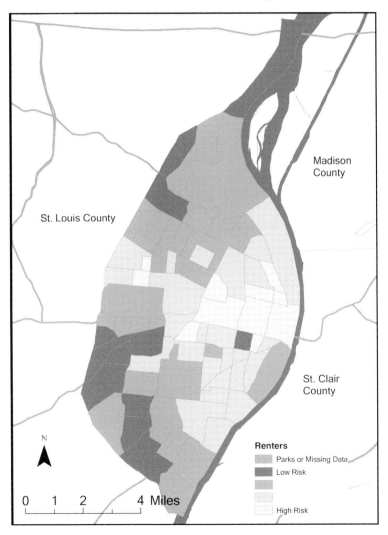

neighborhoods. Based upon analysis of standard deviation units, highly desirable neighborhoods were defined as those with an average sales price of less than $18,638 over the five-year period. Moderately desirable areas were defined as those with average sales prices ranging between $18,639 and the citywide average ($54,979). The data in Figure 10 reveal a familiar array of high-risk neighborhoods clustering in the southern and northern parts of the city.

Community vitality may also be measured by the number of businesses located in the neighborhood. Residents with disposable income are able to support not only community intuitions and voluntary associations but also neighborhood businesses. According to 1996 data, there was an average of 96 businesses in each St. Louis neighborhood, excluding the downtown and the industrial areas along the riverfront. Some neighborhoods reported as few as 3 businesses (Walnut Park West) while others reported more than 750 (Central West End). Figure 11 shows the average number of businesses across all St. Louis neighborhoods. High-risk neighborhoods were defined as those with fewer than 34 businesses. Moderately high-risk neighborhoods were defined as those with more than 34 but fewer than 62 businesses. Neighborhoods with a weak business and economic base tend to cluster in the northern part of the city and in selected parts of south St. Louis.

There is an obvious relationship between the absence of a strong neighborhood economic base and access to local employment opportunities. In order to show this relationship, the ratio of the total number of jobs in a neighborhood to the total number of people living there was calculated. A ratio of 1.00 indicates that there is 1 job for every person living in the neighborhood. A ratio of .10 means that there is 1 job for every 10 persons living in the community. A ratio of 4.0 means there are 4 jobs for every person living in the neighborhood. The average ratio of jobs to residents in all St. Louis neighborhoods was .88. The jobs to people ratios ranged from a low of .01 (1 job for every 100 people) to a high of 9.97 (nearly 10 jobs for every person living in the neighborhood).

Figure 12 shows the comparison of jobs-to-residents ratios for all St. Louis neighborhoods. High-risk neighborhoods were defined as those with ratios ranging between .01 and .10 (less than 1 job for every 10 persons living in the neighborhood). Moderately high-risk neighborhoods were defined as those with ratios ranging between .11 and .19. Low-risk neighborhoods were defined as those with ratios greater than 1.0. Excluding the downtown and the industrial areas along the riverfront, the lowest-risk neighborhoods included Midtown, the Central West End, and those neighborhoods considered part of the central corridor. The highest-risk neighborhoods tended to cluster in the northern and southern parts of the city.

**Figure 10. Average Sales Price of Single-Family Residences, 1993–97.
Neighborhood Average = $54,978; Standard Deviation = $36,341;
Range = $8,000 to $189,062**

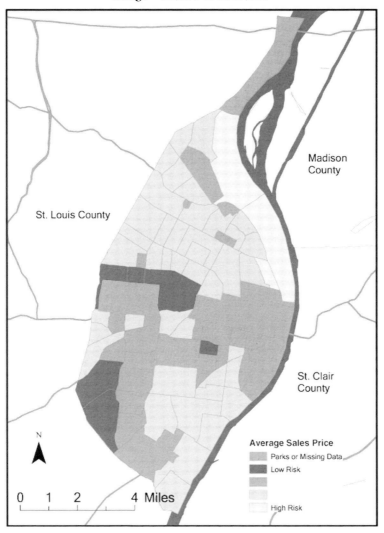

Figure 11. Total Number of Businesses in St. Louis Neighborhoods, 2000.
Neighborhood Average = 96; Range = 3 to 807

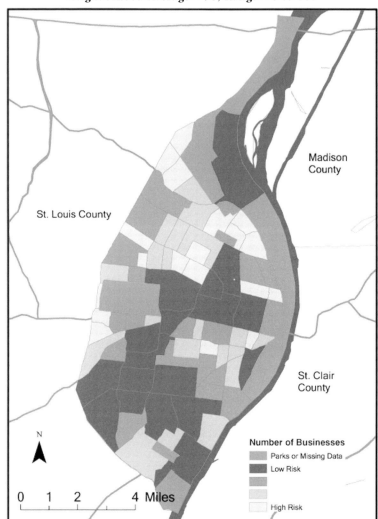

In order to display the reinforcing nature of the deprivation indices, neighborhood instability, and the risk factors shown in Figures 3 through 12, the degree of association among the several indicators was calculated. In addition to the indices appearing in the figures, several other risk indicators were included in the analysis: (1) the total cost of residential building permits in 1997, (2) the total cost of non-residential building permits in 1997, (3) the average assessed value of single-family parcels in

Metromorphosis

Figure 12. Ratio of Jobs to Population in St. Louis Neighborhoods, 2000.
Neighborhood Average = 9:10; Range = 1:100 to 10:1

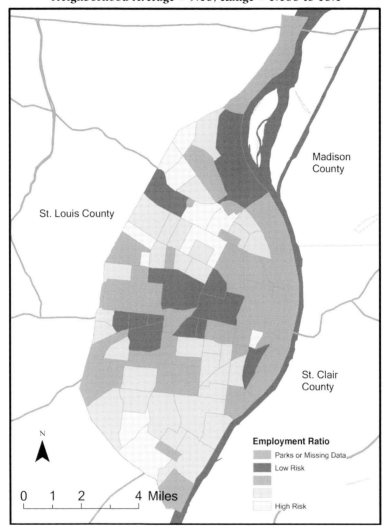

1997, (4) the average assessed value of multi-family parcels in 1997, (5) the average assessed value of industrial commercial parcels in 1997, and (6) the average assessed value of vacant parcels in 1997. All of these additional economic indicators measure variations in a neighborhood's economic and commercial vitality.

The relationships among several of the risk factors examined appear in Table 9. The risk factors are divided into three general categories. The data show that many African American neighborhoods are characterized by exposure to a high degree of community instability. Many highly segregated African American neighborhoods report much higher levels of population decline, have higher levels of renter occupancy, and reveal higher levels of vacant and abandoned housing. These same observations, however, apply to poor white neighborhoods in the city. African American and poor white neighborhoods also reveal the lowest levels of home sale prices, have lower average assessed tax evaluations, and have fewer businesses in the community. The data in Table 9 also show the reinforcing nature of the community development risk factors described by Jargowsky (1997) and Wilson (1996). Neighborhoods with lower assessed housing values tend to have fewer businesses and depressed real estate values. As a result, there is a much lower level of building, construction, and renovation activity (as measured by the low total amount of building permit values). All of these observations reinforce the importance of the overall policy issues raised at the outset of this chapter.

Political Fragmentation and the Future of Racial Inequality in St. Louis

It is currently fashionable in public policy circles to argue that regional solutions to urban problems are preferable to place-specific interventions (Orfield 1997; Rusk 1995, 2001). Advocates of a regional approach to racial inequality, however, acknowledge the difficulties involved in organizing political support across urban and suburban jurisdictions (Orfield 1997; Wilson 1999). These political barriers are even more difficult to overcome when extreme geographic disparities in wealth and income across metropolitan regions are institutionalized in the form of separate political jurisdictions and governments. In St. Louis, political fragmentation is an integral component of a highly contentious and competitive political environment. Unfortunately, the geography of racial segregation and a high degree of concentrated poverty are integral components of the regional political environment.

The political fragmentation in the St. Louis MSA, while extreme, simply reflects existing jurisdictional disparities of wealth and power across the region. The state of Missouri, St. Louis County government, ninety-two municipalities, and a large number of special districts levy taxes separately and provide services directly to residents of the county. Consistent with Jones's (2000) analysis of the St. Louis region, these separate governments insulate the wealthy from the myriad urban problems left behind in St. Louis City. As a result, upper- and middle-income whites have created de facto political and legal barriers between themselves and the African American poor living in the city.

Political fragmentation within the formal structures of city and county government is also mirrored in the organization of public education. According to an East-West Gateway Coordinating Council report (2001), the region's public school system "is one of the most fractured in the nation. In 1992, there were 119 different public school districts in the St. Louis metropolitan area. With 4.7 school districts per 100,000 people, St. Louis is only surpassed by Oklahoma City and Portland in the number of these governmental entities per capita."

When it comes to racial disparities in jobs, income, and access to equal educational opportunity, the perceived and actual interests of city and suburban residents in the St. Louis region are not easily reconciled. According to a recent report published by FOCUS St. Louis (2002), "Mobilizing people around a critical community issue is always a daunting challenge even under the best of circumstances. Those challenges are especially delicate and problematic when it comes to racial equality. Getting people to take action on an issue of this magnitude usually comes down to one key question: 'What's in it for me?'"

The "call to action" issued by FOCUS St. Louis clearly recognized the magnitude of the racial challenge facing the region's leadership structure through its attempt to address the self-interest question. In deference to the self-interest dilemma, the authors of the "call to action" claimed that regional cooperation will: (1) promote economic strength, (2) attract and retain talented youth, (3) increase community pride, and (4) reinforce important moral imperatives. The strategic political problem, however, is how to interest fast-growing suburbs in racial problems that appear to have their origins in the city.

The magnitude of the racial quagmire in St. Louis poses serious challenges to the region's leadership structure. Stone (1998, 9) contends that "urban regime theory posits that policy change comes about only if reformers establish a new set of political arrangements commensurate with the policy being advocated." In the case of St. Louis, the challenge is to mobilize a variety of diverse constituencies and stakeholders behind a common, racial reform agenda. As Stone (1998, 13) explains, however, achieving reforms and policy changes usually "requires more than the discrediting of the old ways in favor of a fresh idea. It involves the difficult shift from a coalition built around distributive benefits to one built on a more complex set of factors." His observations nicely summarize the difficult set of

Table 9. Degree of Association Among Deprivation Indices, Neighborhood Stability, and Community Development Indices

Indicator	X_1	X_2	X_3	X_4	X_5	X_6	X_7	X_8	X_9	X_{10}	X_{11}	X_{12}	X_{13}	X_{14}	X_{15}
Deprivation Indices:															
X_1: Racial Isolation	1.0	.841*	-.585*	-.662*	-.564*	.254*	.579*	-.277*	-.459*	-.004	-.130	-.407*	.007	-.348*	-.430*
X_2: Percentage Unemployed		1.0	-.607*	-.674*	-.475*	.324*	.697*	-.368*	-.433*	-.1	-.233*	-.434*	.025	-.46*	-.386*
X_3: Average Household Income			1.0	.929*	.356*	-.233*	-.577*	.098	.829*	.145	.016	.621*	-.023	.306*	.512*
X_4: Average Per Capita Income				1.0	.386*	-.024	-.491*	.244*	.826*	.277*	.179	.716*	.061	.404*	.562*
Neighborhood Stability:															
X_5 Population Decline (1990 to 2000)					1.0	-.084	-.383*	.138	.306*	-.137	.098	.279*	.081	.335*	.347*
X_6 Percentage of Housing Renter Occupied						1.0	.568*	.241*	.008	.31*	.327*	.131	.44*	.051	-.039
X_7 Percentage of Vacant and Abandoned Properties							1.0	-.143	-.504*	.046	.017	-.321*	.039	-.193	-.496*
Community Development Indices:															
X_8 Number of Businesses in Neighborhood								1.0	.296*	.574*	.762*	.485*	.415*'	.282*	.25*
X_9 Avg Sales Price of Single Family Homes (93-97)									1.0	.345*	.217	.877*	.471*	.312*	.565*
X_{10} Residental Building Permit Costs (1997)										1.0	.553*	.27*	-.012	.193	.16
X_{11} Nonresidential Building Permit Costs (1997)											1.0	.309*	.257*	.484*	.074
X_{12} AAV Single Family Parcels (1997)												1.0	.435*	.46*	.482*
X_{13} AAV Multi-Family Parcels (1997)													1.0	0.16	.047
X_{14} AAV Commercial/Industrial Parcels (1997)														1.0	.144
X_{15} AAV Vacant Parcels (1997)															1.0

* Statistically significant.

responsibilities facing those interested in reducing racial disparities in the region by contending that it is in everyone's self interest to do so.

The economic interests of suburban developers, those promoting revitalization of the downtown, and the political objectives of suburban elected public officials reinforce the desire among localities to solve their own problems, and to perpetuate and protect existing political alliances and coalitions. According to Molotch (1988, 34), "The doctrine of home rule implies that localities can best handle 'their own problems' and the vesting of land use regulation in local authorities, almost the only autonomous realm of governance remaining at this level, guides decision makers toward the development option for dealing with virtually any problem that manifests itself locally."

By implication, Molotch's observations have relevance for the recent "call to action" issued by FOCUS St. Louis. In recognition of the competing political and economic interests across the region, the FOCUS St. Louis (2002, ii) report acknowledges that the issue of racial equality "has not been a regional priority commanding the attention, resources and problem solving skills of people from every sector of the St. Louis region."

What Stone (1993) calls the "capacity to govern" is an important element shaping a jurisdiction's ability to pursue its economic interests and is an integral component of a region's civic infrastructure. In the case of St. Louis, however, it is not clear how to resolve the apparent contradictions between racial inequality and the economic self-interest of the region's multiple political jurisdictions. There are few apparent incentives motivating suburban political and business interests to address urban racial problems. In order to achieve consensus about how to address racial inequality, a regional regime must manifest the capacity to stimulate the cooperation of numerous private and public actors and be able to organize a governing coalition across multiple jurisdictions. According to Stone, "Responding effectively to a challenge like economic restructuring means bringing about substantial change in established social and economic practices and that means drawing on nongovernmental resources and enlisting nongovernmental actors" (1993, 17). Finding a common issue around which to organize a regional, biracial coalition is a daunting task. Furthermore, it seems apparent that selected suburban jurisdictions are doing quite well in pursuit of a separate economic development agenda.

The policy dilemmas tied to racial inequality are illustrated through recent efforts to initiate work force development reform in the region. As noted by Giloth (2000, 347), "Today's new work force paradigm argues that labor markets are regional and not restricted by city jurisdictional boundaries or by neighborhood sentiments or histories." Despite popular contentions about the need to adopt regional approaches to work force development policy, our analysis shows that deindustrialization and disinvestment have created extreme geographic disparities in St. Louis's regional economy. These extreme geographic disparities complicate policy interventions in the areas of regional transportation planning and work force development and training programs. They also complicate the ability of work force development leaders to mobilize corporate involvement across regional labor markets and to create equitable financial policies to pay for education and training programs.

Regional development disparities also seriously undermine the ability of policy leaders to address the spatial mismatch between those needing jobs (St. Louis City) and the places (St. Louis suburbs) where employment opportunities are being created (Kasarda 1989, 1993), and the associated mismatch between the current skill levels of those needing jobs (young African Americans) and the requirements necessary to compete for the types of jobs being created (Kasarda 1988). Additional problems are derived from the inability of corporate leaders and economic development planners to agree upon the economic sectors that might be targeted for special work force development initiatives. Because of uneven and mixed development across the region, various sectors of the economy are expanding and contracting at different rates. This analysis also shows that a clearer understanding of regional growth and development disparities are needed in order to formulate and sustain long-term work force development changes in the St. Louis region, and thereby address those components of racial inequality linked to these disparities.

It is not clear, however, how to establish a calculated and politically acceptable mix between a place-based and a regional strategy of work force development and training program delivery. Recently, the Initiative for a Competitive Inner City (ICIC) issued a report outlining a strategy to revitalize the City's urban economy. The ICIC report (2000) proposed a "work force readiness" strategy and identified several sectors of the City's economy with high potential for job creation and expansion: metal manufacturing, commercial services, transportation and logistics, and construction. Michael Porter (2000) has consistently advocated revitalization of urban economies. While he argues (Porter 1998a, 1998b) that urban economies exist within and must compete within larger regional markets, the recent ICIC report tends to be more of a "place-based" approach to work force development and job creation in St. Louis City. As such, it may not be altogether consistent with a more regional approach to this policy question. Moreover, the ICIC approach has captured considerable popular support among certain elements of the city's political leadership and appears widely supported by the minority business community and political leadership (Nicklaus 2000; "Real Strategy" 2000). Not surprisingly, the future of the ICIC initiative in the St. Louis region is problematic. The suburbs do not appear interested.

While more African Americans now live in St. Louis County (193,306) than in the city (153,565), they compose only around 19 percent of the county's population, and a lower proportion of the region's population. African Americans, therefore, are more of a lobbying force in city as opposed to county and regional politics. Nonetheless, low turnout among African American voters reduces their influence at the polls. And even though St. Louis is now a majority African American city, voting age whites still outnumber those blacks eligible to vote in city elections. The consequences of these political demographics were seen in the last mayoral election when Francis Slay was elected. Slay, a white candidate, defeated two African American candidates for the Democratic nomination, largely due to bloc voting among whites and widespread support for his candidacy among the downtown corporate community.

Racial politics, directly or indirectly, dominate many public policy issues facing the city and region. Many residents view St. Louis City and East St. Louis as having intractable racial problems. Although no public official would likely admit to such a proposition, the counties and political jurisdictions surrounding these two cities would undoubtedly prefer to keep racial issues and problems confined to the inner city. Yet, this unspoken agenda is not at all compatible with those elements of local leadership who are aggressively promoting the transformation of the downtown and seeking to reverse St. Louis's image as a racially polarized region. An absence of consensus among downtown and suburban development interests often undermines the capacity of the St. Louis regime to govern, to wield power in an efficient manner, and to agree upon a common work force development agenda. To the extent that work force development reform in St. Louis continues to be perceived as a "black issue" or a "black program," it is likely that political debate over this component of racial inequality will mirror the class and racial divisions that split city and suburban interests in the region.

Despite the strategic difficulties involved, the region does have an important stake in resolving urban racial problems. Even though the FOCUS St. Louis arguments about self-interest and economic motivation might not be overly compelling, their "call to action" is timely and surely warranted. Cities with high levels of racial disparity, and that manifest a wide array of urban problems, including high rates of crime, unemployment, and poverty, are also places that have great difficulty attracting new businesses and retaining existing establishments. In the wake of the Rodney King riots in 1992, Los Angeles not only lost millions of dollars in business and tax revenues but also lost billions of dollars in national and international investment dollars to competitor cities like San Francisco, Sacramento, Portland, and Seattle (Baldassare 1994; "Could it Happen Again?" 2002; Kasler 2000). The relevance of the Los Angeles experience for the St. Louis region is apparent.

In his recent book discussing how to build multiracial political coalitions, Wilson (1999, 43) observed: "it is imperative that the political message underscore the need for economic and social reform that benefits all groups, not just America's minority poor." While Wilson is promoting political alliances across racial and ethnic divisions among the nation's working poor and urban underclasses, it is perhaps more significant to stress the idea that suburban entrepreneurs, investors, and suburban commercial and business elites also have a direct financial stake in creating a region free from the kinds of intractable urban problems that create serious impediments to the kinds of prosperity and economic security we are all seeking.

References

Adelman, R., C. Jaret, and L. W. Reid. *Metropolitan Area Social and Economic Structure Data Set.* Atlanta: Georgia State University, Department of Sociology, 2003.

Baldassare, M. *The Los Angeles Riots: Lessons for the Urban Future.* Boulder, Colo.: Westview Press, 1994.

Bendavid-Val, A. *Regional and Local Economic Analysis for Practitioners.* New York: Praeger, 1991.

Bluestone, B., and B. Harrison. *The Deindustrialization of America.* New York: Basic Books, 1984.

Checkoway, B. "Revitalizing an Urban Neighborhood: A St. Louis Case Study." In *The Metropolitan Midwest: Policy Problems and Prospects for Change,* edited by B. Checkoway and C. V. Patton. Urbana: University of Illinois Press, 1992.

"Could It Happen Again?" *Guardian Unlimited* [online]. August 24, 2002 [cited April 2003]. Available at http://www.guardian.co.uk/g2/story/ 0,3604,689486,00.html.

East-West Gateway Coordinating Council. "Public Education in the St. Louis Region." In *Where We Stand.* St. Louis: Author, 2001.

___. "The Strategic Assessment of the St. Louis Region." In *Where We Stand* (4th ed.). St. Louis: Author, 2002.

FOCUS St. Louis. *Racial Equality in the St. Louis Region: A Community Call to Action.* St. Louis: Author, 2002.

___. *St. Louis Currents: A Guide to the Region and Its Resources.* St. Louis: Missouri Historical Society Press, 1997.

Giloth, R. P. "Learning from the Field: Economic Growth and Workforce Development in the 1990s." *Economic Development Quarterly* 14, no. 4 (2000): 340–59.

Hawkins, J. D., and R. F. Catalano. *Communities That Care: Action for Drug Abuse Prevention.* New York: Jossey-Bass Social and Behavioral Science Series, 1992.

Hoover, E. M., and F. Giarranti. *An Introduction to Regional Economics.* 3rd ed. New York: Alfred A. Knopf, 1984.

Initiative for a Competitive Inner City. *St. Louis Inner City Competitive Assessment and Strategy Project: Creating Jobs, Income, and Wealth in the Inner City.* St. Louis: The Project, 2000.

Jaret, C., L. W. Reid, and R. Adelman. "Black-White Income Inequality and Metropolitan Socioeconomic Structure." *Journal of Urban Affairs* 25 (2003): 305–33.

Jargowsky, P. *Poverty and Place: Ghettos, Barrios, and the American City.* New York: Russell Sage Foundation, 1997.

Jones, E. T. *Fragmented by Design.* St. Louis: Palmerston and Reed, 2000.

Kasarda, J. "Inner-City Poverty and Economic Access." In *Rediscovering Urban America: Perspectives on the 1980s,* edited by I. J. Sommer and D. A. Hicks. Washington: Office of Housing Policy Research, U.S. Department of Housing and Urban Development, 1993.

___. "Jobs, Migration and Emerging Urban Mismatches." In *Urban Change and Poverty,* edited by L. E. Lynn, Jr., and M. G. H. McGeary, 148–98. Washington: National Academy Press, 1988.

___. "Urban Industrial Transition and the Urban Underclass." *Annals of the American Academy of Political and Social Sciences* 501 (1989): 26–47.

Kasler, D. *Odds Against Inner-city Firms: Barriers to Capital Hold Back Struggling Entrepreneurs* [online]. *Sacramento Bee* January 24, 2000 [cited April 2003]. Available at //www.sacbee.com/static/archive/news/projects/leftbehind/.

Kerner Commission Report. *Kerner Report: The 1968 Report of the National Advisory Commission on Civil Disorder.* New York: Pantheon Books, 1968.

Losos, C. W. Introduction to *St. Louis Currents: A Guide to the Region and Its Resources,* by FOCUS St. Louis, 1–2. St. Louis: Missouri Historical Society Press, 1997.

Manning, M. "Lost Souls, Lost Dollars." *St. Louis Business Journal* [online]. July 17, 1998 [cited April 2001]. Available at stlouis.bcentral.com/stlouis/stories/ 1998/07/20/story2.html.

Molotch, H. "Strategies and Constraints of Growth Elites." In *Business Elites and Urban Development*, edited by S. Cummings, 25–47. Albany: State University of New York Press, 1988.

Nicklaus, D. "Inner City Presents Exciting Possibilities to Noted Thinker." *St. Louis Post-Dispatch*, September 13, 2000, pp. C1-3.

Orfield, M. W. *Metropolitics: A Regional Agenda for Community and Stability*. Washington, D.C.: Brookings Institution, 1997.

Porter, M. E. *Competitive Strategy: Techniques for Analyzing Industries and Competitors*. New York: Free Press, 1998a.

___. *Competitive Advantage: Creating and Sustaining Superior Performance*. New York: Free Press, 1998b.

___. "Regional Prosperity Depends on Prosperity That Benefits Our Inner City." *St. Louis Post-Dispatch*, September 17, 2000, p. B4.

Primm, J. N. *Lion of the Valley: St. Louis, Missouri*. Boulder, Colo.: Pruett Publishing Co., 1981.

Putnam, R. J. *Bowling Alone: The Collapse and Rival of American Community*. New York: Touchstone Books, 2001.

"Real Strategy for City Development." *St. Louis Business Journal*, September 15, 2000.

Rusk, D. *Cities without Suburbs*. Washington, D.C.: Woodrow Wilson Center Press, 1995.

___. *Inside Game/Outside Game: Winning Strategies for Saving Urban America*. Washington, D.C.: Brookings Institution, 2001.

Shaw, W. *A Tale of Two Cities: The Best of Times, the Worst of Times. Inequality in St. Louis's Metro East*. Southern Illinois University–Edwardsville, 2000 [cited July 2001]. Available at www.siue.edu/~wshaw/esl.htm.

Stein, L. *St. Louis Politics: The Triumph of Tradition*. St. Louis: Missouri Historical Society Press, 2002.

Stone, C. N. *Changing Urban Education*. Lawrence: University of Kansas Press, 1998.

___. "Urban Regimes and the Capacity to Govern: A Political Economy Approach." *Journal of Urban Affairs* 15 (1993): 1–28.

Von Hoffman, A. *Why They Built the Pruitt-Igoe Project* [online]. Iowa State University–Sociology, 2003 [cited April 2003]. Available at http://www.soc.iastate.edu/sapp/PruittIgoe.html.

Wagman, J. "District's New Leader Confronts Critics of Cost Cutting Head-on: Turnaround Chief Meets with Teachers, Public, Those Targeted for Firing." *St. Louis Post-Dispatch*, 2003, p. A1.

Wilson, W. J. *The Bridge over the Racial Divide: Rising Inequality and Coalition Politics*. Berkeley: University of California Press, 1999.

___. *The Truly Disadvantaged: The Inner City, the Underclass, and Public Policy*. Chicago: University of Chicago Press, 1987.

___. *When Work Disappears: The World of the New Urban Poor*. New York: Alfred A. Knopf, 1996.

Chapter 6

African American Entrepreneurship in the St. Louis Metropolitan Region: Inner City Economics and Dispersion to the Suburbs

Scott Cummings
Saint Louis University

Introduction

The rapidly changing demography of the St. Louis region has important ramifications for both the history and the current status of African American business enterprise. The region's hyper-segregation is described extensively in Chapter 8. High rates of segregation and the growth of African American communities in the region have significant implications for the number and distribution of minority business enterprises. Have African American firms been confined, both historically and at present, to African American neighborhoods? Have contemporary African American firms been able to expand their markets to include white as well as black communities? Are African American firms located in the suburbs more profitable than those remaining in the City?

This chapter examines the history and current state of African American business enterprise in light of the changing demographics of the St. Louis region. Using historical evidence and data drawn from the five-year economic censuses conducted between 1977 and 1997, the chapter shows that growth rates of African American firms in the suburbs exceed those located in the city. The loss of prosperous African American firms to the suburbs has important policy ramifications for public officials and community activists interested in revitalizing urban neighborhoods by stimulating minority business enterprise.

Enclave Economics and Minority Business Enterprise

An important theme in research addressing minority entrepreneurship in American cities revolves around the business costs and benefits provided by a segregated enclave. Several economists and sociologists contend that many minorities gained an entrepreneurial foothold in cities because of their geographic concentration in urban neighborhoods (Bates 1989, 1993, 1995; Bonacich and Modell 1980; Light 1972; Silverman 2000; Wilson and Martin 1982). In numerous urban communities, such as Little Italy in New York, Chinatown in San Francisco, and Greek Town in Chicago, minority entrepreneurs were able to benefit from ethnic business networks and ethnic group patronage to achieve self-employment. While residential segregation and discrimination may have limited access to investment capital and reduced access to non-ethnic markets in the larger urban economy, racial and ethnic enclaves provided unique competitive advantages to many minority entrepreneurs.

Students of minority business enterprise have also examined the entrepreneurial advantages associated with segregated African American communities. Classic studies of race relations in American cities and southern small towns identify numerous entrepreneurial benefits provided by a segregated enclave. While southern racial traditions greatly disadvantaged black entrepreneurial development in small towns (Davis, Gardner, and Gardner 1941; Dollard 1949; Loewen 1971), many researchers contend that segregation did provide protected and accessible markets for many black professionals and selected merchants. In large cities, segregation provided an even greater array of economic advantages and business opportunities.

The "Great Migration" to northern cities created a protected, albeit segregated, market for African American merchants. According to Drake and Clayton (1945, 434), black entrepreneurs in Chicago "became increasingly conscious of the purchasing power of several hundred thousand people solidly massed in one compact community." Similar observations appear in other classic studies of race relations in northern cities (Drake and Clayton 1945; Myrdal 1944; Spear 1967). According to the protected market theory, immigrant and racial enclaves help support a sense of ethnic solidarity and promote a collective approach to community development (Cummings 1980). As explained by Light and Rosenstein (1995, 20), "By enhancing the scope and integration of social networks, ethnic solidarity confers important business resources…" Included among these resources are transmission of strategic business information, promotion of mutual aid and financial networking, consolidation of market power and penetration, cultivation of trust in business transactions, and encouragement of customer allegiance through ethnic bonds and loyalty (Light and Rosenstein 1995).

In addition to business advantages, some researchers suggest that workers within ethnic and racial enclaves derive greater benefits than their co-ethnics who are employed outside the ghetto (Portes and Bach 1985; Portes and Jensen 1987; Wilson and Portes 1980). While these findings have been questioned by Sanders and Nee (1987), Zhou and Logan (1989, 809) explain that "a key proposition in the theory of ethnic enclave economies is that the enclave opens opportunities for its members that are not easily accessible in the larger society." Despite the alleged advantages derived from conducting business in a protected ethnic market, others contend that there are numerous disadvantages associated with enclave economies. These disadvantages have particular significance for African American entrepreneurs.

Historically, African American businesses have been disproportionately confined to the ghetto (Feagin and Imani 1994; Green and Pryde 1990). Unless minority entrepreneurs can acquire significant capital and expand their business activities into the wider urban economy, their developmental possibilities are severely constrained. While residential segregation may be a prime factor promoting enclave enterprise, it very likely undermines business growth and development. According to Brimmer and Terrell (1971), ghetto entrepreneurs are destined to be less successful than those minority merchants who expand their business activities into the larger, urban economy. They contend that African American entrepreneurs who depend exclusively upon a segregated (protected) market have high potential for failure. And unlike many Asian and immigrant enterprises, African American entrepreneurs have not been able to attract non-black consumers into the ghetto to patronize local businesses. It is apparent that businesses depending exclusively upon an enclave market, or that are unable to draw non-ethnic consumers into the enclave, will likely fail in the face of desegregation and group dispersion, or at best remain small and undercapitalized (Brimmer 1966, 2002).

There are other reasons to question the benefits of enclave enterprise as they relate to African American entrepreneurs. Despite potential advantages, a protected, enclave market is partly a result of historical and legal exclusion of African American consumers from purchasing goods and services from, and shopping at, majority-owned establishments. Aldrich, Cater, Jones, McEvoy, and Velleman (1985) explain that a "protected" market results from residential concentration, spatial isolation, and sufficient social distance between enclave residents and the larger economy. Tabb (1970) contends that African American entrepreneurs who limit business activities to ethnic and racial enclaves face numerous disadvantages: smaller markets, lower-income consumers, higher insurance rates, inability to access credit, higher rates of theft, and limited access to capital. Other researchers tend to agree with the observations of Tabb, and report that business development within African American enclaves has not kept pace with the growth rates of small business in the larger society (Bates 1989; Brimmer 1966, 2002; Schwalbert 1991).

It is also not reasonable to assume that contemporary majority merchants and firms are motivated to disregard growing African American markets. While earlier racial practices and traditions may have compelled some majority merchants to turn their backs on minority markets, contemporary entrepreneurs are surely more rational. Established market research firms contend that the total buying power of African Americans is expected to reach $628 billion by 2006, an increase of nearly 30 percent from current levels (Packaged Facts 2002). As the socioeconomic position of African Americans increases, majority merchants will likely cultivate and pursue rather than ignore and disregard the potential profits to be harvested in this growing and significant urban market. It is more reasonable to assume, therefore, that African American merchants will now have to compete more aggressively to hold whatever slight historical advantage they may have held in the enclave economy. It is unlikely that ethnic and racial loyalty will hold the allegiance of African American consumers in the face of more competitive prices available outside the enclave economy.

Additionally, historical and contemporary evidence suggests that other minority entrepreneurs often serve as "middle-man merchants" and capture significant market shares within African American enclaves (Loewen 1971). Korean, Jewish, Chinese, and Asian Indian merchants, as well as other immigrant entrepreneurs, have often been present within African American enclaves (Bonacich 1973; Lee 1999). While the presence of other minority entrepreneurs within African American enclaves has often produced inter-group antagonism and conflict (Baldasarre 1994), they continue to occupy selected market niches among African American consumers (Bonacich and Modell 1980). Based upon both historical and contemporary evidence, it does not appear reasonable to assume that the marketplace within black enclaves has been the exclusive domain of African American entrepreneurs. Nor is it reasonable to assume that contemporary African American purchasers will confine their shopping activities to a racial enclave where market dynamics severely restrict consumer choices and offer less than competitive prices (Caplovitz 1967; Sturdivant 1969).

African American Business Enterprise in the St. Louis Region

All of these observations have direct relevance to the history and current status of African American business enterprise in the St. Louis region. Its history was partly shaped by the larger patterns of urban development and decline described in Chapters 1 and 5. The demographic shifts that accompanied urban development and decline in St. Louis City resulted in the demolition of many traditional African American settlements, and the displacement of residents from one part of the City to another. Suburban development was also accompanied by African American movement into neighborhoods previously occupied by other ethnic and racial groups. Regional demographic trends and internal population movements had both positive and negative consequences for African American entrepreneurs and consumers. While no single source chronicles the history of African American enterprise in St. Louis, numerous accounts suggest that an enclave economy initially provided important competitive advantages to early minority merchants and craftsmen.

Early Business Development

Wright (2002) describes the early history of African American business development in St. Louis as strongly influenced by residential segregation, and later development as largely shaped by widespread patterns of displacement, internal migration, and targeted urban renewal. Although a limited number of African Americans owned considerable property in pre–Civil War St. Louis, many clustered in riverfront communities dominated by shacks and dilapidated tenement houses. During the postwar era, many blacks were also drawn to the riverfront and lived in wharf boats or squatted in camps along the water. The primary geographic location of the city's early black population was the central corridor: Mill Creek Valley and Midtown. According to Wright (2002, 23), "Mansions and tenements, shops, businesses, factories, dance halls, taverns and clubs, restaurants, churches, schools, hotels, and other institutions crowded into this area."

By 1850, Mill Creek Valley emerged as the heart of St. Louis's African American community and is considered by some historians as the genesis of its entrepreneurial heritage. An important honky-tonk and entertainment district emerged along Chestnut and Market Streets, as well as numerous black churches, educational institutions, and voluntary associations (Wright 2002). One of the city's oldest and best-established African American newspapers, the *St. Louis American*, also has its origins in Midtown.

Another geographic area central to the emergence of the early African American business community was Elleardsville, later abbreviated to "the Ville." Initially occupied by German and Irish immigrants, the area experienced movement of African Americans into the community shortly after the Civil War. While restrictive real estate covenants prevented blacks from moving into many other parts of the city, the Ville was an important exception. According to Wright (2002), between 1920 and 1950 the Ville changed from 8 percent to 95 percent African American. During that time, it emerged as a prominent center of black enterprise, and included an entertainment district, arts and cultural facilities, educational institutions, social services, and a variety of retail and service establishments. Wright notes that the Ville was the home of Annie Pope Malone, who became one of the world's wealthiest black women during the 1930s and 1940s.

Several other geographic areas (Pagedale, Wellston, and Beverly Hills) attracted a limited number of African American residents at the turn of the century. During the 1940s and 1950s, however, many black professionals relocated along Whitney Avenue "and it became a center for social affairs" (Wright 2002, 119). One of the most significant areas linked to early African American business development in the St. Louis region is Kinloch (Wright 2000). It became a significant destination point after the East St. Louis riots of 1917 and during the post–World War I period. In response to increased black migration, white residents of Kinloch voted to divide the community; in 1937, whites established the separate community of Berkeley, and in 1948 Kinloch was established as the first all-black city in Missouri (Wright 2000).

Wright (2002) also identifies Elmwood Park, Overland, Creve Coeur, and Maryland Heights as significant to African American business development. Originally settled by African Americans after the Civil War, these areas were initially agricultural communities. The black settlements in these areas remained small and primarily linked to farming and agriculture until the 1950s. At that time, they were significantly impacted by urban renewal, annexation, and displacement. These themes not only characterized the more recent history of the Elmwood Park area but also shaped the collective fates of other areas discussed by Wright.

While black business enterprise is not a central feature of Wright's analysis of African American history in St. Louis, he does consistently stress the negative impact of urban renewal and displacement on community institutions and neighborhood welfare. He notes that in Mill Creek Valley and Midtown, urban renewal during the 1950s and 1960s displaced approximately 20,000 individuals, 95 percent of whom were African American. The impact of urban renewal upon African American business and commercial enterprises in these two areas was extensive. In Kinloch the expansion of Lambert–St. Louis International Airport resulted in the demolition of approximately 776 homes and the displacement of their African American occupants (Wright 2000). In the 1950s, urban renewal also displaced numerous African American residents in the Elmwood Park area to make way for new development.

Smith (1988) provides a more detailed account of African American business development in north St. Louis. Her history also stresses the impact of segregation, urban renewal, and displacement upon African American business enterprise. Consistent with the enclave enterprise interpretation, Smith (1988, 3) contends that residential segregation was initially an asset for early African American entrepreneurs: "Businesses owned and operated by blacks in St. Louis began by providing services. In some cases these businesses services were provided for white consumers, but for the most part these services were sold to black consumers." While black domestics sold their services primarily to white consumers, other services such as barbering, grocery stores, tailoring, restaurants, laundries, and mortuaries were typically confined to African American consumers within African American communities.

Also consistent with enclave economics, Smith (1988, 27) observes that during the years of legally sanctioned segregation in St. Louis, black communities were much more than simply geographic areas in which African Americans were compelled to live: they were places where families spent much of their time. Within the geographic boundaries of these neighborhoods were located churches, educational institutions, social activities, businesses, and services. The Ville, Mill Creek Valley and the neighborhoods inclusive of Enright, Finney, and Cook, and Grand Avenue are some of the more historic neighborhoods of home owners, businesses, and service facilities.

Smith's history of more recent black business development is also consistent with that presented by Wright and other local historians (Montesi and Deposki 2001; Primm 1981). Emphasizing the impact of urban renewal, clearance, and displacement, Smith (1988) contends that redevelopment pressures in Mill Creek Valley eventually undermined numerous business and community institutions located there, and ultimately transformed the heart of this historic African American community. Prior to urban renewal, the Valley contained 839 businesses and institutions, including churches, theaters, community centers, grocery stores, and a baseball park for the St. Louis Stars, the city's historic Negro League baseball team (Fagerstrom 2000). As a result of urban renewal, these historic facilities, structures, and business districts were completely demolished.

Despite later patterns of demolition and displacement, the early history of black business development in St. Louis appears consistent with the enclave economy interpretation. The strategic advantages associated with the residential concentration of African Americans in several St. Louis neighborhoods enabled merchants to access minority consumers and cater to a racially targeted market. Ethnic and racial loyalty assisted business development. As a result, numerous African American merchants, professionals, and service providers were able to establish a small but important entrepreneurial foothold in St. Louis's urban economy. In the face of widespread segregation and racial discrimination, black enclaves did provide some advantages for African American entrepreneurs. Regardless of these early competitive advantages, however, urban renewal, demolition, and displacement often undermined the institutional basis of business support that linked neighborhood identity to racial loyalty in the marketplace.

The more recent history of black enterprise in St. Louis is also partly consistent with business advantages found in enclave economies. While many traditional black enclaves were disrupted or demolished and residents were displaced to other parts of the city, the magnitude of racial segregation in St. Louis has remained fairly constant over time (see Chapter 8). Since 1970, the total number of African Americans residing in the St. Louis metropolitan area has dramatically increased, as has the total amount of geographic space they occupy. In St. Louis City, the African American population grew from 154,223 residents in 1950 to 195,523 residents in 2000, a growth rate of 26.8 percent. In St. Louis County, the African American population grew from 17,067 residents in 1950 to 235,485 residents in 2000, a growth rate of nearly 1,280 percent.

The African American population has grown significantly in every county surrounding St. Louis City since 1950. These trends mean that the size of the African American enclave has expanded both in terms of the number of households included within it and the amount of geographic space that the enclave encompasses. What is not clear is whether the spatial expansion of St. Louis's segregated enclave has conferred businesses advantages to African American entrepreneurs in the contemporary era.

Later Business Development

Between 1970 and 2000, radical population shifts occurred within many north St. Louis neighborhoods. Chapter 5 explained the larger patterns of economic growth and development that shaped neighborhood and community development in north St. Louis and the demographic shifts that accompanied these changes. Many north St. Louis neighborhoods are currently characterized by high rates of housing vacancies and equally high rates of abandoned commercial structures. Several communities, however, have experienced considerable redevelopment activities between 1970 and 1990, especially in housing, social services, and commercial renovation. Some of the recent redevelopment activities have targeted African American communities with many major projects being led by African American entrepreneurs, developers, community activists, or community development corporations headed by neighborhood leaders. Federal funding financed some of the redevelopment efforts; private foundations, private sector investors, and commercial lenders funded others.

Smith (1988) reports that significant redevelopment of Mill Creek Valley followed in the wake of the massive urban renewal project of 1959. A new development, Laclede Town and Laclede Park, was constructed during the 1970s. By the mid-1980s, however, the area had once again become a one-race community. Despite redevelopment of the area in the 1980s, Laclede Town was demolished during the 1990s to make way for the expansion of Saint Louis University and Harris-Stowe State College (Reinert and Shore 1996). Significant movement into the adjacent community of JeffVanderLou occurred as a result of the displacement produced by the demolition of Laclede Town (Smith 1988). Additional housing and community development occurred in the Murphy-Blair neighborhood.

Smith (1988) also reports that significant redevelopment occurred in the Norwood Square and Kings Heights communities between 1960 and 1975. Considerable redevelopment was also initiated by the Union Sarah Economic Development Corporation (Berndt 1977) in the area adjacent to the Central West End. According to Smith (1988, 42), this redevelopment effort peaked in 1984. Consistent with other recent redevelopment efforts, however, the benefits received by minority contractors, vendors, and merchants from enclave revitalization are not clear.

While many housing initiatives during the 1960s and 1970s were initially focused on residential areas such as Norwood Square, the redevelopment of other black neighborhoods by community development corporations such as JeffVanderLou, Inc., the West End Community

Conference, as well as the Union-Sarah Economic Development Corporation, was also extensive. Several historic districts were targeted for redevelopment during the 1970s and 1980s, including Visitation Park. Smith (1988) notes that Visitation Park became the first predominantly black community to be designated a historic district. By 1982, Lewis Place, West Cabanne Place, and Fountain Park were designated as national historic districts. All these areas were primarily African American. The adjacent communities of Penrose Park, Fairground Park, O'Fallon Park, and Enright Avenue were also impacted by internal black migration and racial transition. Again, however, the specific benefits derived by African American entrepreneurs from these redevelopment and revitalization efforts are not clear.

During the mid-1990s, the JeffVanderLou neighborhood was targeted for major redevelopment. The Vashon/JeffVanderLou Initiative (2001) identified a large section of the community for housing, social service, and business redevelopment. The redevelopment plan is organized around the construction of a new high school, a neighborhood park, and a wide array of strategic community amenities (Vashon/JeffVanderLou Initiative 2001). While Vashon High School has been completed, the comprehensive JVL Initiative is ongoing and linked to a number of other housing and community development projects in this predominantly African American neighborhood. Because of the Initiative's magnitude, it is reasonable to expect significant economic multipliers, market expansions, and related business benefits to be generated on behalf of minority entrepreneurs operating in this section of the city's larger black enclave. While the size of African American business expansion linked to the Initiative remains ambiguous, the publicly stated objective is "to bring sustained improvement to the lives of the individuals and families who live, work and worship in JeffVanderLou by working in partnership with residents, business and government to stimulate physical, economic and social revitalization" (Vashon/JeffVanderLou Initiative 2001, 4).

Likewise, other parts of the city's African American enclave have been targeted for redevelopment by various federal programs and initiatives in recent years. In response to the needs of its most distressed communities, St. Louis City has targeted several at-risk neighborhoods for intensive community development efforts. Approximately eighteen neighborhoods make up the St. Louis Enterprise Community and Empowerment Zone areas of the city, and have been designated Neighborhood Revitalization Areas by the U.S. Department of Housing and Urban Development (HUD). As a result, these neighborhoods are able to use Community Development Block Grant (CDBG) funds more flexibly. Funding for the Empowerment Zone initiative, however, has been severely curtailed under the Bush administration. Nonetheless, the target communities remain as development priorities within the city.

Several other city neighborhoods have been targeted for special attention by St. Louis 2004, a civic advocacy group closely tied to the Danforth Foundation. The Sustainable Neighborhoods Initiative is a partnership of residents, community groups, financial institutions, local foundations, and state and local government to revitalize nine St. Louis–area neighborhood clusters. According to St. Louis 2004 (2002), the Sustainable Neighborhoods Initiative "combines physical development and infrastructure improvements with human service support and community-based economic development." Each sustainable neighborhood cluster is required to design and develop a strategic plan as part of the Sustainable Neighborhoods Initiative. Despite the lofty goals of the Sustainable Neighborhoods Initiative, uneven development has characterized revitalization efforts in the target neighborhoods.

Over the past two decades, several local CDCs and related organizations such as DeSales Housing Corporation, Pyramid Construction, the Charles Vatterot Co., the Regional Housing and Community Development Alliance (RHCDA), as well as private developers like McCormack-Baron, have been active in numerous St. Louis neighborhoods. The St. Louis Association of Community Organizations (SLACO) is composed of fourteen neighborhoods and sixteen churches; SLACO has been an active force in both community development and neighborhood planning in the city. Numerous urban churches and faith-based organizations also target particular neighborhoods for strategic interventions and community development activities. Whether these initiatives have produced expansions in local minority enterprise is not clear.

Two new public housing programs have produced major redevelopment activities in several St. Louis neighborhoods. In July 2000, Phase I of the first HOPE VI project, Near Southside Redevelopment Plan, King Louis Square, was officially launched on the site of the former twenty-seven-acre Darst-Webbe housing project. The site is located south of downtown St. Louis and is close to several important historic districts including Soulard, Benton Park, and Lafayette Square. Primary funding was secured through HUD's HOPE VI program; additional funds were provided through several sources, including the City of St. Louis, MHDC, Fannie Mae (FNMA), Firstar Community Development Corporation, Bank of America, and the syndication of federal and state tax credits through the St. Louis Equity Fund. According to the *St. Louis Construction News* ("Construction Begins" 2003), the $42 million grant provided by HUD to the City of St. Louis and the St. Louis Housing Authority was leveraged to create a $160 million development area. A second HOPE VI project was recently awarded to St. Louis and is currently underway. The redevelopment of the Arthur Blumeyer Housing Development in the Covenant/Blu neighborhood entails a $35 million grant designed to leverage $104 million in public and private investment to build 815 new units. While expectations are high, it is too soon to know if either of these mega-projects will stimulate the expansion of minority enterprise in the target areas.

The Current State of African American Business Enterprise

While much is known about patterns of internal migration within St. Louis's African American population (see Chapter 8) and the regional developmental changes associated with them, it is not clear if the spatial expansion of the region's black enclave has produced more or fewer business opportunities for minority entrepreneurs. We also know that significant and numerous development initiatives have been undertaken in many predominantly African American neighborhoods, especially those located in St. Louis City. Has expansion of the black enclave stimulated the growth of minority enterprise? If African American business has expanded in response to the growth of the region's black population, what types of enterprises have benefited? What parts of the black enclave have grown most rapidly? Does African American business expand more rapidly in areas that benefit from targeted interventions like HOPE VI development, the JVL Initiative, or the Sustainable Neighborhoods program? Has African American business expanded more in St. Louis County or in St. Louis City? Are more African American firms operating outside the enclave?

In order to examine these important questions more thoroughly, the Economic Census, Survey of Minority Owned Business Enterprises (SMOBE) was analyzed. The SMOBE data files have been gathered every five years beginning in 1977 (U.S. Bureau of the Census 1977, 1982, 1987, 1992, 1997). Data examined were drawn from all national surveys conducted since 1977 (1977, 1982, 1987, 1992, 1997). The data files make it possible to compare business performance in St. Louis with national trends and benchmarks. These five-year intervals cover critical periods in the modern period of African American business enterprise in the St. Louis region. The SMOBE databases contain a wide array of information about minority businesses, including total number of African American firms, total number of African American firms with paid employees, average number of employees per firm, average size of payroll, and total receipts per firm.

In addition to specific rates of business performance, it is also possible to determine overall rates of business ownership among African Americans and calculate standardized rates of performance. Rates of ownership represent the total proportion of firms in a region or city owned by a minority entrepreneur. Table 1 shows longitudinal rates of business ownership among African Americans in the St. Louis region between 1987 and 1997. In 1987, there were approximately 5,736 firms owned by African Americans. Most (4,753) were located in either St. Louis City or St. Louis County. In 1992, African Americans in the St. Louis region owned 7,321 firms and by 1997 they owned approximately 9,675 firms. In 1992 and 1997, the bulk of African American–owned firms were located in the City or the County, 5,981 and 7,913 respectively. In 1987, African Americans in St. Louis City and St. Louis County owned about 1.62 percent of all Missouri firms. By 1992, rates of ownership among City and County entrepreneurs had increased to 1.71 percent of all Missouri firms, and by 1997 rates of ownership had increased to 1.92 percent of all Missouri firms. According to the 1992 data, African Americans owned approximately 6 percent of all firms in the St. Louis region, a figure well below their actual presence in the local population.

Table 2 shows the ten states with the largest number of firms owned by African Americans, along with several other measures of business performance. Overall, Missouri falls considerably below the ten states appearing in Table 2 on nearly all measures of business performance. Table 3 compares African American firms in the St. Louis region with ten other metropolitan areas with the largest number of black-owned firms. These benchmark cities are pertinent to the St. Louis circumstances since the bulk of Missouri's African American population resides in the St. Louis metropolitan region. Moreover, the 1997 data show that nearly 71 percent of all black-owned firms in Missouri (13,678) are located in the St. Louis metropolitan region (9,675). Despite this, the St. Louis region falls consistently below the other regions, both in terms of the total number of firms and the total receipts measured in millions of dollars. Within the St. Louis region, a number of important trends can be identified across various parts of the black enclave.

Table 1. Overall Rates of Business Ownership among African Americans in the St. Louis Metropolitan Region

	1987	1992	1997
Total number of firms in Missouri	293,131	348,978	411,403
Total number of firms owned by African Americans in the St. Louis metropolitan region	5,736	7,321	9,675
Total number of firms owned by African Americans in St. Louis City and County	4,753	5,981	7,913
Proportion of Missouri firms owned by African Americans in St. Louis City and County	1.62%	1.71%	1.92%

Table 2. Ten States with Largest Number of Black-Owned Firms Compared to Missouri

State	Black-Owned Firms (Number)	All Firms (Number)	Black as a Percent of All	Black Sales and Receipts (Million Dollars)	All Firms Sales and Receipts (Million Dollars)
New York	86,469	1,509,829	5.7%	5,067	1,488,913
California	79,110	2,565,734	3.1%	6,395	2,178,292
Texas	60,427	1,525,972	4.0%	6,857	1,415,536
Florida	59,732	1,301,920	4.6%	4,092	828,429
Georgia	55,766	568,552	9.8%	4,111	580,345
Maryland	47,614	400,203	11.9%	3,965	285,924
Illinois	41,244	882,053	4.7%	3,913	933,117
North Carolina	39,901	570,484	7.0%	2,299	518,649
Virginia	33,539	480,122	7.0%	3,408	415,093
Ohio	26,970	781,284	3.5%	3,947	796,506
Missouri	13,678	411,403	3.3%	1,261	382,797

Figure 1 shows general trends in the total number of firms owned by African Americans within the St Louis region between 1977 and 1997. In the region as a whole, the number of firms has grown from 3,765 in 1977 to 9,675 in 1997. The slowest rate of growth occurred in St. Louis City. Between 1982 and 1987, the total number of firms doing business in St. Louis County eclipsed the total number located in the City. By 1992, there were approximately 3,500 firms located in St. Louis County and 2,481 located in the City. By 1997, there were 4,482 firms located in the County and 3,431 in the City. The evidence shows, therefore, that African American firms are either increasingly moving to the suburbs, or that rates of business growth in the suburbs are greatly exceeding growth rates in the city, or both.

Table 3. Ten Metropolitan Areas with Largest Number of Black-Owned Firms Compared to Black-Owned Firms in the St. Louis Metropolitan Area

Metropolitan Area	Firms (Number)	Receipts (Million Dollars)
New York, NY, PMSA	69,410	4,003
Washington, DC-MD-VA-WV	48,709	5,410
Los Angeles-Long Beach, CA	38,277	3,322
Chicago, IL	35,569	3,375
Atlanta, GA	34,592	2,959
Houston, TX	24,286	1,846
Philadelphia, PA-NJ	17,863	1,660
Detroit, MI	17,692	3,507
Miami, FL	16,918	1,070
Baltimore, MD	16,712	1,360
St. Louis	9,625	797

Figure 2 shows the total number of firms with paid employees between 1977 and 1997. These firms obviously have the potential to exert greater influence on community and neighborhood development because they provide jobs and income for residents. As with Figure 1, the evidence shows that St. Louis County eclipsed the City around 1992. While growth rates for the region as a whole reveal sharp increases in the number of firms with paid employees since 1992, the trajectory in the County is especially steep. By 1997, there were 4,351 firms with paid employees in the County and 3,365 in the City. Not only are African American firms growing faster in the suburbs but those firms are also employing more people. Despite targeted neighborhood development in numerous parts of the City, African American business development in the suburbs appears much more accelerated.

Figure 3 shows the analysis of total gross receipts of firms owned by African Americans in the St. Louis region. In 1977, the total gross receipts for firms located in the City were $75,656,000. In the County, the total gross receipts per firm were $25,075,000 in 1977. By 1997, however, gross receipts for the County were $438,075,000 as compared to $255,471,000 for the City. While total gross receipts for both the City and County increased, the rate of growth in the County has escalated more sharply since 1992. While total gross receipts do not necessarily mean suburban firms were more profitable, it is highly likely that they were.

Another way to compare rates of African American business performance within the region is to calculate average receipts per firm for all firms. Figure 4 shows that by 1987, the average receipts per firm were

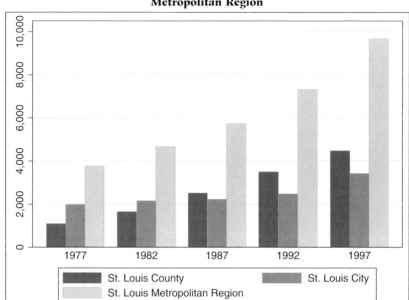

Figure 1. Total Number of Firms Owned by African Americans in the St. Louis Metropolitan Region

nearly identical between the City and County. While the business cycle produced a drop in average receipts per firm between 1987 and 1997, and a sharp increase after that time, by 1997 the average receipts per firm in the County were markedly different from those revealed in the City.

Very similar patterns were revealed in the analysis of average receipts per firm for firms with paid employees (Figure 5). By 1987, rates of performance were nearly identical between the City and the County. After that time, rates of performance continued to widen between the two areas. By 1997, performance rates for County firms with paid employees were higher than regional averages and increasing at a much sharper rate than those revealed among City firms with paid employees.

Figure 6 shows the average number of employees per firm only for firms with paid employees. By 1992, County and City firms were employing a comparable number of people. By 1997, County firms employed an average of 7.37 individuals; on the other hand, City firms employed an average of 6.75 individuals. County averages also exceeded regional figures (7.27).

Average annual payroll figures are shown in Figure 7. The data show very little difference between City, County, and regional averages. A sharp increase in the size of all payrolls is revealed after 1992. By 1997, average payrolls in the County ($120,000), City ($124,400), and region ($123,500) were very close. These figures are of interest because they suggest that labor costs in the county are lower, a fact probably linked to higher levels of total receipts and higher number of individuals employed among County firms.

Figure 2. Total Number of Paid Employees in Firms Owned by African Americans in the St. Louis Metropolitan Region

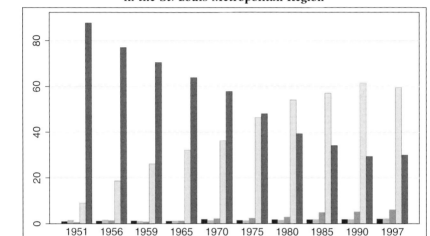

Figure 3. Total Gross Receipts of Firms Owned by African Americans in the St. Louis Metropolitan Region (1000s)

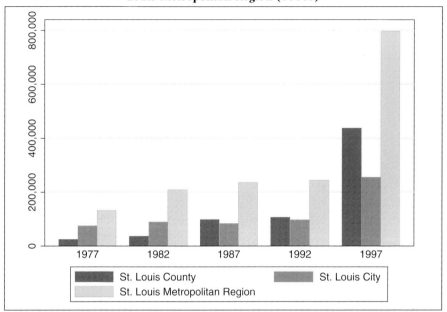

Figure 4. Average Gross Receipts per Firm for All Firms Owned by African Americans in the St. Louis Metropolitan Region (1000s)

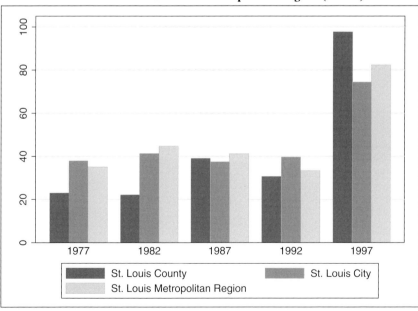

Metromorphosis

Figure 5. Average Gross Receipts per Firm for Firms with Paid Employees Owned by African Americans in the St. Louis Metropolitan Region (1000s)

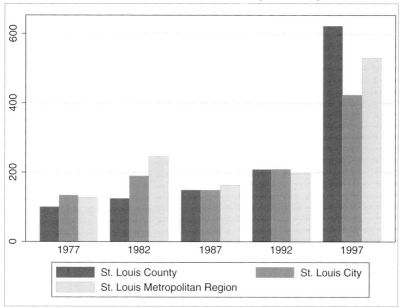

Figure 6. Average Number of Employees per Firm for Firms with Paid Employees Owned by African Americans in the St. Louis Metropolitan Region

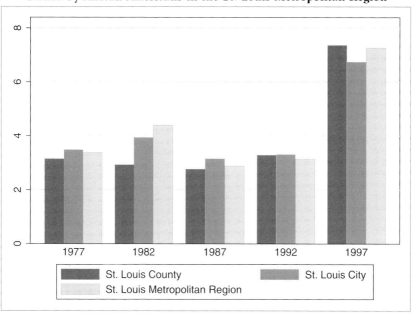

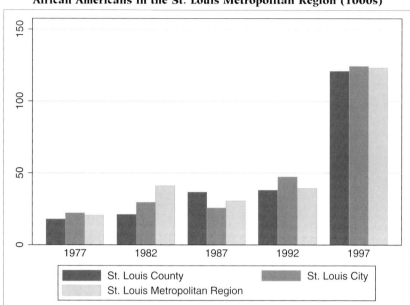

Another way to compare rates of business development within the region's black enclave is to measure rates of performance per 1,000 African American population. Figure 8 shows the average number of firms in the region per 1,000 African American population. When measured in this manner, business development indices within the County escalate at a much sharper rate than those appearing in the City. From these data, it also appears clear that African American firms doing business in the suburban portion of the region's black enclave appear to be outperforming their counterparts remaining within the City. The findings are reinforced by Figure 9, which shows the average gross receipts per firm only for firms with paid employees per 1,000 African American population.

According to this measure, rates of business performance in the County began to eclipse those revealed in the City after 1982. By 1997, County businesses were clearly ahead of those remaining in the City.

What is not clear from Figures 8 and 9 is whether the African American firms located within the County are exclusively confined to the enclave or are doing business outside the black community. In order to address this question, certified African American firms were geo-coded according to their business address and spatially located in the City and County based upon the percentage of African Americans residing in a zip code. These

Figure 8. Average Number of Firms Owned by African Americans in the St. Louis Metropolitan Region per 1,000 Black Population

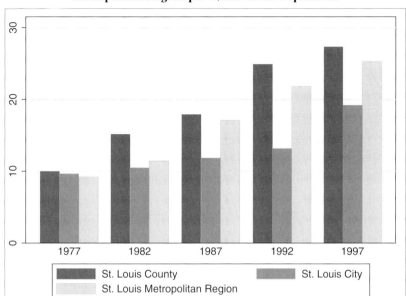

data do not include all African American firms in the City and County, but only those that sought formal certification as a minority-owned firm. The percentage of African Americans residing in a zip code was based upon the 1990 census data because the list of certified minority firms used in the analysis was based upon 1998 data.

The spatial analysis of certified African American firms was based upon five ranges of racial concentration: under 20 percent, 20–39 percent, 40–59 percent, 60–79 percent, and more than 80 percent African American. In the City of St. Louis, nearly all African American firms tend to cluster within the racial enclave or within close proximity to the inner city. Very few African Americans are located in south St. Louis (only 3 firms), a predominantly white area. In the County, however, more than 65 percent of African American firms are located in areas where the white population exceeds 80 percent. While many St Louis County firms are located in the inner ring suburbs where numerous African Americans reside, other minority firms are apparently doing business outside the enclave.

These latter findings are important for a variety of reasons and can be explored in more detail by examining the recent appearance of African American firms in St. Charles County. In 1992, there were 166 firms owned by African Americans located in St. Charles County; this was the first year that the SMOBE database reported African American firms appearing there. In the 1987 database, no African American firms were reported for St. Charles County. By 1997, however, the total number of African American firms in St. Charles County had increased to 201, a growth rate of approximately 21 percent since 1992. Table 4 shows the comparison of all African American firms doing business in St. Louis city, St, Louis County, and St. Charles County in 1997. Based upon average gross receipts per firm for all firms, businesses located in St. Charles County ($130,423) outperformed those located in the St. Louis City ($74,460) and in St. Louis County ($97,740) by a wide margin. African American firms located in St. Charles County also employed more people on average (16.3) than those firms located in St. Louis County (7.37) and in St. Louis City (6.75). Average rates of employment in St. Charles were more than double the rates for the City and County. St. Charles firms also revealed higher average payrolls ($196,906) than firms located in the City ($124,402) or in St. Louis County ($120,898). Additionally, they reported higher average gross receipts ($725,938) than African American firms located in St. Louis City ($423,442) or in St. Louis County ($621,792).

Figure 9. Average Gross Receipts per Firm with Paid Employees Owned by African Americans in the St. Louis Metropolitan Region per 1,000 Black Population

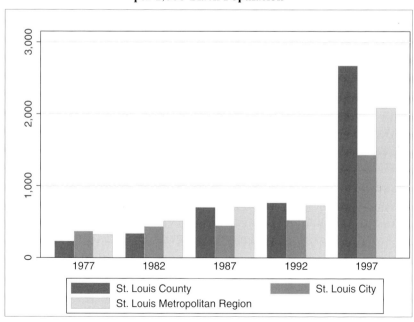

Planning and Policy Implications

The movement of African American firms to the inner ring suburbs of St. Louis County and deeper into the region's suburban fringes has important planning and public policy implications. It is apparent that arguments about the supposed business advantages derived from a protected market within an enclave economy do not fit contemporary St. Louis. In the case of contemporary African American entrepreneurs, the findings suggest that locating outside the enclave economy is associated with higher levels of business performance. The findings are not surprising, considering the greater access to higher levels of disposable income in the suburbs. Though it is surely premature to dismiss the enclave theory of minority enterprise altogether, the evidence presented in this chapter suggests that for contemporary African American business development in the St. Louis region, a much broader interpretation is warranted.

Table 4. A Comparison of Business Performance among African American Firms in St. Louis City, St. Louis County, and St. Charles County, 1997

	St. Louis City	St. Louis County	St. Charles County
Total number of firms	3,431	4,482	201
Gross receipts for all firms	255,471,000	438,075,000	26,215,000
Average gross receipts for all firms	74,460	97,741	130,422
Total number of firms with paid employees	498	590	32
Number of employees for firms with paid employees	3,363	4,351	522
Average gross receipts for firms with paid employees	423,442	621,792	725,938
Annual payroll of firms with paid employees	61,952,000	71,330,000	6,301,000
Average annual payroll of firms with paid employees	124,402	120,898	196,906
Gross receipts for firms with paid employees	210,874,000	366,857,000	23,230,000
Average number of employees for firms with paid employees	6.75	7.37	16.30

The evidence and argument presented here, however, do not lead to the conclusion that enclaves serve no important business or economic development functions for African American entrepreneurs. On the contrary, the historical evidence strongly suggests that enclaves were probably very important sources of early African American enterprise. Additionally, contemporary businesses within the enclave, whatever their degree of efficiency and profitability, are meeting the immediate retail and commercial needs of the residents there, especially in St. Louis City. Nor would it be appropriate to conclude that African American merchants within the enclave would be better advised to close their shop doors and move to the suburbs. Nonetheless, the findings do suggest strongly that the developmental prospects of enclave businesses are probably severely constrained by the enclave itself. As a result, their ability to attract capital to the community and to provide jobs for residents is limited as well. The evidence shows that suburban firms employ more people and generally appear more profitable than those located in the city.

It is not clear, however, if African American suburban firms started within the enclave, achieved some success, and later moved to a suburban market. If such a pattern were the case, one could argue that the St. Louis city enclave served as a business incubator preparing selected minority firms and entrepreneurs for entry into larger metropolitan and regional markets. It also is possible that suburban firms serve inner-city enclave markets through wholesaling or other distributional activities. Likewise, African American business networking between cities and suburbs may promote and sustain economic activity within the enclave. Unfortunately, the databases do not provide insights into these intriguing possibilities.

It follows from the findings, however, that African American entrepreneurs interested in growth and expansion should consider locating outside the enclave to achieve more success. Within the inner-city enclave, the limited purchasing power of residents establishes real economic constraints restricting the potential of business enterprises to expand. Markets are limited, thereby severely restricting not only development potential but also the ability to create jobs and to attract capital to the enclave. Unless African American entrepreneurs reach broader, metropolitan markets, their businesses are destined to remain small, undercapitalized, and marginally profitable. Most significant, public policies that confine business and economic development to limited geographic areas, whether intentionally or as an unforeseen consequence, will probably restrict rather than expand the opportunities for minority entrepreneurs to enter the business mainstream and undermine their ability to reduce the increasingly high levels of unemployment in the enclave economy. These observations pose a policy paradox for public officials interested in promoting community and neighborhood development.

Boston and Ross (1996, 342) contend that there "is a growing 'misperception' that virtually all successful black-owned businesses are moving to the suburbs." They insist that "an important element of any strategy to revitalize inner cities, at least where African Americans reside, must be a focus on the promotion of African American-owned businesses." They present evidence and arguments showing that, in Atlanta, many successful African American entrepreneurs prefer the city to the suburbs.

In St. Louis and in many other parts of the nation, their observations appear questionable (Cummings 1999).

It seems clear from the St. Louis findings that policy interventions designed to stimulate economic development only at the community and neighborhood levels have serious limitations. Blakely (1994) identifies several forms of community-based economic development: community development corporations, community cooperatives, local enterprise agencies, employee-owned enterprises, and community employment and training boards. After discussing the costs and benefits of each intervention, he concedes that the performance record of community-based development is one of limited and marginal success: "My experience … is that community initiatives are generally small and oriented toward the provision of household services, community services and facilities.…" (Blakely 1994, 227).

Teitz (1989) reaches similar conclusions. He observes that community or neighborhood economic development is problematic by its very nature. The geographic separation of work from place of residence poses serious difficulties for developing community-based businesses. Though the neighborhood remains the locus for political advocacy and collective mobilization (neighborhood planning), a confined geographic space is a less effective locus for economic development. Cummings and Glaser (1983, 1985) and Stoecker (1997) develop comparable arguments. Community-based or neighborhood interventions such as community development corporations may help to provide housing within ethnic and racial enclaves (Schwartz, Bratt, Vidal, and Keyes 1994), but they do not appear effective at developing or incubating other types of business enterprises (Cummings and Glaser 1985). In the case of St. Louis, African American firms in the suburbs are consistently outperforming those confined to the inner-city enclave economy. Indeed, many of St. Louis's most successful minority firms are located in the suburbs (Nicklaus 2000, 2001), including World Wide Technology, recently ranked as the largest black-owned firm in the nation.

For economic development and equity planners, it appears wiser to promote minority enterprise within a region or metropolitan area rather than confine such efforts to the enclave (Hutchinson and Follman 1997) or to an even smaller geographic area like a neighborhood. Planners and public officials might do better to design and promote programs that stimulate regional minority enterprise without confining such initiatives to the neighborhood or community level (FOCUS St. Louis 2001). A better mix of strategic interventions, with more regional and metropolitan objectives, would promise greater results for the future of urban neighborhoods and their minority inhabitants.

Michael Porter (1997, 12) observed:

> a sustainable economic base can be created in inner cities only as it has been elsewhere: through private, for-profit initiatives, and investments based on economic self-interest and genuine competitive advantage instead of artificial inducements, government mandates, or charity, A sound economic strategy must focus on the position of inner cities as part of regional economies, rather than treating inner cities as separate, independent economies; otherwise economic activity there will not be sustainable.

The evidence and argument presented in this chapter favor Porter's formulation of the strategies required for minority economic development. It also seems apparent that the suburbanization of many African American firms in the St. Louis region reinforces the wisdom of his observations, and that this wisdom has been reflected in the private location decisions of numerous African American entrepreneurs.

References

Aldrich, H., et al. "Ethnic Residential Concentration and the Protected Market Hypotheses." *Social Forces* 6 (1985): 996–1009.

Baldassare, M. *The Los Angeles Riots: Lessons for the Urban Future.* Boulder, Colo.: Westview Press, 1994.

Bates, T. *Assessment of State and Local Government Minority Business Development Programs, Report 1–16.* Washington, D.C.: U.S. Department of Commerce, Minority Business Development Agency, 1993.

___. "Small Business Viability in the Urban Ghetto." *Journal of Regional Science* 29 (1989): 625–43.

___. "Why Do Minority Business Development Programs Generate So Little Minority Business Development?" *Economic Development Quarterly* 9 (1995): 3–14.

Berndt, H. *New Rulers in the Ghetto.* Westport, Conn: Greenwood Press, 1977.

Blakely, E. J. *Planning Local Economic Development.* Thousand Oaks, Calif.: Sage Publications, 1994.

Bonacich, E. "A Theory of Middleman Minorities." *American Sociological Review* 38 (1973): 583–94.

Bonacich, E., and J. Modell. *The Economic Basis of Ethnic Solidarity.* Berkeley: University of California Press, 1980.

Boston, T., and C. Ross. "Local Preferences of Successful African-American Owned Businesses in Atlanta." *The Review of Black Political Economy* (Fall/Winter 1996): 337–57.

Brimmer, A. "Competition and Integration of Black Enterprises in the American Economy." *Review of Black Political Economy* 29, no. 3 (2002): 9–50.

___. "The Negro in the National Economy." In *American Negro Reference Book*, edited by J. David. Englewood Cliffs, N.J.: Prentice-Hall, 1966.

Brimmer, A., and H. Terrell. "The Economic Potential of Black Capitalism." *Public Policy* 19 (1971): 289–307.

Caplovitz, D. *The Poor Pay More.* New York: Free Press, 1967.

City of St. Louis. *Community Information Network. St. Louis Five-Year Consolidated Plan Strategy* [online]. City of St. Louis, 2002. Accessed through http://stlouis.missouri.org/5yearstrategy/app_a.html (accessed December 2003).

"Construction Begins on King Louis Square to Create New Residential Community at Site of Former Darst-Webbe Public Housing." *Saint Louis Construction News*, July 24, 2000. Available at www.slfp.com/Cnews0811M.htm (accessed September 2003).

Cummings, S., ed. "African American Entrepreneurship in the Suburbs: Protected Markets and Enclave Business Development." Journal of the American Planning Association (Winter 1999): 50–61.

___. "Selecting Sound Investments for Community Development Corporations." *Journal of Applied Sociology* 3 (1986): 51–62.

___. *Self-Help in Urban American Patterns of Minority Business Enterprise.* London: Kennikat Press, 1980.

Cummings, S., and M. Glaser. "An Examination of the Perceived Effectiveness of Community Development Corporations." *Journal of Urban Affairs* 5 (1983): 315–30.

___. "Neighborhood Participation in Community Development." *Population Research and Policy Review* 4 (1985): 267–87.

Davis, A., B. B. Gardner, and M. R. Gardner. *Deep South.* Chicago: University of Chicago Press, 1941.

Dollard, J. *Caste and Class in a Southern Town.* New York: Doubleday Anchor, 1949.

Drake, S. C., and H. R. Cayton. *Black Metropolis: A Study of Negro Life in a Northern City.* New York: Harcourt, Brace and Company, 1945.

Fagerstrom, R. *Mill Creek Valley: A Soul of St. Louis.* St. Louis: Fagerstrom, 2000.

Feagin, J. R., and N. Imani. "Racial Barriers to African-American Entrepreneurship: An Exploratory Study." *Social Problems* 4l (1994): 562–73.

FOCUS St. Louis. *Racial Inequality in the St. Louis Region: A Community Call to Action.* St. Louis: Author, 2001.

Green, S., and P. Pryde. *Black Entrepreneurship in America.* New Brunswick, N.J.: Transaction Publishers, 1990.

"Hope VI Funds New Urban Neighborhoods." *New Urban News* [cited September 2003], January/February, 2002. Available at www.newurbannews.com/hopeVI.html.

Hutchinson, S., and Cindy Follman. "Joining Hands to Aid Minority Business." *St. Louis Post-Dispatch*, March 28, 1997, p. 7B.

Lee, J. "Retail Niche Domination among African American, Jewish, and Korean Entrepreneurs: Competition, Co-Ethnic Advantage, and Disadvantage." *The American Behavioral Scientist* (June/July 1999): 1398–1416.

Light, I. *Ethnic Enterprise in America.* Berkeley: University of California Press, 1972.

Light, I., and C. Rosenstein. *Race, Ethnicity and Entrepreneurship in Urban America.* New York: Aldine Grayton, 1995.

Loewen, J. *The Mississippi Chinese.* Cambridge, Mass.: Harvard University Press, 1971.

Montesi, A., and R. Deposki. *Images of America: Downtown St. Louis.* Chicago: Arcadia, 2001.

Myrdal, G. *An American Dilemma.* New York: Harper and Row, 1944.

Nicklaus, D. "African-American Businesses Break out of Categories That Bound Them in the Past While Black Entrepreneurs Have Expanded beyond Niche Markets." *St. Louis Post-Dispatch*, February 28, 2001, p. C1.

___. "Homegrown Values Cultivate Success for Firm; Tech Company Ranks No. 1 among Black-Owned Businesses." *St. Louis Post-Dispatch*, June 14, 2000, p. C1.

Packaged Facts. "The U.S. African American Market." MarketResearch.com, January 2002 [cited September 2003]. Available at http://www.marketresearch.com/map/prod/261606.html.

Porter, M. "New Strategies for Inner-City Economic Development." *Economic Development Quarterly* 11, no. 1 (1997): 11–27.

Portes, A., and R. L. Bach. *The Latin Journey.* Berkeley: University of California Press, 1985.

Portes, A. and L. Jensen. "What's an Ethnic Enclave?" *American Sociological Review* 52 (1987): 768–971.

Primm, J. N. *Lion of the Valley: St. Louis, Missouri.* Boulder, Colo.: Pruett Publishing Co., 1981.

Reinert, P. C., and P. Shore. *Seasons of Change.* St. Louis: University of Saint Louis Press, 1996.

Sanders, J. M., and V. Nee. "Limits of Ethnic Solidarity in the Enclave Economy." *American Sociological Review* 52 (1987): 745–67.

Schwalbert, C. "Making Good in Retailing." *The Crisis* 98, no. 5 (1991): 15, 16, 32.

Silverman, R. M. *Doing Business in Minority Markets.* New York: Garland Publishing Inc., 2000.

Smith, JoAnn Adams. *Selected Neighbors and Neighborhoods of North St. Louis and Selected Related Events.* [St. Louis]: Friends of Vaughn Cultural Center, 1988.

Spear, A. *Black Chicago.* Chicago: University of Chicago Press, 1967.

St. Louis 2004. *Sustainable Neighborhoods.* 2002 [cited December 2002]. Available at http://www.stlouis2004.org/html/ap_neighborhoods.html.

Stoecker, R. "The CDC Model of Urban Redevelopment: A Critique and Alternative." *Journal of Urban Affairs* 19 (1997): 1–22.

Sturdivant, F. D. *The Ghetto Marketplace.* New York: Free Press, 1969.

Tabb, W. *The Political Economy of the Black Ghetto.* New York: W. W. Norton and Company, Inc., 1970.

Teitz, M. "Neighborhood Economics: Local Communities and Regional Markets." *Economic Development Quarterly* 3, no. 2 (1989): 111–22.

U.S. Bureau of the Census. *Economic Census.* Survey of Minority-Owned Business Entrepreneurs, Black. Washington, D.C.: U.S. Government Printing Office, 1977, 1982, 1987, 1992, 1997.

Vashon/JeffVanderLou Initiative. *Subcommittee Report: Plan for Action.* St. Louis: Danforth Foundation, 2001.

Wilson, K. L., and W. A. Martin. "Ethnic Enclaves: A Comparison of the Cuban and Black Economies in Miami." *American Journal of Sociology* 88 (1982): 135–60.

Wilson, K. L., and A. Portes. "Immigrant Enclaves: An Analysis of the Labor Market Experiences of Cubans in Miami." *American Journal of Sociology* 86 (1980): 305–19.

Wright, J. A., Sr. *Discovering African American St. Louis: A Guide to Historic Sites.* St. Louis: Missouri Historical Society Press, 2002.

___. *Kinloch: Missouri's First Black City.* Chicago: Arcadia, 2000.

Zhou, M., and J. Logan. "Returns to Human Capital in Ethnic Enclaves: New York City's Chinatown." *American Sociological Review* 54 (October 1989): 807–20.

Chapter 7
The St. Louis Transportation Transformation

Mark Tranel
University of Missouri–St. Louis

> Before 1843 St. Louis walked. Beginning
> with November 1843, St. Louis rode.
> —Forrest A. Swyers

What a ride it has been! Over the course of 160 years what St. Louisans rode in, who rode, and where they rode has transformed the very essence of what St. Louis is. While St. Louis's geographic advantage puts it at the national crossroads of inter-metropolitan air, river, and road transportation systems (Missouri State Highway Department 1947), the intra-metropolitan transportation system is at the intersection of technology, demographics, and public policy.

The St. Louis area experienced dramatic physical change over the last century and a half. For nearly one hundred years St. Louis grew in population, largely in the central city, conveyed by an evolving multi-modal transportation system. Then from 1960 to 2000 St. Louis grew in area, stagnated in population, and rebuilt itself primarily for an automobile transportation system.

These changes occurred in a policy context of federal, state, and local design. Federal policy initially was not a factor in urban transportation, as the City of St. Louis controlled franchises for the operation of transit systems. When it entered in the 1930s, the federal government gave exclusive support to the automobile and the building of an infrastructure to provide for its use. Then efforts were made to finance rehabilitation of existing systems in addition to relentless expansion of new peripheral roadways. In the last decade two federal initiatives created a pot of money and left determination of its application to state and metropolitan authorities. Although guidelines and goals were established, there was no federal enforcement.

This chapter details the developments in technology, demography, and public policy in the transformation of the St. Louis transportation system.

The three elements are intertwined. Any discussion of the current state of transportation in metropolitan St. Louis must be based on an understanding of the interaction among these three aspects of urban transportation. The transportation dynamics addressed in this chapter are limited to means for personal movement; commercial transportation is not addressed.

Changes in Transportation Technology

St. Louis is a classic illustration of the national eras of transportation technology growth and transport development (Muller 1995). In the mid-nineteenth century transportation technology beyond walking started with many people being moved by one horse. Ironically, today more often than not one person is being moved by the power equivalent of about two hundred horses. Vehicular transportation in St. Louis began November 2, 1843. A private entrepreneur initiated omnibus service (Swyers n.d.). The omnibus was an open-air buckboard wagon with bench seating for about 12 people. By 1858 there were 145 wagons, many of them double-decker, moved by 681 horses on 11.5 route miles carrying an average of 14,000 passengers a day (Swyers n.d.).

One year later the City of St. Louis granted seven franchises for the construction and operation of street railroads. Street railroads initially were horse-drawn cars that rode on rails rather than the unimproved street surface. On July 4, 1859, the first street railroad began operation. By 1867 there were 114 cars in service that annually carried a total of 1.3 million passengers (Young 1988). As a technology, the animal-powered street railroads were excessively costly. Horses were expensive to buy, required large stable facilities, and could work only four hours a day, necessitating a high ratio of horses to each vehicle. Horse car line operators could not afford to add capacity to keep up with the rising demand (Smerk 1965). There was a brief interlude with cable-drawn cars beginning in 1887, but the cable system proved to be too costly and mechanically unreliable.

On February 6, 1888, a third transportation transformation started: the first electric streetcar went into service. In less than a decade there were no horse-drawn cars in service except the floats of the Veiled Prophet parade, which were horse-drawn until the mid-twentieth century. Within twenty years of the first electric streetcar there would be 1,400 cars riding on over 450 miles of track (350 miles in the City of St. Louis and 100 miles in St. Louis County). At their peak, streetcars collected 300 million passenger fares a year (Young 1988).

One reason for the rapid development of new transportation technology was the explosive growth in the St. Louis population. Between the introduction of the street railroad in 1859 and the electric streetcar in 1888, the population of St. Louis increased from just over 160,000 residents to 452,000. While the railed horse cars were an improvement over the omnibus, they were too small, too slow, and too expensive to service the needs of a population approaching a half million. As technology advanced, so did the reach of the transportation system. In 1875 a narrow-gauge steam railway went into service; by late fall of 1879 it was providing service to Florissant. The nascent development of the suburbs had already begun (Young 1988).

The most revolutionary change in transportation technology came at the end of the nineteenth century, starting mostly as a hobby. J. D. Perry Lewis built the first "horseless carriage" in St. Louis in 1893. It was a two-person buggy with a battery powered electric motor. Lewis received the first St. Louis automobile license (no. 1) in 1902. By 1908 there were 1,900 licensed automobiles in St. Louis. St. Louis entered the era of the manufactured automobile Thanksgiving Day 1898 with the incorporation of the St. Louis Motor Carriage Company. It delivered its first two twin-cylinder gasoline motorcars in 1899. Within a decade there were nine automobile plants in St. Louis, turning out 2,400 cars in 1910 (St. Louis Society of Automobile Pioneers 1930).

Gasoline-powered vehicle technology initially was applied to personal vehicles. Before long, however, engines powerful enough for mass transit vehicles were being built. The first prototype of a bus built in St. Louis was an eight-passenger electric-powered vehicle. Its builders, the brothers Ashley and Semple S. Scott, operated it as the first bus line in St. Louis during the streetcar strike that same year, 1898 (Swyers n.d.).

Within twenty years, the internal combustion engine would challenge streetcars. In 1922, People's Motor Bus Company was given permission to operate on the same routes as streetcars. A year later streetcar ridership was down 13.5 million (Young 1988). As was the case with the previous two transportation technologies, multiple private companies operated bus services. There was plenty of business for all of them. The City's population continued to grow, peaking at 856,000 in 1950.

While buses are still the dominant form of mass transportation in St. Louis, private ownership ended in 1963 when the Bi-State Development Agency purchased the fifteen private transit companies then supplying service. Bus transportation experienced a precipitous decline as the shape of the metropolitan area began to change. More households were living in single-family housing units on larger lots built in serpentine or cul-de-sac developments. Bus routes no longer ran close to such homes, creating an unacceptably long walk to a bus stop. And as employment locations spread out, buses no longer conveniently served the workers' destinations. In 1957 the bus transit system carried approximately 115 million passengers. Within fifteen years less than half that number of passengers would be riding on the bus (McKenna and Veatch 1975). As ridership declined, the cost per passenger increased five-fold, making revenue operations unsustainable (Antonio 1983).

Local public funding has kept transit alive since 1973. Bi-State Transit, known as Metro beginning in 2003, announced in April 1973 it would shut down bus service in ninety days unless it received a subsidy. The Missouri legislature responded by authorizing the governing bodies to impose a sales tax for public mass transit system operations. In June the St. Louis Board of Aldermen and St. Louis County Council each approved a half-cent transportation sales tax that went into effect July 1, 1973. Initially the tax annually provided Bi-State with about $12 million in operating funds. The 2002 National Transportation Database recorded that the sales tax provided 65 percent of the operating funds for Bi-State, over $100 million. Public support of transit was increased in 1994 with an additional sales tax to support operation of a light rail system in St. Louis City and County. The sustainability of mass transit service in St. Louis is a key example of the nexus of technology, demography, and public policy.

Demography

Transportation technology experienced a multiphase evolution between 1850 and 1950, in part driven by the needs of a growing population. After 1950, transportation technology stabilized with the hegemony of the automobile. Just as transportation technology was stabilizing, the population growth of metropolitan St. Louis practically ground to a halt, but the characteristics of users of the automobile began a cycle of evolution. This affected who was traveling where.

As Table 1 shows, while the change in total population has languished since 1960, the growth in both the number of households and the number of workers has been persistent.

Table 1 also documents:

In 1960, 34 percent of the metropolitan population lived in the City of St. Louis, and 22 percent of workers traveled to work by public transportation or other means. By 2000, 13 percent of the population lived in the City and 4 percent of workers traveled by public transportation or alternatives.

All alternative transportation modes dwindled over this forty-year period: carpooling, public transportation, and walking/biking.

There were almost a half-million more workers in 2000 in St. Louis than there were in 1960, an increase of 65 percent. The census did not begin distinguishing among workers who drove alone and those who carpooled until 1980. In 1980 about two-thirds of St. Louis workers traveling in a car, truck, or van drove alone. By 2000 that had increased to over 90 percent. The increase in the number of workers driving alone combined with the overall increase in the number of workers resulted in an increase of almost 350,000 single-passenger vehicles on metropolitan St. Louis roads in the twenty years between 1980 and 2000.

At the same time there has been an increasing number of workers on the road and a disproportionate increase in the number of vehicles, the mean travel time to work has increased only marginally, from 23 minutes in 1980 to 25.5 minutes in 2000.

Table 1. Metropolitan St. Louis Demographic Trends, 1960–2000

	1960	1970	1980	1990	2000
MSA population	2,060,103	2,363,017	2,335,460	2,444,099	2,603,607
MSA population in central city	750,026	622,236	452,801	396,685	348,189
MSA population in suburbs	1,310,077	1,740,781	1,882,659	2,047,414	2,255,418
MSA households	624,886	737,325	837,997	923,639	1,013,341
Commuting to Work (MSA)					
Workers 16 years and over	751,618	883,200	1,004,321	1,144,336	1,238,964
Car, truck, or van—drove alone	dnc*	dnc*	676,043	912,509	1,023,647
			(67%)	(80%)	(83%)
Car, truck, or van—carpooled	dnc*	dnc*	214,514	137,883	122,219
			(21%)	(12%)	(10%)
Car, truck, or van	507,542	737,324	890,557	1,050,392	1,145,866
	(68%)	(84%)	(89%)	(92%)	(93%)
Public transportation, including taxi	119,858	71,646	57,483	33,994	29,915
	(16%)	(8%)	(6%)	(3%)	(2%)
Walk or bicycle	48,612	42,459	33,785	25,981	20,061
	(7%)	(5%)	(3%)	(2%)	(2%)
Mean Travel Time to Work (Minutes)	dnc*	dnc*	23	23.3	25.5

*Data not collected.
Source: U.S. Census Bureau; MIDAS.

Thus, within a fairly stable overall population base there was a dramatic increase in the number of households, expanding the number of points of origin in the transportation system. These changes appreciably augmented the demand for automobile-based transportation infrastructure. Drivers in early twenty-first century metropolitan St. Louis take 7 million trips a day, which was up by 40 percent since 1990. It has been projected that trip-making will grow another 20 percent to 8.3 million by the year 2015, with daily vehicle-miles traveled rising from 48 million to 67 million (East-West Gateway Coordinating Council 2002).

Why so many trips? In addition to the increases in households and workers, the development pattern that has evolved in the past fifty years makes multiple daily trips a necessity. Most of the St. Louis area consists of spatially separated, highly specialized land uses. The single-family, owner-occupied housing that is the majority of the housing built since 1950 was developed in subdivisions, isolated from banks, drug stores, grocery stores, hospitals, libraries, and schools. For households to obtain the goods and services they need, household members must drive from location to location to location. For households with children, the increased participation of women in the work force has meant two trips each workday to a daycare center. Most urban travel occurs as a byproduct of trying to accomplish some other (nontravel) activity such as work, shopping, or mailing a letter (Muller 1995).

While St. Louis has hardly grown in population, all this travel has redefined the St. Louis area. In 1950, the Census Bureau identified four counties and the City of St. Louis as the St. Louis MSA (Figure 1). Over the last half of the twentieth century eight more counties were added, as households used the interstate highways as arteries to move from the central city and then the inner suburbs farther into undeveloped land on the periphery (Figure 2). As a result of the continued expansion documented in the 2000 Census the metropolitan St. Louis area expanded by three more counties to a total of fifteen counties (OSEDA 2003). The Office of Management and Budget has established commuting patterns as the means for defining metropolitan areas. Based on this definition, there are sufficient numbers of residents of Bond and Calhoun Counties in Illinois and Washington County in Missouri who travel to places of employment within the St. Louis area to be reclassified as metropolitan counties.

The demographic-driven transportation evolution in St. Louis created a transportation planning anomaly. East-West Gateway Coordinating Council, the area's metropolitan planning organization, was organized in 1965, based on a study defining the St. Louis metropolitan area as seven counties (Voorhees 1965). The metropolitan area has grown in the last few decades to the extent that almost half of its land mass is outside the jurisdiction of the "metropolitan" transportation planning organization.

One of the effects of this growth is a wide range of commuting times masked by metropolitan average data. Table 1 showed that mean travel time to work had increased by only 2.5 minutes over twenty years. Table 2 provides evidence that, with so many points of origin and destinations spreading over such a large geography, there is significant variation in travel time within different communities in the St. Louis metropolitan area. The sharpest contrast is between Webster Groves and Wildwood. The mean travel time to work for Webster Groves residents is 40 percent (twelve minutes) less than those in Wildwood. More than half (52.7 percent) of Wildwood workers spend over thirty minutes traveling to work, compared to 16 percent of Webster Groves workers. The shifting pattern of both people and jobs is illustrated in the data on workers who travel more than thirty minutes to work. The percentage of St. Louis City workers who travel more than thirty minutes to work (31.2) is closer to the percentage for the Illinois cities in the sample (34.6) than it is to the inner suburban cities (Maryland Heights, University City, and Webster Groves) in St. Louis County (20.4).

Figure 1. Map of the St. Louis Metropolitan Area, 1950

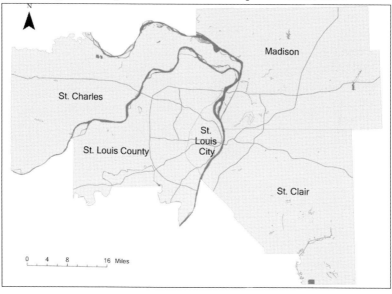

Another aspect of local travel revealed in the travel-to-work data from the census is a notable difference between white and African American workers in the percentage that drives alone to work. While the percentage of white workers who drive alone is fairly consistent—in the mid-80s—in a number of communities the percentage of African Americans who drive alone is notably less: 25 percent lower in Lake St. Louis, 17 percent lower in Webster Groves and the City of St. Louis, 16 percent lower in Belleville and Edwardsville, 11 percent lower in Alton and Collinsville. While there is no extant research on commuting patterns of African Americans in St. Louis, national research indicates that both preference for and reliance on mass transit compared to single-occupancy vehicles contributes to lower rates of African Americans driving alone (Krovi and Barnes 2000).

Figure 2. Map of the St. Louis Metropolitan Area, 2000

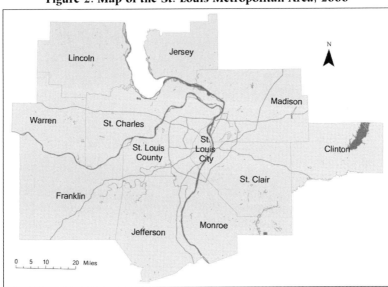

A Few More People, but a Lot More Congestion

St. Louis generally is regarded favorably for its comparatively low housing costs; however, households are not necessarily better off because of affordable housing. The unmentioned penalty is excessive transportation cost. Data for 1998 verify that St. Louis residents paid almost $600 more a year for transportation than for housing. As shown in Table 3, St. Louis is one of a small number of metropolitan areas that spends more on transportation than on shelter. The average household in St. Louis traveled over 25,000 miles by car, spending almost $6,500 on transportation. That is not only a higher percentage of household income but also a larger dollar cost than the average household in Boston, Chicago, or San Diego spends on transportation.

An explanation for the excessive transportation costs in St. Louis is broadcast on area radio and television stations. It is a feature of contemporary life in large American metropolitan areas for the electronic media to carry live reports of traffic congestion on major highways every weekday in the morning and in the evening. Traffic reports are a standard feature on St. Louis stations. If St. Louis grew in geography but not in population, how could there be so many people on the same roads at the same time?

Table 2. Travel Time to Work

City	Mean	>30 Minutes	>45 Minutes	Drive Alone
				Pct. of Workers White/Black
St. Louis	25.1	31.2	11.8	76.5/59.4
St. Louis County				
Florissant	24	34.9	8.8	88.5/79.5
Maryland Heights	21	24.9	6.8	90.2/80.4
University City	20.5	20.3	4.7	78.2/76.1
Webster Groves	18.8	16	3.5	85.3/67.5
Wildwood	30	52.7	21.2	87.7/85.7
St. Charles County				
Lake St. Louis	28.5	46.3	16.8	85.8/60.5
O'Fallon	28.1	48.6	19.1	85.7/88.6
St. Peters	25.8	41.4	13.5	88.6/91.2
Jefferson County				
Arnold	26.2	44.4	15	87.0/0
Illinois				
Alton	23	33.7	16.2	83.4/71.9
Belleville	23.7	32.5	14.5	84.2/67.8
Collinsville	24.5	39.7	12.7	86.2/74.5
Edwardsville	24.3	38.9	15.6	85.5/69.0
Godfrey	25	33.3	19.1	87.6/84.7
O'Fallon	22.8	29.4	12.9	87.1/81.7

Source: U.S. Census Bureau.

As shown in Table 4 the number of travelers on the road at peak driving times increased by 9 percent and the urban area of metropolitan St. Louis increased by 74 percent. Over the course of the almost two decades covered by this data, the physical capacity of the highway system (lane miles) increased by 50 percent and the capacity of the main connector streets by 34 percent. What causes the media to have daily reports of traffic congestion is that daily vehicle-miles of travel on highways increased by 93 percent. Use of the roadway system outpaced its expansion.

The Texas Transportation Institute (TTI) prepares an annual report on metropolitan-area congestion. The report includes various measures of the extra time drivers spend on the road due to congestion and how much that congestion costs. Table 5 records the development of traffic congestion on highways and principal arterial streets in St. Louis and two groups of comparison regions for 1982 to 2000. TTI uses the percentage of peak period person-miles of travel that are congested to measure what people experience as congestion and percentage of lane-miles of roadway that are congested in the peak period to measure how physically crowded roadways are.

Table 3. Comparative Transportation Costs

Metro Area	Annual Household Spending		Percent of Total Household Expenditures	
	Transportation	Shelter	Transportation	Shelter
Boston	$5,788	$9,370	15.2%	24.6%
Chicago	$5,436	$7,695	14.9%	21.1%
Milwaukee	$5,800	$8,114	16%	22.3%
San Diego	$6,319	$10,037	15.8%	25.1%
Cleveland	$6,384	$6,345	17.5%	17.4%
Kansas City	$6,489	$6,036	18.1%	16.8%
Pittsburgh	$6,331	$5,329	17.5%	14.7%
St. Louis	$6,489	$5,911	17.6%	16%

Table 4. Metropolitan St. Louis Area Roadway Data

	1982	1990	1994	2000	Increase
Urban area[1] (sq. mi.)	650	760	940	1,130	74%
Peak road travelers (000)	879	921	935	959	9%
Highway					
Daily vehicle-miles of travel (000)	13,365	17,670	22,460	25,740	93%
Lane-miles	1,190	1,500	1,635	1,780	50%
Principal Arterial Streets					
Daily vehicle-miles of travel (000)	9,000	11,180	12,205	11,040	23%
Lane-miles	1,450	1,720	2,200	1,945	34%

Source: Texas Transportation Institute.
[1]The Texas Transportation Institute uses data from the Federal Highway Administration's Highway Performance Monitoring System (HPMS). The HPMS applies the U.S. Bureau of the Census designations of urbanized areas (UZA) from the decennial census.

Table 5. Peak-Period Congestion, 1982–2000

	Person-Miles of Congested Travel					
	Highway			Principal Arterial Street		
	1982	1990	2000	1982	1990	2000
St. Louis	17	25	54	40	46	71
75-area average	30	52	65	37	54	68
Large area average	20	42	62	32	49	65
	Lane-Miles of Congested Roadway					
St. Louis	15	25	55	40	45	65
75-area average	27	43	54	39	50	61
Large area average	21	38	53	35	47	57

Source: Texas Transportation Institute.

The data in Table 5 confirm that the foremost congestion issue in metropolitan St. Louis occurs not on the interstate highways that ribbon the area but instead on the principal arterial roads. In 2000, 71 percent of peak period person-miles of principal arterial street travel were congested compared to 54 percent of highway. The same year, 65 percent of principal arterial lane-miles were congested in the peak period, compared to 55 percent of highway lane-miles. Over time the gap between highways and principal arterial streets has narrowed by about 50 percent, but arterial congestion continues to be more extensive.

Comparing St. Louis to other metropolitan areas, the percentage of congested highway lane-miles nearly reached parity over the eighteen-year period in both the 75-area sample and the large-area sample. In 1982 highway lane-mile congestion was 80 percent greater in the 75-area sample and 40 percent greater in the large-area sample than in St. Louis. By 2000, highway lane-mile congestion in St. Louis was about 2 percent greater than the 75-area sample and 4 percent greater than the large-area group. Congestion on principal arterial streets has always been greater in St. Louis than in either sample of metropolitan areas, although the gap widened comparing St. Louis to the 75-area sample. The data also show that traffic congestion in St. Louis has accelerated in recent years. As shown in Figure 3, highway and arterial congestion increased at over twice the rate between 1990 and 2000 that it did between 1982 and 1990.

What these measures of person-miles and lane-miles of congestion indicate is that more people are experiencing added congestion and that there are more miles of crowded roads. Since the population of metropolitan St. Louis has shifted more than it has grown, this is an indication of how much faster the development of residential and commercial destinations has occurred than the road building in the new areas.

Figure 3. Peak Period Congestion

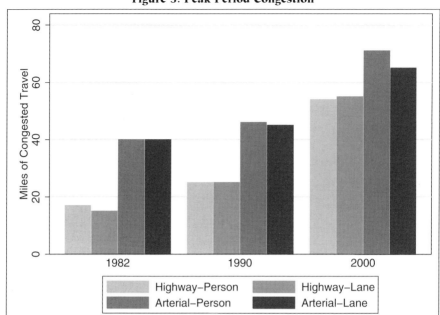

While congestion overall has increased in St. Louis, peak travel congestion continues to be the most severe. As detailed in Table 6, peak period travel in congestion over the eighteen-year period has stayed fairly consistently about twice the level of all daily travel in congestion. Daily congestion was at 13 percent in 1982, increasing to 29 percent in 2000. Peak congestion in 1982 was at 26 percent, increasing to 59 percent by 2000. Compared to its peers in the TTI large-area sample, daily congestion in St. Louis increased by 123 percent while the large-area sample rose by 146 percent. St. Louis had slightly higher peak congestion than the large-area group in 1982, but St. Louis only increased by 127 percent while the large-area sample increased by 152 percent as of 2000.

The rate of peak period congestion in metropolitan St. Louis is accelerating. Figure 4 illustrates the increase in peak congestion between 1990 and 2000 at almost three times the increase between 1982 and 1990. The rate of increase in daily congestion a little more than doubled comparing the same time periods. The steepest increase was the increase in peak travel during 1990 to 2000.

The fact that more single-passenger automobiles are spending more time going to farther destinations has a cost consequence for metropolitan St. Louis. St. Louis does not have the highest congestion costs in the nation, but it has higher congestion costs than similarly sized metropolitan areas. For example, the annual cost of congestion in St. Louis is one and one-half times the cost in Cleveland and over twice the cost in Kansas City and Pittsburgh (Schrank and Lomax 2003).

Table 6. Congested Travel, Daily v. Peak

Daily	1982	1990	2000
St. Louis	13	17	29
75-area average	17	26	33
Large area average	13	23	32
Peak	1982	1990	2000
St. Louis	26	33	59
75-area average	33	53	66
Large area average	25	45	63
Source: Texas Transportation Institute.			

Table 7 presents data that calculate the cost of congestion based on the value of the extra time and fuel that is consumed during congested travel. For the year 2000, the estimated total cost of congestion in metropolitan St. Louis was $805 million. This is about 11 percent less than the average total cost in all of the metropolitan areas examined by TTI, but it is about 14 percent greater than the average for comparably sized metropolitan areas. The additional congestion cost is just over $800 for every rush-hour driver, which is about 27 percent less than all the metropolitan areas in the TTI sample and about 8 percent less than the comparable size metros. The cost comes to almost $400 per person in metropolitan St. Louis, about 22 percent less than all TTI metros, and about 7 percent less than the comparable size group.

Public Policy

Did St. Louisans become stuck in traffic because they abandoned other forms of transportation over a "love affair with the automobile," or were they responding logically to direction and incentives of public policy? (Vuchic 1999). As the evidence above documents, St. Louisans readily embraced the technologies of mass transportation introduced over the last half of the nineteenth century. Public policy was one factor that did play a role in guiding St. Louis residents into the single-passenger automobile. The City of St. Louis naïvely legislated crippling rules that bankrupted streetcar operations; the State of Missouri established a policy for rural areas that had unintended consequences in St. Louis; and the federal government made a similar mistake, compounding it with a huge amount of money.

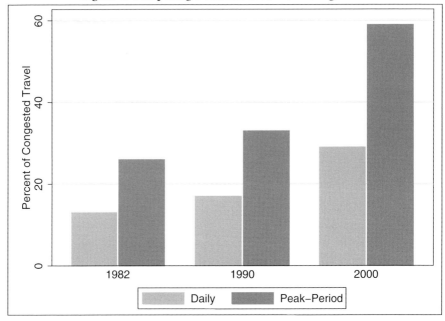

Figure 4. **Comparing Peak and Non-Peak Congestion**

Table 7. **Cost of Congestion, 2000**

	Annual Cost Due to Congestion ($ millions)				Per Peak Road Traveler		Per Person	
	Delay	Fuel	Total	Rank	$	Rank	$	Rank
St. Louis	710	95	805	22	840	28	395	25
75-area average	780	120	900		1,160		505	
Large area average	615	90	705		915		425	
Source: Texas Transportation Institute.								

Local

Through the era of the street railroad, oversight of urban transportation facilities was limited to municipal government. The City of St. Louis granted franchises that regulated the ownership of transportation companies, the location of lines, and the rates charged for fares, and which established a tax on operating revenues. At the same time that the automobile was becoming a more affordable individual expense, the capital cost of maintaining a streetcar system was becoming crippling. The most severe problem was the impact of World War I on the cost of raw materials, especially copper, steel, and electrical products. Automobile production faced the same cost problems, but what gave the automobile the edge was a forty-year-old cap on fares maintained by the City of St. Louis (Young 1988). In addition, the tax on streetcar operations was approximately 10 percent of gross operating revenue. That the taxation of street railways was excessive was noted in a report to the Board of Aldermen by the Transportation Survey Commission it appointed to examine alternatives for the city to respond to the lack of an effective transportation system. The report compared the financial profile of St. Louis railways to Detroit, which had taken public ownership of its system. It found that with 15 percent less revenue than the Detroit railways system, the St. Louis operators were paying two and one-half times as much in taxes. Making the finances of streetcar operations worse, the city required free transit to fire and police personnel. City policies regulating streetcars were financial policies, not transportation policies.

State

The Missouri state government had no direct role in urban transportation until the advent of automobile technology. Even then, the state initially limited its activity to regulation, including the registration of motor vehicles and setting standards for road construction by the counties. In Missouri, road building was the exclusive responsibility of county governments until 1907. The growing need for a system of roads prompted the General Assembly to provide for the appointment of a highway engineer in each county (Missouri State Highway Commission 1922). Federal aid for road construction started benignly in 1916 by empowering the Secretary of Agriculture to provide the states money for construction of "any public road over which the United States mails now are or may hereafter be transported, excluding every street and road in a place having a population, as shown by the latest available Federal census, of 2,500 or more…" In 1917 the Missouri General Assembly passed the Hawes State Road Law adopting the provisions of the federal act (Missouri State Highway Commission 1922).

Missouri expanded its responsibilities after voter approval of a $60 million bond issue in November 1920. To administer the bond funds, the legislature enacted the Centennial Road Law in 1921. It provided for a State Highway Commission empowered to develop a state highway system of 1,500 miles of primary roads and 6,000 miles of secondary roads.

The primary roads were to connect population centers of more than 2,500. This was the first step toward road construction for urban populations. Previously, expenditures for road construction served rural farm-to-market or postal delivery needs.

For the next two decades the state invested in roads that connected cities and towns, but it did not pay for construction or maintenance within city boundaries. That changed at the end of World War II. A constitutional amendment in 1945 authorized expenditure of state revenue for construction in cities "when necessary to continue into and through such city or town."

Before long the state was not just contemplating highway construction in cities, but also advocating highways for an improved quality of life. Consider the following quote from the Missouri State Highway Department written about a decade before the large-scale development of the auto-dependent suburbs.

> Picture yourself on a highway over which it is possible to drive at good speed without encountering the delays and congestion so common today, especially in urban areas; or visualize the possibility of being able to reside in a lovely suburban locality and travel daily to your place of employment in the business district of some large city, without being delayed by congested city streets or interference from opposing or cross traffic. No, this is not an idle dream, but very practical, as has been demonstrated by experience with multiple-lane rural expressways, but up to recent years sufficient thought and consideration have not been given to extending this type of facility into urban areas (Missouri State Highway Department 1947).

Urban dwellers may have responded, but the vision for advancing the application of automobile technology clearly started with the state.

Federal

While the policies of the City of St. Louis may have crippled streetcars and the State of Missouri may have adopted the role of salesman, federal policy had the most pervasive effect on making the automobile the dominant form of urban transportation. The federal government had established a role in investing in transportation systems, including the National Road starting in 1806 and the transcontinental railroad in the 1860s.

By the 1950s there were a number of urban transportation technologies that could have been developed into an integrated, multi-modal system: pedestrian, bus, rail, and automobile (Vuchic 1999). Federal policy instead committed to the development of an automobile-based system (Foster

1981). The design for the interstate highway system was produced by the Bureau of Public Roads as directed by Congress in the Federal-Aid Highway Act of 1938. The resulting study found that a national highway system could not be self-supporting as toll roads. The bureau's report, Toll Roads and Free Roads, established the design concepts for urban highway construction and the routes for the interstate system (Weingroff 1996). The Federal-Aid Highway Act of 1944 authorized construction of the "National System of Interstate Highways" but provided no funding. The 1952 Act authorized $25 million available to the states on an equal share-matching basis. The 1954 Act increased the authorization to $175 million and the federal commitment to provide 60 percent of construction costs (Weingroff 1996).

The Federal-Aid Highway Act of 1956 committed the nation to construction of the interstate system. The Act authorized $27 billion over the next thirteen fiscal years. Over half the available funding was to be spent on the urban portion of the 41,000-mile system (Meyer and Gómez-Ibáñez 1981). The Act also established the Highway Trust Fund. It authorized an increase in the fuel tax, an excise tax on tires, and weight taxes collected on commercial vehicles. These revenues were credited to the Highway Trust Fund, which could only be used for highway construction; it raised the federal share of new highway construction to 90 percent.

As it turned out, the highway system took about forty more years and 22 percent more than the original estimate of $231 billion to complete (Boarnet and Haughwout 2000). More time and money were not, however, the only unintended consequences. As articulated by the Missouri Highway Department, the vision for the highway system was urban travel "without encountering the delays and congestion so common today." The investment in interstate highways only made congestion worse. It fostered a decentralized lifestyle, causing households to become automobile dependent in a physical environment where housing and employment are separated by long distances. An additional miscalculation was the cost of maintaining the system. Even as the system was being completed, its developed roadway was wearing out. There were not enough dollars in the Trust Fund to attempt to expand the system to relieve congestion and to maintain the built system (Humphrey 1995).

Thirty-five years after the federal government established a plan and capital financing for the interstate highway system, including a major commitment to highways in urban areas, it adopted, at least nominally, a new policy approach. The Intermodal Surface Transportation Efficiency Act (ISTEA) of 1991 and then the Transportation Equity Act for the 21st

Century (TEA-21) of 1998 gave states and local governments the resources and the authority to determine their own priorities for transportation investment, considering new construction and maintenance needs as well as the opportunity to invest in alternatives to an automobile-based transportation system (Katz, Puentes, and Bernstein 2003).

The Future

The resources and authority available at the local level are considerable. The East-West Gateway Coordinating Council estimates $14.6 billion (80 percent federal funds) in metropolitan St. Louis transportation system investment through the year 2025 (East-West Gateway Coordinating Council 2002). Legacy 2025, East-West Gateway's transportation plan for the next twenty years of investment in the portion of metropolitan St. Louis for which it is responsible, identifies a number of trends that will influence that investment. Several relate to demography and development.

First, the plan projects the metropolitan St. Louis population to grow by 9 percent, but most of the net increase will be in areas of new development in Franklin, Jefferson, Monroe, and St. Charles Counties. The demand for new or expanded transportation facilities would thus continue to come from the need to serve more area than more people. Second, population diversity as discussed in the plan refers primarily to the aging of the metropolitan population. Not only will there be more senior citizens, but also more will be living into their eighties and nineties. Urban transportation previously has not been designed to meet the needs of a large, active older population. The other aspect of population diversity identified in the plan that will cause demand for nontraditional transportation system design is an increasing number of active persons with disabilities. The requirements of the Americans with Disabilities Act have made many physical aspects of the transportation system accessible to persons with disabilities. A system that operationally meets their needs is, however, an additional challenge. Finally, the plan acknowledges that prior to ISTEA, equity in transportation planning in metropolitan St. Louis referred to equitable distribution of resources among the political jurisdictions served by East-West Gateway. As more responsibility for transportation planning devolved to the local level through ISTEA and TEA-21, equity evolved to incorporate consideration of the income, ethnicity and race, ability and disability, gender, and age of people using the transportation system.

Incorporating these trends into the transportation system for the future of St. Louis requires new goals and a change in the historical allocation of transportation resources. Effectively setting these goals and making these changes can only be done at the metropolitan level. Initially the federal government had no role in urban transportation. Starting in the mid-twentieth century, and for the next forty years, the federal government had the dominant role. In its redirection of planning to the state and local level, federal policy acknowledged that local transportation needs are unique for each region.

The three aspects of urban transportation discussed in this chapter, technology, demography, and public policy, will not influence St. Louis as much in the future as they have in the past. For the foreseeable future there will not be a major evolution in transportation technology (Muller 1995). While the propulsion system may be adapted, the private vehicle will remain the most important form of urban transportation. Other modes of transportation may receive more support than they have in the past, but they are all existing technologies. There is a robust vision for developing several new light-rail service lines in St. Louis City and County and two new lines in Illinois, but the twenty-year projection is based on the same type of service available today.

In the first half of the twentieth century, St. Louis got bigger because it grew in population. In the second half of the twentieth century, St. Louis got bigger because it grew in geography. In the twenty-first century, St. Louis will experience only modest gains in both population and physical size. There should be no surprises in the rate of household formation. All the heads of households making decisions regarding residential location for the next twenty years have already been born. Their demand for housing can readily be incorporated into transportation planning. Immigration has not been a significant factor in metropolitan St. Louis, so demographers can accurately project future population change based on the excess of births over deaths in the region. And the age cohorts that will determine birth and death rates for the next twenty years are established. The only unknown population variable is intra-urban migration. Whether the pace of population movement will be sustained as development reaches a fifty- and sixty-mile radius from the central city remains to be seen.

It is public policy that will have the most influence on the shape of things to come. Federal policy has created the opportunity for develop-ment of a multi-modal transportation system that both is more equitable and addresses maintenance needs as well as expansion of the existing roadways. It is the challenge of local public policy, at both the state and metropolitan levels, to realize the benefits of this opportunity. The previous record is one of major unintended consequences. The Legacy 2025 plan identifies the issues that should be addressed in the future development of transportation in metropolitan St. Louis. Those issues will be dealt with in a series of short-term steps as that future unfolds.

References

Antonio, James F. *Special Review of the Bi-State Development Agency of the Missouri-Illinois Metropolitan District.* Jefferson City, Mo.: Office of the State Auditor, 1983.

Boarnet, Marlon G., and Andrew F. Haughwout. *Do Highways Matter? Evidence and Policy Implications of Highways' Influence on Metropolitan Development.* Washington, D.C.: The Brookings Institution Center on Urban and Metropolitan Policy, 2000.

East-West Gateway Coordinating Council. *Legacy 2025: The Transportation Plan for the Gateway Region.* St. Louis: East-West Gateway Coordinating Council, 2002.

Foster, Mark S. *From Streetcar to Superhighway: American City Planners and Urban Transportation, 1900–1940.* Philadelphia: Temple University Press, 1981.

Humphrey, Thomas F. *Consideration of the 15 Factors in the Metropolitan Planning Process: A Synthesis of Highway Practice.* Washington, D.C.: National Academy Press, 1995.

Katz, Bruce, Robert Puentes, and Scott Bernstein. *TEA-21 Reauthorization: Getting Transportation Right for Metropolitan America.* Washington, D.C.: The Brookings Institution, 2003.

Krovi, Ravindra, and Claude Barnes. "Work-Related Travel Patterns of People of Color." In *Travel Patterns of People of Color.* Washington, D.C.: U.S. Department of Transportation, 2000.

McKenna, Joseph P., and James F. Veatch. *Urban Travel in St. Louis.* St. Louis: University of Missouri Center of Community and Metropolitan Studies, 1975.

Meyer, John R., and José A. Gómez-Ibáñez. *Autos, Transit, and Cities.* Cambridge, Mass.: Harvard University Press, 1981.

Meyer, Michael D., and Eric J. Miller. *Urban Transportation Planning.* New York: McGraw-Hill Book Company, 1984.

Missouri State Highway Commission. *Third Biennial Report of the Missouri State Highway Commission.* Jefferson City, Mo.: Author, 1922.

Missouri State Highway Department. *A Traffic Survey of St. Louis Metropolitan Area.* Jefferson City, Mo.: Author, 1947.

Muller, Peter O. "Transportation and Urban Form: Stages in the Spatial Evolution of the American Metropolis." In *The Geography of Urban Transportation,* edited by Susan Hanson. New York: Guilford Press, 1995.

Office of Social and Economic Data Analysis. *Metropolitan Statistical Areas as of June 2003* [online]. OSEDA, http://www.oseda.missouri.edu/2000_census/new_metroareas_2000html (accessed June 2003).

Schrank, David, and Tim Lomax. *The 2002 Urban Mobility Report.* College Station: The Texas A&M University System, 2002. Available at http://tti.tamu.edu/product/catalog/reports/mobility_report_2002.pdf (accessed June 2003).

___. *The 2003 Annual Mobility Report.* College Station, Tex.: Transportation Institute, 2003.

Smerk, George M. *Urban Transportation: The Federal Role.* Bloomington: Indiana University Press, 1965.

St. Louis Society of Automobile Pioneers. *A History of Automobiles in St. Louis and the Part That City Has Taken in the Development of the Automobile.* St. Louis: St. Louis Society of Automobile Pioneers, 1930.

State Highway Board of Missouri. *1918 Annual Report.* Jefferson City, Mo.: Author, 1918.

Swyers, Forrest A. *Street Railways of St. Louis.* St. Louis: [1950?].

Transact. *Driven to Spend.* Transact, 2000. Retrieved from http://transact.org/states/metro.asp?s=missouri (accessed February 5, 2003).

Voorhees, Alan M., and Associates, Inc. *Prospects for a Land Use and Transportation Planning Program for the St. Louis Metropolitan Area.* St. Louis: East-West Gateway Coordinating Committee, 1965.

Vuchic, Vukan R. *Transportation for Livable Cities.* New Brunswick, N.J.: Center for Urban Policy Research, 1999.

Weingroff, Richard F. *Creating the Interstate System* [online]. Public Roads On-Line, Summer 1996. http://www.tfhre.gov/pubrds/summer96/p96su10.htm (accessed March 20, 2003).

Young, Andrew D. *The St. Louis Streetcar Story.* Glendale, Calif.: Interurban Press, 1988.

Chapter 8
Racial Housing Segregation in the St. Louis Area: Past, Present, and Future

John E. Farley
Southern Illinois University at Edwardsville

Overview

This chapter examines long-term trends of racial housing segregation in St. Louis over the past 150 years. Among the questions addressed are:

How do trends and levels of segregation, both in the United States as a whole and in other metropolitan areas, compare to those in St. Louis?

Are there identifiable "break points" in historical trends in segregation in the St. Louis area and nationally?

What factors account for the above patterns? Can they be linked to African American migration patterns into the St. Louis area? Economic competition? Generalized patterns of racial conflict in society?

What current patterns of segregation have resulted from these past trends?

What do past trends and current segregation patterns suggest about possible future trends in racial housing segregation in and around St. Louis?

St. Louis has a long history as one of the most segregated urban areas in the United States. Racial housing segregation in St. Louis rose from the mid-nineteenth century until around 1930 and did not change much for a half century thereafter. Over the past few decades, segregation has been modestly declining. The decline began first in the suburbs, as the area's African American population suburbanized, and followed in the city. The most recent data suggest that this trend has accelerated in the city and in the Illinois part of the metropolitan area, but it appears to have stalled in the Missouri suburbs.

Housing segregation remains a matter of concern for several reasons. First, it is a key mechanism through which racial inequality is maintained and perpetuated, both nationally (Massey and Denton 1993; Feagin 2000) and in the St. Louis area (FOCUS St. Louis 2001). Housing segregation deprives African Americans of the opportunity to amass wealth through homeownership and appreciation in value of what for most households is the most significant economic asset—the home in which one lives (Conley 1999; Oliver and Shapiro 1995; Yinger 1995). This is because segregation both restricts the ability of African Americans to live in the areas in which the opportunity for value appreciation is greatest, and increases the likelihood of steering and white avoidance of African American neighborhoods. Thus the market for the sale of the homes in which most African Americans live is limited.

Additionally, housing segregation perpetuates unequal education, because it is the driving force behind school segregation. If neighborhoods are segregated and there is a system of neighborhood schools, then schools will inevitably be segregated. In many instances, segregated schools are unequal schools: unequal in funding, unequal in what is ex-pected of students, and unequal in access to college preparatory and advanced-placement courses (National Science Foundation 1996; Alexander, Entwisle, and Thompson 1987; Kozol 1991; National Center for Education Statistics 2000). For a time, the impact of housing segregation on school segregation was partially mitigated by programs using busing to desegregate schools, but these programs have been scaled back in many parts of the country, including St. Louis. The consequence is that, nationally, school segregation levels are on the increase again, and the mitigating impact of school desegregation on the effects of housing segregation is decreasing (Orfield 2001; on the effects of desegregation in St. Louis, see Wells and Crain 1997).

Finally, housing segregation significantly perpetuates the gap in employment rates between whites and African Americans. This is because African American neighborhoods, still located disproportionately in the central city, are far from the areas of greatest job growth, typically in the suburbs. A variety of studies has shown that racial housing segregation perpetuates disproportionate unemployment among African Americans (Kain 1968; Farley 1987; Kasarda 1989a, 1989b, 1990; Ihlanfeldt and Sjoquist 1990, 1991, 1998; Ihlanfeldt 1992, 1993; Holtzer and Ihlanfeldt 1996). The impact of this is increased with urban sprawl, as the distance between the central-city neighborhoods where many African Americans live and the outlying areas with the most job growth steadily increases (Brookings Institution 2000). In the St. Louis area, the impact of segregation and job decentralization was illustrated dramatically in the 1980s, when the General Motors plant on Union Boulevard, located in predominantly African American north St. Louis city, closed and a new plant was opened forty miles to the northwest in Wentzville, in predominantly white St. Charles County.

In addition to all of the ways in which it perpetuates economic inequality between whites and African Americans, housing segregation is also problematic because it deprives whites and African Americans the opportunity for the type of ongoing daily contact that is effective in breaking down prejudices, stereotypes, and misunderstandings. Because of segregation, opportunities for close, meaningful interactions between racial groups are severely limited. For example, though many whites claim to have African American friends, far fewer actually name African Americans when asked to name their closest friends. In a 1998 General Social Survey, when asked "Are any of your good friends that you feel close to Black/White?," 42 percent of whites claimed that one or more of their good friends were black. However, when a different method was used, and whites were asked to name their good friends, and afterwards were asked the race of the people they had named, it turned out that only 6 percent had named even one African American (Smith 1999). Surely one reason for this is that so few whites have sizable numbers of African American neighbors. If only one white person in twenty has close friendship contacts with African Americans, it is not surprising that whites would know little about the day-to-day experience of African Americans. A variety of studies has shown that this lack of knowledge leads whites to underestimate the amount of segregation that African Americans experience (Kluegel 1990; Hoschschild 1995; Blauner 1989; Schuman and Krysan 1999; Gallup Organization 1997). When whites underestimate the amount of discrimination that occurs, they become less likely to support actions and initiatives to remedy such discrimination (Kluegel and Smith 1986; Herring et al. 2000; Pride 2000).

The Measurement of Racial Residential Segregation

The Index of Dissimilarity

The index of dissimilarity (D), often referred to simply as the "segregation index," is a statistical index, based on census data, indicating to what extent two population groups are similarly or dissimilarly distributed across neighborhood areas in a city or metropolitan area (Taeuber and Taeuber 1965). Although there are many measures of segregation available to evaluate various aspects and dimensions of segregation (Massey, White, and Phua 1996; Massey and Denton 1988), the index of dissimilarity remains the most widely used and recognized measure of the degree of overall separation between the two groups and will be the main focus of this analysis.

The index of dissimilarity ranges from 0 to 100. The higher it is, the more segregated the two population groups are. "Segregated" means that people in each group live in neighborhoods with other members of their own group, away from members of the other group. Thus, in the case of segregation between whites and African Americans, a city or metropolitan area would be segregated if most of its white residents live in neighborhoods where most or all of their neighbors are white, while most African American residents live in neighborhoods where most or all of their neighbors are African American. In the hypothetical case of an index of 100 (complete segregation), all whites would live in neighborhoods with no African American residents, and all African Americans would live in neighborhoods with no white residents.

At the other end of the scale, an index of 0 would indicate there is no segregation. In this situation, each neighborhood would have the exact same mix as the overall area. For example, the St. Louis metropolitan area in 2000 was about 18 percent African American and 78 percent white. (Among the remaining 4 percent of the population, about 3 percent was of other races, and just over 1 percent reported two or more races).[1] If there were no segregation, every neighborhood in the area would have that same mix—18 percent African American and 78 percent white. In fact, such neighborhoods are unusual, as will be discussed in greater detail below.

In reality, no city or metropolitan area will have an index of either 0 or 100. Thus, metropolitan areas or cities with complete segregation and ones with no segregation represent ideal-type opposites on the continuum from segregated to integrated. In reality, all cities and metropolitan areas fall somewhere between.

---

[1] In 2000, for the first time in recent history, the census allowed individuals to classify themselves as belonging to more than one race. About 1.2 percent of respondents in the St. Louis area did so. The totals for whites and African Americans are based on the numbers of residents who indicated white only or black/African American only on the census form.

Defining the Neighborhood Unit

Notice that, thus far, we have referred to the racial composition of "neighborhoods." A key problem for sociological researchers, and an even bigger problem for historical researchers, is that there are different ways to define "neighborhood," and the definition that is used makes a substantial difference in how high or low the index comes out. The smaller the area, the higher the index, because using smaller areas will do a better job of detecting very localized or fine-grained patterns of segregation that may exist within larger neighborhood areas. For example, if the east side of a city were predominantly African American and the west side predominantly white, a relatively large neighborhood area would still detect the segregation. But what if, within the east side of a city, there were small clusters of blocks in which all of the residents are white, and others in which all of the residents are African American? Since both kinds of clusters would be found within a large neighborhood area, the area might appear to be relatively integrated. Yet, at a more localized level, most residents live on blocks where the residents of their own block and those of nearby blocks are nearly all of the same race as their own.

Previous studies have used a wide variety of geographic definitions of neighborhood. Roughly going from largest to smallest, these definitions of neighborhood include community areas, census tracts, wards, block groups, and blocks. Different neighborhood units have been used in different studies conducted in different time periods, especially pre-1970. This makes consistent comparisons of the level of segregation across time quite difficult.

In addition to this challenge, it is also the case that some studies compute segregation indices for cities, while other studies report segregation indices for metropolitan areas. This is a problem even when studying the time trend in segregation for just one area, such as St. Louis. One reason is that, as official data entities, metropolitan areas did not exist until 1950. Since the designation of metropolitan areas in 1950, it has been possible to compute segregation indices for the entire St. Louis metropolitan area, as well as the major city around which it is centered, St. Louis. Additionally, indices can be computed for each constituent county and for other municipalities within the metropolitan area, providing that such areas have sufficient diversity within their population to make an index meaningful.

Until metropolitan area data became available in 1950, all studies of segregation used data for cities. But in recent years, national studies of segregation have shifted away from analyses of segregation in cities in favor of studies of entire metropolitan areas. This further complicates the difficulty of getting consistent data from census to census.

Data on the Trends of Segregation in the St. Louis Area

Fortunately, for St. Louis City there are long-term data extending back to 1860. However, two census years (1870 and 1880) are missing, and as noted above, a variety of geographic areas has been used to measure segregation over the years. The data that go back the furthest are for wards, which are somewhat larger in area than the more recently available census tracts but compare more closely with tracts than any other geographic area used recently to compute segregation indices. Additionally, for the City of St. Louis, segregation indices have been computed based on block data in each census from 1940 through 2000. For the St. Louis metropolitan area, the data do not go back as far as they do for the City, but there are trend data for the metropolitan area at the tract level since 1960, and at the block level since 1980. Additionally, county by county trend data are available at the tract level since 1970 and at the block level since 1980. We shall explore the data in the following order:

Studies of segregation in St. Louis City, based on tract or ward data which begin in 1860, and are available decennially from 1890 through 1940 (ward data) and from 1940 through 2000 (tract data). The indices for 1860 and 1890 through 1930 are based on ward-level data (reported by Massey and Denton 1993 and by Cutler, Glaeser, and Vigdor 2001), and the indices for 1950 through 2000 are based on tract-level data, reported by Farley (2002, 1993, 1983) and by Glaeser and Vigdor (2001). The authors cited here are in some cases including results of analyses previously published by others.

Studies of segregation in St. Louis City based on block data, which are available on a decennial basis from 1940 through 2000 (reported by Taeuber and Taeuber 1965, and by Farley 2002, 1993).

Studies of segregation in the St. Louis metropolitan area and its constituent counties based on tract and block data. These data begin at the tract level in 1970 and at the block level in 1980, and continue on a decennial basis to 2000.

In addition, we shall compare patterns, trends, and levels of segregation in the St. Louis metropolitan area to national patterns, trends, and levels, comparing the City of St. Louis to national averages and to other major cities, and comparing the metropolitan area to national trends for metropolitan area.

Findings

Long-Term Trends in Segregation, St. Louis City, 1860–2000

The long-term trend in racial housing segregation in St. Louis City is shown in Figure 1. For comparison purposes, national trends are shown in Figure 2. As described above, these analyses use primarily ward data prior to 1940 and primarily census tract data from 1940 on. While it is true that wards tend to be somewhat larger areas than census tracts (so that ward data tend to produce lower segregation indices than census data), it is striking that the increases in segregation, both in St. Louis and nationally, occur mainly during the period when indices were based on ward data, not when the transition from ward to tract data occurs. Figures 1 and 2 show clearly that there are three distinct periods with respect to segregation: 1) a gradual increase in the late nineteenth century, which accelerated rapidly up to around 1930 (in St. Louis) or 1940 (in much of the rest of the country); 2) a period of steady, high segregation from around 1930 to 1980 in St. Louis, and from around 1940 to 1970 in much of the rest of the country; and 3) a period of declining segregation that began in much of the nation around 1970, and in St. Louis City around 1980. While the latter trend has resulted in a significant reduction in segregation levels both in St. Louis and nationally, it has yet, either in St. Louis or in racially diverse areas nationally, to bring segregation levels back down to what they were in the latter part of the nineteenth century.[2]

Period 1: The Creation of Segregation. Figures 1 and 2 show that housing segregation—both in St. Louis and nationally—is a pattern that largely developed in the early part of the twentieth century. Both in St. Louis and in cities throughout the United States, segregation levels in the latter part of the nineteenth century were below the midpoint of 50 on the index of dissimilarity, and significantly lower than they are today. Although segregation was on the increase in the latter part of the nineteenth century, it was in the first half of the twentieth century that

---

[2] In Figure 2, the average "weighted for African American population" compares indices among areas with similar African American populations. If one looks at all metropolitan areas without such adjustment, the appearance of a downward trend is created by the addition over time of new areas with relatively small African American populations. These areas tend to have lower segregation indices, but relatively few African Americans live in these areas, so they do not represent the residential experience of most African Americans. If one examines only areas with similar African American populations, it is clear that the decline in segregation since 1970 has yet to bring the segregation level anywhere near as low as it was a century ago.

cities were transformed from places where segregation levels were modest to places where white and black Americans lived almost entirely separately from one another. In particular, the period between 1900 and 1930 in St. Louis, and between 1910 and 1940 nationally, was marked by sharp increases in segregation; it was a time in which it could be said that cities were transformed into highly segregated places (Cutler, Glaeser, and Vigdor 2001; see also Massey and Denton 1993).

Figure 1. Trends in Segregation, St. Louis City, 1860–2000

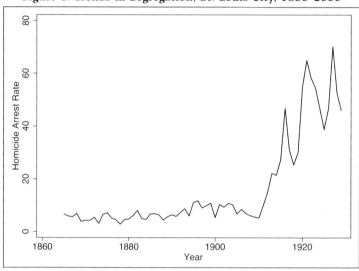

Source: Data for 1860 are from Massey and Denton 1993.
Data for 1890–1960 are from Cutler, Glaeser, and Vigdor 2001.
Data for 1970–2000 are from Farley, 2002.

This trend was somewhat earlier and more pronounced in St. Louis than in the country as a whole. For example, a comparison of Figures 1 and 2 show that while nationally the rapid increase in segregation occurred between 1910 and 1940, a comparable or greater increase occurred in St. Louis in the shorter and earlier (in terms of completion) period of 1900 to 1930. In fact, St. Louis was one of the four cities in the entire country with the most rapid increase in segregation between 1910 and 1930. The other three—Chicago, Milwaukee, and Cleveland—were also, like St. Louis, large and to a substantial extent industrial cities located in the Midwest (Massey and Denton 1993). As shown in Figure 3, the St. Louis pattern of the most rapid increase between 1900 and 1930 generally holds for large, racially diverse cities in the Midwest and

Metromorphosis

Northeast. Elsewhere, the trend is more typical of the nationwide pattern of the increase occurring somewhat later, between around 1910 and 1940. In some places, notably smaller southern cities, this period came even later.

What is it about the 1900–1930 time period and cities with characteristics similar to St. Louis that led to such a sudden surge in segregation? It was precisely during this period that the most rapid south-to-north and rural-to-urban migration of African Americans occurred, and it was industrial cities in the Midwest and Northeast that were the major

Figure 2. Trends in Segregation Index, 1890–2000. National Average and Average Weighted for Black Population

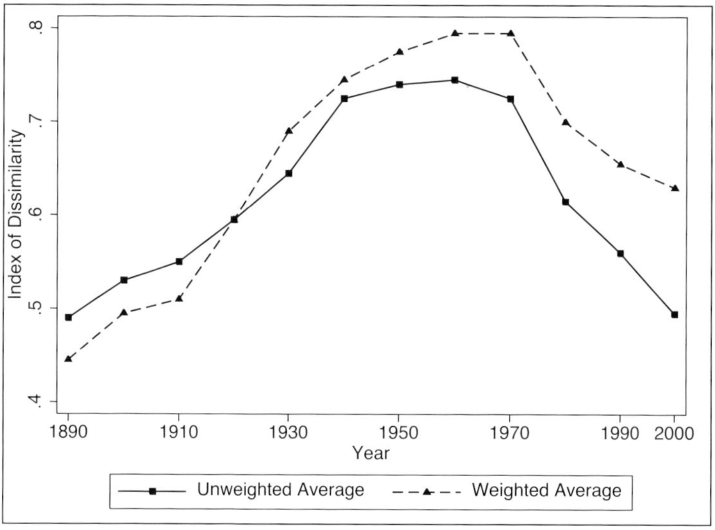

Source: Glaeser and Vigdor 2001, 4. Reprinted by permission.

recipients of this migration. About 525,000 African Americans moved from the South to the North between 1910 and 1920, and another 877,000 African Americans moved from the South to the North between 1920 and 1930 (Massey and Denton 1993, p. 29). St. Louis and Chicago were among the cities receiving the largest numbers of these immigrants. This rapid in-migration by African Americans was seen as a threat by many whites, who perceived the new migrants as competitors for housing, jobs, and education. One way to contain this perceived competition was through segregation—restricting where African Americans could live, where and in what jobs they could work, and where they could attend school.

Another way to contain it was through sheer intimidation—and the period from around 1900 to 1930 was one of the bloodiest in American history in terms of race rioting. Indeed, the second-deadliest riot of the entire twentieth century occurred in the St. Louis area, in East St. Louis, Illinois, in 1917. The East St. Louis riot was one of three deadly outbreaks to hit Illinois in just over a decade, with the others occurring in Springfield in 1908 and Chicago in 1919. Collectively, these three riots took an estimated ninety-three lives, the great majority African American and more than half of the total (forty-eight) in the East St. Louis riot (Farley 2000, 160). Major riots also occurred during the 1910–30 period in Philadelphia and Chester, Pennsylvania; Evansville, Indiana; Omaha, Nebraska; Elaine, Arkansas; Longview, Texas; Tulsa, Oklahoma; and other cities. All of these riots consisted primarily of mobs of whites attacking African Americans, and the great majority of victims were African American, though in some but not all of these uprisings, there were significant instances of retaliation by African Americans. The pattern of violence subsided for a while but did not really come to an end until after a series of riots in 1943, with a particularly serious riot in Detroit, and with a riot in Los Angeles in which the primary group targeted was Mexican Americans (whose population there was growing rapidly, as was the African American population in nearly all of the cities where African Americans were targeted). The Tulsa and Detroit riots were particularly deadly, with at least thirty killed in Tulsa and thirty-four in Detroit (Franklin 1969).

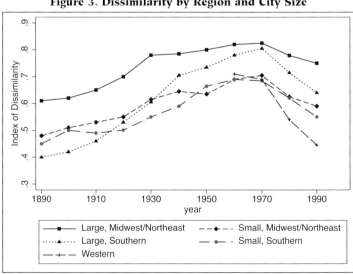

Figure 3. Dissimilarity by Region and City Size

Source: **Reprinted by permission from Cutler, Glaeser, and Vigdor 1999, 463.**

Metromorphosis

It is significant that both the nationwide surge in segregation and the outbreak of race riots initiated by whites against African Americans occurred precisely when the largest numbers of African Americans were arriving in the St. Louis area and in other large cities, especially in the central and northeastern United States. Indeed, most of the south-to-north and rural-to-urban migration of African Americans brought them to large cities in the Midwest and Northeast, including St. Louis.

The white populations of these areas responded with segregation and riots as a way of containing the perceived competition of African Americans and ensuring that blacks would be excluded from the better jobs, neighborhoods, and schools. As the sociologist Joe R. Feagin (2000, 63) said of this time period, "Once again, whites had more or less exclusive access to the economic, housing, and political resources that enabled them and their children to move up the socioeconomic ladder."

In terms of the St. Louis area, the growth of the black population occurred more rapidly than in nearly all other areas between 1910 and 1930, and correspondingly, whites responded with particularly severe segregation and rioting. Thus, the St. Louis area experienced both the most deadly riot of the 1910–30 time period and one of the four most rapid increases in segregation.

Period 2: Persistent Segregation. Once segregation hit its peak in St. Louis and other large midwestern and northeastern cities around 1930, it did not change appreciably for forty or, in the case of St. Louis, fifty years. In St. Louis, segregation levels remained basically the same for the next five decades after 1930. Adjusting for the shift from ward to tract data, this is quite evident in Figure 1. By 1940, the availability of census block and tract data began to make the measurement of segregation better, easier, more widespread, and more consistent. In St. Louis, segregation indices were computed using block data in each census year from 1940 forward. The trend in segregation in the City of St. Louis at this level is shown in Figure 4. Strikingly, these data show no decline in segregation in the City of St. Louis until after 1980. In every census from 1940 through 1980, analysis of block data produced a black-white segregation index within a few points of 90—in other words, 90 percent of the way toward the segregated end of the scale! Even when computed at the tract level (thereby using a larger geographic unit which produces a lower segregation index), segregation indices hovered in the mid-80s throughout this period. There are very few cities anywhere in the United States where levels of segregation were this high or this steady throughout the period, and the few others where they were are all large industrial cities in the Midwest or Northeast—precisely the characteristics associated with the earliest and sharpest increase in segregation in the preceding period.

Also notable is the fact that the period of persistent high segregation lasted longer in the City of St. Louis than in most other large cities. Only after 1980 did segregation decline in the City of St. Louis, whether measured at the tract level or the block level. Nationally, in contrast, the average level of segregation began to fall after 1970, as shown in Figure 2. Undoubtedly these declines in segregation, small as they were, reflect the impact of fair housing legislation and a Supreme Court ruling in 1968 which made housing discrimination illegal. The 1968 Fair Housing law banned discrimination on the basis of race, color, religion, sex, and national origin in the sale and rental of housing, except for buildings of four or fewer units in which the owner resided in one of the units. It also provided procedures for addressing fair housing complaints and penalties for violations. Also in 1968, in the *Jones v. Mayer* case, the Supreme Court ruled that housing discrimination was illegal under the 1866 Civil Rights Act, a long-unenforced law which had prohibited racial discrimination in economic transactions.

Figure 4. Block-Level Segregation Index, City of St. Louis, 1940–2000

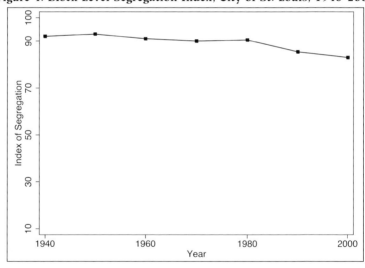

Source: Computed by author from census data.

Significantly, the *Jones v. Mayer* case, like several other landmark fair-housing cases in the Supreme Court, originated in St. Louis. In part, this is because virtually every imaginable technique, legal and illegal, was used to keep St. Louis segregated. Much of the city, like other cities in the Midwest and Northeast, was covered by restrictive covenants until they were overturned in the *Shelley v. Kraemer* case (1948), another important case that began in St. Louis. Under these covenants, a house could never be sold to a member of a specified list of groups (which nearly always included African Americans), and if such a sale occurred, ownership reverted back to the original owner. Restrictive covenants were used in St. Louis and other cities to surround African American neighborhoods with housing that they were forbidden to purchase. Real-estate codes of ethics in this period forbade the sale to African Americans and other minorities of houses in white neighborhoods, state courts enforced the covenants if they were violated, and federal housing policy actively encouraged racial discrimination. Loan and insurance redlining, blockbusting, and discriminatory zoning were other techniques used to maintain and perpetuate housing segregation in the St. Louis area and throughout the country. When these techniques did not work, cross burnings and violent attacks were sometimes resorted to, and these have occurred intermittently in the St. Louis area as recently as 2000 and on several occasions in the 1990s (*St. Louis Post-Dispatch* 2001a; 1999; 1997).

With respect to zoning, a third key Supreme Court case, *United States v. City of Black Jack*, resulted in a 1974 ruling that Black Jack, a north St. Louis County suburb, had effectively engaged in discrimination by passing a zoning ordinance banning multi-family housing. Thus, while a wide variety of techniques were used effectively for fifty years to keep St. Louis segregated, fair housing advocates repeatedly challenged these techniques. As a result, three of the most important fair housing cases to reach the Supreme Court came from St. Louis or nearby areas (Equal Housing Opportunity Council 1998).

To summarize, in St. Louis the rise in segregation came earlier than it did in the nation as a whole, and the decline came later. This reflects the efforts of whites to retain dominance in a context of rapid in-migration of African Americans between 1910 and 1930, and ongoing use of a wide variety of discriminatory techniques for much of the twentieth century. One result is that the period of persistently high segregation in the City of St. Louis lasted for fifty years, from 1930 through 1980, whereas in most cities it lasted thirty or forty years. A more positive result is that many of the legal challenges to housing discrimination that set the stage for a decline in segregation also arose in St. Louis.

Period 3: Declining Segregation. Since 1980, segregation has been on the decline in the City of St. Louis at what appears to be an accelerating rate. Over the past few decades, changing patterns have emerged between the

City and the suburbs. This began to be evident in the 1960s and 1970s, as the African American population began to suburbanize. Indeed, because of this suburbanization, the pattern of declining segregation in the St. Louis area became evident in the suburbs before it became evident in the City, though in some suburban areas it appears to have stalled after 1990. Because the City of St. Louis is an independent city that is not part of St. Louis County, the city is landlocked in a relatively small geographic area between St. Louis County and the Mississippi River. As the urban area expanded outward and the City was unable to annex into St. Louis County or across the river into Illinois, a progressively smaller proportion of the urbanized area was within its boundaries. Because of its landlocked nature, this shift occurred earlier and to a greater extent in St. Louis than in most large cities, which in some cases were able to annex to partially capture the outward moving population. Because of this, St. Louis was one of the earliest regions to suburbanize (i.e., to find an increasing share of its population moving to nearby communities outside its city limits), and it has been and is one of the most suburbanized metropolitan areas in the United States. Indeed in 2000, less than 14 percent of area's population lived in the City of St. Louis—one of the lowest such percentages in the nation.

For much the same reason, St. Louis has been ahead of most of the country with regard to black suburbanization. The majority (about 63 percent) of African Americans in the St. Louis area today live outside the City of St. Louis; more than 40 percent live in St. Louis County, which today is home to over 193,000 African Americans. This distribution reflects the continuation of a trend toward suburbanization that has been evident on a substantial scale among the area's African American population since around 1970.

In 1960, fewer than 20,000 African Americans lived in St. Louis County—less than 3 percent of its population. Between 1960 and 1970, this number more than doubled, to over 45,000. By 1970, almost 5 percent of the county's population was African American, and the number has grown since then. Today, 19 percent of St. Louis County's population is African American, slightly above the percentage for the entire metropolitan area. On the Illinois side of the metropolitan area, increases have also occurred in the portions of St. Clair County outside East St. Louis, as more African Americans today live in the balance of St. Clair County than in East St. Louis, and in Madison County. Although to a large extent African American suburbanization reproduced the segregation patterns of the central city, most African Americans who moved to the suburbs did end up living in modestly less segregated areas. In 1970 and 1980, for example, the segregation index for St. Louis County was lower than that of the City, and it also declined more (Farley 1983).

By 1980, Madison County's segregation index was also below that of St. Louis City.

For three reasons, these changes meant that the segregation index for the overall metropolitan area began to decline before the segregation index in the City. First, the suburbs were less internally segregated than the City, although blacks were a smaller proportion of the population in the suburbs. In other words, blacks and whites who lived in St. Louis and Madison Counties were less separated from one another than blacks and whites who lived in the City. Second, the suburbs began to experience a significant decline in segregation after 1970, especially in St. Louis County. Third, after 1970 the City's black population fell, while the black population of the less internally segregated suburbs continued to rise. Consequently, while segregation in the City did not begin to decline until after 1980, the segregation index (based on tract data) for the metropolitan area as a whole fell from 86.5 to 82.9 between 1970 and 1980.

Figure 5. Recent Racial Housing Segregation Trends Based on Tract Data, St. Louis Metropolitan Area and St. Louis City

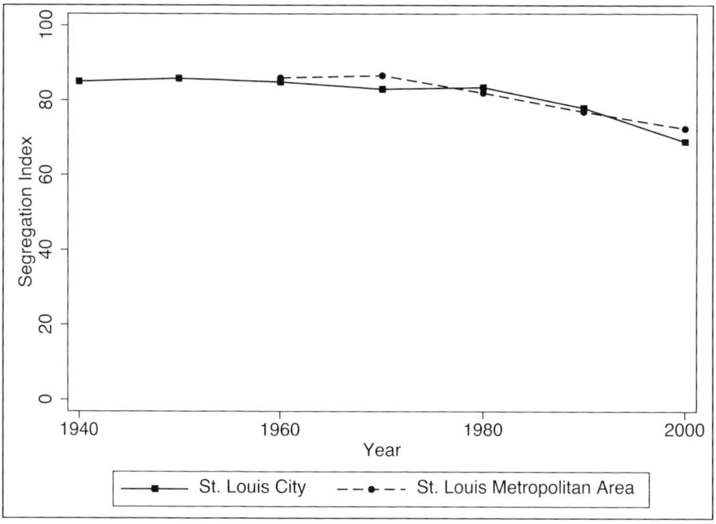

Source: From Farley 2002. Used by permission.

Figure 6. Racial Housing Segregation Trends by County Based on Tract Data, 1980–2000

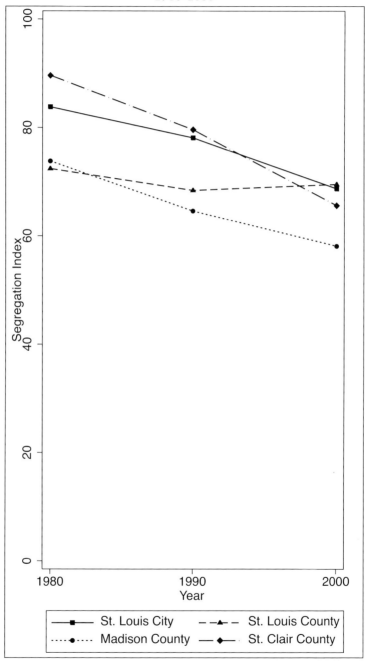

Source: From Farley 2002. Used by permission.

Segregation has continued to decline in the metropolitan area as a whole and in most parts of the metropolitan area, as shown in Figures 5 and 6. Between 1980 and 1990, segregation in the area as a whole declined by six points, from 82.9 to 76.9. The City, St. Louis County, Madison County, and St. Clair County all experienced declines in their levels of segregation. The largest declines, 10 and 9 points respectively, came in St. Clair and Madison Counties, and the smallest, 5.7 points, in the City. However, this was the first decade in which a significant decline in segregation had ever been recorded in St. Louis City, and comparisons of the periods before and after the 1988 Dress Rehearsal Census that was conducted in the City suggest that the rate of decline accelerated over the course of the decade (Farley 1993).

In the most recent intercensal period, 1990–2000, many of these trends continued. The rate of decline of segregation in the City continued to accelerate, with the index dropping 9.4 points in this one decade—almost double its drop in the preceding decade. In fact, in the past decade for the first time, the City's level of segregation declined faster than that of the area as a whole, as can be seen in Figure 5. Also for the first time, the City's segregation index in 2000 was lower than that of the metropolitan area as a whole. Segregation also continued to decline rapidly in the two major suburban counties in Illinois, Madison and St. Clair. St. Clair County's segregation index fell by another 14 points between 1990 and 2000, making for a remarkable 24-point decline between 1980 and 2000. Madison County's index fell by about 6.5 points, making for a decline of nearly 16 points between 1980 and 2000.

There is, however, one very important deviant case, and there are still several suburban counties that are so overwhelmingly white that computation of a segregation index for them is meaningless. The very important deviant case is St. Louis County—with a population of over 1 million, by far the most populous county in the area. Between 1990 and 2000, segregation in St. Louis County actually increased, reversing the recent trend toward reduced segregation. The level of segregation in St. Louis County rose from 68.4 in 1990 to 69.5 in 2000. This is a matter of considerable concern, since nearly 40 percent of the metropolitan area's population as well as 40 percent of its African American population lives in this one county. In seven outlying counties in the metropolitan area, including two of the fastest-growing areas, St. Charles County and Jefferson County, the proportion of African Americans is so low (below 3 percent) as to make computation of segregation indices meaningless. And in the eighth outlying county (Clinton County, Illinois), the percentage is slightly higher (just under 4 percent), but the number of African Americans is only 1,300. Thus, in all of the metropolitan area except for St. Louis City and County and St. Clair and Madison Counties, the population remains overwhelmingly white.

These trends in the segregation index are based on census tract data. Block data show a similar pattern, but slightly different nuances emerge. As do the tract data, the block data show sizable declines in segregation in St. Louis City, St. Clair County, and Madison County. In the City and in St. Clair County, the block data indicate declines of more than 9.0 points in the segregation index between 1990 and 2000, and 7.5 points in Madison County.

As with the tract data, the block data do not show a significant decline in segregation in St. Louis County, though unlike the tract data they do not show an increase either. The block data also suggest that the segregation indices may be converging in the mid-70s in the parts of the metropolitan area that are racially diverse: all four areas described above had block-based segregation indices between 74 and 77 in 2000 (Farley 2002). However, a more likely explanation is that the trend lines are crossing, since segregation in recent years has declined significantly in St. Louis City, St. Clair County, and Madison County, while the decline in segregation appears to have stalled in St. Louis County.

Current Patterns and Future Trends in Segregation in the St. Louis Area

The continuing rapid declines in segregation in St. Louis City and in St. Clair County are significant because both areas have very large African American populations—about 51 percent of the population in St. Louis City and about 29 percent in St. Clair County. About 53 percent of the area's African American population lives in these two areas. While there are parts of the City and of St. Clair Country that are very segregated, and many of these areas' African Americans live in the segregated portions (Farley, forthcoming), there are also a large and growing number who live in the less segregated parts of these areas. And whites in these areas on average have more integrated neighborhood environments than do whites anywhere else in the metropolitan area. This is the good news in recent patterns and trends. The bad news is that it remains true that 1) St. Louis is one of the most segregated metropolitan areas in the country, and 2) in a milder form, the patterns of segregation long established in the City of St. Louis and in East St. Louis and nearby areas have been largely replicated as the African American population has suburbanized. This has been most true in St. Louis County, but is probably becoming less so with time in St. Clair County.

Both of the patterns described above can be seen in Figure 7, a map showing the racial composition of census tracts in the innermost eight counties of the St. Louis metropolitan area in 2000, and in Figure 8, an enlargement of the portion of the map showing St. Louis City and County.[3] With regard to the extension of past patterns of segregation, it is evident that the main sector of the African American population, which once encompassed the northern part of St. Louis City and much of East St. Louis, Illinois, has expanded to include much of north St. Louis County and portions of St. Clair County outside East St. Louis. This type of sectoral pattern is common in the distribution of racial and ethnic groups in urban areas, and is particularly characteristic of the distribution of African Americans, who encounter levels of segregation far beyond those experienced by any other group.

At the same time, however, the maps show significant areas in St. Louis City, in St. Clair County, and in St. Louis County, where the population of neighborhood areas mirrors that of the metropolitan area as a whole.

Figure 7. Racial Composition of Census Tracts, St. Louis Metropolitan Area, 2000

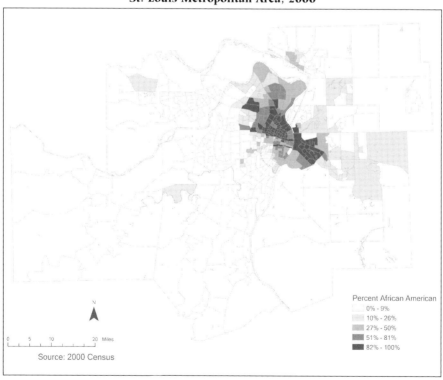

Percent African American
0% - 9%
10% - 26%
27% - 50%
51% - 81%
82% - 100%

0   5   10   20 Miles

Source: 2000 Census

---

[3] St. Louis city, an independent city which is not part of any county and is considered a "county equivalent," is included in the total of eight counties and is one of the geographic areas included in the map.

This can be seen by examining the distribution of census tracts with populations between 10 percent and 25 percent African American. Since the St. Louis metropolitan area's population is just over 18 percent African American, it can be said that these tracts have racial compositions similar to that of the metropolitan area as a whole. The number of such tracts, and the number of people living in them, increased considerably between 1990 and 2000. Much of the urban portion of St. Clair County outside East St. Louis falls into this range, as does much of the southern part of St. Louis City. The increase in such areas undoubtedly accounts to a large extent for the decline in segregation indices seen in the City and in St. Clair County. There are also a growing but smaller number of such tracts in Madison County. Significantly, however, there are virtually no such areas in St. Charles County, Franklin County, Jefferson County, Monroe County, or the western half or southern third of St. Louis County, all of which are overwhelmingly white areas.

The final area where such tracts can be found is in St. Louis County, but there, unlike the other three areas, the large majority of them are on the outer edge of the main sector of African American population. Unlike the other three areas, about half of them are contiguous with tracts consisting of a primarily African American population. There are some exceptions to this pattern such as the part of the county just southwest of the City, but these largely represent tracts with long-standing African American enclaves. Because so many of the 10–25 percent African American tracts in St. Louis County are contiguous to the main sector of African American population—reflecting the lack of decline in segregation in St. Louis County—it is more likely in St. Louis County than elsewhere that these tracts are in transition from predominantly white to predominantly African American areas. Since 1980, however, such transitions have been much less rapid and inevitable than was the case before 1980 in the St. Louis area (Farley 1993).

Despite declines in segregation and the growth in racially integrated areas, the St. Louis area remains one of the most segregated metropolitan areas in the country. On the basis of the index of dissimilarity, the St. Louis area remained the eighth most segregated among the fifty largest MSAs in 2000, and among all 331 metropolitan areas in the United States, it was the thirteenth most segregated (Logan 2001). On the basis of an averaging of multiple indices that measure different aspects of segregation, it ranked the fourth most segregated in a sample of forty-three large U.S. metropolitan areas (U.S. Census Bureau 2003). Despite the encouraging downward trend, Farley's (2002) analysis showed that at the average rate of decline over the past thirty years, it would take more than half a century for the area's level of segregation to reach even the midpoint between total segregation and no segregation. Similarly, it would also take about that long for the level of segregation in the St. Louis area to reach what now is the average level of segregation for all metropolitan areas in the United States. Hence, the progress being made toward becoming a more integrated community, though real, is modest indeed.

Moreover, whether this progress continues, accelerates, or stalls depends largely on very different trends in different parts of the region. In the Illinois part and in the City, the recent trends are encouraging. It appears that in these segments, integrated neighborhoods have increased significantly, even though many whites and African Americans still live in segregated areas. One reason for the progress in these areas is institutional support: diversity has come to be recognized as a marketing point for City life, and real estate agents in St. Louis City understand this and behave accordingly. In Illinois, fair housing training has been incorporated as a mandatory part of continuing education for real estate agents. Vigorous

Figure 8. Racial Composition of Census Tracts, St. Louis City and County

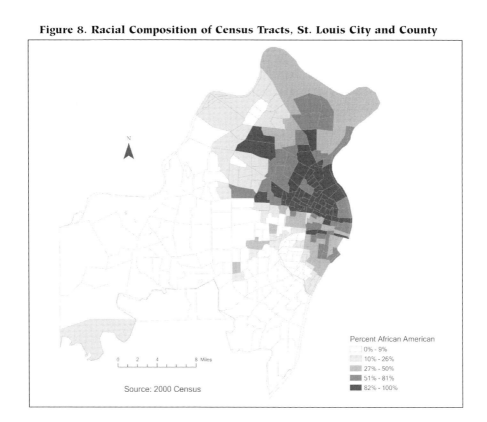

federal enforcement efforts including Justice Department oversight of Belleville through much of the 1990s and efforts by Scott Air Force Base to combat discrimination in surrounding areas seem to have paid off. Undoubtedly, the presence of Scott Air Force Base has helped to promote greater integration in St. Clair County, since national research shows the presence of military institutions to be associated with lower and declining levels of segregation.

In the suburban part of the Missouri side of the metropolitan area, however, progress appears to have stalled after 1990. The reasons for this are more difficult to explain, but fair-housing audits have shown that steering remains a problem in north St. Louis County (*St. Louis Post-Dispatch* 2001b), and unlike Illinois, real-estate agents in this area are not required to receive fair-housing training. Efforts to provide scatter-site, low-income housing have also met strong resistance in St. Louis County, especially when proposed in the western and southern parts of the county. The key to future progress in reducing segregation in the area may depend on the Missouri suburbs, which are home now to the majority of the metropolitan area's population. While progress in the City and in the Illinois part of the area has been significant over the past two decades, progress in the Missouri suburbs appears to have slowed since 1990. Whether or not it can be restored in the coming decade or two will be critical in determining whether the St. Louis area's legacy as one of the nation's most segregated areas is perpetuated or altered.

References

Alexander, Karl, Doris R. Entwisle, and Maxine S. Thompson. "School Performance, Status Relations, and the Structure of Sentiment: Bringing the Teachers Back In." *American Sociological Review* 52 (1987): 665–82.

Blauner, Bob. *Black Lives, White Lives: Three Decades of Race Relations in America*. Berkeley: University of California Press, 1989.

Brookings Institution. *Moving beyond Sprawl: The Challenge for Metropolitan America*. Washington, D.C.: Brookings Institution, 2000.

Conley, Dalton. *Being Black, Living in the Red: Race, Wealth, and Social Policy in America*. Berkeley: University of California Press, 1999.

Cutler, David, Edward Glaeser, and Jacob Vigdor. "Cutler/Glaeser/Vigdor Segregation Data." 2001. http://trinity.aas.duke.edu/~jvigdor/segregation/ (accessed June 3, 2003).

___. "The Rise and Decline of the American Ghetto." *Journal of Political Economy* 107 (1999): 455–506.

Equal Housing Opportunity Council of Metropolitan St. Louis. *The Struggle for Fair Housing in St. Louis: Local Court Cases with National Impact*. 1998. http://stlouis.missouri.org/501c/ehoc/cases.html (accessed June 3, 2003).

Farley, John E. "Excessive Black and Hispanic Unemployment in U.S. Metropolitan Areas: The Roles of Racial Inequality, Segregation, and Discrimination in Male Joblessness." *American Journal of Economics and Sociology* 46 (1987): 129–50.

___. "Housing Segregation in the St. Louis Metropolitan Area, 1980–1990: Comparing Trends at the Block and Census Tract Level." *Journal of Urban Affairs* 15, no. 6 (1993): 515–27.

___. "Interracial Exposure Indices: When 'Average' Is Not Typical." In *Critical Demography*. Vol. 1. New York: Klewer Press, forthcoming.

___. *Majority-Minority Relations*. 4th ed. Upper Saddle River, N.J.: Prentice-Hall, 2000.

___. "Metropolitan Housing Segregation in 1980: The St. Louis Case." *Urban Affairs Quarterly* 18 (1983): 347–59.

___. "Racial Housing Segregation in the St. Louis Metropolitan Area." *Edwardsville Journal of Sociology* 2 (2002). http://www.siue.edu/SOCIOLOGY/journal/FARLEYV2.HTM (accessed January 22, 2003).

Feagin, Joe R. *Racist America: Roots, Current Realities, and Future Reparations*. New York: Routledge, 2000.

Focus St. Louis. *Racial Equality in the St. Louis Region: A Community Call to Action*. St. Louis: Focus St. Louis, 2001.

Franklin, John Hope. *From Slavery to Freedom: A History of Negro Americans*. 3d ed. New York: Vintage Books, 1969.

Gallup Organization. "Special Reports: Black/White Relations in the U.S." 1997. http://www.gallup.com.

Glaeser, Edward L., and Jacob L. Vigdor. *Racial Segregation in the 2000 Census: Promising News*. Washington, D.C.: Brookings Institution, 2001.

Herring, Cedric, Hayward Derrick Horton, Verna Keith, and Melvin Thomas. "Race Traitors, Self-Haters, or Equal Opportunists?: Explaining Support for the 'Wrong Views' on Affirmative Action." Paper presented at annual meetings of the American Sociological Association, Washington, D.C., August 12–16, 2000.

Hochschild, Jennifer L. *Facing up to the American Dream: Race, Class, and the Soul of the Nation*. Princeton, N.J.: Princeton University Press, 1995.

Holzer, Harry J., and Keith R. Ihlanfeldt. "Spatial Factors and the Employment of Blacks at the Firm Level." *New England Economic Review* 65 (May/June 1996).

Ihlanfeldt, Keith R. "Intra-Urban Job Accessibility and Hispanic Youth Unemployment Rates." *Journal of Urban Economics* 33 (1993): 254–71.

___. *Job Accessibility and the Employment and School Enrollment of Teenagers*. Kalamazoo, Mich.: Upjohn Institute for Employment Research, 1992.

Ihlanfeldt, Keith R. and David L. Sjoquist. "The Effect of Job Access on Black and White Youth Unemployment: A Cross-Sectional Analysis." *Urban Studies* 28 (1991): 255–65.

___. "Job Accessibility and Racial Differences in Youth Unemployment Rates." *American Economic Review* 80 (1990): 267–76.

___. "The Spatial Mismatch Hypothesis: A Review of Recent Studies." *Housing Policy Debate* 9 (1998): 849–92.

Kain, John F. "Housing Segregation, Negro Employment, and Metropolitan Decentralization." *Quarterly Journal of Economics* (May 1968): 175–97.

Kasarda, John D. "Structural Factors Affecting the Location and Timing of Urban Underclass Growth." *Urban Geography* 11 (1990): 234–64.

___. "Urban Change and Minority Opportunities." In *The Reshaping of America: Social Consequences of the Changing Economy*, edited by D. Stanley Eitzen and Maxine Baca Zinn. Englewood Cliffs, N.J.: Prentice-Hall, 1989.

___. "Urban Industrial Transition and the Underclass." *Annals of the American Academy of Political and Social Science* 501 (1989): 26–47.

Kluegel, James R. "Trends in Whites' Explanations of the Black-White Gap in Socioeconomic Status, 1977–1989." *American Sociological Review* 55 (1990): 512–25.

Kluegel, James R., and Eliot R. Smith. *Beliefs about Inequality: Americans' Views of What Is and What Ought to Be*. Hawthorne, N.Y.: Aldine de Gruyter, 1986.

Kozol, Jonathan. *Savage Inequalities: Children in America's Schools*. New York: Crown, 1991.

Logan, John. "Ethnic Diversity Grows, Neighborhood Integration Lags Behind." Report by the Lewis Mumford Center, April 3, 2001. Updated December 18, 2001, to include 1980 data. http://mumford1.dyndns.org/cen2000/WholePop/WPreport/page1.html (accessed June 3, 2003).

Massey, Douglas S., and Nancy Denton. *American Apartheid: Segregation and the Making of the Underclass*. Cambridge, Mass.: Harvard University Press, 1993.

___. "The Dimensions of Residential Segregation." *Social Forces* 67 (1988): 281–315.

Massey, Douglas S., Michael J. White, and Voon-Chin Phua. "The Dimensions of Segregation Revisited." *Sociological Methods and Research* 25, no. 2 (1996): 172–206.

National Center for Education Statistics. *The Condition of Education, 2000*. Washington, D.C.: U.S. GPO, 2000a. http://nces.ed.gov/pubs2000/coe2000/ (accessed December 15, 2002).

National Science Foundation. *Women, Minorities, and Persons with Disabilities in Science and Engineering: 1996 (NSF 96-311)*. Arlington, Va.: Author, 1996. Available online at http://www.nsf.gov/sbe/srs/nsf96311/start.htm (accessed January 22, 2003).

Oliver, Melvin L., and Thomas M. Shapiro. *Black Wealth, White Wealth: A New Perspective on Racial Inequality*. New York: Routledge, 1995.

Orfield, Gary, with Nora Gordon. "Schools More Separate: Consequences of a Decade of Resegregation." Civil Rights Project, Harvard University, 2001. http://www.civilrightsproject.harvard.edu/research/deseg/Schools_More_Separate.pdf (accessed January 22, 2003).

Pride, Richard A. "Public Opinion and the End of Busing." *Sociological Quarterly* 41(2000): 207–16.

Schuman, Howard, and Maria Krysan. "A Historical Note on Whites' Beliefs about Racial Inequality." *American Sociological Review* 64 (1999): 847–55.

Smith, Tom W. "Measuring Inter-Racial Friendships: Experimental Comparisons." GSS Methodological Report No. 91. Chicago: National Opinion Research Center, 1999.

St. Louis Post-Dispatch. "Advocacy Group, Florissant, Mo., Reach Agreement in Housing Lawsuit," April 26, 2001b.

___. "Four Cross-Burners Are Given Chance to Avoid Prison," August 5, 1999.

___. "Man Gets 18 Months in Burning of Cross," February 7, 2001a.

___. "Racism Led to Firebomb, Police Say," August 26, 1997.

Taeuber, Karl, and Alma F. Taeuber. *Negroes in Cities*. Chicago: Aldine, 1965.

U.S. Census Bureau. "Housing Patterns—Racial and Ethnic Residential Segregation in the United States: 1980-2000." http://www.census.gov/hhes/www/housing /resseg/papertoc.html (accessed June 3, 2003).

Wells, Amy Stewart, and Robert L. Crain. *Stepping over the Color Line: African-American Students in White Suburban Schools*. New Haven, Conn.: Yale University Press, 1997.

Yinger, John. *Closed Doors, Opportunities Lost: The Continuing Costs of Housing Discrimination*. New York: Russell Sage Foundation, 1995.

Acknowledgments

Support for this research was provided by the Graduate School and the Institute for Urban Research at Southern Illinois University at Edwardsville. Assistance with Geographic Information System analyses and preparation of the maps shown in Figures 7 and 8 was provided by Steve Galinski of the Institute for Urban Research. I am grateful for this support and assistance.

Chapter 9
City Neighborhoods: Housing Stability, Quality, and Affordability

Richard Wesenberg
Washington University

Introduction

The increased complexity of household life patterns and individuals' work careers has changed the composition of St. Louis neighborhoods. The social enclaves represented by the parish, the high school allegiance, and the "old neighborhood," while still present, exist in a more complex and mobile society that demands greater adaptability by individuals and households. The family household is still a majority, but single individuals and female heads of households represent a greater share of all households. These changes affect neighborhoods, since smaller households with fewer resources place greater demands. Affordability is not a problem just for households; it presents a dilemma for neighborhoods and the city. Home ownership supports and stabilizes neighborhoods and helps maintain the quality of neighborhood life. This study examines the changes in households and neighborhood affordability over the last five decades within five St. Louis City neighborhoods.

City Neighborhoods

From the mid-nineteenth to the early twentieth century, St. Louis neighborhoods near the riverfront, such as Soulard, Carondelet, Hyde Park, and College Hill, were developed to provide economical row housing and apartments for the city's factory and transportation workers. Many of the residents in these working-class neighborhoods were immigrants with similar ethnic and racial backgrounds and religious affiliations. These residents shared social affiliations, supported the stability of the neighbor-hoods, and helped to define the "fenced-off corners"[1] of the city's different ethnic communities. In the early decades of the twentieth century, new housing developments such as the Shaw neighborhood and the Fairground Park area created new single-family and duplex houses designed for middle-class and upper-middle-class office and retail employees and managers, as well as professionals working in the city. The houses in these neighborhoods were located away from the city center on public transportation lines offering families quieter, family-friendly streets.

Most city neighborhoods changed very little from the early twentieth century until the 1950s, when the employment and economic changes described in accompanying chapters began to affect their composition. Between 1950 and 1970 most families enjoyed prosperity that offered the middle class more choices of neighborhoods and housing. The distinctions in the ethnic, racial, and religious boundaries of many city neighborhoods began to blur as older residents moved to new suburban homes. The significant losses in population and in employment in the city during the 1960s and 1970s affected many neighborhoods negatively.

It is difficult to overestimate the effects on city neighborhoods as the number of households declined from 258,412 to 147,286 households between 1950 and 2000. Significant demographic changes in the size and composition of city households affect the demand for housing in city neighborhoods. The changes in household composition as non-family households and female-headed households became a larger percent of total households led to smaller family and household sizes. In St. Louis between 1950 and 2000, married-couple households declined from 78 percent of all households to 26 percent. The ratio of family to non-family households in the city declined from 9:1 in 1950 to approximately 1:1 in 2000.

As the percent of nontraditional households and younger and highly mobile households increases in a neighborhood originally formed by social identity or affiliation, the area is transformed into a compositional form of neighborhood that hosts a population with a variety of household categories and ethnic backgrounds. Nontraditional households need affordable housing and amenities and services that vary with the size and type of household. Young single individuals seek neighborhoods with

---

[1] Eric Sandweiss (*St. Louis: The Evolution of an American Urban Landscape*, Philadelphia: Temple University Press, 2001) uses this term to describe the tightly knit neighborhoods formed around social identity and cohesion that characterize the older neighborhoods of St. Louis and other U.S. cities until the 1950s. The tightly knit neighborhood still exists, but its influence has been reduced by the increased mobility and compositional change in younger generations of households.

Metromorphosis

opportunities for socializing and recreation. Single-parent and married households with children need neighborhoods with convenient shopping and open-space recreation, low traffic flows, and household mobility. Low- and moderate-income households need affordable housing in locations that offer public transportation. All households desire secure, clean, attractive settings. The variety of house types in the city neighborhoods provides a number of options to meet the needs of these households. The dilemma is that many households cannot afford rising urban housing costs.

The neighborhoods with many young, individual, and single-parent households require affordable housing as these households are smaller than family households and have lower incomes. The precipitous decline in demand for city housing after 1960 created a more affordable housing market for less affluent households but resulted in diminished social and economic stability in many neighborhoods. A minimum level of household income is required to maintain the quality of neighborhoods and housing.

The Neighborhoods

To examine the effect of the social changes on neighborhood stability, quality, and affordability, five neighborhoods—Carondelet and Patch, College Hill, Vandeventer, a portion of the Central West End, and Shaw[2]—were selected. The neighborhoods are presented in Figure 1. The first two are working-class neighborhoods, the third a black neighborhood, the fourth a mix of upper-middle-class and lower-income households, and the last an educated middle-class neighborhood that has experienced some degree of social integration over the study period. These neighborhoods were selected to evaluate how the household changes, differences in quality of the housing and the neighborhood, and affordability and appreciation of housing to the neighborhood's residents have changed over the last five decades.

Carondelet

The Carondelet neighborhood, located on the Mississippi River at the south border of St. Louis, was first settled in the late eighteenth century.

---

[2] The neighborhoods' boundaries correspond approximately to the U.S. Census tract boundaries: Carondolet (census tract 1018), College Hill (census tract 1097), Vandeventer (census tract 1111), Central West End (census tract 1092), and Shaw (census tract 1172). The statistical data in the neighborhood descriptions are U.S. Census data from the population and housing tables of 1950 to 2000.

The area studied includes the "Patch" neighborhood and the south portion of the Carondelet neighborhood. Named for the French governor of Louisiana,[3] the area has always been a working-class neighborhood with an ethnically diverse population. The main street, South Broadway, is lined with many nineteenth-century commercial storefront buildings. It is a neighborhood with the character of a turn-of-the-century small town. Building owners are rehabilitating the main buildings, and local businesses are active on Broadway. The neighborhood residences are smaller houses or two- to three-story apartments located on quiet streets with a hilly topography. The median value of owner-occupied houses in 1950 was 56 percent of the city median value. By 2000 the value of owner-occupied houses in the tract was 48 percent of the median city value, and 20 percent of the houses were vacant.

Figure 1. St. Louis Neighborhoods Selected for Study

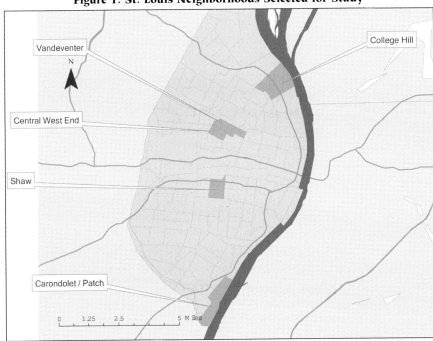

In 1950 this working-class neighborhood had a population of 8,057 white residents living primarily in single-family residences. By 2000, the

---

[3] Robert E. Hannon, *St. Louis: Its Neighborhoods and Neighbors, Landmarks and Milestones* (St. Louis: Buxton and Skinner, 1986). French colonialists called the neighborhood "Vide Poche" or "empty pockets" as many of its early residents were poor immigrants and Native Americans working on the river and other transient occupations.

population had declined to 3,119 residents, living in 1,318 households. Of the 3,585 workers in the labor force in 1950, 1,716 were machine operators and craftsmen, many employed in riverfront transportation or in steel foundries, rail shops and yards, and shipbuilding. By 1990, in the labor force of 1,961, approximately 1,000 workers were employed in occupations similar to those in 1950, as machine operators, craftsmen, or in service sector occupations. In 2000, despite the decline in population, income, and house values, most houses and properties were actively maintained. It is a neighborhood that still provides working families an affordable home with convenient access to the city.

College Hill

The College Hill neighborhood is on the north edge of the Hyde Park area and is bounded on the east by north Broadway and on the west by Florissant Avenue. The two historic water towers and the Bissell Mansion are prominent features, as is the neighborhood's height above the surrounding area. College Hill was developed in the 1880s as housing for European immigrant families and individuals working in the chemical plants, lumber mills and wood shops, rail yards, and stockyards of north St. Louis.[4] The houses located on the heights of the neighborhood on the axis of the water tower are attractive brick townhomes. Most of the remaining units are row houses and small three- to four-story apartments, or closely spaced single-family residences.

In 1950 the neighborhood's population was 14,857. As white residents moved to suburban housing in the 1960s and 1970s, the neighborhood became the destination for African American households with low and moderate incomes. In 2000, 1,275 households lived in the neighborhood. The median house value in 1950 was 67 percent of the city median value; by 2000 the value was 55 percent of the city median; and as of 2004 one-third of housing units were vacant.

The neighborhood has a unique charm and architectural character in streets on the heights near the water towers. Some of the houses are being rehabilitated, but most of the lower neighborhood is in marginal condition. The poor condition of the buildings and the disorderly environment indicate the toll caused by benign neglect. The existing high rate of household poverty suggests the demand for housing will be limited

---

[4] James Neal Primm, *Lion of the Valley: St. Louis, Missouri, 1764–1980*, 3d ed. (St. Louis: Missouri Historical Society Press, 1998). The German population that settled in College Hill provided many of the craftsmen that made the woodwork and constructed the houses of St. Louis neighborhoods.

to affordable houses until substantial investment is made to upgrade the neighborhood's condition and infrastructure. The neighborhood is an example of the dilemma of balancing affordability and quality.

Vandeventer

The Vandeventer neighborhood was developed late in the nineteenth century for African American workers employed in service and domestic-service occupations. Many large, attractive, substantial brick and masonry two- and three-story houses, built as rooming houses, line the streets. The current poor condition of residences and the number of vacant houses can be attributed to the out-migration in the 1960s and 1970s of black households as they moved from overcrowded housing to other city neighborhoods.

In 1950 12,833 blacks and 853 whites lived in the neighborhood; by 2000 there were 1,900 blacks and 9 whites. Much of the housing has significant architectural quality but is declining in condition due to the low income and the aging-in-place of residents. In 1950 the median house value was 87 percent of the city median value; in 2000 the value was 66 percent of the city median, and 30 percent of all housing units were vacant.

There are small industrial factories and shops in the eastern third of the Vandeventer neighborhood and scattered along the western end of Pinney and Fairfax Streets. The Ranken Institute, a large technical training school, is located on the west border of the neighborhood. Although many vacant lots and neglected and deteriorated houses are scattered throughout the neighborhood, the quality of the stock of existing houses and the central location of the neighborhood, near the Barnes-Jewish Hospital Medical Center and the Lindell and Euclid commercial areas, are major advantages. The revival of the neighborhood will depend on the success of current developments, such as the market-rate townhouses constructed on Belle Street, and the rehabilitation that is occurring in houses scattered throughout the neighborhood. Because of its proximity to the Central West End and the Grand Center neighborhoods, it has potential for redevelopment as a residential neighborhood with a variety of housing types.

Central West End

The fourth neighborhood is the portion of the Central West End bounded by Enright, McPherson, Sarah, and Taylor Streets. This is an urban neighborhood with a stock of older mansions and townhouses, as well as large apartment buildings of substantial architectural quality. Current development includes market-rate townhouses and detached housing. It is a heterogeneous neighborhood of young professionals, middle-class, and upper-middle-class residents. In 1950 there were 6,739 white and 1,497 black residents; in 2000 there were 1,300 black and 345 white residents living in the neighborhood.

The neighborhood includes the portion of Olive Street that was the Gaslight Square entertainment district in the 1960s, now demolished and being redeveloped. New housing has been constructed on Boyle and Westminster, and there is renovation of existing nineteenth and early twentieth century houses on Delmar and Washington. The vitality and stability of this neighborhood is due to its location between St. Louis University and Grand Center, and its proximity to the Central West End, the Barnes-Jewish Hospital complex, Forest Park, and the Euclid-Maryland restaurants and shops. It is a neighborhood that represents the potential for reintegrating middle-class households into the pattern of contemporary city life.

Shaw

The Shaw neighborhood is a community developed by Henry Shaw and other developers in the late nineteenth century for the middle class and upper middle class (Hannon 1986). Shaw planned Flora Place as a boulevard of mansions placed on the axis of the entrance to the Shaw Botanical Gardens. On either side of Flora Place, side streets of duplex and single-family, two-story homes were developed as housing for the office employees and professionals working in the city.

The presence of a middle-class population has been a constant in the neighborhood. In 2000, 29 percent of the residents were employed in professional and managerial positions. In 1950 there were 14,411 white and 118 black residents. In 2000 there were 1,873 white and 4,568 black residents living in 2,538 households. The social transition of the neighborhood has not affected the demand for its housing. The median house value in 1950 was 141 percent of the city median value, and in 2000 the value was 139 percent of the city median.

The Shaw neighborhood is home to many students and professionals because of its convenient access to the medical and academic campuses of St. Louis University and Washington University. The attraction of the neighborhood is aided by the quality of the houses and proximity to the Missouri Botanical Garden and Tower Grove Park. The nearby restaurants, specialty shops, and commercial services on South Grand Avenue create a sense of place with the functional aspects of a complete urban neighborhood.

Neighborhood Stability

Neighborhood stability is relative. Change is happening even if residents remain in place because their aging influences the conditions of the neighborhood. Neighborhood stability can be defined as social stability, racial mix, household incomes, or household prices. Filtering, the rate of change in neighborhood conditions, implies the temporal aspect of neighborhood stability. Myers (1990) defines filtering as the "longitudinal joining of supply and demand," i.e. the matching of household needs and means with housing choices and neighborhood qualities.[5]

The conventional definition of filtering in the housing market is an economic one: housing units "trickle down" in price and condition as they become affordable to lower-income households as prices decline over time in relation to household incomes. This condition may occur in the city neighborhoods where low-income households and substandard houses are concentrated. Without sufficient economic demand, housing will tend to remain affordable, but if effective demand can be created, housing filters up in the market. In gentrification active efforts by real-estate developers and housing lenders create "signature neighborhoods" with amenities that influence affluent households to purchase housing.

The successful revival of city neighborhoods depends on the quality of the housing stock, the neighborhood setting, and the demand for those qualities. Pozdena (1988, 19–46) emphasizes that neighborhood filtering is the result of general conditions, "such as changes in the distribution of wealth among households." He explains that as wealth or income in segments of the population change, the demand for a particular type of housing or neighborhood may increase or decrease and affect the price of all comparable housing. When the household wealth of a social group increases, their housing demand rises and, unless the market supplies more units at the former level of affordability, lower-income and higher-income households compete for the same neighborhood housing. Myers states the neighboring filtering process can be influenced by the following conditions:

> The life-cycle of neighborhoods or housing styles, as housing deteriorates to levels of affordability, or as younger generations find some older types of housing fit their lifestyles and tastes for aesthetic qualities.

---

[5] Dowell Myers, ed., *Housing Demography: Linking Demographic Structure and Housing Markets* (Madison: University of Wisconsin Press, 1990). See pp. 274–96 for a thorough discussion of neighborhood filtering theories, gentrification, the effects of household and neighborhood life cycles, racial transitions, and government policy on the long-term dynamics of neighborhood "filtering."

Regional effects, housing inflation or deflation, or regional income and occupational shifts in the economy.

Cohort effects, such as baby boomers' changes in lifestyle, or household composition.

Housing price is the dependent variable in most life-cycle theories of filtering, i.e. falling rents or prices indicate the filtering down of housing.

Myers states, however, rents or housing prices can remain constant even as housing demand drops in neighborhoods. As the income of younger cohorts rises, the change will be reflected in housing price and rent increases. The decline or increase in housing prices may reflect a change in the demand for the housing stock, or may reflect the change in the ability of residents to afford the housing stock.

The stability of neighborhoods is influenced by a combination of social and economic factors, including the lifestyles and incomes of residents, changes in occupational and educational contexts in the regional or national economy, and changes in the tastes and values of social groups for the qualities of housing and neighborhoods.

Housing Affordability

Financial institutions and the U.S. Department of Housing and Urban Development use the ratio of income to housing price or payments to define housing affordability. This formula works well when household income and housing costs are close to the median range of values, but is not an accurate measure of affordability for lower-income households. It is necessary to examine the distribution of income and housing prices in neighborhoods to determine the actual affordability of housing to different households. The basic affordability ratio or percent of income to housing costs in the study neighborhoods between 1950 and 2000 is illustrated in Table 1.

The high ratio of income to housing costs in the Carondelet and College Hill neighborhoods during the study period indicates the high level of affordability that existed in the 1960 and 1970 decades. This ratio is explained by the low value of houses in these neighborhoods in the 1960s. The ability to afford the housing depends on the total value of household expenses and housing costs in relation to household income. Low house prices indicate the lack of demand for housing in the neighborhood by higher-income households. One trend that is apparent in all neighborhoods is the nadir of demand for city housing that occurred from approximately 1960 to 1980 following the period of the greatest social transition.

Table 1. Affordability. Median Income as a Percent of Median House Price, 1950 to 2000

Area	1950	1960	1970	1980	1990	2000
St. Louis City	29%	36%	45%	44%	38%	42%
Carondelet	56%	61%	77%	54%	51%	51%
College Hill	48%	59%	64%	73%	50%	49%
Vandeventer	18%	25%	39%	51%	40%	35%
Central West End	17%	24%	34%	16%	23%	21%
Shaw	25%	37%	48%	38%	29%	31%

The stability of housing markets in lower-income neighborhoods depends on the continuity of household income. As Belsky and Duda (2002, 212) state, "lower-cost homes are more sensitive to changes in interest rates, income, and employment, all of which affect low-income buyers' ability to overcome income and wealth constraints to ownership." The high interest rates of the 1980–90 period acted as an additional deterrent to home ownership, as did the reluctance of financial institutions to provide credit to low-income applicants and to those in neighborhoods with a high percentage of black residents.

Testimony before the Senate in 1988[6] indicates that when the Association of Community Organizations for Reform Now had negotiated agreements with five local St. Louis banks to provide credit within low-income areas in the City of St. Louis, they found the agreements were blocked by the underwriting standards of FNMA and FHLMC lending policy. These requirements mandated a $30,000 minimum loan, prohibited lending in neighborhoods with more than 15 percent of houses abandoned, required two years of continuous employment with one employer immediately preceding an application, and stipulated that no more than 40 percent of a down payment be provided by next-of-kin relatives. These requirements prevented many female and minority households during the 1970s and 1980s from obtaining mortgages in city neighborhoods. The increased level of ownership in many minority and moderate-income city neighborhoods during the 1990s was due to the promotion of ownership through vigorous federal enforcement of the Credit Recovery Act, the increase in household incomes, and the decline in mortgage interest rates.

To measure housing costs-to-income ratios, the FHA mortgage interest rates for each decade between 1950 and 2000 and the median household income and house price in each neighborhood were used to calculate the ratio of mortgage payments to income (see Table 2).

---

[6] U.S. Senate, Hearings Before the Committee on Banking, Housing, and Urban Affairs, "The Community Reinvestment Act," S. Hrt.100-652 (Washington, D.C.: U.S. Government Printing Office, 1988).

Table 2. Affordability. Annual Mortgage Payments as a Percent of Household Income, 1950 to 2000

Area	1950	1960	1970	1980	1990	2000
St. Louis	21.9%	18.1%	20.3%	31.2%	27.6%	20.7%
Carondelet-Patch	11.5%	11.8%	11.9%	25.2%	20.7%	17.1%
College Hill	13.5%	12.8%	14.3%	18.8%	21.2%	18.1%
Vandeventer	35.0%	28.8%	23.8%	26.8%	26.6%	25.2%
Central West End	37.3%	30.5%	26.9%	86.0%	46.0%	42.4%
Shaw	26.0%	19.7%	19.1%	36.1%	36.8%	28.0%

Note: Percentages calculated by author from U.S. Census Tables, 1950–2000.

The differences in the ratios of income and mortgage payments were greater in 1980 than in any other decade. The extensive redevelopment that began in the late 1970s in the Central West End explains the inflated ratio of housing costs in 1980. The overall trend in disparity of housing costs and income was highest in 1950 and trended down to a low in 1990, but has since begun to increase. This indicates the increased disparity in housing prices between the high-income and low-income neighborhoods. In spite of the changes in neighborhoods between 1950 and 2000, the relationship of values among neighborhoods has remained remarkably similar.

When evaluating affordability housing, household composition is one of the most significant variables, as it together with occupation determines the level of household income. Goeber states that household composition affects housing affordability as female, individual, and non-family heads of households typically have lower incomes.[7] To determine how affordability varies in 2000 by the composition, race, and gender of households in each of the five neighborhoods, two formulas[8] were used to evaluate household income and house prices in the city and each of the five neighborhoods:

The FHA loan qualification formula (affordable monthly mortgage payment = .28 x gross income/month).

---

[7] Goeber (1990, p. 239) lists six forms of households that represent the predominant categories of households in U.S. cities, "(1) married couples with children, (2) childless couples, (3) female single parents, (4) other families... (5) persons living alone, and (6) unrelated individuals living together." Household income can vary significantly within these six categories of household.

[8] Source: U.S. Census Bureau, Statistical Abstract of the United States, 2001. The formulas used a mortgage interest rate of 8 percent, an approximate average of the interest rates available during the 1990 decade. The household categories were taken from the 1990 and 2000 census SF-1, SF-2, and SF-3 tables, as were the median income and median house and rent values. The mortgage interest values and amortization values used are from the 32 Edition of the Realty Bluebook. The moderate house value is from U.S. Department of Housing and Urban Development (Code of Federal Regulations, Title 24, Volume 1).

The U.S. Bureau of Labor Statistics cost of living for the average household in St. Louis in 1998–99 and the annual costs of an 8 percent mortgage for the median house price. See Table 3 for the results.

The values used in the affordability formulas[9] are based on a household paying the median rent or purchasing the median-price house in each neighborhood. The FHA standard formula for mortgage qualification uses the minimum annual income required to pay the mortgage for the median price of the house. Using the values of the median-price house in each census tract, the monthly payment for an 8 percent, thirty-year loan was calculated and compared with 28 percent of the median income to compute the minimum annual income needed for each category of household to meet the mortgage payments.

To investigate affordability for lower-income households, the U.S. Bureau of Labor Statistics costs of living, $17,356, for the average St. Louis size household of 2.5 individuals, are added to the 2000 mortgage costs for the median price house in each tract. When the normal costs of living are added to mortgage costs, the income needed to afford the median price house is calculated to be $22,216, and $21,124, $20,488, $21,088, $23,611, and $29,655 respectively in the city at large and the Carondelet, College Hill, Vandeventer, Shaw, and Central West End neighborhoods. Using the cost-of-living formula reduced the number of households able to afford the costs of ownership in three of the tracts. In the Carondelet neighborhood only white family households meet the affordability standard, and in the College Hill neighborhood only black households without children meet it.

To compare rent costs with ownership costs, the median 2000 annual rent for both white and black households in each neighborhood was added to the U.S. Bureau of Labor cost of living values ($17,356) for the average St. Louis household to compare differences in rent affordability.

The minimum income levels in the Carondelet, College Hill, Vandeventer, Shaw, and Central West End neighborhoods meeting rentaffordability are, respectively for white and black households: ($22,156, $23,008), ($20,908, $22,084), (NA, $21,808), ($22,972, $23,008), and ($28,756, $20,572). The cost of rent in each neighborhood is approximately equivalent to the cost of ownership of the median-price house in the Carondelet, College Hill, Vandeventer, Shaw, and Central West End neighborhoods. The advantages of home ownership to households and the community suggest the policy of supporting home ownership is an important aspect of maintaining and improving the stability and quality of neighborhoods.

---

[9] See Nicolas P. Retsinas and Eric S. Belsky, eds., *Low-Income Homeownership* (Washington, D.C.: Brookings Institution Press, 2002), 234–35, for an alternative formula for affordability.

Table 3. Home Ownership Affordability. Median 2000 Annual Incomes by Family Composition, Gender, Race, and Tenure

Household Median Incomes	City of St. Louis	Carondelet-Patch	College Hill	Vande-venter	Central West End	Shaw
All households	$27,156	$22,040	$17,191	$17,102	$32,917	$27,930
White households	$33,514	$21,587	$13,056	NA	$94,851	$36,795
Black households	$20,785	$28,611	$17,330	$16,648	$23,333	$22,623
White family households	$44,427	$24,718	$19,375	NA	$125,000	$58,359
Black family households	$24,503	$17,778	$16,611	$23,000	$39,500	$21,719
White NF households	$25,508	$17,201	$11,500	NA	$71,667	$27,740
Black NF households	$13,885	$100,338	$16,563	$9,479	$9,881	$20,896
Male individual income	$28,366	$18,787	$18,261	$12,650	$23,527	$20,589
Female individual income	$21,299	$12,682	$11,451	$14,825	$21,250	$16,571
White per capita income	$21,830	$12,936	$9,977	$16,333	$50,068	$25,653
Black per capita income	$11,582	$10,251	$7,675	$9,722	$15,291	$9,757
Owner HH income	$38,787	$29,152	$21,083	$28,787	$65,156	$49,318
Renter HH income	$19,054	$17,036	$13,859	$12,036	$12,574	$21,928
Families w/ children	$26,800	$25,720	$12,254	$21,429	$36,750	$22,604
Families w/o children	$38,760	$22,898	$25,074	$25,724	$54,205	$43,665

Source: U.S. Census Bureau Summary Tape Files 2000: SF 1, SF 2, & SF 3.
Note: Household incomes qualifying for mortgages under FHA loan standards are in *italics*.
Note: Household incomes above the COL affordability formula combining mortgage costs and the U.S. Bureau of Labor average household costs of living in St. Louis in 1999 are in **boldface**.

Appreciation and Housing Costs

The price of housing is influenced by the ratio of supply and demand. Supply is relatively inflexible in the housing market. Only a small percent of houses sold each year are new to the market, typically less than 5 percent. The remaining sales of existing houses indicate the relative influence of appreciation on house prices, i.e. the elasticity of demand and price. The long-term costs of housing include the returns of appreciation and asset accumulation during ownership. The rate of appreciation is influenced not only by the relative supply of housing stock, but also by the demand for neighborhood qualities. Housing prices and appreciation are influenced by the amount and quality of community public and commercial services, the quality of primary and secondary education in the community, and the aesthetic and recreational amenities of the neighborhood that influence the demand for houses in neighborhoods.

The "user cost of housing" is explained in economic terms by Pozdena (1988) to equal the net mortgage interest costs as affected by the federal tax policy plus the expected changes in house appreciation or depreciation.

Pozdena's formula[10] includes the federal income tax rate, the mortgage interest deduction, the general rate of inflation, and the capital gains realized due to house appreciation in a formula for the cost of housing over the period of ownership. Over the long term, appreciation and the income tax deduction for ownership can affect housing costs and prices significantly.

Case and Marynchenko's (2002) review of housing appreciation studies did not reveal consistent patterns in appreciation between upper- and lower-priced houses for Boston, Chicago, Houston, and Los Angeles over the 1980–95 period. Their finding indicates that the effect of appreciation operates across the housing market. Case and Marynchenko's conclusion is that appreciation is conditional and depends on the "time of purchase, conditions in the regional economy, and the dynamics of supply and demand at the local level."

The flight of white residents in the 1960s and 1970s meant the supply of existing houses exceeded the population demand from households as their numbers declined from 258,412 to 147,286, leaving many units available. This deflation or depreciation is reflected in the high ratio of income to housing prices in the Carondelet and College Hill neighborhoods in the 1970s and 1980s, as house prices plummeted when alternative housing was available in the city. The decline in the number of households in St. Louis between 1950 and 2000 has been a substantial restraint on the price of city housing. The excess supply of houses together with the decline in income of households relative to the St. Louis region has depressed effective economic demand for housing in many city neighborhoods.

To determine the rate of appreciation in constant dollars for houses purchased at the beginning of each decade the U.S. Bureau of Labor Statistics consumer price index (CPI) was used to adjust all of the prices to 2000 dollars. Table 4 indicates the rate of appreciation of the median-priced house in each neighborhood from the decade of purchase to their value in 2000.

---

[10] Randall Johnston Pozdena, *The Modern Economics of Housing: A Guide to Theory and Policy for Finance and Real Estate Professionals* (New York: Quorum Books, 1988), 88. User cost of housing = after-tax interest costs minus after-tax capital gains = (P) [(1-t) $(r + e) – (1 – t_c)(h)$], where: P = price of a housing unit; t = the tax rate on ordinary income; i = r + e = the nominal interest rate; r = the real interest rate; e = expected inflation of general prices; t_c = the tax rate on capital gains; k = expected capital gains; k/P = h = expected housing price inflation (appreciation). The nominal interest rate is represented by the factors (1-t) times (r + e) which equal the cost of housing, less the "after tax interest costs" (or the mortgage interest subsidy for ownership) and the effect of the general inflation rate. The federal mortgage interest deduction may be represented by (t) times the mortgage interest rate times the individual household's income tax rate. The appreciation or depreciation costs in house value are represented by (k/P).

Table 4. Median House Appreciation in Percent from Initial Decade of Purchase to 2000. CPI Adjusted Values, 1950 to 2000

Initial Decade of Purchase	1950	1960	1970	1980	1990	2000
St. Louis City, all houses	-	91%	111%	120%	96%	100%
St. Louis City, white households	-	-	-	117%	97%	100%
St. Louis City, black households	-	-	127%	136%	100%	100%
Carondelet-Patch	128%	95%	113%	109%	85%	100%
College Hill	78%	72%	93%	147%	120%	100%
Vandeventer	74%	77%	109%	181%	107%	100%
Shaw	105%	109%	144%	140%	99%	100%
Central West End	192%	207%	323%	136%	184%	100%

Source: *The CPI Detailed Report*, February 2003. Table 24 for All Urban Consumers (CPI-U).
Note: The DU appreciation percents were calculated using U.S. Bureau of Labor Statistics CPI to adjust the rate of appreciation calculated from the census median house values for the City of St. Louis and each neighborhood census tract for the decades from 1950 to 2000.

Although the appreciation rate of the median house price in the city declined by 4 percent between 1990 and 2000, the potential differences in appreciation and return in equity by neighborhood are illustrated. The difference in appreciation in recent decades between black and white households and neighborhoods is notable. Appreciation reflects the combined effects of demand, market costs and timing, and neighborhood and service flow effects, and it influences the true costs of housing for households within the neighborhoods.

How can the differences in appreciation be explained? The issues of school quality and segregation by economic, social, or race factors are complex and are not tested in the present evaluation of affordability and appreciation. Although the difference in incomes between white and black households in the city is sizable across all categories of families and households, where income is comparable, race by itself does not seem to have affected house values in St. Louis. Belsky and Duda's (2002) studies in 1982 and 2000 revealed little or no changes in appreciation due to race, when income was controlled, regardless of the price level of housing in the neighborhoods considered.

When housing dollars invested in St. Louis between 1970 and 1990 are compared, the CPI adjusted rates of appreciation have been greater for black-owned houses than for white households. The "catching up" of prices of houses owned by black households probably reflects the greater confidence of the market and financial institutions in their economic stability. The stability of housing price appreciation in the Shaw neighborhood as it went from a predominantly white neighborhood to a racially mixed neighborhood indicates that race is not the factor it was during the decline in house prices that occurred in the 1960s. A detailed study of distribution of black and white household incomes would have to be evaluated against the changed value of houses in other city neighborhoods to expand on this limited statement. It is probable that income, household composition, and housing service flows have a larger influence on trends in housing prices in the current market than does race.

What are other factors that can explain the appreciation of housing in St. Louis neighborhoods? First, some of the increase is due to the quality of the housing stock itself. St. Louis has a large inventory of quality residential architecture. The style, architectural character, size, and functionality of an attractive neighborhood's housing stock can provide a substantial base for appreciation. Second, neighborhoods with curb appeal and commercial and public services are attractive to potential residents with high incomes. Without buyers with sufficient income willing to purchase housing in the Central West End neighborhood the appreciation in prices realized between 1990 and 2000 would not have occurred.

When increases in households with high income demand are joined with a supply of high quality housing stock and an attractive neighborhood-services flow, the potential for significant appreciation in house prices exists. This potential can be seen if the increases in income and house values are compared in the 1990s in the Central West End. The median income of families increased from $17,604 to $46,250 between 1990 and 2000; the white per capita income in 2000 was $50,068 and the black per capita income was $15,291. These numbers explain the price appreciation in the basic market sense.

Conclusions

Neighborhoods remain in our consciousness as the places where we reside. But unlike earlier neighborhoods formed around social cohesion and identity, many contemporary neighborhoods are compositional. They accommodate a variety of households and residential lifestyles. Young mobile professionals, married couples, nontraditional families, couples with and without children, and older adults are among the households who enjoy the cultural aspects and convenience of city living. There are affordable neighborhoods for working households that represent the working city. There are active neighborhoods that are the "place to be" in city life.

The city offers a variety of neighborhoods in social, economic, and aesthetic terms that are not available elsewhere. Building service flows in neighborhoods is important from the basics of retail services, daycare, education and job counseling, to aesthetic and environmental amenities. Greening of the city, creating recreational opportunities and aesthetic environments, supports the housing market for young single, partnered, or married professional households. Going green has a double benefit, for environmental reasons and to attract residential investments by households who can return some of the economic base and social diversity that was lost in the last half of the twentieth century. After the era of suburbanization and the social transformations of desegregating city neighborhoods, it is important to recognize that many of the empty places may never be filled. It is time to consider the "re-composition" of the city and to build a portfolio of neighborhoods that are able to accommodate more of the complexities of contemporary society.

St. Louis residents are fortunate in that housing has remained affordable in comparison with many other cities. Households overburdened by housing costs are at risk socially and economically. The balance between affordability and neighborhood quality is an issue that underlies the future of many city neighborhoods. The sense of place that is created by public amenities, parks, plantings, recreational spaces, and, most important, local services supports the social connections that created the neighborhoods we remember for their sense of place and identity. The city needs neighborhoods where people decide to put their feet on the ground and leave their keys in their pocket in order to build social and economic stability.

References

Belsky, Eric S., and Mark Duda. "Asset Appreciation, Timing of Purchase and Sales, and Returns to Homeownership." In *Low-Income Homeownership*, edited by Nicolas P. Retsinas and Eric S. Belsky. Washington, D.C.: Brookings Institution Press, 2002.

Brown, Clair. *American Standards of Living: 1918–1988*. Oxford, Eng.: Basil Blackwell Ltd., 1994.

Case, Karl, and Maryna Marynchenko. "Home Price Appreciation in Low and Moderate-Income Markets." In *Low-Income Homeownership*, edited by Nicolas P. Retsinas and Eric S. Belsky. Washington, D.C.: Brookings Institution Press, 2002.

Goodman, A. C. "Neighborhood Impacts on Housing Prices." In *Urban Neighborhoods: Research and Policy*, edited by Ralph B. Taylor. New York: Praeger Publishers, 1982.

Hannon, Robert E. *St. Louis: Its Neighborhoods and Neighbors, Landmarks and Milestones*. St. Louis: Buxton and Skinner, 1986.

"Housing Opportunity: What Can You Afford?" *Consumers' Research Magazine* 75, no. 3 (March 1992). http://web4.epnet.com/citation .asp?tb=1& ug=dbs+0+1n+en percent2Dus+sid+24C638EB percent2D (accessed December 12, 2002).

Kain, John F. "The Influence of Race and Income on Racial Segregation and Housing Policy." In *Housing Desegregation and Federal Policy*, edited by John M. Goering. Chapel Hill: University of North Carolina Press, 1986.

Kain, John F., and William C. Apgar, Jr. *Housing and Neighborhood Dynamics: A Simulation Study*. Cambridge, Mass.: Harvard University Press, 1985.

Kendig, H. L. "A Life Course Perspective on Housing Attainment." In *Housing Demography: Linking Demographic Structure and Housing Markets*, edited by Dowell Myers. Madison: University of Wisconsin Press, 1990.

Longman, Phillip. "The Mortgaged Generation: Why the Young Can't Afford a House." *The Washington Monthly* 18 (April 1986). http://web1.infrotrac.galegroup.com/itw/infomark/246/134/27487316w1/purl=rc1_EAIM_0 (accessed September 25, 2002).

Meyerson, A. "The Changing Structure of Housing Finance in the United States." In *Housing Issues of the 1990s*, edited by Sara Rosenberry and Chester Hartman. New York: Praeger Publishers, 1989.

Myers, Dowell. *Analysis with Local Census Data: Portraits of Change*. San Diego: Academic Press, 1992.

___, ed. *Housing Demography: Linking Demographic Structure and Housing Markets*. Madison: University of Wisconsin Press, 1990.

Pozdena, Randall Johnston. *The Modern Economics of Housing: A Guide to Theory and Policy for Finance and Real Estate Professionals*. New York: Quorum Books, 1988.

Primm, James Neal. *Lion of the Valley: St. Louis Missouri, 1764–1980*. 3d ed. St. Louis: Missouri Historical Society Press, 1998.

Roistacher, E. A. "The Rise of Competitive Mortgage Markets in the United States and Britain." In *Housing Markets and Policies under Fiscal Austerity*, edited by Willem Van Vliet. Westport, Conn.: Greenwood Press, 1987.

Roistacher, E. A., and J. Spratlin Young. "Two-Earner Families in the Housing Market." In *Housing Policy for the 1980's*, edited by Roger Montgomery and Dale Rogers Marshall. Lexington, Mass.: Lexington Books, 1980.

Rosenberry, Sara, and Chester Hartman, eds. *Housing Issues of the 1990s*. New York: Praeger Publishers, 1989.

Sandweiss, Eric. *St. Louis: The Evolution of an American Urban Landscape*. Philadelphia: Temple University Press, 2001.

Spain, D. "Housing Quality and Affordability Among Female Households." In *Housing Demography: Linking Demographic Structure and Housing Markets*, edited by Dowell Myers. Madison: University of Wisconsin Press, 1990.

U.S. Department of Housing and Urban Development. Code of Federal Regulations, Title 24, Volume 1. http://www.hud.gov/offices /cpd/ affordablehousing/lawsandregs/regs/home/subf/ 92254.cfm (accessed February 12, 2003).

Chapter 10

Family and Household Types, 1950 to 2000: Where Have All the Cleavers Gone?

Lois Pierce
University of Missouri–St. Louis

Most people, when asked about families in the 1950s, immediately picture a *Leave It to Beaver* family with two married parents, two children, and a dog. June stayed home and took care of the house and children. Ward's salary provided the family with everything they needed to be happy. Today's family, which is one of the most rapidly changing social institutions (Anderson 2000), is much more difficult to summarize in one image.

During the past fifty years families in the St. Louis MSA have changed as well. The change in St. Louis City has been the most dramatic, but all counties in the region have seen other types of families replace married couples (see Tables 1 and 2). In 1950, St. Louis City and St. Charles County had similar proportions of married couples—approximately 3 of every 4 households. Twenty years later, only half of St. Louis City's households were married couples, and thirty years after that, in 2000, married couples were only 1 in 4 of City households. In contrast, the proportion of married-couple households in St. Charles County remained relatively high, approximately 2 of every 3. From 1970 to 2000 each county in the region experienced a fairly dramatic decrease in the number of married-couple households.

The decrease in married-couple households in St. Louis City has been mirrored by increases in non-family households, half of the City households in 2000, and single heads of households—1 of every 4 households in 2000. Again, using St. Charles County as a comparison, approximately 1 in 4 households are non-family households and slightly more than 1 in 10 are single heads of households. Other counties have experienced the same changes. Assumptions about families as married-couple households are quickly becoming obsolete.

Table 1. Share of Household Types, St. Louis MSA Core Counties, 1970

	Franklin	Jefferson	Madison	Monroe	St. Clair	St. Charles	St. Louis County	St. Louis City
Family Households	85%	90%	83%	86%	82%	88%	87%	69%
Married couple	76%	82%	74%	78%	67%	81%	78%	52%
Married with own children under 18	51%	59%	50%	51%	48%	63%	54%	34%
Single head	11%	8%	12%	10%	16%	8%	10%	26%
Female head of household	6%	5%	7%	5%	11%	5%	6%	15%
Female with own children under 18	3%	3%	4%	2%	7%	3%	3%	8%
Non-family Households	15%	10%	17%	14%	18%	12%	13%	31%
Total Households (Number)	16,978	29,777	78,470	5,757	86,347	25,926	283,139	215,479

Note: Percentages presented unless otherwise noted.

Table 2. Share of Household Types, St. Louis MSA Core Counties, 2000

	Franklin	Jefferson	Madison	Monroe	St. Clair	St. Charles	St. Louis County	St. Louis City
Family Households	74%	76%	69%	76%	70%	76%	67%	52%
Married couple	60%	61%	53%	65%	48%	63%	51%	26%
Married with own children under 18	38%	39%	33%	42%	31%	43%	34%	21%
Single head	18%	20%	23%	14%	31%	17%	24%	50%
Female head of household	9%	10%	12%	7%	17%	9%	13%	21%
Female with own children under 18	6%	6	7%	4%	10%	6%	7%	12%
Percent in poverty	39%	43%	54%	61%	49%	58%	56%	63%
Non-family Households	26%	24%	31%	24%	30%	24%	33%	48%
Householder living alone	22%	19%	26%	21%	26%	19%	28%	40%
Householder 65 and over	9%	6%	11%	10%	10%	6%	10%	13%
Total Households (Number)	34,945	71,499	101,953	10,275	96,810	101,663	404,312	147,076

Note: Percentages presented unless otherwise noted.

Census Data and Definitions

To examine these shifts, census data from the last fifty years are used to determine changes in the number of families and married couples as a proportion of overall households, and the number of married couples as a proportion of families.

A household includes all people occupying a housing unit. Usually the householder is the person in whose name the housing unit is owned, being bought, or rented. Households are defined by the sex of the householder and the presence of relatives and are either family or non-family households (U.S. Bureau of the Census 2003).

Families are defined by the Census Bureau as "a group of two persons or more (one of whom is a householder) related by birth, marriage or adoption and residing together" (U.S. Bureau of the Census 2003). A married couple is defined as a "husband and wife enumerated as members of the same household." Married couples without children usually are young two-earner families, older "empty nester" couples, or elderly couples who may have their grandchildren living with them (Frey 2001). Children refer to a parent's own children under the age of eighteen.

A non-family householder is a householder living alone or with non-relatives only. Non-relatives usually are foster children, housemates or roommates, boarders, or an unmarried partner (U.S. Bureau of the Census 2003).

Changes in other family and non-family types are also compared. Other families with children are usually single-parent households, and other families without children include single adults with their parents living in their home, single parents with children over eighteen living with them, and adult relatives living in the same household (Frey 2001). Because past studies have found differences between inner cities and the suburbs in terms of where various family types live, this analysis will compare St. Louis City with seven surrounding counties of the MSA: St. Louis, St. Charles, Franklin, and Jefferson Counties in Missouri, and Madison, St. Clair, and Monroe Counties in Illinois.

Family Changes

Why worry about family structure? Casper and Bryson (1998) suggest that family structure is closely related to economic well-being. Family income and poverty are characteristics based not only on total income for the family, but also on marital status, family members in the work force, and number of dependents in the family. Each of these components has changed during the past fifty years, and these adjustments have made a difference in family well-being.

Today, few families fit the traditional image of a father working and a mother staying home with the children. These changes have occurred for several reasons, most notably changes in family life cycles. New life cycle patterns have evolved since 1950, and the result is an increase in family structures other than married parents with children (Carter and McGoldrick 1999). A number of married parents become single parents at some time during their children's lives, and some of these remarry, adding their spouse and his or her children to the mix. Others have children, but never marry. As grandparents live longer, more are living with their grandchildren. Gay and lesbian couples now participate in commitment ceremonies, formalizing families that have existed for many years. Although they are still considered non-families by the Census Bureau, they are counted. One of the most obvious consequences of changing life patterns has been the decrease in married couples and married couples with children.

Women's Changing Roles

As women pursue careers, they wait longer to marry and to have children, or decide not to have children at all. Women's roles in family economics have changed, so that a woman adding her paycheck to the family is now often a necessity. Teachman, Tedrow, and Crowder (2000) suggest that the decline of the participation of married men in the work force from 90 percent in 1960 to 78 percent in 1997 has contributed to the importance of a wife's income to the economic survival of their families. Women in the work force often wait until later to have children. Moreover, women's ability to support themselves financially means that for them, marriage is less valued as a source of economic stability (Teachman, Tedrow, and Crowder 2000).

Married women who work are generally more economically independent than those who do not. This independence, when combined with divorce laws that make it easier to leave a partner, has resulted in more divorces and, consequently, more single parents. Men's roles in families have also changed and, as they increase the time spent in child care and housework, men also increase their possibility of retaining physical custody of their children if the marriage ends in a divorce. As a result, more families now, compared to the 1950s, are headed by a single parent, and a larger percentage of these parents are fathers.

Single-parent households have also increased because as women earn more, they are more likely to put off marrying (Teachman, Tedrow, and Crowder 2000). This is particularly true for white women for whom increased earning power explains 70 percent of the decline in marriage. Teachman, Tedrow, and Crowder also suggest that as women spend fewer of their childbearing years in marriage, they are more likely to have children outside of marriage.

Although adoption has always been a solution for couples who want to have children and are unable to conceive, now single people are encouraged to adopt children, increasing the number of single-parent families. In Missouri, the number of single African American women adopting children has increased significantly (personal communication, Joy Hughes, DFS 2002).

Longer Life

Because Americans are living longer, more parents will spend as much time as "empty nesters" as they do raising children. The proportion of people over sixty-five is predicted to increase from 12.8 percent of the population in 1995 to 20.7 in 2040. Longer life means a greater chance of spending time in three-, four-, and five-generation families. For women especially, this means more time caring for older parents, aunts, uncles, disabled children, grandchildren, or great-grandchildren (Moen and Forest 1995). It also means that many women, who are likely to outlive their husbands, will spend more time living alone than in the past.

During the past fifty years, the Census Bureau has gradually acknowledged changing family types by refining its definition of households. For example, in 2000 the Census Bureau, in recognition of the growing number of grandchildren now being raised by their grandparents, included a question on family relationships to enable collection of data on grandparent/grandchildren families. In 1950, the Census Bureau had three categories for marital status: single, married (including separated), and widowed or divorced. By 2000, the categories included: never married; now married, spouse present; now married, spouse absent; now married, separated; now married, other; widowed; and divorced.

Changes: Families and Households

Although there have been major changes in American families in the past fifty years, Frey (2003) suggests that the decline in traditional married-couple families, which began in the1960s, has slowed. He attributes this, to a major extent, to the population growth of Asians and Hispanics, who are more likely to form traditional families, and Generation-Xers, whose preference for traditional families has not shown the same decline as seen in previous decades.

In the St. Louis region, except in St. Louis City, the number of families has, for the most part, increased every year. St. Louis City lost 67 percent of its families from 1950 to 2000. The loss has been fairly steady, peaking with a 28 percent loss in families from 1970 to 1980. The loss of families has leveled off somewhat, with a 16 percent and 15 percent decrease in the two decades since 1980.

Monroe County lost families a little earlier with a 36 percent loss from 1960 to 1970, but that loss was offset by a 116 percent increase in families the previous decade. Since 1970, the number of families has increased steadily, with a 25 percent increase in families between 1990 and 2000. St. Clair County is the only other county that has lost families at some point, but the number of families there increased by 28 percent from 1950 to 2000.

St. Charles County had the largest increase in families—930 percent—from 1950 to 2000. Jefferson County also experienced a substantial growth in families, with a 466 percent increase during the past fifty years. However, most of this growth occurred prior to 1980. During the past decade growth in families has slowed considerably. Monroe County experienced the most growth in families, a modest 10 percent increase.

Even though numbers of families in suburban counties have increased, the growth in households has been greater, indicating more people are living alone or in non-family situations. The growth in households has been significant, a 1,095 percent increase in St. Charles and a 543 percent increase in Jefferson County. Only St. Louis City has lost households—43 percent from 1950 to 2000.

Central Cities

Chow and Coulton (1998), using Cleveland as an example, describe how changing labor markets, continued suburbanization of the population, and growth of poverty contribute to an increase in social problems, including what they call "family distress." One component of family distress is family structure. Their analysis found that prolonged unemployment and dependence on welfare assistance weakened the social conditions of the neighborhoods. These changes were compounded by selective out-migration of traditional, married-couple families to outer ring, more affluent suburbs and an increase in female-headed households in the city. Others (Garfinkel and McLanahan 1986; McLanahan and Sandefur 1994) have found that children raised in female-headed families are also more likely to be school dropouts and single parents themselves.

In many ways the changes in Cleveland are similar to those in St. Louis City and graphically describe how family structure is affected by economic and other social factors. Chow and Coulton (1998) point out that because social distress touches all aspects of city residents' lives, it will affect not just neighborhoods but also the entire metropolitan area, contributing to a decline in the overall quality of life for everyone. They argue that it is important to be aware of the rapid decline of social conditions in urban areas so that this decline may be addressed.

Although the following does not address social conditions specifically, it will examine one of many factors involved in social structure—types of families. As will be seen, within the St. Louis region, St. Louis City and (sometimes) St. Clair County generally move in the opposite direction of the suburban counties.

Married Couples

In 1950, approximately 82 percent of all households in the St. Louis region were married couples. However, there was a difference between St. Louis City and St. Charles County, where 78 percent and 79 percent of households respectively were married couples, and St. Louis County where 90 percent of the households were married couples.

By 2000, the difference among counties is striking (see Table 2). In St. Louis City, only 26 percent of households were married couples, a 300 percent decrease from 1950. St. Charles County now has one of the largest proportions of married-couple families (63 percent), second only to Monroe County (65 percent). St. Louis and St. Clair Counties have also begun to lag behind with just approximately half of their households (51 percent and 48 percent respectively) being married couples. Now only 50 percent of the households in the region are married couples, although the dramatic drop in St. Louis City has an effect on the average for the region. When St. Louis City is left out of the equation, 57 percent of the households in the surrounding counties are married-couple families.

Another way of examining changes in family structure is to compare married couples as a share of families (i.e., married couples and single heads of households) in 1950 to the share of married couples now. In 1950, married couples ranged from 96 percent of the families in St. Louis

County to 87 percent in St. Louis City. In 2000, the number of married-couple families as a percentage of families had fallen to 50 percent in St. Louis City, 76 percent in St. Louis County, and 77 percent in Madison County. The City's decline is comparable to other urban areas with declining populations (Frey 2001).

During the past fifty years, St. Louisans have followed the national trend toward fewer married couples. However, the information in the 1950 census does not allow a close analysis of what might be contributing to the trends. Information from the 1970 to 2000 censuses allows a more comprehensive examination of differences in family and non-family household types, and the rest of the comparisons in this chapter will use 1970 and 2000 census data.

Frey (2001) has compared the 1990 and 2000 census data, and has found that traditional married-couple families are more likely to settle in the South and West of the country. But those married-couple families living in slow-growing Midwest cities, particularly those with children, declined at a much faster rate than other families and non-families. Missouri is one of nineteen states where there was a decline in married-with-children households, although Missouri's decline was only 1.1 percent. On the other hand, Illinois had a 4.3 percent increase in married-couple-with-children families. Frey stresses the importance of married-couple families to urban growth. He found that when cities, including St. Louis, with significant inner-city black populations lost white families, the consequence was smaller "married-with-children shares." But the suburbs of these cities also had smaller growth in the shares of married-couple families and significant growth in non-family households. Tables 1 and 2 describe the changes in family types as a percent of households for each county. As can be seen, the decrease in married-couple families has contributed to the overall decrease in family households, with the greatest change occurring in St. Louis County and St. Louis City.

Not only have married-couple households decreased, fewer married couples are having children. In 1970 married couples with children made up 63 percent of the families in St. Charles and 34 percent of the families in St. Louis City. In the Illinois counties of the region—Madison, Monroe, and St. Clair—married couples with children were about half of the family households. By 2000, the share of married couples with children as a percent of families had dropped in each county. Monroe County had the smallest change in share of married couples with children, dropping from 51 percent to 42 percent. Although St. Louis City started with the smallest share of married couples with children in 1970 (34 percent), by 2000 St. Louis County, St. Charles County, and Jefferson

County each had 20 percent fewer married couples with children as a proportion of families. Although St. Louis started with many fewer married couples with children in 1970, thirty years later the Missouri counties surrounding St. Louis City had lost relatively more married couples with children. St. Louis County now has reached the same share of married couples with children, 34 percent, that St. Louis City had in 1970. In St. Clair County, even fewer, or 31 percent of, families are married couples with children. Percentage changes are actually higher. When St. Louis City's share of married couples with children dropped from 34 percent to 21 percent, this was a 40 percent decrease in the City's share of married couples with children.

Children

Another way to understand families is to examine relationships of those living in families. The 2000 census includes a question that asks the relationship of children living with householders. Although most of the children residing in households are the birth children of the householder (Table 3), it is now possible to see how many children are adopted and stepchildren. Foster children are not counted as part of a family household.

There is some difference among the counties in the number of birth children in families. St. Louis City has the largest share of natural children as a percent of children in the family, 94 percent. St. Clair County has the smallest share, 90 percent. These shares are balanced by shares of stepchildren living with householders. St. Louis City and St. Louis County families have fewer stepchildren, 4 percent. Jefferson County has the largest share, 8 percent. There is little difference among the counties in the share of adopted children in families. Although the number of adopted children is small in comparison to birth children and stepchildren, several federal acts, including the Adoption and Safe Families Act of 1997, have increased the incentives for families to adopt.

Frey (2001) suggests that urban areas that have experienced growth in the last decade have a large percent of married couples with children. He attributes this to an influx of immigrants and expansive borders of the cities, which tend to have more suburban-type areas within their boundaries. But fast-growing areas also have experienced increases in all household types. The St. Louis region has some immigrant families, but the City is completely landlocked. New housing in the Washington Avenue loft area and in other areas may bring some new residents to the city, but for now St. Louis City is one of fifteen urban areas with the greatest decline in its central city population (Frey 2001).

In reality, decisions about where to live depend on where a person is in the family life cycle, proximity to work, and affordability of existing housing. Although many families with children do live in the suburbs, a number of families, with or without children, continue to prefer a city location for their home.

As the counties surrounding St. Louis City and St. Clair County, which include East St. Louis, gain more population and become more urbanized, the families who live there have changed as well. The share of married-couple families is now lower in those counties, and, as described in the following sections, those counties have more non-family households.

Table 3. Relationships of Household Residents, 2000
(percent of family or non-family households)

	Franklin	Jefferson	Madison	Monroe	St. Clair	St. Charles	St. Louis County	St. Louis City
Family Households								
Female householder	17%	19%	23%	15%	30%	17%	26%	49%
Child:	36%	37%	36%	37%	38%	38%	37%	40%
Natural born (% of child)	91%	89%	92%	91%	90%	91%	93%	94%
Adopted (% of child)	2%	2%	2%	3%	3%	2%	3%	3%
Step (% of child)	7%	8%	6%	6%	5%	6%	4%	4%
Grandchild	2%	2%	2%	1%	3%	1%	2%	5%
Parent	0%	1%	1%	1%	1%	0%	1%	1%
Total Number	81,827	175,379	215,393	24,278	217,087	249,830	842,183	255,626
Non-family Households								
Male householder:	41%	43%	37%	39%	38%	38%	35%	40%
Living alone (% of male householders)	78%	76%	80%	81%	81%	74%	81%	82%
Female householder:	43%	38%	47%	46%	47%	42%	50%	45%
Living alone (% of female householders)	90%	87%	88%	92%	90%	87%	89%	88%
Total Number	10,971	20,687	37,797	2,956	34,121	30,273	154,793	81,913

Note: Percentages presented unless otherwise noted.

Family Types

As family structure changes, we would expect to find an increase in the percent of other family types to match the decrease in married couples. As mentioned earlier, the Census Bureau includes in other family households single male- and female-headed households, two-sibling households, and other relatives living together. Because not all of the householders are single parents, these families will be referred to as "other families" or single head of household families. "Parents" will be used when the "with own children" category is being discussed.

Although St. Louis City's share of other families rose from 18 percent in 1970 to 26 percent in 2000, a 47 percent increase in proportion, other counties—St. Louis and Jefferson—had greater overall increases in the proportion of single head of household families, 92 percent and 101 percent respectively. In St. Louis and Jefferson Counties, the share of other families rose from 8 percent to 16 percent and 15 percent respectively. Monroe County's share of single head of household or other families barely budged from 9 percent in 1970 to 10 percent in 2000.

When looking at other family types as a percentage of families, the changes in share of families are more striking. Again, St. Louis City shows the greatest change, with single head of household families increasing from 27 percent to 57 percent. St. Clair County has the next highest share, 37 percent, but it also had one of the highest shares in 1970, 17 percent. When overall change in proportion is compared, Jefferson County again has the highest change, 212 percent, having moved from an 8 percent share to a 25 percent share in single heads of households.

Single fathers head only a small percentage of the families with children, but in St. Louis County their share of family households has increased five-fold from 1 percent in 1970 to 5 percent in 2000. The smallest increases have been 150 percent in St. Charles and Monroe Counties, the counties with the highest shares of married-couple families.

The outcome of these changes for children is that their chances of living in a single-parent home at some point in their lives continue to increase. Although this is not necessarily a negative for children emotionally, single mothers, the largest share of single heads of households, are more likely than others to live in poverty (Chow and Coulton 1998). This brings us back to how family structure matters. In the St. Louis region it matters a great deal. Of those families in poverty (Table 2), the share that is woman-headed households ranges from 32 percent in Monroe County to 63 percent in St. Louis City. Madison, St. Louis, and St. Charles Counties are similar with 54 percent, 56 percent, and 58 percent shares respectively. In the St. Louis region, living with a single mother means that you have a better than average chance of being poor.

Although increases in male- and female-headed families account for some of the decrease in married-couple families from 1970 to 2000, the increase in non-family households appears to explain more. The large majority of non-family households are people living alone (see Table 3), and more than one-third of people living alone are over sixty-five years old (Frey 2001).

Other non-family households are unrelated people living together.

Once more, St. Louis City is the exception in the region. Thirty-one percent of St. Louis City households in 1970 were non-family. This was almost twice the share found in the next highest counties—Madison and St. Clair, where the share of non-family households was 17 percent. By 2000, St. Louis County had experienced the largest increase in non-family households, moving from a 13 percent share of households in 1970 to a 33 percent share of households in 2000, a 145 percent increase. Other counties with large percentage increases were Jefferson County, 120 percent from 11 percent in 1970 to 24 percent in 2000, and St. Charles County, which had a 106 percent increase from 12 percent in 1970 to 24 percent in 2000. Although, in 2000, the percentage shares for the counties range from 24 percent—St. Charles, Jefferson, and Monroe—to 48 percent in St. Louis City, the overall changes are larger than those for any other family structure.

Race and Ethnicity

Census data from 1970 will be used to examine changes in black families, and from the 2000 census to examine black and Hispanic families. In 1970, black households were a small percentage of households in most counties, composing less than 1 percent of households in Franklin, Jefferson, St. Charles, and Monroe Counties. St. Louis City (34 percent) and St. Clair County (21 percent) had the largest share of black households. Because the share of black and Hispanic households is relatively small, this discussion will examine differences at the regional instead of the county level.

Married couples composed 51 percent of the black households in 1970, single heads of households composed 27 percent, and non-family households composed 22 percent (see Table 4). By 2000, the share of married couples had dropped dramatically to 27 percent. Families headed by a single person increased to 40 percent of the black families, and the share of non-family households had also increased to 33 percent. St. Charles County had the largest share of black married-couple households (48 percent); St. Louis City had the smallest (19 percent). Conversely, St. Louis City had the largest share of non-family households, 39 percent; St. Charles County had the smallest, 24 percent.

In 1970, 76 percent of white households were married couples, 9 percent were single heads of households, and 15 percent were non-family households. By 2000, the change in share of white married-couple families had experienced a decrease similar to that of black families. Married couples shares had decreased to 55 percent of white households, although

2 of every 3 white households in St. Charles and Monroe Counties were married couples. However, the share of single heads of households increased only 3 percentage points to 12 percent, while the share of non-family households more than doubled to 33 percent.

Hispanics were not included in the 1970 census, but 2000 census data are available to use as a comparison with white and black families in the region. Frey (2001) suggests that Hispanic families are more likely to be married-couple families, and that is true for the region (Table 4), where 50 percent of Hispanic households are married couples. Nineteen percent of Hispanic families are single heads of households and 31 percent are non-families.

Table 4. Household Type Shares by Race and Ethnicity, 1970 and 2000, St. Louis Region

	1970	2000
Total black households	105,617	171,446
Married couple	51%	27%
Single head	27%	40%
Non-family	22%	32%
Total white households	657,023	770,691
Married couple	76%	55%
Single head	9%	12%
Non-family	15%	33%
Total Hispanic households	NA	11,289
Married couple	NA	50%
Single head	NA	19%
Non-family	NA	31%

Note: NA = Not available.

Overall, whites and Hispanics are more likely to have a larger share of married-couples households than blacks. Baker (1999) examines three theories that have been used to describe an increase in single-parent families. Using a number of independent variables including male employment rate, he finds support for William Julius Wilson's (1990) dislocation theory, which says single families result when there is a decline in eligible black males through unemployment and incarceration. This may explain, to some extent, the larger number of black single-parent families in the counties with larger black populations.

Other Types of Households

Unmarried-partner households were first counted in the 1990 census as a separate type. Nationally, these now account for 5 percent of households, only slightly less than non-family households with 2 or more people (6 percent) and slightly more than multigenerational households (4 percent).

In St. Louis, unmarried-partner households account for 6 percent of the households in St. Louis City and Jefferson County, 5 percent of the households in Madison, St. Clair, Franklin, and St. Charles Counties, and 4 percent in Monroe and St. Louis Counties (see Table 5).

Differences occur with the share of same-sex and opposite-sex couples. St. Louis City has one of the largest shares of unmarried couples. It also has the largest share of same-sex couples, or 16 percent of all unmarried couples. Monroe County has only eleven documented same-sex couples, a 3 percent share of unmarried couples in that county.

Because Americans are living longer, there is a greater possibility for families to live in multigenerational households. As a result, the 2000 census asked about relationships of family members which allowed tabulating grandparent/grandchild families. Multigenerational families are more likely to reside in areas where new immigrants live with their relatives, where there are housing shortages that cause families to double up on their living arrangements, and in areas that have relatively high rates of single-parent families living with their children in their parents' home (Frey 2001). These families are still a very small share of households, and as can be seen (Table 5) the counties for once are fairly similar in their share of multigenerational households.

Although multigenerational families include grandparents, there are about twice as many families where grandparents live with their grand-children without their grandchildren's parents being present. Data on grandparents with their own grandchildren living with them are available as estimates for the St. Louis MSA for 2000 and 2001. Within a year, the number of grandparents responsible for grandchildren under eighteen years old who are living with them has increased from 35 percent in 2000 to 38 percent in 2001.

In the St. Louis region, the percent of grandparents who care for the grandchildren with whom they live is somewhat higher. Half of the grandparents (50 percent) in St. Louis City live with and care for their grandchildren (Table 5). This share is similar to St. Clair (49 percent), Madison (47 percent), and Jefferson and Franklin Counties (46 percent each). Monroe County has the smallest share, or about one-third of grandparents (34 percent) in the county, caring for their grandchildren.

Returning to the St. Louis MSA estimates, a more striking change is in the percent of grandparents who have been caring for their grandchildren for five or more years, an increase from 28 percent in 2000 to 50 percent in 2001. A large percent of the grandparents are married, 69 percent, and are in the labor force, 57 percent, although the percent in the labor force decreased by 9 percent from 2000 to 2001. Not surprisingly the percent of grandparents responsible for their own grandchildren who are in poverty has increased by 9 percent during the same time period.

Table 5. Household Categories from 2000 Census

	Franklin	Jefferson	Madison	Monroe	St. Clair	St. Charles County	St. Louis County	St. Louis City
Total Households (Number)	34,945	71,449	101,953	10,275	96,810	101,663	404,312	147,076
Unmarried partner (number)	1,842	4,270	4,765	367	4,995	4,810	16,135	9,433
Percent	5.3%	6.0%	4.7%	3.6%	5.2%	4.5%	4.0%	6.4%
Same-sex partner (percent of married partners)	7.0%	6.4%	9.5%	3.0%	8.7%	9.1%	10.5%	15.8%
Grandparents living w/ grandchildren (number)	1,598	3,485	4,330	290	5,610	3,731	16,393	9,417
Percent	4.6%	4.9%	4.2%	2.8%	5.8%	3.7%	4.1%	6.4%
Grandparents responsible for grandchildren (pct. living w/ grandchildren)	45.9%	46.5%	46.8%	33.8%	48.7%	40.5%	42.9%	49.6%
Multiple-generation families (number)	579	1,313	1,495	220	1,870	1,664	7,045	3,136
Percent	1.7%	1.8%	1.5%	2.1%	1.9%	1.6%	1.7%	2.1%

Note: Percent of household unless otherwise noted.

Casper and Bryson (1998), in their summary of demographic research on grandparents, found that blacks are more likely to raise their grandchildren, that women are more likely to care for grandchildren than men, and that kinship care is more likely to occur in black and Hispanic families. Children in kinship care families are twice as likely to be receiving public assistance as other children.

In 1997, there were 3.7 million grandparents who were the head of the household containing their grandchildren (Casper and Bryson 1998). Most of these heads of households were grandmothers, 2.1 million. Casper and Bryson have found substantial differences among grandparent family types. For example, grandmothers in grandmother-only households are less likely to have graduated from high school, less likely to be employed, more likely to rent, more likely to be African American, and more likely to be poor when compared to other grandmothers. Although households headed by single grandmothers are only 14 percent of the grandparent-headed families in this region, this group will require more social services than other grandparent families.

In 2000, 26 percent of households in the United States consisted of a single person living alone. The only household type that had a larger household share was married-couple households (52 percent). Areas with a low percentage of married couples were more likely to have one-person households in 2000. This is generally true in the St. Louis region, particularly in St. Louis City, which ranked ninth in the country with the highest percent of one-person households in 2000 (Simmons and O'Neill 2001). Generally, living alone is more likely to occur at certain life stages—when young adults move out on their own, when couples separate or divorce, or when elderly people are widowed.

This increase in single-person households cannot be fully explained by an increase in the number of people over sixty-five as a share of the population. From 1950 to 2000, St. Louis City as well as St. Louis and St. Charles Counties had a decrease in the share of elderly as a percent of the population. Even in the counties where there were gains in this group, the gains in share were modest—9 percent to 13 percent in Monroe County, 8 percent to 12 percent in Franklin County. Madison County has the largest share of people older than sixty-five years in its population, 14 percent (see Figures 1 through 8 for changes in each county).

Neither can the increase in single-person households be attributed to a larger share of people eighteen years moving into adulthood. The share of people eighteen years and under has remained essentially the same or decreased from 1950 to 2000, while the number of single, never married people has changed noticeably in St. Louis City, increasing from about one in five (18 percent) to almost one in three (32 percent). St. Clair and St. Louis Counties also have had increases—14 percent to 21 percent in St. Clair County and 15 percent to 21 percent in St. Louis County—while St. Charles County's share of single people dropped from 20 percent to 17 percent. Other counties either dropped slightly—St. Clair and Jefferson— or rose slightly—Madison and Franklin. The increase in single, never married people in some counties is balanced by decreases in others and cannot be used to explain the increase in single-person households.

The most dramatic change from 1950 to 2000 has been in the number of divorced and widowed people. St. Louis County experienced a 133 percent overall increase in share of divorced or widowed people. The share of the population who were widowed or divorced rose from 6 percent in 1950 to 14 percent in 2000. Madison County also had a relatively large overall increase, 114 percent, going from 7 percent of the population being widowed or divorced in 1950 to 15 percent in 2000. The smallest change in share of divorced or widowed people in the population occurred in St. Louis City—11 percent to 17 percent, an overall change of

55 percent. Even though not everyone who is divorced or widowed lives alone, the large increase in this group helps to explain increases in the population share of single people living alone, except in St. Louis City, which started with fewer married couples and which has seen a larger overall increase in single, never married people.

Another way of examining single persons in non-family households is by gender (Table 3). In each county except Jefferson, females are more likely to be the householder living in non-family households. St. Louis County has the highest share, 50 percent, and Jefferson County has the smallest, 38 percent. What is more striking is the share of female householders who live alone—92 percent in Monroe and 90 percent in Franklin and St. Clair Counties. Even in those counties that have the smallest share of female householders living alone, only 13 percent live with another person. Although only a small share of non-family households have householders who are sixty-five and older (Table 2), a large majority of female householders live alone.

Figure 1. Single, Married, and Widowed/Divorced, St. Louis City, Missouri

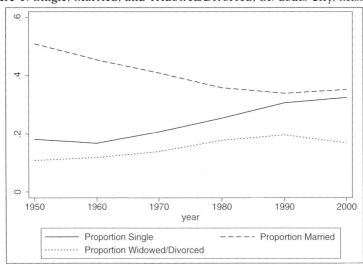

Figure 2. Single, Married, and Widowed/Divorced, St. Louis County, Missouri

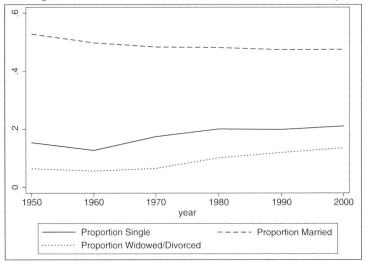

Figure 3. Single, Married, and Widowed/Divorced, St. Charles County, Missouri

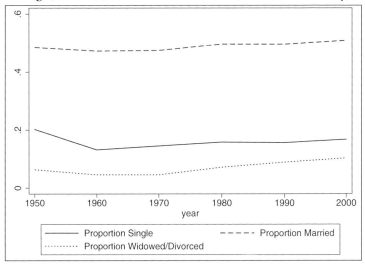

Figure 4. Single, Married, and Widowed/Divorced, Jefferson County, Missouri

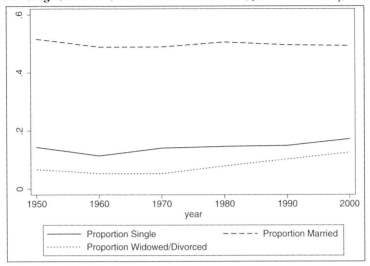

Figure 5. Single, Married, and Widowed/Divorced, Franklin County, Missouri

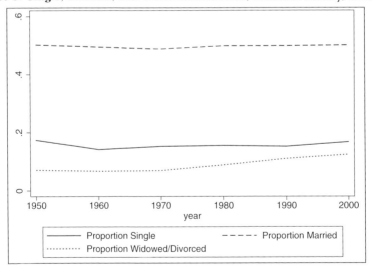

Figure 6. Single, Married, and Widowed/Divorced, St. Clair County, Illinois

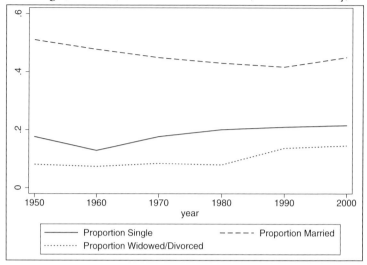

Figure 7. Single, Married, and Widowed/Divorced, Madison County, Illinois

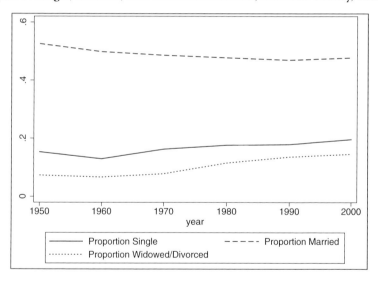

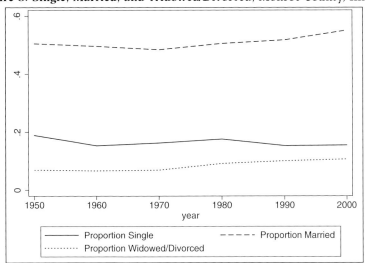

Figure 8. Single, Married, and Widowed/Divorced, Monroe County, Illinois

Changes in family structure are important for many reasons. An increase in families headed by single women is likely to require an increase in a number of social services including Women Infants and Children, Temporary Assistance for Needy Families, and food stamps. As more grandparents take care of their grandchildren, they will need access to schools, child care and, if the children are in kinship care, subsidies. An increase in family size as more generations live together corresponds to different types of housing and affordable housing for large family groups. The relationship of people living together is a key variable for determining the definition of poverty, which is used to determine eligibility for a wide range of state and federal programs.

Knowledge about changes in family structure helps government agencies evaluate programs geared towards particular groups and helps policymakers determine whether or not an issue is important enough to change existing policy or develop new policy (i.e., the increase in grandparent caregivers). Grandparent caregivers who participate in kinship care are now eligible for subsidies which, in many cases, provide them the additional financial support needed to keep grandchildren in their homes.

These days, the Cleavers may not have as many neighbors who look like them, but families like them still make up a large share of families in such counties as Monroe, St. Charles, Franklin, and Jefferson. Parents who are single heads of households will find St. Clair, Madison, and St. Louis City more to their liking. And, people who live alone will probably feel more at home and find the services they need in St. Louis City.

References

Anderson, Margaret. *Thinking About Women: Sociological Perspectives on Sex and Gender.* Boston: Allyn and Bacon, 2000.

Baker, David G. "The Increase of Single Parent Families: An Examination of Causes." *Policy Sciences* 32 (1999): 175–88.

Carter, Betty, and Monica McGoldrick. "Overview: The Expanded Family Life Cycle." *In The Expanded Family Life Cycle: Individual, Family, and Social Perspectives.* 3rd ed. Edited by Betty Carter and Monica McGoldrick. Boston: Allyn and Bacon, 1999.

Casper, Lynn, and Kenneth Bryson. *Co-resident Grandparents and Their Grandchildren: Grandparent Maintained Families.* U.S. Bureau of the Census Population Division Working Paper No. 26, 1998.

Chow, Julian, and Claudia Coulton. "Was There a Social Transformation of Urban Neighbourhoods in the 1980s? A Decade of Worsening Social Conditions in Cleveland, Ohio, USA." *Urban Studies* 35 (1998): 1358–75.

Frey, William H. *City Families and Suburban Singles:* An Emerging Household Story from Census 2000. Census 2000 Series. Washington, D.C.: Brookings Institution, 2001.

___. "Married with Children." *American Demographics* 25 (2003): 17–20.

Garfinkel, Irwin, and Sara McLanahan. *Single Mothers and Their Children: A New American Dilemma.* Washington, D.C.: The Urban Institute Press, 1986.

McLanahan, Sara, and Gary Sandefur. *Growing Up with a Single Parent: What Hurts, What Helps.* Cambridge, Mass.: Harvard University Press, 1994.

Moen, Phyllis, and Kay Forest. "Family Policies for an Aging Society: Moving to the Twenty-first Century." *Gerontologist* 35 (1995): 825–31.

Simmons, Tavia, and Grace O'Neill. *Households and Families: 2000.* Census 2000 brief. Washington, D.C.: U.S. Census Bureau, 2001. Available online at http://www.census.gov.population/www/cen2000/briefs.html.

Teachman, Jay D., Lucky M. Tedrow, and Kyle D. Crowder. "The Changing Demography of America's Families." *Journal of Marriage & Family* 62 (2000): 1234–47.

U.S. Bureau of the Census. American Community Service. Accessed through http://www.census.gov/acs/www/UseData (accessed November 2003).

Wilson, William Julius. *The Truly Disadvantaged: The Inner City, the Underclass, and Public Policy.* Chicago: University of Chicago Press, 1990.

Chapter 11

A Century-or More-of Homicide in St. Louis

Scott H. Decker
University of Missouri–St. Louis

Jeffrey J. Rojek
Saint Louis University

Eric P. Baumer
University of Missouri–St. Louis

Introduction

In both a figurative and a literal sense, St. Louis occupies a central place in the history of the United States. Located in the geographic and current population center of the country, St. Louis provides the opportunity for social scientists, policymakers, citizens, and pollsters to understand national trends in a local context. Certainly the rapid population expansion of the early twentieth century, and the even more rapid contraction of the City's population during the second half of that century, illustrate local exemplars of national trends. The concentration of poverty and the loss of manufacturing jobs in the last two decades of the twentieth century are another example of how the city has become a microcosm—often in exaggerated terms—of national trends.[1] Unfortunately, St. Louis serves as a bellwether to national homicide trends as well, albeit at greatly exaggerated levels. This chapter examines trends in St. Louis homicides, placing them in a national context, as well as the context of population change.

The availability of murder data for St. Louis City beginning in the 1860s provides a remarkable series of homicide data. These data compare favorably with the often-cited Monkkonen series for New York City in

---

[1] Indeed, Morrison (1974) regards St. Louis as one extreme of the growth-decline continuum that American cities experienced in the two decades following World War II.

terms of consistency of definitions, completeness of the series, and availability of complementary data. In addition, the historical span encompasses the most noteworthy demographic changes in the City's history, including major shifts in population size, economic conditions, and ethnic and racial composition. This chapter addresses four related issues. First, we examine trends in St. Louis homicides over the past 140 years. Second, we evaluate the extent to which St. Louis homicide trends converge with or diverge from U.S. national trends. Third, we consider the relationship between changes in racial composition and changes in homicide in St. Louis. Finally, we speculate about the reasons behind the homicide trends reported in the chapter. Before addressing these issues, however, we situate our work in the broader criminological literature on historical homicide trends.

Research on Homicide Trends

There is voluminous literature on homicide covering a wide range of topics, including the role of victim-offender relationship (Wolfgang 1958; Decker 1993), weapon use (Wolfgang 1958), motive (Decker 1996), temporal trends (Zahn 1989; Eckberg 1995, regional variation (Gastil 1971), the role of drugs, alcohol, and gangs (Goldstein 1989; Rosenfeld, Egley and Bray 1999; Parker 1995; Decker and Curry 2002), and the structural correlates of homicide (Messner and Sampson 1991).

Although less prevalent, there also have been some studies of historical homicide trends. Lane (1999) attempts to estimate homicide rates as early as the medieval ages; he concludes from the available data that homicide rates in the United States in its first two centuries were extremely high, perhaps over 20 per 100,000 residents, but generally have declined since that time. During the twentieth century, U.S. homicide rates have exhibited some dramatic peaks and valleys (BJS 2002; Blumstein and Wallman 2000). Homicide rates increased from under 2 per 100,000 at the turn of the century to about 10 per 100,000 by the early 1930s, but then fell to 5 per 100,000 by the early 1940s. Beginning in the early 1960s, however, homicide rates began to rise precipitously; rates peaked by the early 1980s just under 11 per 100,000. Homicide rates fell slightly during the early 1980s to about 8.4 per 100,000, rose substantially during the latter half of the 1980s and early 1990s to about 10.5 per 100,000, and have declined substantially since that time. The U.S. homicide rate for 2002 was 5.5 per 100,000 residents.

Most homicide research, including historical work, has been conducted with cities as units of analysis, owing largely to the concentration of homicide within large cities and, as Lane (1999) suggests, because cities experienced particularly high rates of homicide and large spikes in homicide due to the clash of religion, race, and culture that tends to accompany big city life. The "city context" of homicide is not new; indeed, historical work demonstrates that big cities have higher concentrations of homicide and other forms of violent crime, not only in terms of the raw numbers but also in terms of rates.

City level homicide studies have been conducted in Los Angeles (Maxson, 1999), Chicago (Block and Block 1992), Milwaukee (Rose and McClain 1990), New York City (Goldstein, Brownstein, and Ryan 1992), and Indianapolis (McGarrell and Chermak 2002). There has also been considerable research on homicide in St. Louis, with studies of the role of gangs (Rosenfeld, Bray and Egley 1999; Decker and Curry 2002), victim-offender relationship (Decker 1990, 1993, 1996), witnesses (Decker 1996), neighborhood characteristics (Kohfeld and Sprague 1991), drugs (Rosenfeld 1990), and the relationship between St. Louis and national trends in homicide (Rosenfeld, Decker and Kohfeld 1990). However, there have been few studies of historical trends in St. Louis homicide. Meyers (1954) examined trends in St. Louis homicide rates from 1937 through 1953. He determined that rates were highest during the early 1930s (13.14 per 100,000 in 1930), declined during the late thirties and forties (a low of 6.5 per 100,000 in 1945), only to rise to double digits by 1953 (11.21 per 100,000). The homicide trends for the city, however, have not remained stable since Meyers's research. In fact, St. Louis City gained the nickname "Murdertown" by virtue of ranking first in homicide rates (18.7 per 100,000) in 1965, which suggests the need for an expanded examination of St. Louis homicide trends.

Although relatively little attention has been devoted to historical homicide trends in St. Louis, there has been considerable study of such trends in other major cities. These studies have focused on large cities, most notably London, Amsterdam, Philadelphia, and New York, and describe homicide trends in these areas for several hundred years. Lane (1999) observes that homicide rates in these cities have generally followed a reverse "J" curve pattern; that is, they declined dramatically from a peak in the Middle Ages, to bottom out in the early part of the twentieth century, only to increase again in the 1960s. Monkkonen (2000) notes a dramatic decline in homicides in London from 1250 to 2000, corresponding with what some (Mares 2003) identify as a "civilizing process" (see, for example, Elias 1939). Homicide rates peaked in the early stages of this series, falling to their nadir in the nineteenth century, but rising throughout the twentieth century. At their peak, rates in London were between 10 and 20 homicides per 100,000. This process was replicated in the Low Countries (Mares 2003), Belgium and the Netherlands, between the fourteenth and eighteenth centuries. The reported declines in homicide in the Low Countries (Spierenburg 1994; Eisner 2001; Franke 1994) mirror those of London.

New York City has been the focus of much of the previous research on long-term homicide rates. This may be due to a variety of factors, not the least of which is the richness and quality of death records available for historical analysis. Despite these attributes, New York City homicide data have some deficiencies. As Monkkonen (1997) reports, homicide data from the Uniform Crime Reporting (UCR) Program administered by the Federal Bureau of Investigation (FBI) is available for New York from 1931 onward, but prior to that period a variety of sources must be consulted, including coroner's reports, newspaper reports, and local police data. The use of multiple sources of data in historical homicide research raises a number of issues, including problems with changing definitions, consistency of data collection across record types, and the variability in how homicides are attributed to a particular city, which is especially problematic for port cities such as New York. With these conditions as a backdrop, Monkkonen reports that between 1840 and 1875, New York homicide counts ranged between the upper teens in the late 1840s to a high of nearly 120 in 1865. The overall trend during this period was an increase in the number of homicides in New York. Monkkonen reveals, however, that like European cities, New York and other American cities experienced a decline in violence following the Civil War. This decline occurred despite the presence of massive immigration, crowding, growth, and increases in poverty.

Ferdinand's (1967) study of Boston homicides between 1849 and 1951 reflects patterns similar to those that occurred in New York City during the same period. Despite the dramatic growth in population, ethnic diversity, and volatility in employment, homicide rates in Boston declined during this period. Homicides in Boston peaked in the period of 1855–59 at 7 per 100,000 residents, declined to about 2 per 100,000 during the Civil War, only to rise to 6 per 100,000 during the period immediately after the Civil War. In general, homicide rates showed a pattern of decline in Boston from the post–Civil War years through the 1950s.

The Chicago Historical Homicide Project (Bienen and Rottinghaus 2002) has produced an especially rich set of data on Chicago homicides from 1889 through 1930. This includes entries on more than 11,000 homicides in Chicago during a period when the city underwent a number of significant demographic, economic, and population changes. The homicide count increased from fewer than 50 in 1889 to nearly 700 at the end of the series. There was a dramatic increase beginning in the late teens, with a rapid acceleration in raw numbers during the 1920s. Gun deaths were the largest category during this period, although homicides, gun deaths, and auto accidents appear to be correlated, particularly beginning in 1910. Males predominated as both victims and offenders during this period, composing 79 percent of victims and 90 percent of offenders. Seventy-eight percent of victims were white, and 85 percent of defendants were white. Homicide was a predominantly intra-racial affair for whites, as 96 percent of whites were killed by whites. However, the majority of black victims (54 percent) were killed by white suspects.

The role of race looms large in most historical studies of homicide, even if it has been difficult to gauge precisely with available data. In his comprehensive study of national homicide trends, Lane (1999) notes that although the overall pattern shows that homicide rates in the United States declined in the last half of the nineteenth century, homicide rates for blacks actually rose. Monkkonen (1995) also examined the role of race in homicides over time in New York City. Consistent with Lane's (1999) national-level research, Monkkonen concludes that black and white homicide rates diverged considerably during the nineteenth century. His analysis shows that while white homicide rates declined in the nineteenth century, those for blacks increased, particularly after the Civil War. Nonetheless, it is important to note that for most of this period, homicide remained a largely intra-racial and intra-ethnic form of violence, with most killers choosing victims of their own race or ethnicity. This reflects patterns of opportunity as well as interaction. In highly segregated cities, patterns of routine activities keep racial groups relatively isolated, confining their interactions largely to within-group patterns.

In short, there have been relatively few studies of long-term homicide trends in the United States. The existing research on homicide trends has focused primarily on a few large cities, and although general patterns are difficult to decipher from this work, the weight of the evidence points to five major trends in homicide rates during the past 150 years: 1) a decline in homicide rates from approximately 1850 through the early 1900s; 2) a substantial increase in homicide from the early 1900s through the 1930s; 3) a steady decline from the early 1940s through the early 1960s; 4) a substantial increase in homicide between the early 1960s and the early 1980s; and 5) a substantial increase between the mid-1980s and early 1990s followed by an even greater decline through 2001. These general patterns fit the national portrait of homicide in the United States as well as those observed in the small number of cities for which long-term homicide data are available. One of the goals of this chapter is to evaluate whether similar patterns emerge for the city of St. Louis.

Measuring Historical Homicide in St. Louis

One well-established approach to examining homicide patterns in the present day is though use of the data provided in the UCR, which contains counts of crimes known to the police. The UCR data provide for not only an aggregation of homicide figures at the national level, but also crime estimates for state and local jurisdictions. There is a limitation in using these data for the analysis of historical homicide trends, however, given the fact that this recording mechanism did not start until 1930. One solution for expanding the time series prior to the period covered by the UCR program is to use data on arrests for homicides provided by local police departments, which facilitate the measurement of homicide in the pre-1930 period. Monkkonen (1995) used this strategy for obtaining long-term estimates of homicide rates in New York City. In addition to presenting historical trends as reviewed above, Monkkonen reported that homicide arrest trends in New York were strongly correlated (the Pearson's correlation was approximately .80) with the homicide trends observed with UCR data in the period for which data from both sources are available (i.e., post-1930). This suggests that using arrest data to supplement UCR homicide data is a reasonable approach for gauging historical homicide trends.

We adopt Monkkonen's approach for the analyses reported in the remainder of this chapter. Specifically, we draw from the official records of the St. Louis Metropolitan Police Department (SLMPD) for reported arrests for homicides to supplement data provided by the UCR to present a long-term portrait of St. Louis homicide. The official arrest records for the SLMPD provide a rich data series of homicide counts that date back to 1865. Annual arrest figures are available for crimes ranging from a variety of low-level offenses, such as being drunk in public and loitering, to arrest for serious crime such as homicide. Further, the reports provide details of the race and ethnicity of individuals arrested, though these data are available only from 1931 onward. Consequently, our time series data for overall homicide arrests commences in 1865, while the series for race-specific analyses begins in 1931.

Although the data used for our analyses are innovative, there are some noteworthy inconsistencies in the raw data over time, particularly with respect to the precise definition of murder used. From 1865 to 1930, the SLMPD reported arrests separately for homicide and manslaughter, respectively. To facilitate comparisons with more recent data, we combine these categories into one overall homicide count (see also Monkkonen 1995). With the advent of the UCR program in the 1930s, some changes in the way police agencies report crime emerged. The most notable change relevant to the present analysis occurs in 1947, when many police agencies, including the SLMPD, began reporting separate counts for homicide/non-negligent manslaughter and negligent manslaughter, respectively. We believe it is reasonable to assume that the pre-1930 data used for our analysis includes both negligent and non-negligent manslaughter; accordingly, we chose to combine these two forms of manslaughter, along with homicide counts, to construct overall estimates of homicide for the period of 1947 onward. This strategy seems justified and, given that manslaughter composes a very small proportion of total homicides, it is unlikely to introduce significant bias into our examination of long-term homicide patterns for St. Louis.

One additional consideration in the SLMPD arrest data is that the published reports for annual arrest figures are not available after 1984. To extend our series beyond this date, we obtained overall and race-specific homicide arrest data from the publicly available UCR arrest files. Doing so yields a database that contains overall homicide arrest counts for St. Louis from 1865 through 2000, and race-specific (limited to blacks and whites) homicide arrest counts from 1931 through 2000.

To adjust for changes in population size during the time period considered in our research, we obtained population counts for St. Louis City from the 1860–2000 decennial censuses. Counts for the total population as well as the black and white population of the city were gathered for each decennial period, and annual counts were estimated by using linear interpolation between censuses. We then used the annual population counts to compute homicide arrest rates per 100,000 residents; parallel rates were computed for blacks and whites as well, using the race-specific arrest data described above and race-specific census population estimates. Standardizing the arrest counts in this way facilitates a more meaningful comparison of the relative incidence of homicide during the period examined in our study.

Trends in St. Louis Homicide

We begin by examining trends in St. Louis homicide arrest rates between 1865 and 2000. For ease of presentation, we divided these data into two graphs: Figure 1 shows homicide arrest rates from 1865 to 1929, and Figure 2 shows homicide arrest rates from 1930 to 2000. In both cases, homicide arrest rates (homicide arrests per 100,000 persons) are presented on the y-axis and year is presented on the x-axis. Figure 1 reveals two distinct patterns in the trend in homicide arrests for the period 1865 through 1929. The first pattern is the relatively stable homicide arrest rates observed from 1865 through the end of the first decade of the twentieth century. There is a slight upward trend in homicide arrest rates during this period, but the main story that emerges is that despite substantial demographic, social, and economic change in St. Louis in the last of half of the nineteenth century, homicide arrest rates remained remarkably stable. Such stability is surprising given that the period spans the end of the Civil War, the influx of European immigrants into St. Louis, the beginnings of industrialization, and the westward expansion of the city. Moreover, the city population increased from about 270,000 in 1865 to nearly 700,000 in 1912.

The stability observed in homicide arrest rates during the latter half of the nineteenth century and the early years of the twentieth century appears to reflect the "calm before the storm." As Figure 1 reveals, there was a striking spike in homicide arrest rates beginning in 1912 that appears to signal a general upward trend in rates that lasts through the late 1920s. Some potentially important intervening peaks and valleys are evident in the years before and after World War I, but the general portrait seems to be a dramatic increase in homicide arrest rates between 1912 and 1927, with rates more than seven times higher in the latter year than the former.

Figure 2 provides data for both the homicide arrest rate and the homicide offense rate for the period 1930–2000. These data complement Figure 1 by extending the time series on arrest rates an additional seventy-one years, as well as adding data on the homicide offense rate—the number of homicide incidents recorded by the police, irrespective of whether or not an arrest was made—data that were not available for the earlier time series.

Three features are immediately clear from Figure 2. First, the graphs of the two data series appear to be highly correlated. Indeed, statistical analysis demonstrates that the Pearson's correlation between homicide rate and homicide arrest rate is very strong ($r = .88$), exceeding that of Monkkonen for New York City. This lends confidence in the assumption that one series of data can be reliably substituted for the other, and suggests that the arrest data shown in Figures 1 and 2 are a valid approximation of actual homicide offending rates. Second, and more relevant to the issues explored in our study, the decline in homicide arrest rates that begins in 1927 (see Figure 1) appears to signal the beginning of a substantial, prolonged drop in rates that does not level off until about 1960. The magnitude of the drop during this thirty-three-year period is staggering, with homicide arrest rates declining from about 70 per 100,000 in 1927 to less than 5 per 100,000 in the late 1950s. Third, there are two distinct eras of homicide arrest "booms and busts" during the second half of the twentieth century. As Figure 2 reveals, homicide arrest rates increased steeply between the late 1950s and the early 1970s, but declined sharply from then until the mid-1980s. Somewhat similarly, homicide arrest rates increased considerably between the mid-1980s and the early 1990s, but have fallen precipitously since that time. As noted above, homicide offense rates closely mirror the arrest trends for this period.

Figure 1. Trends for St. Louis Homicide Arrest Rates, 1865–1929

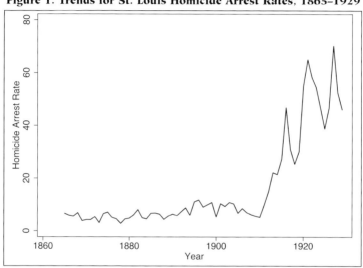

Figure 2. Trends for St. Louis Homicides and Homicide Arrests 1930–2000

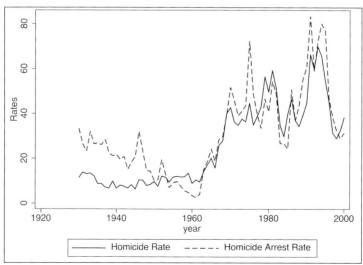

The dramatic changes in St. Louis homicides during the twentieth century may be less exceptional when viewed in comparison with other large cities or the nation overall. For example, as dramatic as the spikes in the St. Louis arrest rates were in the teens, 1970s, and 1990s, they may simply mirror national trends or trends reflected in the dynamics of other large cities. We explore these issues in Figures 3a and 3b.

Figure 3a displays St. Louis homicide arrest rates for the years 1901–2000 and the U.S. reported homicide rate for the same time period.[2] To more readily facilitate comparisons with the trend observed in St. Louis, we multiplied the U.S. arrest rate by a factor of 5 (see also Blumstein and Wallman 2000). Three general conclusions can be drawn from Figure 3a. First, the St. Louis homicide rate is exceptionally high when compared to the U.S. rate, roughly by a consistent factor of 5. Second, the patterns of change in United States and St. Louis homicide rates are remarkably consistent with respect to the timing of major increases and decreases. Not surprisingly, the homicide booms and busts are considerably steeper for the St. Louis data than the national data, owing to the smoothing effect introduced by the large number of jurisdictions which contribute to the U.S. trend line. It is interesting to observe that the decline in St. Louis homicide arrests beginning in the 1930s appears to be steeper than that for the nation. But this comparison masks the fact that big-city homicide rates tend to be higher than those for the nation as a whole, and as such, national homicide rates may not be the most appropriate comparison to set St. Louis trends in a broader context. Indeed, a better means of gauging historical homicide trends in St. Louis would be to compare them to other major U.S. cities.

Figure 3b shows 1934–98 reported homicide offense rates for four cities: St. Louis, Kansas City, Chicago, and New York. We selected the latter three cities because they introduce both stability and variability in the types of structural and cultural conditions evident during this period in the United States. Kansas City and Chicago are both midwestern cities, subject to many of the same historical pressures and changes as St. Louis. Yet, unlike St. Louis and Kansas City, Chicago experienced much greater levels of immigration and demographic change during the period. In

---

[2] It is important to reiterate that the data used for Figure 3a for St. Louis are for homicide arrests, while data for the U.S. are for homicide offenses recorded by the police. We use different measures because a comparable set of data on arrests for the U.S. and reported homicides for St. Louis are not readily available for this period. As noted above, trends in arrests and homicide incidents are very highly correlated for the period during which both figures are available in St. Louis. This suggests that comparing St. Louis homicide arrest rates and national homicide offense rates is a reasonable way to gauge the relative trajectories exhibited during the twentieth century.

addition, New York was the largest U.S. city for most of the period and is unique in historical terms because it experienced many of the social, economic, and demographic transitions thought to be relevant to the production of crime well before St. Louis; moreover, New York City typically accounts for 10 percent of all U.S. homicides annually.

Figure 3a. Comparison of Reported Homicide Rate in the United States (x5) and Homicide Arrest Rate in St. Louis, 1901–2000

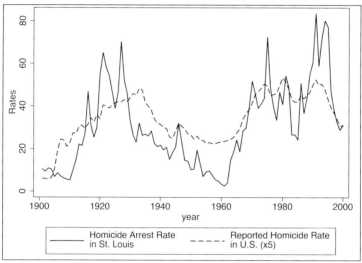

Figure 3b. Comparison of St. Louis Homicide Rate to Other Cities

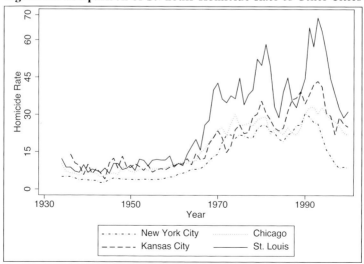

Interestingly, despite the different historical contexts reflected in these four cities, Figure 3b reveals strong similarities in reported homicide rate trends across these cities between 1934 and 1998. All four cities seem to exhibit a relatively stable homicide rate across the first five years of the time series, and each experiences a dramatic increase in homicide in the mid-1960s. Moreover, the cities display similar trajectories during the 1980s and 1990s, with homicide rates declining in the early 1980s, increasing between the mid-1980s and early 1990s, and falling throughout the remaining years of the 1990s. It is also noteworthy, however, that despite exhibiting generally parallel trends, since the early 1960s St. Louis consistently ranks well above the other three cities in terms of its level of homicide. Thus, one broad conclusion we draw from Figures 3a and 3b is that although St. Louis homicide trends during much of the twentieth century are quite similar to those observed for the United States as a whole and for other large cities, the conditions that pushed homicide rates up in the early 1960s and beyond appear to have been more intense in St. Louis than elsewhere. From 1960 onward, homicide rates in St. Louis follow a similar trajectory to those in the other large cities considered, but they do so at a much higher level.

Examining overall homicide trends ignores the substantial role that race plays in levels and trends in city crime rates. Are the patterns shown for St. Louis similar for blacks and whites? To begin to address this question, in Figure 4 we present homicide arrest rates for 1930–2000 disaggregated by race. Three trend lines are shown, which represent total homicide arrest rates and black and white homicide arrest rates, respectively.

Figure 4. Homicide Arrest Rates: Total, Black and White, 1930–2000

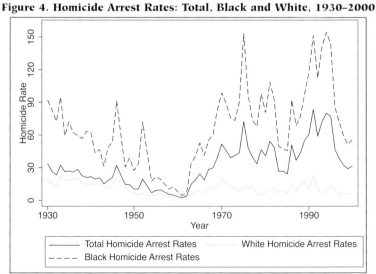

Metromorphosis

Three important observations emerge from inspection of Figure 4. First, the trend in homicide arrest rates for whites is relatively stable throughout the period, fluctuating no more than 10 per 100,000 over the last seventy years of the twentieth century. Second, consistent with findings reported in previous historical studies of homicide in the United States and in New York (Lane 1999; Monkkonen 1995), homicide arrest rates for blacks are generally much higher than the rates observed for whites, and they remain higher throughout the period. Indeed, black arrests account for over half of all arrests from 1950 on, a period of time when blacks accounted for less than one-third of the city's population. And since 1970, blacks have accounted for 80 percent of homicide arrests except for a single year. Not surprisingly, one product of the combination of higher homicide arrest rates for blacks and relatively stable rates for whites is that the trend in overall homicide arrests rates is driven largely by black arrest rates. To elaborate, the correlation between the black arrest rate and total arrest rate is .96, while the correlation between the white arrest rate and the total arrest rate is much weaker (.36). This suggests that the forces responsible for driving homicide arrest rates during much of the twentieth century in St. Louis were apparently more relevant for blacks than whites. Finally, perhaps the most interesting pattern that emerges in Figure 4 is that during the first thirty-two years of the period, from 1930 to 1962, homicide arrest rates for blacks and whites in St. Louis show clear signs of convergence, whereas between 1963 and 2000 the trends diverge considerably. In both cases, the relative gap in homicide arrest rates for blacks and whites is primarily a function of changes in rates for blacks. Most intriguing, however, is that the changes in the relative gap in arrest rates for the two groups are counter to the expectations outlined in much of the social science literature on race, crime, and race relations. This literature anticipates a general increase in the extent to which black and white crime and arrest rates converge during the twentieth century, largely because racial gaps in many of the social conditions believed to drive crime and arrest rates have diminished, especially during the last four decades. In contrast, the data used for our analysis indicates a growing divergence between black and white rates during that period.

Although the full meaning of the race-specific trends shown in Figure 4 would move us well beyond the scope of this chapter, it is noteworthy that the year in which black and white homicide arrest rates begin to diverge considerably—1963—is a unique year in the demographic history of St. Louis. As shown in Figure 5, 1963 is the first year in which the City's black population approaches about one-third of the total population, a proportion that has been identified as an important "tipping point" in social science research on racial segregation (Schelling 1971), and whites' expressed neighborhood residential preferences, perceived threat from blacks, and fear of crime (e.g., Stults and Baumer 2003).

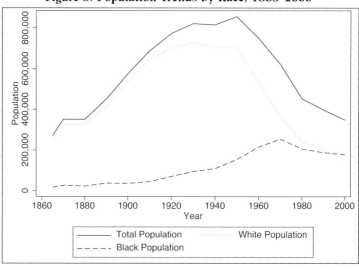

Figure 5. Population Trends by Race, 1865–2000

Conclusions

What are we to make of these findings? St. Louis clearly is an important location in which to study homicide. The dramatic increases in homicide in St. Louis over the past 150 years make it clear that both in terms of the rapidity of change and overall prevalence, St. Louis homicide rates may provide important lessons for other major cities and the nation. Indeed, homicide and violence more generally have plagued the city over much of the last century. Accounting for the underlying causes is somewhat more difficult, however, than documenting those changes. Given the descriptive nature of our analysis, we can only speculate about those causes; more definitive answers must await future research.

Demography clearly plays a role in the changes in homicide over time, but its role is not immediately evident. The most obvious explanation for the patterns of increase and decrease in homicide in St. Louis may be the rapid shifts in population. After all, St. Louis grew dramatically in population in the later part of the nineteenth and early twentieth centuries. However, demographic changes move slowly and incrementally, words that are not accurate in describing the three dramatic increases in

St. Louis homicide rates between 1865 and 2000. And it is difficult to accept the assertion that population increases—or decreases for that matter—account for the sudden upturns and downturns in homicide. For example, the 1980s and 1990s were decades of substantial population loss in the city, yet homicide rates exhibit both substantial increases and decreases during this period. This questions the importance of the role of population change, per se, on changes in homicide trends.

It is also doubtful that changes in other demographic attributes such as age and gender composition account for much of the observed change in homicide trends in St. Louis. Although these components of population structure do change considerably in the City over the period covered in our analysis, they did not shift sufficiently to fuel the three increases in homicide noted in Figures 1 and 2. Nor does it seem likely that changes in social conditions and economic well-being were responsible for much of the observed changes in homicide trends; like most of the demographic variables, these conditions tend to change somewhat slowly, at least relative to the rapidity with which homicide trends in St. Louis appear to increase and decrease.

Race is a demographic variable with an apparent major relationship to changes in homicide rates. There is a strong correlation between changes in black homicide rates and the overall homicide rate in the City of St. Louis between 1930 and 2000. The timing of the most substantial increase in black homicide arrests during this period, and the beginning of the divergence between black and white rates, began and grew substantially at a time when the city population changed from about one-third to about one-half black. To be clear, the data used for our research do not enable us to address why black and white homicide arrest rates diverge from the early 1960s onward. The fact that the divergence is driven by a substantial increase in the number of black arrests during a period in which blacks compose a steadily growing proportion of the population is supportive of theoretical arguments that link greater levels of crime control applied to blacks in response to growing racial threat perceived by whites. However, the trends observed in our study are also consistent with theories that emphasize the importance of structural disadvantages (e.g., concentrated poverty, joblessness) in generating high levels of homicide. It has been well documented that blacks have experienced a disproportionate share of these disadvantages in St. Louis and elsewhere (FOCUS St. Louis 2001). What is clear from our work is that a comprehensive understanding of historical homicide trends requires a close inspection of race-disaggregated rates, and a closer consideration of the forces that may have generated the patterns of convergence between the early 1930s and the early 1960s, and the patterns of divergence thereafter.

A final city level variable that may provide one clue for the explanation of the dramatic increases in homicide relative to the nation and the three comparison cities during the 1960s is the fixing of city borders. As Jones (2000) notes, unlike other cities, the St. Louis border has not expanded since 1876. As a consequence, St. Louis has the second smallest central city population of any MSA, ranking only behind Atlanta. Practically speaking, this has the effect of concentrating the poor and potentially the underclass of the MSA within the City. Moreover, the "border politics" that characterize the St. Louis geographic landscape have created a potentially misleading denominator for use in the calculation of homicide rates. Such rates are computed by using residential city populations, which in many instances gives a valid representation of the number of persons at risk for a specified outcome. More than is the case in other cities, however, the residential population of St. Louis City since the 1960s has vastly underestimated the number of persons who work and play within the city limits and, as a result, should technically be considered in the denominator of crime rate calculations. Although we lack reliable estimates of the annual daily population for St. Louis City during the period covered by our study, it is nonetheless important to note that the elevated levels of homicide revealed in our study, and to a lesser extent the excess increase observed relative to other cities, may be partly a function of differences in the geographic composition of the metropolitan area in which St. Louis is situated.

Overall, our analysis has documented some of the major homicide booms and busts experienced in St. Louis during the past 135 years. For the most part, the trends observed for St. Louis parallel those observed in other major cities and for the nation as a whole. The analysis also documents important race differences in homicide trends, especially during the last four decades of the twentieth century. The study contributes to the historical homicide literature and to what we know about St. Louis, past and present. Yet, it raises many questions that cannot be addressed with the data currently available, such as: Why was there such stability in homicide arrest rate trends between 1865 and 1911, a period that could not easily be characterized as stable in terms of demographic, social, and economic change? What accounts for the substantial increase in homicide during the pre- and post–World War I era, and what drove the equally substantial decline in the 1930s, 1940s, and 1950s? Finally, what were the precise factors that led to the major increases in homicide rates in the 1960s for blacks in St. Louis and elsewhere?

References

Bienen, Leigh B., and Brandon Rottinghaus. "Learning from the Past, Living in the Present: Understanding Homicide in Chicago, 1870–1930." *Journal of Criminal Law and Criminology* 92 (2002): 437–534.

Block, Carolyn, and Richard Block. "Overview of the Chicago Homicide Project." In *Questions and Answers in Lethal and Non-Lethal Violence*, edited by Carolyn Block and Richard Block. Washington, D.C.: National Institute of Justice, 1993.

Decker, Scott H. "Deviant Homicide: A New Look at the Intersection of Motives and Victim Offender Relationships." *Journal of Research on Crime and Delinquency* 33 (1996): 427–49.

___. "Exploring Victim Offender Relationships in Homicide: The Role of Individual and Event Characteristics." *Justice Quarterly* 10 (1993): 585–612.

___. "Reconstructing Homicide Events: The Role of Witnesses in Fatal Encounters." *Journal of Criminal Justice* 23 (1996): 439–50.

Decker, Scott H., and G. David Curry. "Gangs, Gang Homicide and Gang Loyalty: Organized Crimes of Disorganized Criminals." *Journal of Criminal Justice* 30 (2002): 1–10.

Eckberg, Douglas Lee. "Estimates of Early Twentieth-Century U.S. Homicide Rates: An Econometric Forecasting Approach." *Demography* 32 (1995): 1–16.

Eisner, Manuel. "Modernization, Self-Control, and Lethal Violence." *British Journal of Criminology* 41 (2001): 618–38.

Elias, Norbert. *The Civilising Process: Sociogenetic and Psychogenetic Investigations*. London: Blackwell, 1939.

Ferdinand, Theodore N. "The Criminal Patterns of Boston Since 1849." *American Journal of Sociology* 73 (1967): 688–98.

Fields, Larry, "City May Earn New Title—Murdertown." *St. Louis Globe-Democrat*, May 4–5, 1968, p. 15.

FOCUS St. Louis. *Racial Equality in the St. Louis Region*. St. Louis: FOCUS St. Louis, 2001.

Franke, Herman. "Violent Crime in the Netherlands: A Historical-Sociological Analysis." *Crime, Law, and Social Change* 21 (1994): 73–100.

Gastil, Robert. "Homicide and a Regional Culture of Violence." *American Sociological Review* 36 (1971): 412–27.

Goldstein, Paul. "Drugs and Violent Crime." In *Pathways to Criminal Violence*, edited by N. A. Weiner and M. E. Wolfgang. Beverly Hills, Calif.: Sage Publications, 1989.

Goldstein, Paul, Henry Brownstein, and Paul Ryan. "Drug-Related Homicide in New York: 1984 and 1988." *Crime and Delinquency* 38 (1992): 459–76.

Gurr, Ted Robert, ed. *Violence in America: The History of Crime*. Vol. 1. Newbury Park, Calif.: Sage, 1989.

Jones, E. Terrence. *Fragmented by Design: Why St. Louis Has So Many Governments*. St. Louis: Palmerston and Reed, 2000.

Kohfeld, Carol, and John Sprague. "The Organization of Homicide Events in Time and Space." In *The St. Louis Homicide Project: Local Responses to a National Problem*, edited by Richard Rosenfeld, Scott Decker, and Carol Kohfeld. St. Louis: University of Missouri–St. Louis, 1991.

Lane, Roger. "Murder in America: A Historian's Perspective." In *Crime and Justice: A Review of Research*, edited by Michael Tonry. Chicago: University of Chicago Press, 1999.

Leonard, Ira M., and Christopher C. Leonard. "The Historiography of American Violence." *Homicide Studies* 7 (2003): 99–153.

Mares, Dennis. "Civilization, Economic Change, and Trends in Interpersonal Violence in the Netherlands, England and the United States." Ph.D. diss. proposal, University of Missouri–St. Louis, 2003.

Maxson, Cheryl L. "Gangs and Gang Homicide: An Extension of the Literature." In *Homicide: A Sourcebook of Social Research*, edited by M. Smith and M. Zahn. Thousand Oaks, Calif.: Sage, 1999.

McGarrell, Edmond, and Steven Chermak. "Problem Solving to Reduce Gang and Drug-Related Violence in Indianapolis." In *Policing Gangs and Youth Violence*, edited by Scott Decker. Belmont, Calif.: Wadsworth, 2002.

Messner, Steven, and Robert Sampson. "The Sex Ratio, Family Disruption, and Rates of Violent Crime." *Social Forces* 69 (1991): 693–713.

Meyers, Arthur C. "Murder and Non-Negligent Manslaughter: A Statistical Study." *St. Louis University Law Journal* 3 (1954): 18–34.

Monkkonen, Eric. "Diverging Homicide Rates, England and the United States, 1850–1875." In *Violence in America*, edited by Ted Robert Gurr. Newbury Park, Calif.: Sage, 1989.

___. "Homicide over the Centuries." In *The Crime Conundrum*, edited by Lawrence M. Freedman and George Fisher. Boulder, Colo.: Westview, 1997.

___. *Murder in New York City*. Berkeley: University of California Press, 2000.

___. "New York City Homicides: A Research Note." *Social Science History* 19 (1995): 201–14.

___. "Racial Factors in New York City Homicide, 1800–1874." In *Ethnicity, Race, and Crime: Perspectives across Time and Space*, edited by Darnell Hawkins. Albany, N.Y.: University of Albany Press, 1995.

Morrison, Peter. "Urban Growth and Decline: San Jose and St. Louis in the 1960s." *Science* 185 (1974): 757–62.

Parker, Robert Nash. *Alcohol and Homicide: A Deadly Combination of Two American Traditions*. Albany, N.Y.: SUNY Press, 1995.

Rose, Harold, and Paula McClain. *Race, Place, and Risk: Black Homicide in Urban America*. Albany, N.Y.: SUNY Press, 1990.

Rosenfeld, Richard. "Anatomy of a Drug-Related Homicide." In *The St. Louis Homicide Project: Local Responses to A National Problem*, edited by Richard Rosenfeld, Scott H. Decker, and Carol Kohfeld. St. Louis: University of Missouri–St. Louis, 1991.

Rosenfeld, Richard, Tim Bray, and H. Arlen Egley, Jr. "Facilitating Violence: A Comparison of Gang-Motivated, Gang-Affiliated, and Non-Gang Youth Homicides." *Journal of Quantitative Criminology* 15 (1999): 495–516.

Rosenfeld, Richard, Scott H. Decker, and Carol Kohfeld. "Different Levels, Common Causes: St. Louis Homicide Rates in National Perspective." In *Questions and Answers in Lethal and Non-Lethal Violence*, edited by Carolyn Block and Richard Block. Washington, D.C.: National Institute of Justice, 1993.

Spierenburg, Pieter. "Faces of Violence: Homicide Trends and Cultural Meanings: Amsterdam, 1431–1816." *Journal of Social History* 27 (1994): 701–16.

Wolfgang, Marvin. *Patterns in Criminal Homicide*. Philadelphia: University of Pennsylvania Press, 1958.

Zahn, Margaret. "Homicide in the Twentieth Century: Trends, Types, and Causes." In *Violence in America*, edited by Ted Robert Gurr. Newbury Park, Calif.: Sage, 1989.

Chapter 12
The Municipal Market in the St. Louis Region: 1950–2000

E. Terrence Jones
University of Missouri—St. Louis

The Setting

The modern U.S. metropolitan area is a public marketplace. The principal collective competitors are municipalities, each seeking to succeed in the contest for a viable combination of residents, shoppers, and workers. Those that do well create higher property values and stronger tax bases. The former benefit resident-owners directly, and the latter can provide citizens with either lower internal levies for existing services or higher revenues for additional ones (Lewis 1996; Ostrom et al. 1961; Schneider 1989; Weiher 1991).

Through regulatory policies, especially zoning, and expenditure policies, particularly the types and styles of public goods and services offered, municipalities possess strategic tools for positioning themselves and, if circumstances change, for repositioning themselves. With 10 to 20 percent of households changing locations annually, it is a dynamic market.

Sharing with Pittsburgh the distinction of having the most local governments per capita, the St. Louis metropolitan area is an especially appropriate region to examine how the municipal market works over an extended time. The analysis focuses on the eight counties (City of St. Louis, Franklin, Jefferson, St. Charles, and St. Louis in Missouri and Madison, Monroe, and St. Clair in Illinois) that have been part of the region the longest. Among the questions addressed are: Is the region becoming more municipal, with larger numbers of incorporated areas and greater shares of citizens living within them? What are the levels of entry into and exit from the municipal market? How are various cities faring in the competition for housing values? Do the same jurisdictions always end up on top or is there movement over time? Do income trends follow housing patterns? Are cities' populations become more economically diverse or similar? Racially, are cities becoming more integrated or segregated?

The Players

The core eight-county St. Louis metropolitan area now has 195 incorporated municipalities (see Figure 1). They fall into three general types. First is the City of St. Louis, the original central city, founded in 1809. Second are older communities which once had their own independent existence but, over time, have been drawn into the expanding metropolitan boundary. Examples, with their founding dates, include Alton (1837), Belleville (1850), Festus (1887), Florissant (1786, the earliest), St. Charles (1809), and Union (1851). Third are the suburbs, by far the most numerous, which started slowly but, in the twentieth century, multiplied.

Most of the municipal growth spurt occurred during the 1930s and the ten years immediately following World War II. In St. Louis County, now

Figure 1. Municipal Map, St. Louis Eight-County MSA, 2000

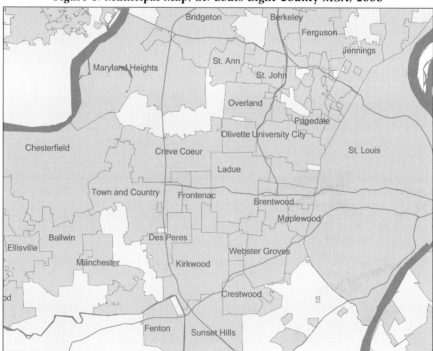

the home of almost half the region's municipalities, there were only 6 cities (Bridgeton, Fenton, Ferguson, Kirkwood, Florissant, Webster Groves) prior to 1900. Even over the next thirty years, as the County's population moved toward 200,000, only 12 more (Brentwood, Clayton, Glendale, Huntleigh, Maplewood, Oakland, Olivette, Richmond Heights, Rock Hill, Shrewsbury, University City, Valley Park) were born.

By 1950, however, the region had 160 municipalities, then 180 in 1960. After that, the number stabilized at 180 in 1970, crept up to 188 in 1980, 191 in 1990, and now 195 in 2000. Incorporation, however, does not necessarily lead to eternal life. Between 1950 and 2000, 48 new municipalities appeared and 13 went out of existence, leaving a net increase of 35.

With one exception (Times Beach, killed by dioxin, and Marvin Terrace), all the remaining cities which either merged or disincorporated had fewer than one thousand residents and most had less than five hundred.

Population Trends

Excluding the City of St. Louis from the calculations, the average municipal population has grown substantially between 1950 and 2000. As Table 1 shows, the median population has more than doubled, going from 1,116 to 2,712, and the mean count has almost doubled, rising from 3,837 to 7,134. Moreover, the entire distribution has risen, indicating that growth is not simply caused by a few jurisdictions booming. Dividing the group into quartiles, the dividing line between the smallest one-quarter and the remainder has risen about two-thirds, going from 378 to 624, while the least populous of the top one-quarter has almost tripled, rising from 3,006 to 8,459.

Table 1. Municipal Population: 1950–2000, Excluding the City of St. Louis

Year	Mean Size	Distribution		
		25%	50% (Median)	75%
1950	3,837	378	1,116	3,006
1960	5,291	526	1,763	5,251
1970	6,117	630	2,168	6,951
1980	5,799	618	2,313	6,164
1990	6,393	680	2,665	7,472
2000	7,134	624	2,712	8,459

Source: U.S. Census of Population, 1950–2000.

In 1950, as the City of St. Louis's population peaked at 856,796, more than four out of every five regional residents lived in an incorporated area (see Table 2). As the City's size dropped precipitously over the next three decades, the incorporated share declined also, hitting its lowest point at two-thirds in 1980. Since then, it has crept back up to 69.8 percent. The other municipalities have become by far the prevailing cities of choice. In 1950, just 35.0 percent of the region's population lived in an incorporated area other than the City of St. Louis. By 2000, 55.8 percent call one of these municipalities home. The modal regional resident lives in a municipality other than the central city.

Steady growth or regular decline is the exception, not the rule, for the region's municipalities. For those cities that have existed from 1950 to the present, 78 percent have had at least one decade of population loss during that period. Only 18 percent have posted gains in each decade and an even smaller 4 percent have experienced drops every ten years. The six municipalities within the latter group are all in the inner core: the City of St. Louis, East St. Louis and Brooklyn in St. Clair County, and Beverly Hills, Hillsdale, and Wellston in St. Louis County.

Conversely, the twenty-seven that have risen steadily are scattered over the entire region. Every county except the City of St. Louis has at least two entrants in the grow-grow-grow column: Franklin County (New Haven, St. Clair, Union, Washington); Jefferson County (DeSoto, Festus); Madison County (Collinsville, Edwardsville, Glen Carbon, Highland, Maryville, Troy); Monroe County (Columbia, Waterloo); St. Charles County (O'Fallon, St. Charles, St. Peters); St. Clair County (Caseyville, O'Fallon, Shiloh, Smithton); and St. Louis County (Creve Coeur, Des Peres, Ellisville, Fenton, Town and Country).

Table 2. What Share Live in Municipalities? 1950–2000

Year	Region's Population	Proportion Incorporated		
		Total	City of St. Louis	Other Cities
1950	1,768,614	83.40%	48.40%	35.00%
1960	2,120,176	80.50%	35.30%	45.20%
1970	2,381,407	72.60%	26.00%	46.60%
1980	2,323,819	66.70%	19.50%	47.20%
1990	2,389,439	67.40%	16.60%	50.80%
2000	2,482,935	69.80%	14.00%	55.80%

Source: U.S. Census of Population, 1950–2000.

Housing Values

Although most municipalities compete for shoppers and many vie for workers, the contest for residents is the prevailing game. With the exception of a handful of Illinois cities founded as industrial towns—Alorton and Monsanto (now Sauget) are the two leading examples—the remainder want to be attractive places for people to live. The stronger the demand, the higher the property values. That pleases the existing residents, making them more supportive of their local jurisdiction, and produces real property taxes for special districts and for those cities wishing to use them.

One excellent means for keeping score on which municipalities are doing best in the race for residents is the median value of owner-occupied homes. Although this measure has been part of the census since 1950, it has only been calculated for all municipalities—no matter what their size—since 1980. Only forty-seven cities have values from 1950 to 2000, but eighty exist for 1960 to 2000, all for units that have maintained a minimum population. To ease comparisons among the various censuses, each municipality's median housing value is expressed as a ratio of the regional median: 1.00 means that the municipality has the same median value as the overall region, 2.00 indicates it has twice the value, 0.50 half the value, and so forth.

Table 3. Top Ten Municipalities, Owner-Occupied Housing Median Value, 1960–2000. Highest Value Ranked First

1960	1970	1980	1990	2000
Frontenac	Frontenac	Ladue	Ladue	Ladue
Creve Coeur	Ladue	Frontenac	Frontenac	Frontenac
Clayton	Creve Coeur	Creve Coeur	Clayton	Clayton
Ladue	Clayton	Clayton	Creve Coeur	Creve Coeur
Olivette	Des Peres	Des Peres	Des Peres	Des Peres
Des Peres	Olivette	Sunset Hills	Sunset Hills	Sunset Hills
Glendale	Sunset Hills	Glendale	Glendale	Glendale
Kirkwood	Glendale	Ballwin	Olivette	Olivette
Crestwood	Crestwood	Olivette	Ballwin	Kirkwood
Sunset Hills	Bridgeton	Ellisville	Kirkwood	Webster Groves

Note: Only includes 80 municipalities which met minimum population requirements for each census.
Source: U.S. Census of Population, 1980–2000.

Table 3 shows the ten municipalities having the highest median owner-occupied housing values for each decade from 1960 through 2000. There is at best modest movement across this forty-year span. Among the eighty candidates, only fourteen make the top ten for even one of the decades. The prevailing quartet—Creve Coeur, Clayton, Frontenac, Ladue— remains in place throughout the period. With the exception of Bridgeton's securing the tenth slot in 1960, all the other cities are within central, west, or southwest St. Louis County.

Shifting the focus to all 80, 64 percent are either above the median all five times (24 percent) or below it (40 percent). Another 20 percent, all in northern St. Louis County, started the period above the median but ended beneath it. Seven municipalities moved from below to above: four in Illinois (Columbia, O'Fallon, Swansea, Waterloo) and three in Missouri (O'Fallon, Valley Park, Wentzville). Five Illinois cities (Belleville, Edwardsville, Highland, Lebanon, Mascoutah) initially were below, then went above the median in 1970 or 1980 or both, then slipped back below it. Rock Hill had the opposite experience: above in 1960 and 1970, below in 1980, then above since then.

Table 4 lists the top twenty finishers among municipalities for 1980, 1990, and 2000. The leaders every time are two West County enclaves— Huntleigh and Country Life Acres—each having a small number of homes, 129 for the former and just 24 for the latter. Even beyond this pair, the listings have more continuity than change with sixteen municipalities appearing in all three years. That number might have been slightly higher but Chesterfield, incorporated in 1988, is only eligible for 1990 and 2000 and Wildwood, founded in 1995, can just be on the 2000 list.

The central corridor locations—those extending along U.S. 40 from inner St. Louis County (e.g., Clayton) out into St. Charles County (e.g., Weldon Springs)—prevail. No Illinois cities come anywhere close to the top twenty. One North County municipal miniature—Bellerive, sharing a name with the once adjacent country club which moved to West County forty years ago making way for the University of Missouri–St. Louis campus—makes the 1980 and 1990 lists but slips off in 2000. Two South County small cities—Grantwood Village and Lakeshire—make the group in 1980, and Grantwood Village, perhaps helped by the aura of Grant's Farm and the Busch legacy, maintains its standing throughout the period.

From a more comprehensive perspective, there is only modest movement in the rankings across decades. Of the 183 cities existing from 1980 to 2000, 82 percent stayed either above the regional median (27 percent) or below it (55 percent) for the entire period. Nineteen cities (10 percent) slipped from above the regional median to below it while an even smaller number, 10 (5 percent), went from the bottom to the top half. The remaining 3 percent were either above or below the median in 1980 and 2000 and below or above it in 1990.

Metromorphosis

The nineteen municipalities moving downward across the median are scattered across the region. Six (Belleville, Fairview Heights, Lebanon, Mascoutah, New Baden, Hecker) are in St. Clair County; four (Black Jack, Florissant, Glen Echo Park, Hazelwood) are in north St. Louis County; four (Mackenzie, Marlborough, St. George, Wilbur Park) are in south St. Louis County; three (Edwardsville, Hamel, Highland) are in Madison County; and one each is in west St. Louis County (Winchester) and Jefferson County (Arnold).

Table 4. Top Twenty Municipalities, Owner-Occupied Housing Median Value, 1980–2000. Highest Value Ranked First

1980	1990	2000
Huntleigh	Huntleigh	Huntleigh
Country Life Acres	Country Life Acres	Country Life Acres
Clarkson Valley	Westwood	Westwood
Westwood	Ladue	Ladue
Ladue	Clarkson Valley	Town and Country
Town and County	Town and Country	Frontenac
Frontenac	Frontenac	Clayton
Creve Coeur	Clayton	Clarkson Valley
Clayton	Creve Coeur	Creve Coeur
Grantwood Village	Des Peres	Des Peres
Des Peres	Chesterfield	Weldon Springs
Weldon Springs Heights	Warson Woods	Warson Woods
Warson Woods	Grantwood Village	Weldon Springs Heights
Bellerive	Bellerive	Wildwood
Lake St. Louis	Sunset Hills	Chesterfield
Crystal Lake Park	Crystal Lake Park	Grantwood Village
Sunset Hills	Weldon Springs Heights	Flint Hill
Manchester	Glendale	Crystal Lake Park
Glendale	Weldon Springs	Sunset Hills
Lakeshire	Lake St. Louis	Glendale

Source: U.S. Census of Population, 1980–2000.

Six of the ten upward bound, however, are in St. Charles County. They are Cottleville, Flint Hill, Foristell, New Melle, O'Fallon, and Wentzville. The remaining five include two from St. Louis County (Rock Hill and Valley Park), one from Jefferson County (Kimmswick), and one from Monroe County (Valmeyer). Because of the 1993 flood, Valmeyer moved both literally from lower to higher ground and monetarily from below to above the median.

Just 12 of the 183 cities rose 0.50 or more on the relative-to-region scale between 1980 and 2000, most of which represented the best getting even better and thereby separating themselves even more from the pack. The dozen experiencing the rapid rises (and the scale amount) are Huntleigh (+4.00), Country Life Acres (+3.79), Westwood (+2.25), Ladue (+ 2.01), Clayton (+1.47), Flint Hill (+1.42), Cottleville (+0.97), Town and County (+0.93), Frontenac (+0.77), St. Paul (+0.69), Kimmswick (+0.60), and Valley Park (+0.54).

Only one municipality—Black Jack—declined more than 0.50, dropping 0.56 points. Nine others fell more than 0.30 but less than 0.50. These include three cities (Clarkson Valley, Lake St. Louis, St. Peters) which remain above the regional median but have lost some relative ground, five north St. Louis County municipalities (Bellefontaine Neighbors, Bellerive, Dellwood, Moline Acres, Pasadena Hills), and one Illinois city (Belleville).

A more systematic assessment demonstrates that there is expanding differentiation: those municipalities above the regional median in 1980 have for the most part risen faster than the norm, and those finishing below have fallen further. Using the standard deviation to measure the variability in the rankings, how much they cluster around the regional norm, that measure of variation has risen from .77 in 1980 to 1.04 in 1990 to 1.16 in 2000, a 52 percent increase over the twenty years. As citizens choose where to invest their home purchase dollars, their aggregated individual choices are pushing municipality residential property values further apart, not closer together. In the municipal market for owner-occupied housing, the rich are getting richer and the poor poorer.

Family Income

Family income provides another way to assess municipal competitiveness. Although obviously positively correlated with housing value, it differs in two ways. First, incomes apply to all families in the city, not just home owners. Second, they emphasize current dollar flows, while housing stresses accumulated assets. Median family incomes are available for 80 cities from 1960 to 2000 and for all the municipalities in 1990 and 2000. Again, as with housing values, municipal median family incomes for each census are measured as the ratio to the region's figure at that time.

Table 5 lists the top ten for each decade from 1960 through 2000 for the eighty cities having data for each year. Similar to housing values, there is very little movement at the top. Only fourteen separate jurisdictions have made this list and, if one removes Moline Acres—the only north St. Louis County entry—from the 1960 set, just thirteen others prevail for the remaining four decades. The players are also the same crew represented in the top ten housing value list. Doing best continues to be essentially a central corridor phenomenon, with Sunset Hills in southwest St. Louis County being the sole exception.

Table 5. Top Ten Municipalities, Median Family Income, 1960–2000. Highest Value Ranked First

1960	1970	1980	1990	2000
Clayton	Ladue	Ladue	Ladue	Ladue
Ladue	Frontenac	Frontenac	Frontenac	Frontenac
Frontenac	Creve Coeur	Creve Coeur	Creve Coeur	Clayton
Creve Coeur	Des Peres	Des Peres	Clayton	Des Peres
Glendale	Clayton	Clayton	Des Peres	Creve Coeur
Olivette	Olivette	Glendale	Sunset Hills	Glendale
Des Peres	Glendale	Olivette	Ellisville	Sunset Hillls
Moline Acres	Crestwood	Sunset Hills	Olivette	Ballwin
Kirkwood	Webster Groves	Ellisville	Ellisville	Ellisville
Webster Groves	Kirkwood	Kirkwood	Ballwin	Webster Groves

Note: Only includes 80 municipalities which met minimum population requirements for each census.
Source: U.S. Census of Population, 1960–2000.

The most common path along the median income trail between 1960 and 2000 was downward: 36 percent of the cities went from above the regional median to below it during this period. Thirty-one percent remained below the median, 21 percent stayed above it, 4 percent rose from below to above, and 8 percent had up-and-down experiences.

Seventeen of the cities going from above to below average are in north St. Louis County, two (Maplewood, University City) are in central St. Louis County, eight (Alton, Belleville, Bethalto, Cahokia, Dupo, East Alton, Granite City, Wood River) are in Illinois, and one (Crystal City) is in Jefferson County. The three who moved in the opposite direction—down to up—are all in Illinois: Columbia, Mascoutah, and Waterloo. Four cities (Collinsville and Swansea in Illinois, Rock Hill and Shrewsbury in Missouri) started the period above the median, dipped below it sometime during the forty years, then ended above it in 2000. Two others—Highland and Lebanon in Illinois—experienced the reverse: below at the beginning, above at some point (1980 for both), then beneath again.

Table 6 provides the municipalities having the highest twenty median family incomes for the only two censuses, 1990 and 2000, which have estimates for all cities. Again, there is little change at the top. Seventeen cities are on both lists, three small jurisdictions (Twin Oaks in west

St. Louis County and Glen Echo Park and Pasadena Hills in north St. Louis County) drop off between 1990 and 2000, to be replaced by post-1990 entrant Wildwood along with Glendale and Sunset Hills. The 1990 presence of three North County enclaves and the continuation of one of them, Bellerive, in 2000 suggests that even though their housing values might be slipping relative to the rest of the region, they are still able to attract and retain high-income households.

Shifting substantially on the median family income scale is rare. Only six cities shifted more than plus or minus 0.30 (that is, gained or lost 30 percent relative to the regional median) between 1990 and 2000, three up and three down. The three risers are Eureka (+0.40) in west St. Louis County, Glendale (+0.37) in central St. Louis County, and Kimmswick (+0.37) in Jefferson County, while the declining trio are all cases of high fliers having a modest fall: Glen Echo Park (-0.43) in north St. Louis County, Grantwood Village (-0.37) in south St. Louis County, and Twin Oaks (-0.32) in west St. Louis County.

Based on the 1990 and 2000 data, municipalities vary among themselves much more in housing values than in median family incomes. Moreover, unlike housing values where separation among cities is on the rise, there is convergence rather than divergence for median family incomes.

Because both factors are measured as ratios on the same scale (i.e., 1.00 equals the regional mean), one can directly compare their standard deviations. In 1990 and 2000, the housing value standard deviation is almost twice as high as the median family income's: 1.04 for housing and 0.55 for income in 1990, 1.16 for housing and 0.52 for income in 2000. Second, housing variation rose 12 percent during this period while income variation declined 5 percent. Even though there is greater sorting out among cities in how they fare in the housing competition, it has not led to more disparity in residents' household incomes.

Income heterogeneity also was on the rise between 1990 and 2000 within municipalities. In both censuses, the grouped family income distribution allows calculating the mean and standard deviation.[1] By using the coefficient of variation (the standard deviation divided by the mean), one can then compare diversity across decades and municipalities without having the results distorted by the absolute size of the values. The higher the coefficient of variation, the greater the diversity.

For all municipalities, the mean as well as the median coefficient of variability rose 11 percent between 1990 and 2000, indicating that the typical city had increased its income diversity during the past ten years.

---

[1] For the highest category in the grouped ranges (e.g., $200,000 or more), the mean value is set at 1.25 times the lower level (e.g., $250,000 for $200,000).

For each of the two years, larger cities are moderately but statistically significantly more likely to be diverse than are smaller ones.[2]

Table 6. Top Twenty Municipalities, Median Family Income, 1990 and 2000. Highest Value Ranked First

1990	2000
Country Club Acres	Country Club Acres
Westwood	Huntleigh
Huntleigh	Ladue
Ladue	Town and Country
Town and Country	Clarkson Valley
Clarkson Valley	Westwood
Frontenac	Frontenac
Creve Coeur	Clayton
Grantwood Village	Des Peres
Chesterfield	Chesterfield
Clayton	Weldon Springs
Des Peres	Wildwood
Crystal Lake Park	Creve Coeur
Bellerive	Bellerive
Weldon Springs	Crystal Lake Park
Twin Oaks	Warson Woods
Warson Woods	Grantwood Village
Glen Echo Park	Glendale
Pasadena Hills	Sunset Hills
Lake St. Louis	Lake St. Louis

Source: U.S. Census of Population, 1990 and 2000.

Among cities with populations 5,000 and greater, fourteen had their income diversity, as measured by the coefficient of variation, increase 20 percent or more between 1990 and 2000. These range from upper-income municipalities (Creve Coeur, Kirkwood, Ladue, Lake St. Louis, Manchester, St. Peters, Town and Country) to more middle-income communities (Dellwood, Ferguson, Jennings, St. Ann, University City, Washington). Only two cities become noticeably less diverse over the decade, each moving in the opposite direction. Wentzville became more homogenous toward the upper end while Washington Park did so toward the lower.

Table 7 lists the most income-diverse municipalities in 1990 and 2000. This group suggests there are two principal ways for achieving this status. The first—and the one which probably best represents the prevailing

---

[2] An ordinal measure of association—Kendall's tau-b—was used in order to minimize the impact of the most populous cities. The relationship is significant at the .05 level in 1990 and the .01 level in 2000.

sense of what diversity is all about—is a community with a substantial middle-income population with modest numbers of both upper- and lower-income residents. Actual examples would include Alton, Richmond Heights, and University City.

This statistical normal distribution, however, is the less common means to generate a high diversity score. The more frequent is skewed toward the lower end of the income spectrum with a gradual tail extending out all the way to the upper segment. This is how Centreville, East St. Louis, Jennings, St. Louis itself, and others reach the top ten.

Table 8 presents the ten most income-homogeneous cities for 1990 and 2000. The group is about split among those which are dominated by upper or upper middle income households (e.g., Chesterfield, Des Peres, Ladue, Town and Country, Wildwood) and those clustered closely around the middle or lower middle mark (e.g., Dellwood, Florissant, O'Fallon).

Table 7. Ten Most Income-Diverse Municipalities
(Population > 5,000), 1990 and 2000. Most Diverse Ranked First

1990	2000
Washington Park	East St. Louis
Centreville	Centreville
East St. Louis	St. Louis
East Alton	University City
DeSoto	Jennings
Wentzville	Richmond Heights
University City	Alton
Richmond Heights	Cahokia
Union	Shrewsbury
Granite City	Washington Park

Source: U.S. Census of Population, 1990 and 2000.

Table 8. Ten Least Income-Diverse Municipalities
(Population > 5,000), 1990 and 2000. Least Diverse Ranked First

1990	2000
Ladue	Town and Country
Town and Country	O'Fallon (Missouri)
St. Peters	Ladue
Dellwood	St. Peters
Manchester	Dellwood
Chesterfield	Eureka
Des Peres	Des Peres
Florissant	Wildwood
Glendale	Columbia
Maryland Heights	Manchester

Source: U.S. Census of Population, 1990 and 2000.

Metromorphosis

Race

John Farley's examination of residential segregation in the St. Louis region in Chapter 8 demonstrates its persistence throughout the past fifty years. He largely utilizes census tracts as the units of analysis. When one shifts the focus from tracts to municipalities, what patterns emerge? Have cities begun and remained as predominantly black or white or is there substantial racial transition and, if so, in what direction? Once transition begins, especially from white to black, does it reach an integrated equilibrium or does it progress until the city is largely African American? This discussion looks first at the 113 municipalities having data for each census between 1960 and 2000 and then at the 181 possessing information for the last three decades, 1980 to 2000.[3]

In 1960, the St. Louis region had yet to begin dismantling much of the legal segregation affecting housing patterns. Although restrictive covenants had been declared unconstitutional in 1948, the legacy of past segregation continued, and more affirmative fair housing legislation banning private discrimination would not be passed until later in the 1960s. It is not surprising, as Table 9 shows, that 84 percent of the municipalities were predominantly white (i.e., less than 5 percent black) and only 6 percent were more than one-fifth African American, with one-third of these being two historically all-black communities: Brooklyn and Kinloch.

From 1970 forward, however, many municipalities have experienced substantial racial transition. Table 9's categories reflect six different types of racial mixes with the breaking points based on social science research. Those having less than 5 percent black populations are not only predominantly white but also unattractive options for African Americans to enter (Farley et al. 1993; Massey and Denton 1993). The same analyses indicate that, at least since 1980, whites are unlikely to avoid areas or flee them when the African American share exceeds 5 percent but remains under one-fifth. They do, however, become increasingly nervous as the proportion goes past one-fifth and toward one-half. Shifting to political power, both because they are on average younger and because their political participation rates are lower, blacks have some but less than proportional control when their share exceeds a majority but is less than about two-thirds. African Americans then typically achieve public control

---

[3] The examination of race deals only with whites and blacks. For most of this period, the two combined constituted more than 98 percent of the region's population. Although the census definition of race has changed over time, most notably in 2000, it does not affect general patterns. Thus this analysis accepts whatever definition was used for each census.

above 65 percent (Grofman et al. 2001) and, once the community exceeds 95 percent, it is essentially as single race as the 95 percent+ white cities.

Table 9. Municipality Distribution by Percent African American, 1960–2000. N = 113

Percent African American	1960	1970	1980	1990	2000
0.0%–4.9%	84%	74%	63%	48%	42%
5.0%–19.9%	10%	12%	12%	22%	21%
20.0%–49.9%	2%	8%	14%	12%	11%
50.0%–64.9%	2%	1%	1%	4%	4%
65.0%–94.9%	0%	3%	7%	11%	13%
95.0%–100.0%	2%	2%	3%	3%	9%
Source: U.S. Census of Population, 1960–2000.					

Between 1960 and 2000, over half the cities developed at least a visible (i.e., 5 percent or higher) black population and only a minority—although a substantial one at 42 percent—remain predominantly white. For some municipalities, the transition from white to black was rapid. Each decade witnessed cities having their African American share increase 30 percentage points or more, indicating that racial tipping—a dramatic shift from white to black—has not gone out of style. Here are some examples: for 1960 to 1970, Alorton (18 percent to 80 percent black) and Wellston (8 percent to 69 percent); for 1970 to 1980, Berkeley (9 percent to 49 percent), Pagedale (23 percent to 79 percent), Pine Lawn (29 percent to 81 percent), and Washington Park (0 percent to 48 percent); for 1980 to 1990, Bel Ridge (25 percent to 61 percent) and Moline Acres (32 percent to 64 percent); for 1990 to 2000, Dellwood (9 percent to 58 percent), Jennings (48 percent to 78 percent), and Cahokia (5 percent to 38 percent). Over the forty years, eighteen cities went from less than 1 percent black to more than 65 percent African American: Bel Ridge, Berkeley, Cool Valley, Country Club Hills, Flordell Hills, Greendale, Hanley Hills, Hillsdale, Jennings, Moline Acres, Normandy, Northwoods, Pagedale, Pasadena Hills, Pine Lawn, Velda City, Velda Village Hills, and Washington Park.

Is racial tipping inevitable? Once the black share began to increase, has any city been able to stabilize at some equilibrium short of two-thirds or more black? Yes, but the numbers are few. Only two have gone past 30 percent black and not passed 60 percent black within two decades: the City of St. Louis, which went from 29 percent black in 1960 to 41 percent in 1970 but now is just ten points higher (51 percent) in 2000, and University City, which leapt from 0 percent to 43 percent between 1960 and 1980 but has stayed much the same (45 percent in 2000) since then.

Seven others have moved past 10 percent but not risen above 30 percent. The most notable is Rock Hill, which jumped from 8 percent in 1960 to 28 percent in 1970 but is still at 27 percent in 2000. The others, with their 1960/1970/1980/1990/2000 black percentages, are Alton (6 percent/16 percent/21 percent/23 percent/25 percent), Breckenridge Hills (8 percent/11 percent/14 percent/19 percent/29 percent), Hazelwood (1 percent/2 percent/4 percent/11 percent/16 percent) Maplewood (2 percent/3 percent/8 percent/13 percent/16 percent), Olivette (2 percent/1 percent/16 percent/20 percent/22 percent), and Wentzville (7 percent/5 percent/5 percent/14 percent/12 percent). One other municipality, Lebanon, has remained in the teens throughout the period: 14 percent in 1960 to 18 percent in 2000.

Even during the past two decades when there has been heightened awareness about the social costs of residential segregation and the negative consequences of rapid racial transition and awareness of recent examples such as University City about what policies might achieve a stable racial mix, the prevailing pattern has been: once a municipality passes 30 percent African American, it accelerates toward becoming overwhelmingly black. Table 10 shows the relatively small share of cities between 20 percent and 65 percent African American and the growing proportion exceeding 65 percent. During this period alone, seventeen cities went from majority white to majority black. Most have been mentioned in the 1960–2000 discussion, but additional ones from this later group are Black Jack (18 percent in 1980 to 71 percent in 2000), Glen Echo Park (43 percent to 87 percent), Pasadena Park (17 percent to 53 percent), and Vinita Terrace (40 percent to 74 percent).

Concluding Comments

The municipal marketplace is both dynamic and static. Change is prevalent for population, which goes up and down for most cities. Housing value rankings remain much the same over time, but the gap between the market winners and losers has expanded significantly. Residential income standings also are relatively constant, but economic diversity has crept upward during the past two decades. For all but a few cities, race either is a constant—staying predominantly white or, after rapid racial transition, becoming heavily black. But there are a few municipalities, such as Alton, Rock Hill, and University City, that have sustained a racially diverse population.

As actors in this market competition, one suspects that most of the cities initially were more passive than active. Those who have performed best on measures such as housing values probably have benefited more from where they are located than from what they have done. Being in the central corridor, for example, makes success much easier than being in north St. Louis County.

Table 10. Municipality Distribution by Percent African American, 1980–2000. N = 181

Percent African American	1980	1990	2000
0.0%–4.9%	70%	61%	56%
5.0%–19.9%	10%	15%	16%
20.0%–49.9%	10%	10%	8%
50.0%–64.9%	1%	3%	3%
65.0%–94.9%	6%	8%	11%
95.0%–100.0%	2%	2%	6%
Source: U.S. Census of Population, 1980–2000.			

Passivity is most apparent in racial composition. As they move from nearly all-white to, say, one-fifth black and four-fifths white—a proportion that mirrors the region's overall racial mix—very few cities overtly desire to become all-black, especially if the transition is rapid. Yet if the municipalities fail to take positive policy actions, if they instead let the cumulative individual preferences in the marketplace work their collective will, then that is the ultimate outcome.

Over time, however, an increasing number of municipalities are becoming more active in and aware of the competitive environment. If St. Louis remains a slow or steady growth region, what it has been for the past half century and the most likely scenario for the foreseeable future, the competitive intensity within the municipal marketplace should increase. Unlike rapid growth, which provides the opportunity for most or even all to gain, stasis more closely approximates a zero-sum game where one city's win means another municipality's loss. In such a context, cities must be not only lucky—like being sited in a desirable area—but also smart by pursuing and implementing well-designed policies.

References

Farley, Reynolds, et al. "Continued Racial Residential Segregation in Detroit: 'Chocolate City, Vanilla Suburbs' Revisited." *Journal of Housing Research* 4 (1993): 1–38.

Grofman, Bernard, et al. "What Minority Populations Are Sufficient to Afford Minorities a Realistic Chance to Elect Candidates of Choice?" *North Carolina Law Review* 79 (2001): 1,383–1,405.

Lewis, Paul. *Shaping Suburbia: How Political Institutions Organize Urban Development.* Pittsburgh: University of Pittsburgh Press, 1996.

Massey, Douglas S., and Nancy A. Denton. *American Apartheid: Segregation and the Making of the Underclass.* Cambridge, Mass.: Harvard University Press, 1993.

Ostrom, Vincent, et al. "The Organization of Government in Metropolitan Areas." *American Political Science Review* 55 (1961): 831–42.

Schneider, Mark. *The Competitive City: The Political Economy of Suburbia.* Pittsburgh: University of Pittsburgh Press, 1989.

Weiher, Gregory R. *The Fractured Metropolis: Political Fragmentation and Metropolitan Segregation.* Albany: State University of New York Press, 1991.

Chapter 13

Education and Race in St. Louis City and County

Daniel B. Keck
Saint Louis University

Overview

Because comparisons of school systems today rely so heavily on state legislation and on common databases dictated by state accreditation requirements, this chapter will compare St. Louis City schools and St Louis County schools only. Four major issues have dominated public education in St. Louis City and County over the past three decades. They are:

1. The court-ordered desegregation of the city and suburban school districts in St. Louis.
2. The introduction of the Missouri School Improvement Planning (MSIP) process, a data and accountability driven system.
3. The continuing struggles to provide equitable and adequate levels of state funding for public education.
4. Mounting pressures to narrow the discrepancy in levels of achievement between children of lower socioeconomic status, ethnic minorities, and the majority white population.

Of these, the issue of desegregation is arguably the single dominant factor of the past thirty years in St. Louis. It has openly presented the region with a need to confront a series of issues that have permeated its history. These include equity, race and race relations, and access to equal educational opportunity. Desegregation of the schools has become a force in bringing the issues of accountability and social justice to the fore. The federal government's recently passed legislation mandating that "no child be left behind" signals the nation's continuing commitment to a system of inclusive education.

Three decades of attempts to do away with a dual system of public education in St. Louis have effectively linked the national issue of educational accountability to that of narrowing the achievement gap between majority and minority students across the region. All these events have come together at a time when the technology of information gathering, retrieval, and analysis have made it possible to compile and store significant data for comparative studies in education. With common data sets for urban, suburban, and rural schools, researchers now have the capacity to conduct meaningful longitudinal studies on a local, regional, and statewide scale.

The Historical Foundation

In a review of education in St. Louis, Katherine T. Corbett points out the early dominance of parochial and private systems of education in the St. Louis region. It was not until 1847 that the City of St. Louis introduced its first school tax to finance a public system of education which excluded black children. In fact, the education of black children was illegal in Missouri until after the Civil War.

It was the parochial systems of education offered by Lutheran and Catholic parents that led the way toward integration of the races in schools. The Catholic Church desegregated its archdiocesan schools in 1947 while the St. Louis City public schools remained segregated until 1954 when the U.S. Supreme Court declared separate but equal (or dual) systems of education to be unconstitutional. However, the controversy over segregation within the City schools continued, culminating in 1972 in legal action (Corbett 1977, 7).

Desegregation

In 1972 Minnie Liddell, a parent in the St. Louis City School system, along with a group of north St. Louis citizens, brought suit against the St. Louis City Public Schools (SLPS) and the State of Missouri for illegally operating a segregated system. In 1981 the suit was expanded to include twenty-three separate St. Louis County suburban school systems. Two years later the plaintiffs reached a settlement agreement, which included the SLPS, the U.S. Department of Justice, the State of Missouri, the twenty-three suburban school districts named in the suit, the NAACP, and the Liddell plaintiffs.

Under the terms of the original agreement the courts imposed five remedies:

1. A voluntary city-county interdistrict desegregation program would be designed to allow up to 15,000 African American students to

transfer from the SLPS to majority white suburban school districts.

2. The SLPS would provide a magnet school program sufficient to accommodate up to 14,000 students.

3. The SLPS would undertake the improvement of educational quality in all schools, with emphasis on quality improvement in non-integrated schools.

4. The SLPS would begin a program of capital improvement in its physical facilities.

5. The suburban schools would begin efforts to recruit and integrate their staffs (FOCUS St. Louis 2001, 109).

These five remedies led to the establishment in 1983 of the Voluntary Interdistrict Transfer Program, to be financed by the State of Missouri and the St. Louis Public Schools. The program continued under the court-imposed remedies until 1999, at which time the State of Missouri sought relief.

Figure 1. School Districts, St. Louis City and St. Louis County

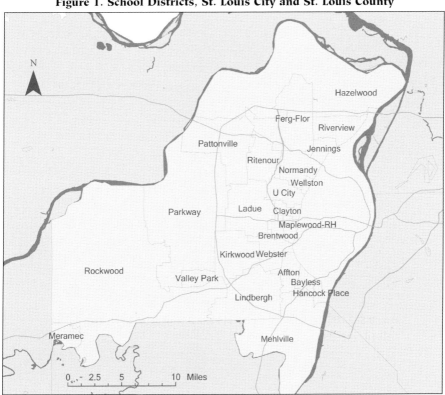

1983—The First Settlement Agreement

The five remedies imposed remained in effect for a decade and each produced a series of results. A review of each remedy and the results that it produced are described as follows.

Remediation 1

"The voluntary transfer of up to fifteen thousand African American students to transfer from the City of St. Louis Public School District to suburban school districts. Transfers to continue until the suburban district had achieved an African American student population of up to a minimum of fifteen percent" (Civic Progress Task Force on Desegregation 1995, 3).

Results

In 1999, the last year of the settlement agreement, 13,263 African American students from the city school system were participating in the voluntary transfer program.

During the initial years of the Voluntary Student Transfer Program, students transferring into the suburban schools from the city were not evenly spread by grade level. An analysis of the 1997–98 transfer group showed that elementary students made up 29 percent of the total transfer population of 11,764 students, while 32.4 percent were middle school transfers and 38.6 percent were high school students. That same year, 1,411 students transferred into the City schools from the county.

Twenty-three suburban districts participated in the program. However, seven districts reached an African American student population of 25 percent or more over the life of the agreement through natural population growth. These seven districts—Ferguson-Florissant, Jennings, Maplewood-Richmond Heights, Normandy, University City, Riverview Gardens, and Wellston—did not participate or stopped accepting City students (FOCUS St. Louis 2001, 110).

The Ferguson-Florissant School District was already involved in a court-ordered merger for the purpose of desegregating the Berkeley and Kinloch School Districts. Although not a party to the original suit, the Ferguson-Florissant School District contained a significant white majority student population, and its boundaries were contiguous to Kinloch and Berkeley, which were predominantly black majority districts. The court merged all three districts to achieve a remedy. The single merged district was declared unitary in late 1983.

Table 1. Voluntary Transfer Program District Attendance Rates, Final Two Years of the 1983–99 Agreement

District	1997–98	1998–99
Affton	334	404
Bayless	158	174
Brentwood	189	216
Clayton	418	476
Hancock Place	323	377
Hazelwood	6	4
Kirkwood	650	723
Ladue	380	456
Lindbergh	932	1,069
Mehlville	1,280	1,481
Parkway	2,878	3,159
Pattonville	1,058	1,070
Ritenour	205	145
Rockwood	2,374	2,750
Special School	NA	NA
Valley Park	136	248
Webster Groves	443	511
Total	**11,864**	**13,263**

Source: Voluntary Interdistrict Coordinating Corporation.
Note: The Hazelwood School District achieved unitary status in 1995 and stopped accepting transfer students at that time.

Remediation 2

"The voluntary transfer of white suburban students to City magnet schools or regular schools and the expansion of the magnet schools to accommodate a total of 14,000 students" (Civic Progress Task Force on Desegregation 1995).

Results

Of the total magnet school population enrolled, 1,640 were to be white suburban students. SLPS magnet schools have the capacity to accommodate slightly more than 14,800 students. White suburban students accounted for 1,351 of those enrolled in 1999.

Table 2. County to City Transfer Student Count, 1997

District	County to City Transfers
Affton	70
Bayless	45
Brentwood	11
Clayton	8
Ferguson-Florissant	117
Hancock Place	101
Hazelwood	145
Kirkwood	37
Ladue	16
Lindbergh	53
Maplewood-Richmond Hts.	224
Mehlville	115
Parkway	84
Pattonville	44
Ritenour	213
Riverview Gardens	3
Rockwood	24
Valley Park	7
Webster Groves	94

Source: Voluntary Interdistrict Coordinating Council.

Remediation 3

"The City schools will focus on the improvement of educational quality in all SLPS, with emphasis of quality improvement in non-integrated schools" (Civic Progress Task Force on Desegregation 1995).

Results

This goal was partially accomplished by reducing class size in the non-integrated schools on average from 30 to 20 students.

Remediation 4

"The Saint Louis City Public Schools would begin a program of capital improvement of its physical facilities" (Civic Progress Task Force on Desegregation 1995).

Results

The State of Missouri and the St. Louis City Schools spent nearly $14 million on building and infrastructure improvements over the life of the original settlement agreement.

Remediation 5

"The suburban school districts would begin efforts to recruit and integrate their staffs" (Civic Progress Task Force on Desegregation 1995).

Results

The goal agreed upon was 15.8 percent African American teachers and 13.4 percent African American administrators. No suburban district achieved this goal.

Financing the Settlement Agreement

Actual cost of the original settlement agreement program was substantial. The cost for the St. Louis program alone was reported to have reached nearly $2 billion by 1998.

How the monies were spent over the life of the agreement was the subject of study and some controversy. Transportation costs were a particular target of criticism. An analysis of a typical budget for the original settlement agreement is shown in Table 4. The budget has seven major expenditure categories.

A New Settlement Agreement: 1999–2010

In 1993, ten years after the implementation of the voluntary transfer agreement, the State of Missouri sought relief when it petitioned the courts to declare the St. Louis City Public School District to have reached unitary status (FOCUS St. Louis 2001, 109). Unitary status is declared when a dual system of schools that intentionally segregated students by race is declared to have created a unitary system that has eliminated to the extent practicable the vestiges of the dual system (Civic Progress Task Force on Desegregation 1995).

Table 3. St. Louis Voluntary Interdistrict Transfer Program Net Expenditures, 1981–98

Year	Net Expenditure	Year	Net Expenditure
1981	8,530,000	1991	130,974,000
1982	12,754,000	1992	136,607,000
1983	17,190,000	1993	133,060,000
1984	30,653,000	1994	133,276,000
1985	55,773,000	1995	136,974,000
1986	59,363,000	1996	148,330,000
1987	80,859,000	1997	147,600,000
1988	91,854,000	1998	158,800,000
1989	118,084,000		
1990	117,896,000	Total	$1,718,550,000

Source: The Missouri Department of Elementary and Secondary Education.

Table 4. St. Louis Settlement Agreement, 1996 (Budget) by Category and Percent. Total Budget for 1996: $148,330,000

Category	Percent
Transfer program payments	43%
Intracity plan	5%
Settlement plan	8%
Magnet plan	19%
City capital improvements	4%
Transportation	19%
Other	2%

Note: Percentages are rounded.

The court appointed Dr. William Danforth as the settlement coordinator to review the issue and draft a new agreement. The proposal was drafted after three years of negotiations involving all parties to the suit and was presented to the court in 1996. Part of the new agreement stipulated that the State would find a way to make up for any loss suffered by the State for St. Louis City Schools.

Settlement efforts continued, and in 1998 the state legislature passed Senate Bill 781. This legislation modified the state education funding formula resulting in the replacement of any state funds lost by SLPS (FOCUS St. Louis 2001, 109).

The bill's final implementation rested on the contingency that the City of St. Louis pass a two-thirds of a cent sales tax increase. Voters passed the tax in February 1999. The district court then approved a second settlement agreement in March 1999. This agreement remains in effect until 2010. Under its provisions, funding will continue from the State to finance requests of African American students from SLPS to St. Louis County districts choosing to participate in the program. This funding will remain available for a minimum of ten years. In 2009–10 each participating district will have the option to continue or end its participation.

Districts continuing in the voluntary transfer program are Affton, Bayless, Brentwood, Clayton, Hancock Place, Kirkwood, Lindbergh, Mehlville, Parkway, Pattonville, Rockwood, Valley Park, and Webster Groves. The Hazelwood School District stopped accepting new transfer students in 1997, having reached unitary status through natural population growth. Under terms of the new agreement, districts must give two years notice to cease participation. The Ladue School District was later exempted from participation in the new agreement under these terms.

Under the original 1983 agreement, City students could choose to enroll in any suburban school district for transfer. New transfer students are to be assigned to a receiving suburban school by geographic zone to reduce transportation costs.

A new oversight body, the Voluntary Interdistrict Choice Corporation (VICC), was formed under the direction of the participating school district superintendents. VICC now manages the transfer agreement. The St. Louis City Public School District was directed to stop all mandatory busing programs. New racial balance goals were established, seeking a 60 percent African American to 40 percent white balance with an allowable variance of plus or minus 5 percent.

The St. Louis City School District will receive $180 million for capital improvements (St. Louis Community Monitoring and Support Task Force 2001). Currently, students are continuing to participate in the Voluntary Student Transfer program (see Table 5), though the numbers have declined in recent years.

Accountability in Education: Missouri School Improvement Planning (MSIP)

Ten years after the formulation of the original 1983 Settlement Agreement, Governor Mel Carnahan signed Senate Bill 380 establishing the Outstanding Schools Act. The act was given a real sense of urgency when on January 15, 1993, Missouri judge Byron Kinder ruled the system of state funding for schools to be unfair, unequal, and unconstitutional. The juxtaposition of these two events joined the issues of accountability for raising levels of student achievement and additional funding for education in the State.

The Outstanding Schools Act established a Commission on Performance. The primary charge given to the commission consisted of three tasks: to establish a management information system to track student academic progress, to provide for establishing measures of accountability, and to establish a public system of reporting results. The commission was to provide advice and counsel to the State Board of Education in accomplishing these tasks.

The resulting accountability system is the Missouri School Improvement Program (MSIP). It was under the authority of this program that the school reporting system in use today came about. This accountability and public reporting system was implemented in 1997 and has provided a comparatively steady and consistent flow of data ever since.

MSIP made longitudinal data available to the public, the schools, and researchers. The establishment of this accountability system in 1997 and the negotiation of the 1999 Voluntary Transfer Agreement closely coincide, providing us with an opportunity to study the issue of educational progress in St. Louis City and in St. Louis County. It also allows us to begin a longitudinal assessment of student academic progress under the latest transfer agreement.

Development of the MSIP program not only provides a basis of comparison within school districts through individual school accounting, but also provides a comparison among districts. The comparison among districts led to the State's recognition that demographics may differ significantly among and within student populations. Data are also now available disaggregated by race and ethnicity. To this end, the State has established a system of data collection to describe student academic progress within demographic anomalies. In doing so, the State tacitly recognizes that demographic factors may play a significant role in a child's life, both developmentally and academically.

The Annie E. Casey Foundation annually publishes the *Kids Count Data Book*, which provides a comparison of demographic characteristics of student populations. It also includes student academic progress through Missouri Assessment Program (MAP) test scores and selected measures of effective district management.

Table 5. Voluntary Transfer Program District Attendance Rates, 2000–2003, of the 1999 Agreement

District	1999–2000	2000–2001	2001–02	2002–03
Affton	330.5	303.5	309.5	278
Bayless	180.14	191.5	167.78	160
Brentwood	208	211.5	222	207
Clayton	478.5	478.38	475.38	512
Hancock Place	316.78	290	297	304
Hazelwood	1	0	0	0
Kirkwood	661.86	659.15	652.56	649
Ladue	359	275.75	229	159
Lindbergh	935	908.5	871.53	671
Mehlville	1,338	1,412	1,453	1,411
Parkway	2,845.55	2,722.44	2,683.41	2,675
Pattonville	882	720	616	453
Ritenour	97.5	63	36	32
Rockwood	3,095	2,537.5	2,406.5	1,495
Special School	541.5	223.5	113.5	22
Valley Park	244	253	251.5	241
Webster Groves	463.67	447.92	411.99	390
Total	12,978	11,693.6	11,196.6	10,649

Source: Voluntary Interdistrict Coordinating Corporation.

Notes: **Special School District** numbers initially included Phase II students (those who received services outside their regular classroom more than half-time). This changed in 2000–2001, and Phase II students were counted by the local district instead of by the Special School District.

Following the 1999 Settlement Agreement, the Maplewood-Richmond Heights School District stopped allowing new students to transfer to city schools. Students already enrolled were allowed to complete the grades in the schools where they were currently enrolled. Under the 1999 Settlement Agreement, preschool seats were no longer available to students transferring from the county. Beginning in the 2003–04 school year, new students from Hazelwood will not be allowed to transfer to magnet schools due to their changing residential demographics.

1998–99 was the last year under the original settlement agreement. Students under that agreement could live anywhere in the city and attend any participating school district in the county. This is the year that is used as the baseline enrollment for the enrollment goals under the new 1999 Settlement Agreement.

1999–2000 was the first year under the new settlement agreement. Attendance areas were drawn for city students transferring to county schools, but existing students were given three years to move into the proper attendance area. Relatively few students chose to make the transition the first year. New applicants were generally assigned to school districts paired within their residential attendance area.

2001–02 was the final year for existing students to receive transportation to an out-of-area school. An exception was made for existing students who were entering high school for the 1999–2000 school year. They were given a fourth year of transportation to out-of-area schools, so that they could complete their high school education at one school.

Ladue and Ritenour transfer student numbers have been decreasing since they are no longer accepting any new transfer students. Pattonville's numbers are also declining as that district is accepting fewer new city students than in the past due to the impact of the airport expansion on its residential population and its schools.

Pupil Attendance

One factor of high interest to the state and the public is student attendance rates. This factor generates a score on the MSIP assessment, and coupled with other factors can affect a district's accreditation by the State. Districts continue to place great emphasis on student attendance, and overall attendance rates continue to improve (see Table 6), in most cases surpassing the State average.

Another area of interest is how many students remain in our high schools and eventually graduate. Longitudinal studies of high school attendance indicate that more students are staying in school longer. The State calculates dropout rates by recording the September enrollment count, adding students who enroll late, deducting students who transfer out, and deducting those who leave but do not transfer to another school (dropouts). As Table 7 shows, dropout rates have declined across both the City and County, just as they have declined across the State. City dropout rates declined dramatically from 15.7 percent in 1998–99 to 7.8 percent in 2002–03.

Funding Education in St. Louis Schools: Providing for a System of Adequate and Equitable Resources

The issue of resources takes on real significance in light of Judge Kinder's 1993 ruling on inequity in state school funding. Funding within St. Louis City and County school systems over the past five years continues to exhibit disparities. In 2003 the amount spent on each pupil ranged from a low of $5,754 in the Bayless School District to a high of $13,885 in the Clayton School District. The average range across the State of Missouri was $5,624 to $6,911 (see Table 8).

Funding public schools is a complex issue in any state. Funding is often determined by applying a series of increasingly complicated correction formulas that are designed to equalize the state's resources across urban, suburban, and rural school districts. There are three common sources of resource generation for public schools: local revenues, state revenues, and most recently, the federal government. Districts in the St. Louis area utilize all three sources, but most suburban districts rely heavily on local funding in the form of property tax revenue. Table 9 presents a breakdown of St. Louis City and suburban St. Louis County districts and shows the percentage of funding generated by all three sources.

It is obvious that school districts located in communities with healthy local tax bases rely heavily on their local wealth and community support to fund their school programs. Examining selected St. Louis districts shows how equalization of resources occurs. The examples first presented are the Clayton, Ladue, and Brentwood School Districts (see Table 10). These districts can generate significant financial resources from solid property tax bases and moderate tax rates.

Conversely, St. Louis County suburban districts such as Riverview Gardens, Wellston, and Normandy, with lower local property tax bases, rely more heavily on additional levels of support from the state to equalize their ability to provide adequate funding for their schools. Table 10a shows the percentage of funding by source, while Table 10b shows expenditures in dollars for each pupil for these low-wealth districts after equalization.

It is through this local, state, and federal funding ratio that the State attempts to compensate low-wealth school districts so that they may maintain an adequate level of expenditure to support their individual educational programs. The State constitution uses "adequate" as the term to describe Missouri's required level of funding for its schools.

This should assume that the State acts to exactly equalize funding levels across districts. In Missouri, the state has the obligation to define a level considered adequate and assist districts to meet that defined level of support. Local effort beyond that adequate level is a function of local option and is accomplished by increasing local tax rates through local levy elections. In the cases cited for comparison, the low wealth districts can also offer reasonable per pupil expenditure levels in range of $7,000 to $10,000 per pupil, per year, with State support. Districts with a solid local tax base and a tax rate voted by the public may still generate higher revenues while receiving lower levels of State funds.

Funds received from the federal government are most often tied directly to a particular federal program and cannot be used for purposes other than the program to which the funding is attached. Even commingling federal funds across federal program lines is not allowed. This is often referred to as categorical funding.

While no state's system of funding is perfect, most do attempt to meet the state's obligation to provide adequate funding levels for education. Most state funding programs are a system of managed disequity since, ultimately, property bases vary widely in value between farmland, suburban land, and scarce urban land. Each local school must answer the question of whether the current system of public education in Missouri is capable of producing acceptable levels of student academic performance.

Table 6. Average Rates of Pupil Attendance in Percent in St. Louis City and County School Districts, 1998–2003

District	1998–99	1999–2000	2000–2001	2001–02	2002–03
Affton	94.4	93.9	94.1	94.2	94.2
Bayless	93.6	93.6	94.1	93.3	93.8
Brentwood	97.4	99.6	94.5	95.5	94.8
Clayton	94.9	93.1	95.5	95.5	95.5
Ferguson-Florissant	93.1	92.9	93.1	92.8	93.4
Hancock Place	92.8	91.9	91.1	91.9	92.7
Hazelwood	93.6	93.8	93.2	92.0	93.6
Jennings	92.4	92.2	94.3	90.6	94.0
Kirkwood	93.2	92.8	94.0	94.0	94.1
Ladue	93.9	93.9	93.4	94.2	94.0
Lindbergh	93.1	92.9	94.0	94.2	94.6
Maplewood-Richmond Hts.	92.5	90.5	91.9	93.1	93.8
Mehlville	94.8	94.4	95.0	94.7	95.0
Meramec Valley	94.1	93.1	93.4	92,9	92.7
Normandy	88.4	89.4	90.2	90.3	91.0
Parkway	94.0	94.8	94.4	94.1	94.5
Pattonville	95.1	92.0	95.3	93.6	94.8
Ritenour	93.2	92.8	93.8	91.3	94.0
Riverview Gardens	93.5	92.6	93.6	93.2	94.0
Rockwood	93.5	93.0	93.5	94.3	95.0
University City	90.4	88.1	90.1	89.1	89.9
Valley Park	93.9	94.0	94.0	94.2	94.1
Webster Groves	94.4	93.2	95.0	93.8	94.1
Wellston	93.8	82.2	90.0	86.5	85.7
Special School District	87.6	89.1	89.1	86.7	89.2
City of Saint Louis	89.1	90.2	89.5	87.9	88.3
Missouri (Avg.)	93.1	93.0	93.6	93.3	93.8

Source: Missouri Department of Elementary and Secondary Education.

Metromorphosis

Table 7. High School Dropout Rates in St. Louis City and County School Districts, 1998–2003

District	1998–99	1999–2000	2000–2001	2001–02	2002–03
Affton	4.8	4.2	4.0	3.8	3.8
Bayless	8.6	7.7	2.1	3.4	2.7
Brentwood	3.3	2.8	2.2	3.8	1.3
Clayton	1.8	2.4	1.1	1.8	1.3
Ferguson-Florissant	5.4	4.8	3.9	2.6	1.3
Hancock Place	5.3	5.1	5.0	5.7	4.7
Hazelwood	3.9	4.3	2.7	3.4	4.6
Jennings	5.0	4.8	4.5	4.3	3.8
Kirkwood	5.4	3.0	3.2	2.9	1.9
Ladue	1.2	1.3	0.8	1.2	0.5
Lindbergh	2.9	3.4	3.6	1.9	3.4
Maplewood-Richmond Hts.	15.1	10.5	3.8	2.9	2.0
Mehlville	4.5	5.3	3.2	3.6	3.3
Meramec Valley	5.4	3.9	5.2	4.6	3.9
Normandy	6.7	5.7	6.2	5.6	4.0
Parkway	2.4	2.1	1.9	1.8	1.1
Pattonville	2.7	2.8	2.1	2.5	2.7
Ritenour	2.5	3.1	1.9	1.3	3.0
Riverview Gardens	6.6	5.8	5.2	4.8	3.4
Rockwood	2.9	2.3	2.8	2.5	1.9
University City	6.5	6.5	7.5	10.2	8.0
Valley Park	4.7	7.4	3.6	1.9	2.6
Webster Groves	1.3	2.6	1.7	3.8	3.6
Wellston	11.3	1.9	5.1	22.5	3.7
Special School District	0.5	0.2	0	2.0	2.0
City of Saint Louis	15.7	13.2	9.1	8.6	7.8
Missouri (Avg.)	5.0	4.8	4.5	4.3	3.8

Source: Missouri Department of Elementary and Secondary Education.

Table 8. District Average per Pupil Expenditure in Dollars, 1998–2003

District	1998–99	1999–2000	2000–2001	2001–02	2002–03
Affton	5,934	6,233	6,116	6,361	6,757
Bayless	4,900	5,276	5,400	5,358	5,754
Brentwood	8,206	8,735	9,540	10,385	11,106
Clayton	10,498	11,239	11,626	12,980	13,885
Ferguson-Florissant	6,495	6,796	7,344	7,984	8,479
Hancock Place	4,697	5,558	5,840	5,640	5,819
Hazelwood	5,567	5,838	6,488	7,064	7,238
Jennings	4,792	5,472	6,572	7,077	8,849
Kirkwood	6,700	6,952	7,375	7,717	8,110
Ladue	8,921	9,347	10,183	11,154	11,198
Lindbergh	6,547	6,994	7,334	7,336	7,595
Maplewood-Richmond Hts.	6,439	7,229	8,770	9,368	10,250
Mehlville	5,072	5,545	5,905	5,972	6,297
Meramec Valley	4,344	4,798	4,961	5,402	5,721
Normandy	6,487	6,485	7,179	7,340	7,313
Parkway	6,743	7,828	7,506	8,113	7,956
Pattonville	7,530	8,143	8,527	9,358	9,455
Ritenour	5,217	5,470	6,046	6,454	6,808
Riverview Gardens	5,584	5,889	6,247	6,507	6,868
Rockwood	5,442	5,739	6,123	6,312	6,805
University City	7,070	6,658	7,154	7,531	8,252
Valley Park	6,721	7,329	7,373	7,385	7,742
Webster Groves	6,185	6,389	6,788	7,462	8,039
Wellston	8,123	8,341	9,258	10,115	10,678
Special School District	29,070	31,996	35,634	86,908	106,473
City of Saint Louis	7,079	7,564	8,951	9,572	10,606
Missouri (Avg.)	5,624	5,911	6,303	6,767	6,911

Source: Missouri Department of Elementary and Secondary Education.

Metromorphosis

Table 9. District Funding by State and Local Levels as Percent of Revenue

District	Year 1998	1999	2000	2001	2002
AFFTON					
Local	79.07	80.11	79.44	89.32	90.04
State	19.00	18.40	18.53	8.80	7.83
Federal	1.92	1.49	2.03	1.88	2.12
BAYLESS					
Local	66.68	62.77	63.39	70.13	77.57
State	29.60	32.77	31.93	25.31	17.81
Federal	3.72	4.46	4.68	4.56	4.62
BRENTWOOD					
Local	76.88	75.73	73.15	91.24	94.10
State	21.73	22.98	25.53	7.56	4.66
Federal	1.39	1.28	1.32	1.20	1.24
CLAYTON					
Local	82.25	82.50	82.71	95.56	96.18
State	16.63	16.52	16.03	3.78	3.07
Federal	1.12	0.98	1.26	0.66	0.75
FERGUSON-FLORISSANT R-II					
Local	70.89	68.20	66.33	61.32	60.29
State	24.62	27.85	29.32	34.03	33.58
Federal	4.49	3.95	4.35	4.65	6.13
HANCOCK PLACE					
Local	37.91	34.90	35.71	40.42	46.10
State	55.13	57.73	55.34	50.03	44.75
Federal	6.96	7.36	8.94	9.55	9.15
HAZELWOOD					
Local	77.96	76.18	74.42	69.86	69.70
State	19.30	21.33	23.13	26.82	26.83
Federal	2.73	2.49	2.45	3.32	3.47
KIRKWOOD R-VII					
Local	82.20	83.27	82.89	90.10	92.04
State	15.71	14.80	15.09	8.00	6.15
Federal	2.10	1.93	2.02	1.90	1.81

LADUE					
Local	84.39	83.69	85.75	94.22	95.96
State	14.83	15.67	13.52	5.02	3.37
Federal	0.78	0.64	0.73	0.76	0.67
LINDBERGH R-VIII					
Local	75.68	76.38	75.97	89.58	90.54
State	22.90	22.06	21.99	8.46	7.44
Federal	1.42	1.56	2.04	1.95	2.02
MAPLEWOOD-RICHMOND HEIGHTS					
Local	79.29	80.48	79.87	78.22	82.41
State	13.64	12.71	14.52	16.22	12.63
Federal	7.07	6.80	5.61	5.55	4.96
MEHLVILLE R-IX					
Local	72.55	73.69	73.66	79.35	82.97
State	25.39	24.52	24.52	18.46	14.75
Federal	2.06	1.79	1.82	2.19	2.28
MERAMEC VALLEY R-III					
Local	52.37	54.22	55.98	54.67	57.28
State	41.57	39.06	37.97	39.39	36.40
Federal	6.06	6.72	6.06	5.94	6.32
NORMANDY					
Local	42.57	43.46	38.73	36.02	35.04
State	48.29	48.45	52.93	55.68	55.14
Federal	9.14	8.09	8.35	8.29	9.82
PARKWAY C-2					
Local	80.49	80.97	90.54	91.16	91.76
State	18.19	17.72	7.87	7.32	6.42
Federal	1.32	1.30	1.59	1.52	1.82
PATTONVILLE R-III					
Local	77.54	79.77	79.70	90.79	91.77
State	20.36	18.26	18.06	7.00	6.43
Federal	2.10	1.97	2.23	2.21	1.81
RITENOUR					
Local	67.38	62.64	59.85	59.57	60.57
State	27.55	32.76	35.06	35.42	33.86
Federal	5.06	4.60	5.09	5.01	5.57

RIVERVIEW GARDENS					
Local	45.21	39.99	38.06	34.98	33.04
State	49.32	54.00	55.66	59.14	60.09
Federal	5.47	6.01	6.28	5.88	6.87
ROCKWOOD R-VI					
Local	80.16	80.51	87.25	87.78	88.63
State	18.27	17.95	11.02	10.57	9.45
Federal	1.57	1.54	1.72	1.65	1.92
UNIVERSITY CITY					
Local	70.67	70.43	68.77	66.88	68.76
State	23.76	24.03	25.30	25.76	23.87
Federal	5.57	5.54	5.93	7.36	7.37
VALLEY PARK					
Local	71.08	71.32	69.00	84.65	87.43
State	25.68	25.42	27.20	11.12	8.58
Federal	3.24	3.27	3.80	4.23	3.99
WELLSTON					
Local	36.85	39.46	32.41	31.98	27.17
State	51.03	47.69	54.20	55.74	58.05
Federal	12.13	12.85	13.39	12.28	14.78
SPECIAL SCHOOL DISTRICT, ST. LOUIS COUNTY					
Local	59.23	54.44	53.72	60.04	64.95
State	32.31	36.41	37.16	29.27	24.07
Federal	8.46	9.16	9.12	10.69	10.98
ST. LOUIS CITY					
Local	43.08	42.13	44.67	44.40	50.66
State	45.43	47.85	45.01	43.94	36.07
Federal	11.48	10.02	10.32	11.66	13.27
MISSOURI					
Local	54.71	55.14	56.17	55.93	57.21
State	38.99	38.35	37.22	37.03	35.00
Federal	6.30	6.51	6.62	7.04	7.78

Table 10. High-Wealth Districts: Per Pupil Expenditure after State Equalization

District	Year				
	1998	1999	2000	2001	2002
Clayton	10,498	11,239	11,626	12,980	13,885
Ladue	8,921	9,347	10,183	11,154	11,198
Brentwood	8,206	8,735	9,540	10,385	11,106

Table 10a. Ratio of State to Local Funding as a Percent of Revenue in Low-Wealth Districts in St. Louis County

District	1998	1999	2000	2001	2002
			Year		
RIVERVIEW GARDENS					
Local	45.21	39.99	38.06	34.98	33.04
State	49.32	54.00	55.66	59.14	60.09
Federal	5.47	6.01	6.28	5.88	6.87
WELLSTON					
Local	36.85	39.46	32.41	31.98	27.17
State	51.03	47.69	54.20	55.74	58.05
Federal	12.13	12.85	13.39	12.28	14.78
NORMANDY					
Local	42.57	43.46	38.73	36.02	35.04
State	48.29	48.45	52.93	55.68	55.14
Federal	9.14	8.09	8.35	8.29	9.82

Table 10b. Low-Wealth Districts: Per Pupil Expenditure after State Equalization

District	1998	1999	2000	2001	2002
			Year		
Riverview Gardens	5,584	5,889	6,247	6,507	6,868
Wellston	8,123	8,341	9,258	10,115	10,678
Normandy	6,487	6,485	7,179	7,340	7,313

Measuring Academic Performance: Closing the Achievement Gap for All Children

Analyzing student performance over prolonged periods has been difficult, if not impossible, since the testing instruments used to measure student performance in the past tended to change all too frequently. Without some way to consistently measure student achievement levels over time, comparisons can be faulty or even invidious.

The new State testing programs can provide enough stable comparison points over time to produce some usable trend data. Measures of this type should not be used singly without caution; however, as multiple snapshots of student progress they can provide meaningful insights.

There are two testing instruments, of which MAP is one. The other is called the Terra Nova test. The MAP test assesses knowledge, skills, and application of knowledge in a variety of areas defined by the state. It requires problem solving, writing and meta-cognitive skills since students respond to a number of items with in-depth answers requiring not only the solution to a problem, but also written descriptions of the method they used to solve it. The MAP test measures learning directly tied to Missouri standards.

The MAP test has two parts, mathematics and communication arts. The mathematics portion is administered to students in grades 4, 8, and 10. The communication arts component is administered at grades 3, 9, and 11. Both parts place emphasis on writing proficiency, analytic skills, and problem solving.

Students who take the MAP test are placed in one of five categories or levels of proficiency by the scores they earn on the test:

Step 1: Students are substantially behind in terms of meeting the Show-Me Standards. They demonstrate only a minimal understanding of fundamental concepts and little or no ability to apply that knowledge.

Progressing: Students are beginning to use their knowledge of simple concepts to solve basic problems, but they still make many errors.

Nearing Proficient: Students understand many key concepts, although their application of that knowledge is limited.

Proficient: This is the desired achievement level for all students. Students demonstrate the knowledge and skills called for by the Show-Me Standards.

Advanced: Students demonstrate in-depth understanding of all concepts and apply that knowledge in complex ways (Department of Elementary and Secondary Education 2003).

The California Test Bureau (CTB), a nationally recognized testing firm with a long-standing reputation for integrity and quality, developed the Terra Nova test. It provides a multiple-choice format and measures Missouri student scores against national performance standards, or norms. This resembles traditional standardized tests used in the past.

MAP test results for the years 2001 and 2002 are shown in Table 11a. Terra Nova results for the same period are shown in Table 11b. Both provide performance results over the past several years for school districts in the City and County.

Because of the recent emphasis placed on comparing student progress along racial and ethnic lines, results are reported in that way. The MAP test results for 2001 and 2002 represent an in-depth assessment, not the multiple-choice format found in the Terra Nova instrument. Scores on the MAP represent the percent of students reaching the proficient level, as defined earlier.

The second set of test data shown in Table 11b represents the test results on the Terra Nova multiple-choice test. Scores here are reported in percentile figures. Numbers are based on the average scores for the group of St. Louis students taking the test. For example, a score of 65 would indicate that the St. Louis group scored as well as or better than 65 percent of the national comparison group of students, but lower than 35 percent of the same group.

It is evident from these data that a significant discrepancy in the levels of student achievement between black and other students exists as measured by both the MAP test and the Terra Nova test. Black students score significantly below their Asian and white counterparts on both. This has been the pattern from the first administration of the tests, and it continues with little difference today. This pattern is not evident just in St. Louis area schools; it occurs on a national scale.

In today's climate of educational accountability, racial discrepancy in levels of student performance stands out in the comparisons of student test scores both among and within districts. St. Louis–area schools are not unique in trying to deal with these issues. There is a great need to determine the factors that may help educators correct these discrepancies to the greatest extent possible. The trend data show slight improvement in overall test scores for all ethnic groups over time, but racial and ethnic discrepancies persists. "Closing the gap" has become a national issue. Research seems to indicate this discrepancy is not attributable to one single factor; it seems to be the product of a complex series of factors.

Dr. John Ogbu of the University of California at Berkeley conducted an extensive study of five thousand youth in the Cleveland suburb of Shaker Heights, Ohio (Ogbu 2003). The six-year study was initiated by a group of black parents in the racially diverse and relatively affluent school district. Working with both parents and students, he uncovered some factors that may help build insight. His work suggests that a fundamentally good school system coupled with parental support and involvement are the building blocks for success. But he also found that student peer pressure could be a competing factor in black student success, just as peer pressure can be a factor for any student. Peer pressure builds beginning late in elementary school and is significant by middle-school age.

The studies of Ogbu and others attempt to understand what is happening in St. Louis's efforts to provide quality education for all students. Today, both the City and suburban schools have formed partnerships to build and fund detailed plans aimed at helping teachers work with students to close the achievement gap.

St. Louis–area school districts acknowledge that all underachieving students must be the targets of their effort. Plans stress that parent and citizen engagement in schools is critical to success. Building understanding and dismantling racism are the keys to progress. Defining and maintaining high standards and improving the quality of instruction in all classrooms are common goals (Webster Groves School District 2003).

Table 11a. St. Louis City and County Schools MAP Communication Arts Test Scores, 2001–02, Disaggregated by Race and Ethnicity, Grade Level 11

District	Asian	Black	White
Affton	0.0	8.3	34.1
Bayless	50.0	14.3	27.4
Brentwood	50.0	21.4	41.7
Clayton	66.7	10.5	42.2
Ferguson-Florissant	0.0	6.8	30.1
Hancock Place	NA	0.0	13.1
Hazelwood	16.7	7.0	21.6
Jennings	0.0	4.7	42.9
Kirkwood	100.0	11.1	41.6
Ladue	50.0	14.8	53.1
Lindbergh	33.3	3.4	26.0
Maplewood-Richmond Hts.	NA	4.8	21.1
Mehlville	38.5	1.0	26.0
Normandy	NA	8.9	66.7
Parkway	42.3	10.7	40.4
Pattonville	22.2	17.7	38.5
Ritenour	25.0	8.4	22.7
Riverview Gardens	NA	1.7	18.4
Rockwood	56.8	11.4	40.7
University City	NA	7.6	67.9
Valley Park	0.0	0.0	29.7
Webster Groves	50.0	5.7	46.1
Wellston	NA	22.7	NA
Saint Louis City	7.3	4.2	15.3
Missouri (Avg.)	31.9	6.8	26.3

Source: Missouri Department of Elementary and Secondary Education; *St. Louis Post-Dispatch*, October 24, 2002.

But schools today have taken on a daunting task as they embrace all children in their classrooms. To understand what teachers face we can turn to Vision for Children at Risk, an organization that for years has tracked a variety of human, social, and demographic factors throughout the St. Louis region that place children at high risk. This organization tracks and reports on factors such as poverty, abuse and neglect, crime, and a lack of

Table 11b. A Comparison of State Test Scores on the Terra Nova Test, 2000–2002, Disaggregated by Ethnicity

| | Mathematics | | | | Communication Arts | | | |
| | Black | | | White | Black | | | White |
District	2000	2001	2002	2002	2000	2001	2002	2002
Affton	37	42	41	66	43	53	46	63
Bayless	35	40	46	57	40	37	46	61
Brentwood	46	45	49	74	53	51	52	73
Clayton	45	45	50	83	47	53	51	78
Ferguson-Florissant	40	43	45	68	45	48	47	66
Hancock Place	34	25	31	52	31	38	43	54
Hazelwood	44	41	44	67	48	47	47	64
Jennings	42	42	39	57	46	43	44	62
Kirkwood	40	42	45	77	44	48	44	75
Ladue	47	52	47	82	54	55	50	78
Lindbergh	40	43	41	73	43	45	44	68
Maplewood-Richmond Hts.	32	38	32	62	45	46	48	65
Mehlville	39	35	37	68	42	43	42	67
Normandy	34	36	35	41	46	43	49	57
Parkway	42	41	40	74	44	46	46	71
Pattonville	41	40	45	67	50	49	54	71
Ritenour	37	41	40	58	46	45	45	58
Riverview Gardens	38	39	41	62	43	45	45	61
Rockwood	36	39	41	76	39	41	44	72
University City	42	43	41	81	49	49	49	81
Valley Park	46	43	42	66	37	35	45	59
Webster Groves	42	38	41	78	45	47	47	74
Wellston	45	45	34	NST	39	35	46	NST
City of Saint Louis	36	36	36	53	31	38	43	54
Missouri (Avg.)	39	39	39	64	42	44	44	62

family support systems that plague many urban centers across the nation. It reports on the critical developmental factors affecting disadvantaged children, such as low birth weight, lack of prenatal care, low levels of affordable childcare, poor nutrition, and high lead levels in the blood. In St. Louis, all children do not enter school equally prepared to learn:

> In the St. Louis region … a quarter of a million children live in zip code areas where the risk levels are high. How children are doing depends to a great extent on where in the metropolitan area they live and attend school. Problems exist where there is poverty and the inability or failure to provide critical resources and supports. Disparities among groups of children in the

Saint Louis area often are more severe than in other metropolitan areas. There are as well children who live in the most distressed and disadvantaged areas who do quite well. Through their innate abilities, family and community support, and their own resiliency, they are model children who achieve in school and will succeed in life (Vision for Children at Risk 2001).

References

Annie E. Casey Foundation. *The 2003 Kids Count Data Book Online* [online]. Baltimore, Md., 2003. http://www.aecf.org/ kidscount/databook/ (accessed 2003).

Bower, Carolyn. "Gaps Remain between Blacks, Whites on State's Education Tests." *St. Louis Post-Dispatch*, October 24, 2002.

Civic Progress Task Force on Desegregation. *Desegregation: A Report from the Civic Progress Task Force on Desegregation of the St Louis Public School System.* St. Louis: Civic Progress, 1995.

Corbett, Katherine T. "St. Louis History." *In St. Louis Currents: A Guide to the Region and Its Resources,* edited by James E. O'Donnell. St. Louis: Missouri Historical Society Press, 1997.

Department of Elementary and Secondary Education. *Achievement Level Descriptors* [online]. Jefferson City, Mo., 2003. http://www.dese.state.mo.us/divimprove/assess/Descriptors/index.html (accessed 2003).

FOCUS St. Louis. *Focus on Desegregation: Questions and Answers About the Implication of the Citywide Vote on February 2, 1999.* St. Louis: Author, 1999.

___. *Racial Equality in the St. Louis Region: A Community Call to Action (Full Report).* St. Louis: Author, 2001.

Ogbu, John U. *Black American Students in an Affluent Suburb: A Study of Academic Disengagement.* Mahwah, N.J.: LEA Publishers, 2003.

Project Respond. *The Children of Metropolitan St. Louis 1995: A Report to the Community from Project Respond.* St. Louis: Author, 1995.

St. Louis Community Monitoring and Support Task Force. *Annual Report to the Community.* Saint Louis: n.p., 2001.

Vision for Children at Risk. *The Children of Metropolitan St. Louis: A Report to the Community, 2001.* St. Louis: Project Respond, 2001.

Webster Groves School District. *Achievement Gap: Recommended Actions.* Webster Groves, Mo.: Author, 2003.

Wells, A. S., and R. L. Crain. *Stepping over the Color Line: African American Students in White Suburban Schools.* New Haven, Conn.: Yale University Press, 1997.

Chapter 14

How St. Louis's Past Frames Its Future

E. Terrence Jones and Brady Baybeck
University of Missouri–St. Louis

During the past half century, the St. Louis region has achieved many accomplishments. Parking lots masquerading as a riverfront have been transformed into a testament to St. Louis's role in western expansion, capped by the Gateway Arch, which has become a globally recognized icon for the metropolitan area. Washington University, once a respectable streetcar college, has become one of the world's premier research and teaching establishments. The region's cultural institutions, especially the St. Louis Zoo and the Missouri Botanical Garden, are universally recognized as among the very best. In 2004, as the region looks even further back—two centuries to Lewis and Clark's journey of discovery and one century to the World's Fair—the St. Louis metropolitan area has much to celebrate since it became part of the United States.

In the midst of the justifiable rejoicing in the region's rich past, this book raises concerns about its future. The chapters intentionally focus on statistical trends, aggregations of numbers marching through the decades. Taking advantage of an informational treasure chest, they probe for underlying forces and systemic shifts. That approach can overlook episodic pluses—monuments and institutions and sports championships—but it makes one confront certain basics: how the economy is faring, whether equity prevails, how space is structured, how the social fabric is woven.

During the past half century, the United States and indeed the globe have become a metropolitan world. As the first two chapters on demography and density note, in 1950 the City of St. Louis alone had more than half of the region's residents and an even greater share of its jobs. The region was monocentric, revolving around its core on both sides of the Mississippi River. Then came the suburban expansion, first filling up St. Louis County and then extending into eastern Madison and St. Clair Counties in Illinois and Franklin, Jefferson, and St. Charles

Counties in Missouri. Now, similar to most other regions, St. Louis is polycentric. Its original central city no longer stands alone but instead is one of several concentrations of residents and jobs.

This dispersal has multiple consequences, all requiring a broader metropolitan perspective. As the region competes economically with others, it must harness factors from a larger geography. As it becomes more diverse, it must be increasingly alert to growing inequity among its residents. As it disperses spatially, it must think harder about how growth is shaped. As it deliberates regional priorities and policies, it must involve more stakeholders.

Competing Economically

As Mark Tranel notes in his chapter on economic transformation (Chapter 3), the St. Louis region's performance is respectable, especially when measured by traditional norms. Although some sectors have risen and others declined; although like in other U.S. regions jobs have shifted from manufacturing and wholesale trade to service; and although growth is less than rapid, the economy remains diversified. Heavily committed to aircraft and automobile assembly two decades ago, the region has survived dramatic declines in those areas and expanded in others, most notably health care.

Doing okay economically can and does lead to complacency, a condition all too common among St. Louisans. During most of the past half century, that was the region's posture. With numerous corporate headquarters providing reassuring glitter and solid industries such as automobile (Chrysler, Ford, and General Motors assembly plants), beverages (Anheuser-Busch), chemicals (Mallinckrodt and Monsanto), defense (McDonnell Douglas), and food (Ralston Purina) forming the base, sounding an alarm about economic deterioration was a difficult task.

But in an intensifying race, running steady means falling behind. By the early 1990s, a small but expanding number of civic leaders determined economic development as usual was not good enough. As a consequence, the Greater St. Louis Economic Development Council was formed in 1994. Composed of top officials from both the public and private sectors and including representation from the largest jurisdictions in Illinois and Missouri, it was linked to a transformed Regional Commerce (now Chamber) and Growth Association (RCGA). Capping this shift was the hiring of Richard Fleming, an experienced economic development professional with a demonstrated track record in Denver and Atlanta, to head both entities.

Economic development in the St. Louis region post-1995 is very different from before. It is much more regional, involving especially the next three largest counties (Madison, St. Charles, St. Clair) along with the City of St. Louis and St. Louis County. There is less job and firm poaching within the metropolitan area and more efforts both to build emerging industries from within the area and attract promising firms from outside the region. It is also more strategic, as Tranel describes toward the end of Chapter 3. Although not abandoning tactical pursuit of ad hoc opportunities, the region has done its cluster analysis homework and settled on a long-term direction emphasizing the plant and life sciences, now branded as the "BioBelt."

These efforts are a start whose finish is yet to be determined. The region is concentrating much of its civic and financial capital on the initiative. The Donald Danforth Plant Science Center is the primary research arm, but other university and industry labs are also included. The Nidus Center for Scientific Enterprise and the Center for Emerging Technology house incubating firms, many of which are the prime recipients of venture capital. The Danforth Foundation, the region's foremost philanthropy, is putting all of its remaining chips on this thrust, an amount well into nine figures.

All of this is a sharp departure from St. Louis's past approach to growing its economy. It is long term, looking ahead decades rather than months. It is risky, placing a disproportionate share of the region's capital on relatively few ventures. It is high tech, stressing scientific talent rather than natural resources or assembly lines. It is broadly regional, stretching even beyond the metropolitan boundaries to include the University of Illinois at Champaign-Urbana, 150 miles to the east, and the University of Missouri at Columbia, 120 miles to the west.

As this initiative evolves, one of its major challenges will be attracting knowledgeable workers. Both FOCUS St. Louis and the RCGA have addressed this issue, discussing what might be done to make the region more of a magnet for the bright twenty- and thirty-somethings who will staff these ventures. These reports have helped get this issue on the agenda but, to date, there has been much more rhetoric than action.

As David Laslo's chapter on labor force trends (Chapter 4) emphasizes, the region faces a gap between its plant and life sciences aspirations and the profile of its current work force. This in turn reflects a disconnect between the region's economic development strategy and its post-secondary teaching programs. Although bridges have been built in the past few years to link university scientists with entrepreneurial firms, much less has been done to ensure that local higher education institutions develop, fund, and implement associate's, bachelor's, and master's degree programs that will adequately staff the new economy.

The still unmet challenge is linking economic development strategies and education program development so that both K-12 and post-secondary systems mesh productively. Although educational administrators talk the economic development talk, they find it much more difficult to reshape their institutions so that the latter walk the walk. Colleges and universities are both autonomous and decentralized. They march to their own internal drummers, and many within their walls are reluctant to envision themselves or their institutions as part of the regional enterprise. But, to state the obvious, in a knowledge economy those who produce the knowledge workers matter much. They need to be more a part of an economic team than they are at present.

Addressing Inequity

Although economic development has its conflicts and disagreements, how to enhance the St. Louis region's economic competitiveness is the least controversial theme addressed here. There are legitimate differences about tactics and strategies, but all embrace the goal: a larger gross metropolitan product. Without a bigger pie, much of life within the metropolitan area becomes a zero-sum game where each internal winner has an accompanying loser.

Countering inequity, the topic for this section, and managing space, the subject for the next one, are more nettlesome. Equity—having a community where all do better as time progresses, where prosperity is widely shared rather than narrowly held—is elusive. The lesson that until members of all groups have an equal shot at success, the region as a whole suffers is a difficult one to grasp for many in the St. Louis area. Although a sound strategy well executed is crucial for economic development, it will not succeed fully unless it incorporates all the region's talent.

In St. Louis's context, achieving greater equity more than anything else means overcoming racial inequity. Scott Cummings's chapters on economic restructuring (5) and African American enterprises (6), John Farley's analysis of residential segregation (8), Jones's account of racial transition in municipalities (12), Scott Decker and his colleagues' examination of race and homicide (11), and Dan Keck's narrative about race and education (13)—these individually and collectively underscore how the St. Louis region has still not fully faced up to its racially discriminatory past.

Although there are a few positive signs—slightly less residential segregation in many parts of the region and growth in black-owned firms outside predominantly African American neighborhoods, for example—race still matters all too much. Blacks and whites living separately is still the norm and, once white-to-black transition passes a certain point, almost all municipalities then proceed to an all-black city.

This book is far from the first study to call St. Louis's attention to how much race matters. FOCUS St. Louis has issued two reports, the first in 1989 (*A New Spirit for St. Louis: Valuing Diversity*) and the second in 2001 (*Racial Equality in the St. Louis Region: A Community Call to Action*). The latter patiently and painfully documents racial gaps in economic, housing, and educational opportunity. The East-West Gateway Coordinating Council *Where We Stand* series of reports (1992, 1996, 1999, 2002) starkly and numerically stresses the extent of racial disparity within the region. On every measure, St. Louis ranks among the most disparate compared to other major metropolitan areas within the United States.

These studies and others have led to several initiatives, all well intentioned but most involving those already committed to racial justice. It has been difficult to break out of the circle of usual suspects and involve the larger community. For many, the assumption is that all it takes to achieve progress is to end individual acts of prejudice. This perspective fails to appreciate fully the inertia created by a century of slavery (1760s to 1860s) followed, on the Missouri side, by almost another century of legally mandated segregation (1860s to 1950s). The deleterious effects of public policies implemented for almost two hundred years do not vanish after a few decades. Eradicating them requires positive policies to undo the impact. Eliminating the negative laws is not enough.

Neither the region's mainstream civic nor political leadership has championed new policies to lessen racial disparities. In education, the area's most sweeping initiative to enhance educational opportunities for African Americans, the Voluntary Interdistrict Program discussed in Dan Keck's essay (Chapter 13), originated in the federal courts and not among local or state decision makers. After less than two decades, its scale will decline following the 1998 agreement, leaving the City of St. Louis and St. Louis County's public schools more single race than they have been throughout most of the 1980s and 1990s.

Although nonprofit organizations such as the Metropolitan St. Louis Equal Housing Opportunity Center serve as watchdogs for racially based housing discrimination, exceedingly rare is the municipality that has instituted programs and practices to achieve racial balance. In business, on the other hand, the principal players—Civic Progress and the Regional

Business Council acting through the Regional Chamber and Growth Association—have recently established the St. Louis Business Diversity Initiative. Started in 2001, it has been most effective in expanding the region's larger firms to do more subcontracting with and purchasing from minority-owned firms.

Managing Space

How a region manages its spatial resources—land, water, and other geographic features—is an important component of a region's sustainability. Spatial resources are finite and sticky. A change in land use lasts for a relatively long time so developmental decisions cast lengthy shadows over the environment. That is why the debate over urban sprawl or urban choice—even the terms characterizing the discussion have become controversial—is so vitally critical to the region's future.

On many spatial indicators, the St. Louis metropolitan area ranks near the bottom compared to other regions. Parts of this book explore the reasons why. Jones's discussion (Chapter 12) of the municipal market captures some of the dynamics within the fragmentation of political jurisdictions. Laslo's chapter on demography (1) quantifies the extent to which people have moved away from the central city and inner suburbs; Baybeck's analysis of density (2) demonstrates how people have become spread among previously rural areas. Taken together, these point to the defining geographic characteristics for the St. Louis region: decentralization and fragmentation. The question then becomes: Can St. Louis sustain itself as a geographically decentralized and fragmented region?

The glib answer is yes. St. Louis is not going to vanish. Its core strengths ensure it some future. There will always be a major metropolis at the confluence of the Missouri and Mississippi Rivers. Nor is St. Louis going to abandon having numerous local governments. Having government nearby, strengthening local control, providing options in taxation and public service levels, creating a small-town atmosphere within a cosmopolitan metropolitan area—all this is part of what makes St. Louis distinctive and special.

But decentralization and fragmentation have a dark side. Their negative consequences must be managed without destroying their positive attributes. Exurban development is zero-sum, a process where growth at the periphery often comes at the expense of the core. When that happens, it erodes the region's natural beauty and undermines its historic center. Better management of the region's spatial resources, done cooperatively rather than dictatorially, must occur to compensate for decentralization and fragmentation.

To date, St. Louis's ability to coordinate action in pursuit of a common regional good, especially one involving space, has been effectively nonexistent. Joint action must overcome fragmentation's imperative that political jurisdictions compete for residents and decentralization's impulse to create even more fragmentation. Since we assume that fragmentation is both inevitable and in many ways desirable, the answer must lie in political jurisdictions coordinating on some matters—and space is definitely one— while they compete on others.

Is the St. Louis region up to this challenge? At first glance, the prospects look bleak. Examining growth from a regional perspective has not been able to even find a place on the regional agenda. The Brookings Institution's *Growth in the Heartland: Challenges and Opportunities for Missouri*, released with some flourish early in 2003, documented clearly and graphically the costs of decentralization. Despite some sporadic efforts to use this analysis as a trigger for action, the study's impact on stimulating a public debate has been nil. The *St. Louis Post-Dispatch*, both in its news coverage and on its editorial page, has also bemoaned sprawl and promoted change, but that too has had little or no effect.

In short, a critical mass of elected officials has yet to agree that a growth management problem exists, the requisite first step for developing solutions. Conversely, some interest groups, by their actions if not by their rhetoric, find the status quo acceptable and have adopted the strategy of opposing even establishing task forces to examine the issue. Nevertheless, there are a few promising signs. The inner ring suburbs, particularly those within St. Louis County, have started to coalesce as a political force on this issue. Taking their cue from earlier coalitions in Minneapolis-St. Paul and Cleveland, they have received a sympathetic hearing from the state legislators representing their communities in an effort to adopt legislation which, through tax credits and other devices, strengthens their position in competing for development. On a more regional scale, the region's five largest counties, three in Missouri (City of St. Louis, St. Charles, St. Louis) and two in Illinois (Madison, St. Clair) passed a one-tenth cent sales tax in 2000, all earmarked for open space. This initiative, now entitled Great Rivers Greenway on the Missouri side and Metro East Park and Recreation District for the Illinois component, has as its signature project Confluence Greenway, an ambitious and visionary plan to protect and enhance the region's rivers, benefiting the environment and linking the metropolitan area.

Regional Decision Making

Competing economically, addressing inequity, and managing space—as it struggles with each, the St. Louis area must learn how to do better thinking and acting regionally. Over the past few decades, St. Louisans have been making steady progress at this. From the 1950s through the present, they have established special districts to tackle many issues: wastewater treatment, community college education, cultural institutions, and open space. Starting in the 1970s, local governments started to initiate joint ventures. Today these cover numerous matters including criminal justice information, tourism, and the arts. Then came public-private partnerships such as the economic development initiative described earlier.

There are now many more institutions that place a regional perspective at the center of their mission. It has become a long list and it continues to expand: the East-West Gateway Coordinating Council, the United Way of Greater St. Louis, the Regional Chamber and Growth Association, FOCUS St. Louis, the University of Missouri–St. Louis, Southern Illinois University at Edwardsville, and the Regional Business Council are among the most prominent. Like most other metropolitan areas within the United States, St. Louis has rejected an overarching metropolitan government and instead opted for ad hoc metropolitan governance, using multiple processes and a mix of public and private institutions to decide when and how to act regionally.

Such an approach respects what makes St. Louis so special. In survey after survey, when citizens are asked what they most like about the region, the prevailing theme is that it is a cosmopolitan area with a small-town atmosphere. That can only happen, of course, if there are numerous small communities, each with its own special flavor and appeal. In acting more regionally, St. Louis cannot abandon its local roots. Regionalism and localism cannot be opposites—they must be allies, balancing one with the other.

Despite doing much more to respond regionally than it did a half century ago, this book's findings suggest that on many fronts the St. Louis area is at best holding its own and more often is slipping behind. Reversing those trends will require everyone within the region to work better together. This will not happen until even more citizens appreciate the region's importance to themselves and their families, and realize that they owe simultaneous and equal commitments to their local community and their metropolitan area.

Index

About the Editors

Brady Baybeck is Assistant Professor of Political Science and Public Policy Administration and Public Policy Research Fellow at the University of Missouri–St. Louis. A specialist in urban politics and geographic information systems, his articles have appeared in *Political Analysis*, *Political Geography*, and *Publius: The Journal of Federalism*.

E. Terrence Jones is Professor of Political Science and Public Policy Administration and Public Policy Research Fellow at the University of Missouri–St. Louis. His most recent books are *Fragmented by Design: Why St. Louis Has So Many Governments* (Palmerston and Reed, 2000) and *The Metropolitan Chase* (Prentice Hall, 2003).